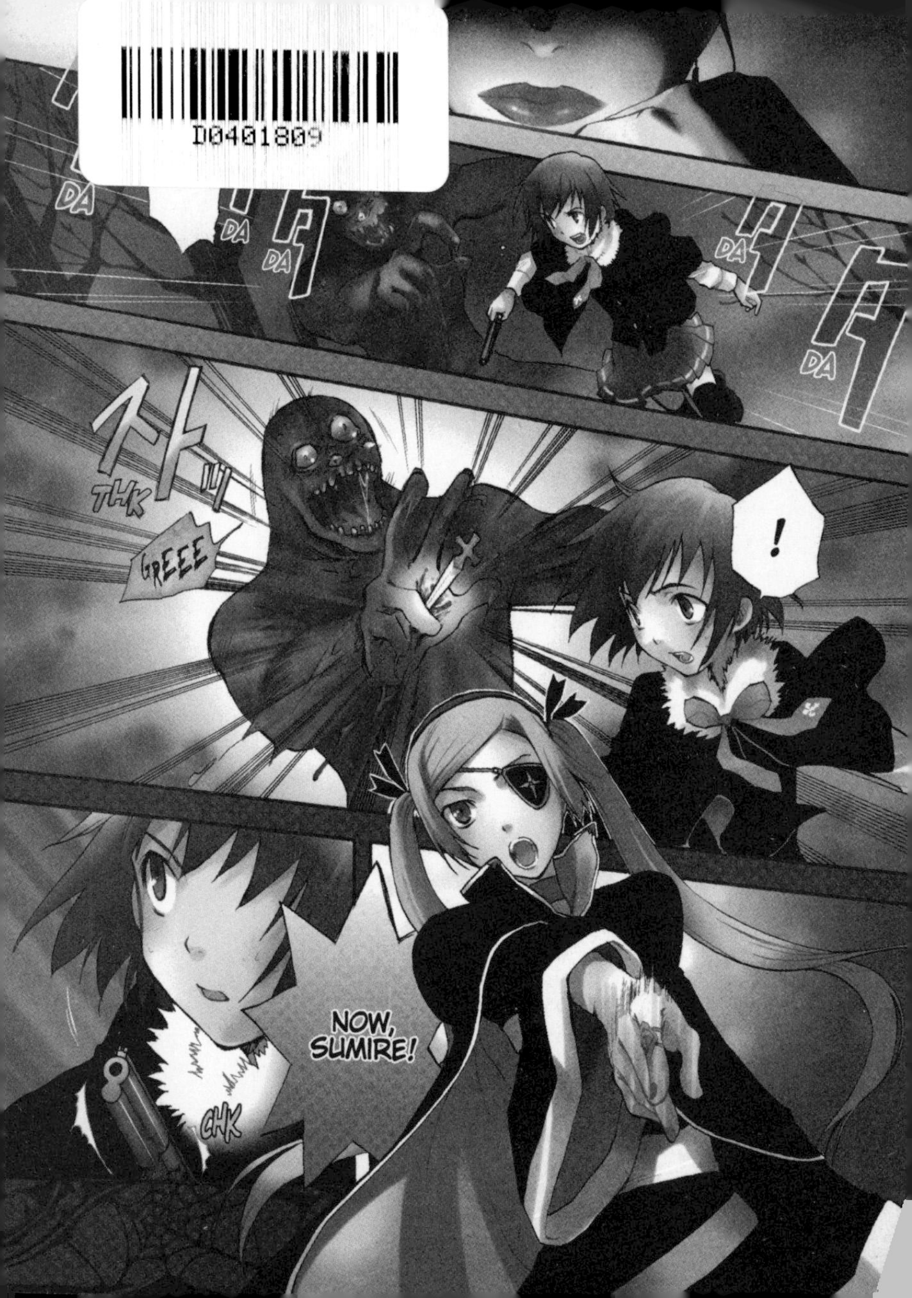
DA
DA
DA
DA
DA
!
THK
GREEE
NOW, SUMIRE!
CHK

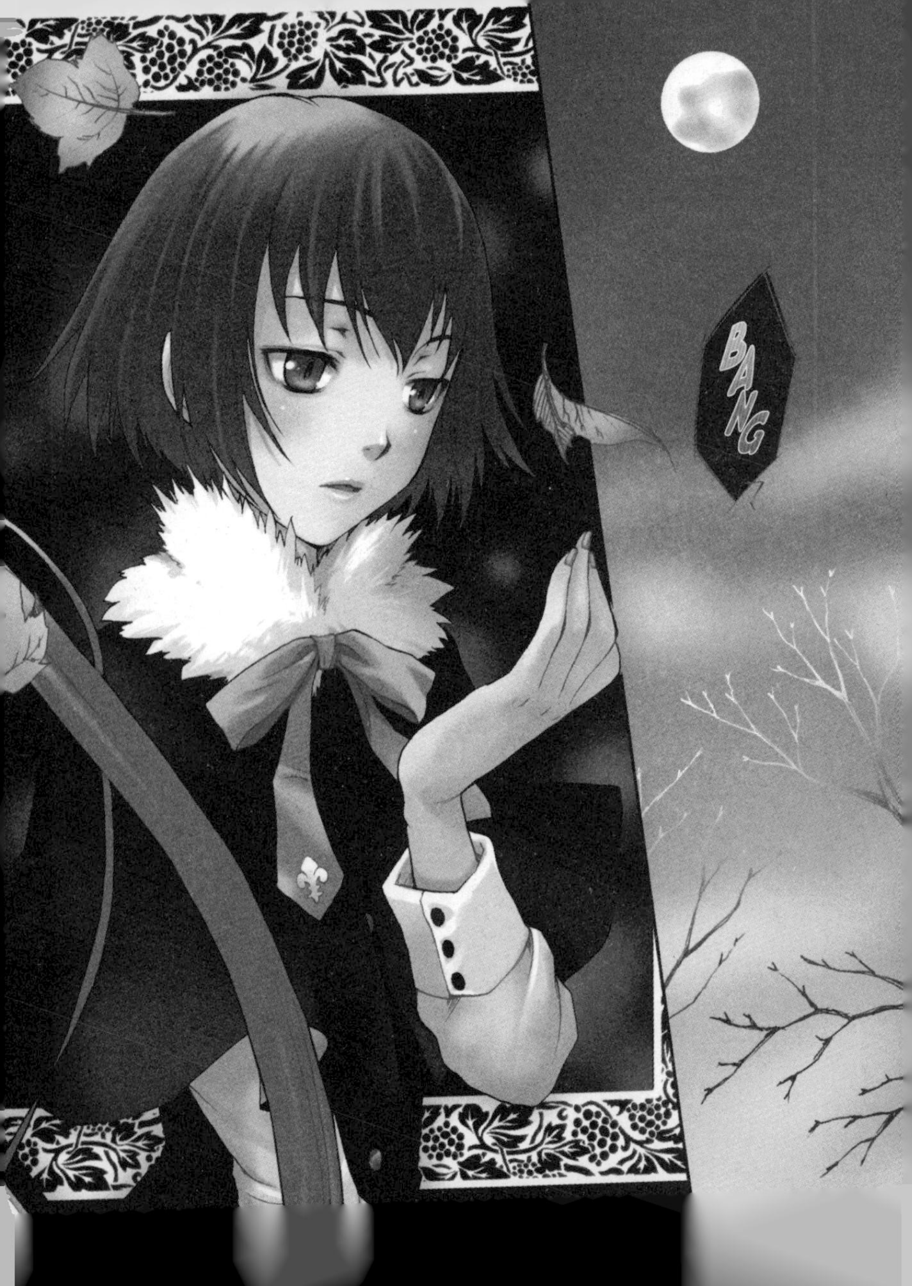
BANG

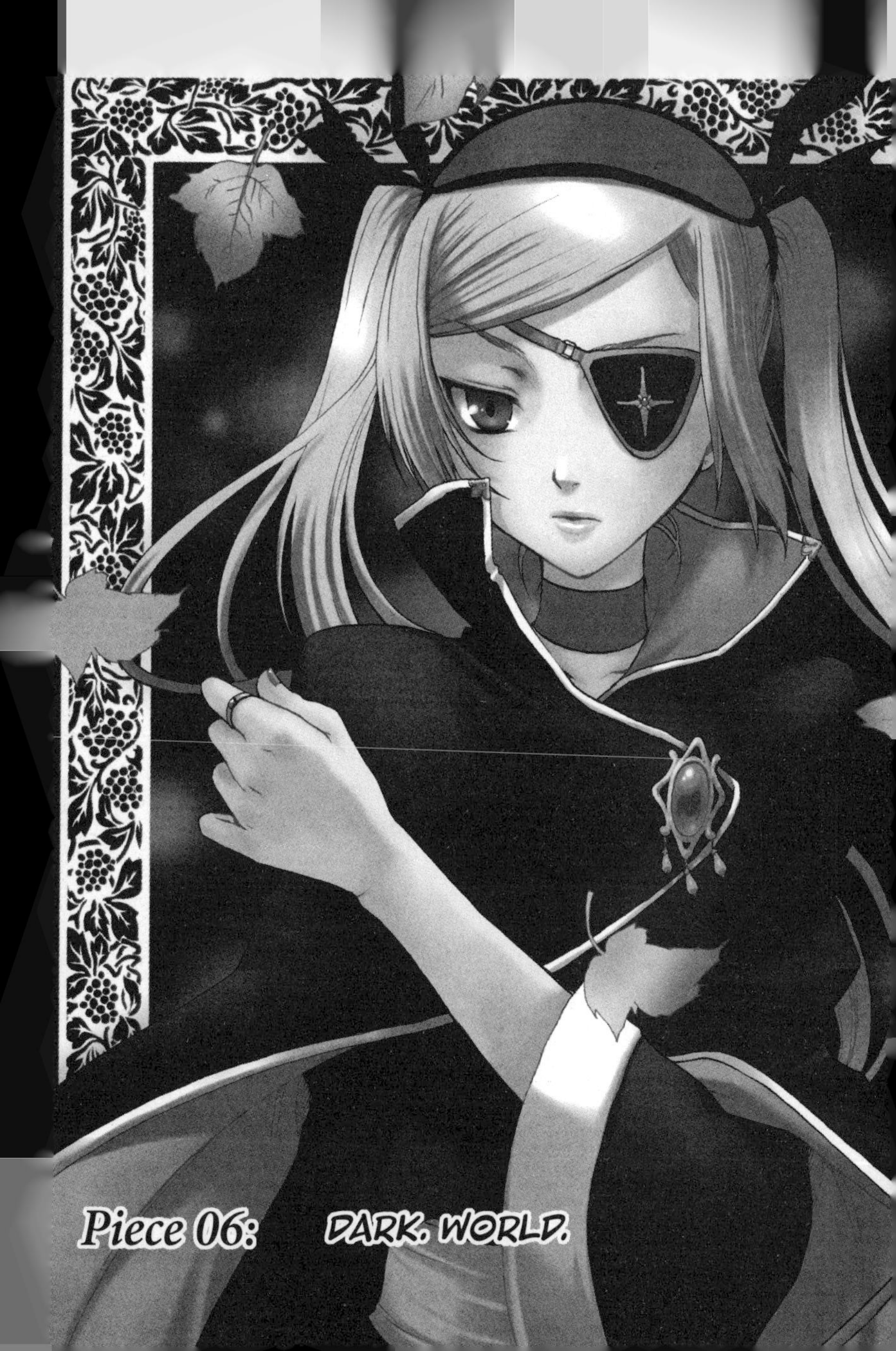

Piece 06: DARK. WORLD.

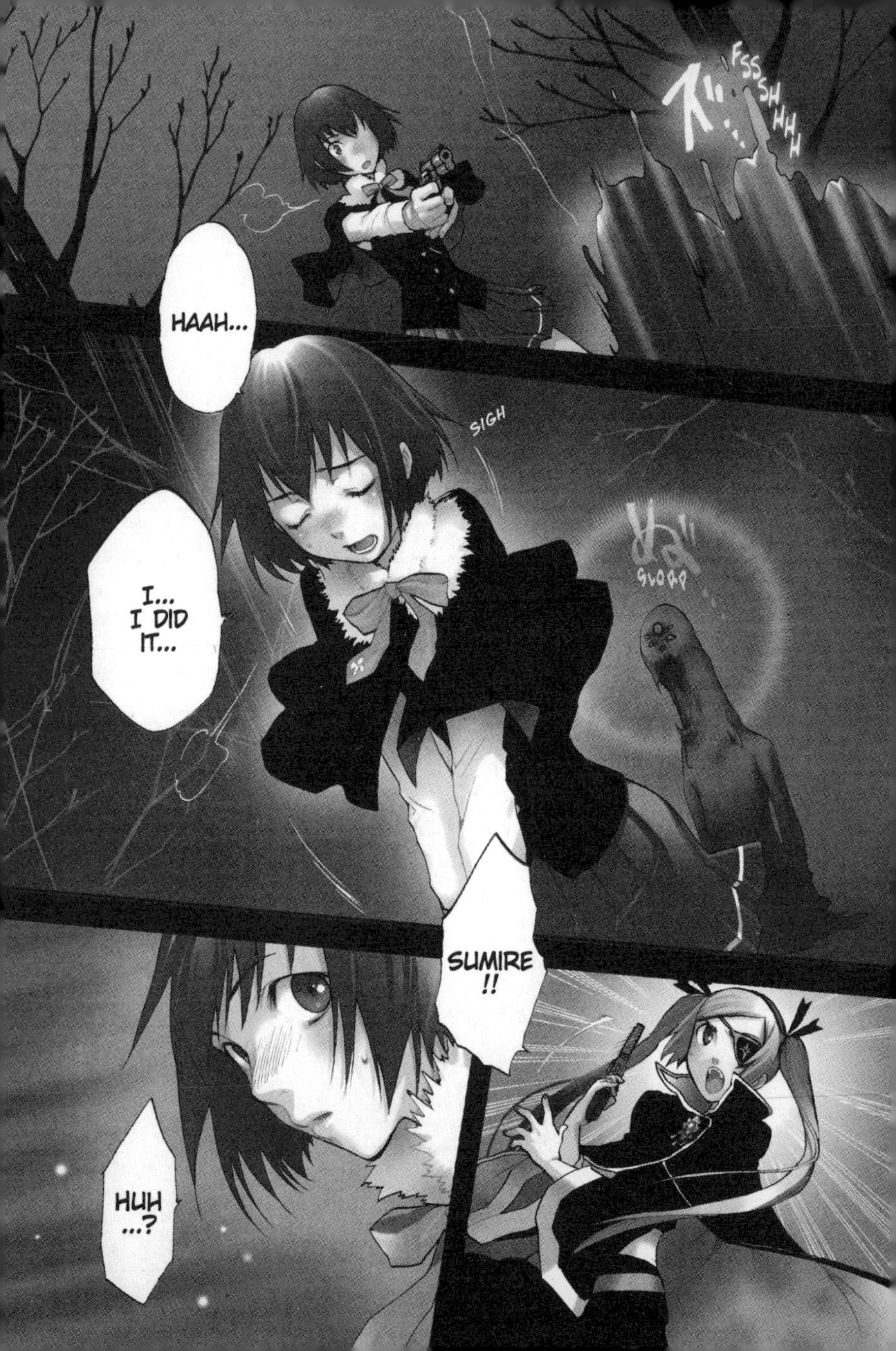
FSSSHHHH
HAAH...
SIGH
SLOOP
I... I DID IT...
SUMIRE !!
HUH ...?

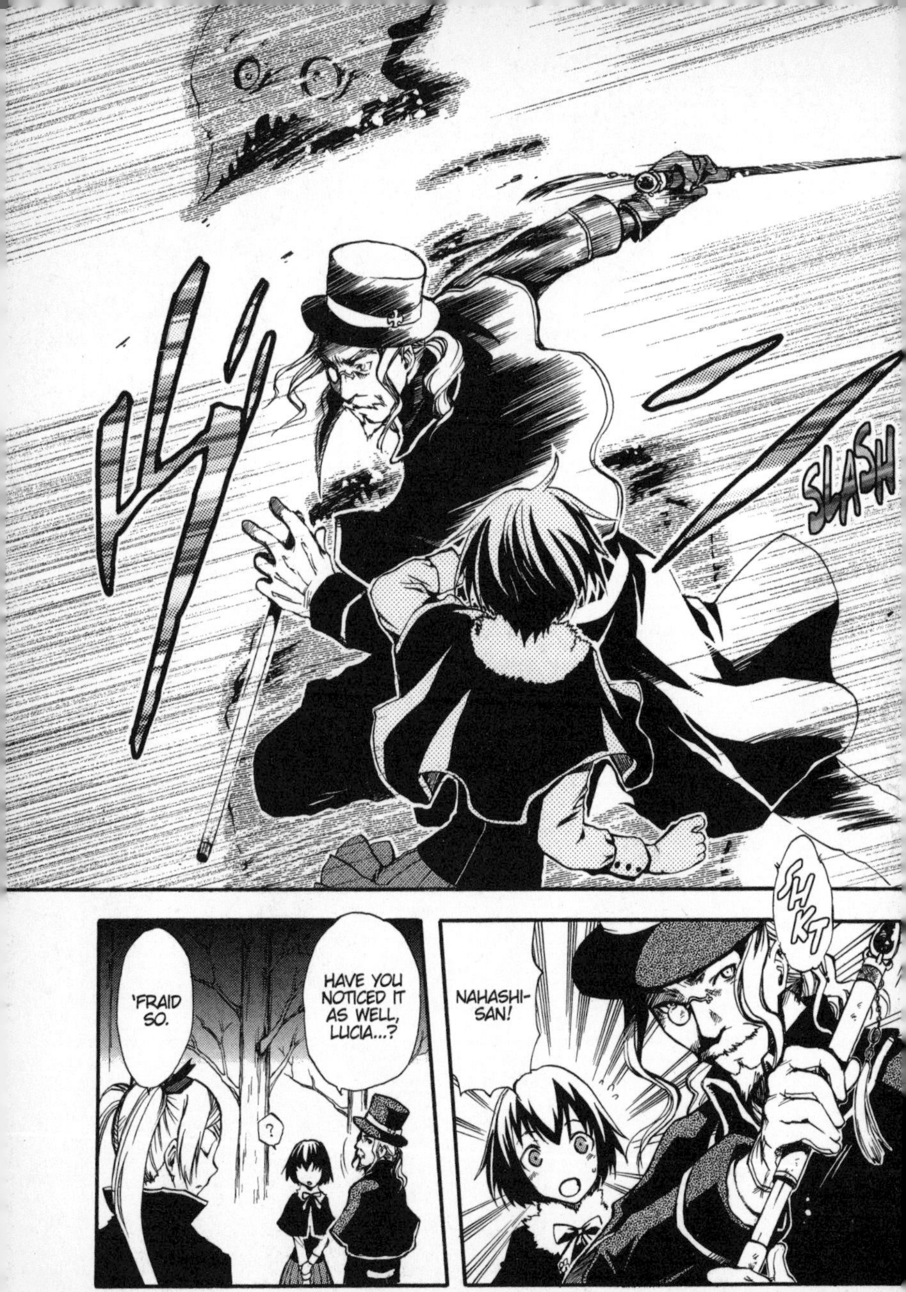
SLASH
SHKT
NAHASHI-SAN!
HAVE YOU NOTICED IT AS WELL, LUCIA...?
?
'FRAID SO.

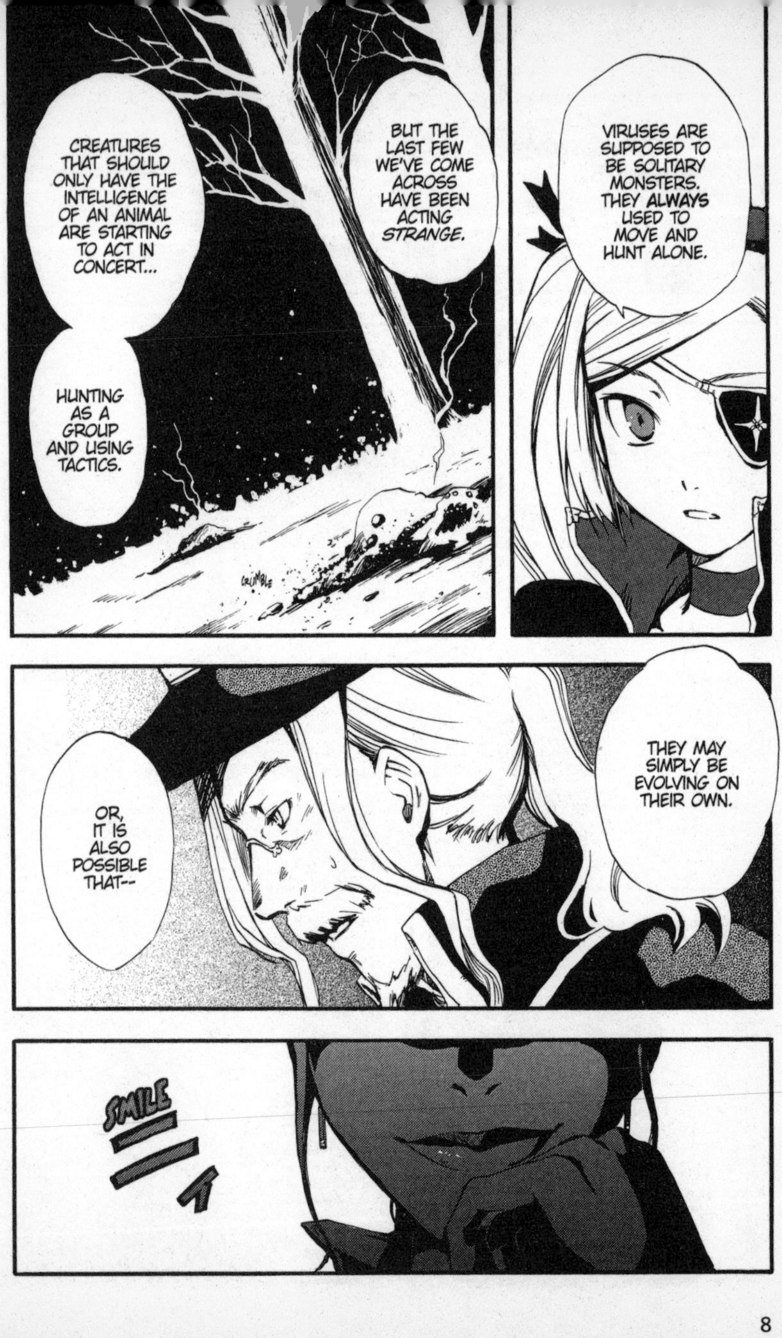
VIRUSES ARE SUPPOSED TO BE SOLITARY MONSTERS. THEY ALWAYS USED TO MOVE AND HUNT ALONE.
BUT THE LAST FEW WE'VE COME ACROSS HAVE BEEN ACTING *STRANGE*.
CREATURES THAT SHOULD ONLY HAVE THE INTELLIGENCE OF AN ANIMAL ARE STARTING TO ACT IN CONCERT...
HUNTING AS A GROUP AND USING TACTICS.
CRUMBLE
THEY MAY SIMPLY BE EVOLVING ON THEIR OWN.
OR, IT IS ALSO POSSIBLE THAT--
SMILE

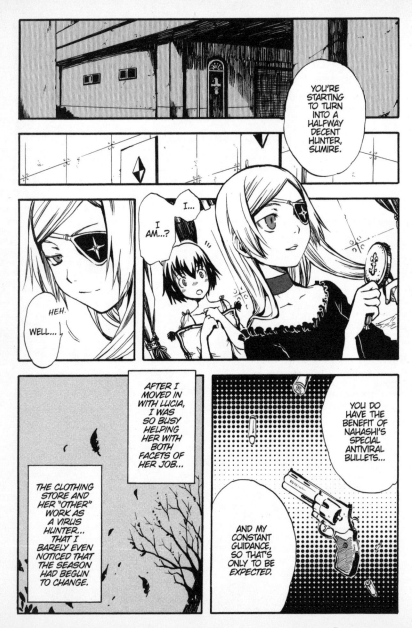

YOU'RE STARTING TO TURN INTO A HALFWAY DECENT HUNTER, SUMIRE.
I...
I AM...?
HEH.
WELL...
YOU DO HAVE THE BENEFIT OF NAHASHI'S SPECIAL ANTIVIRAL BULLETS...
AND MY CONSTANT GUIDANCE, SO THAT'S ONLY TO BE EXPECTED.
AFTER I MOVED IN WITH LUCIA, I WAS SO BUSY HELPING HER WITH BOTH FACETS OF HER JOB...
THE CLOTHING STORE AND HER "OTHER" WORK AS A VIRUS HUNTER... THAT I BARELY EVEN NOTICED THAT THE SEASON HAD BEGUN TO CHANGE.

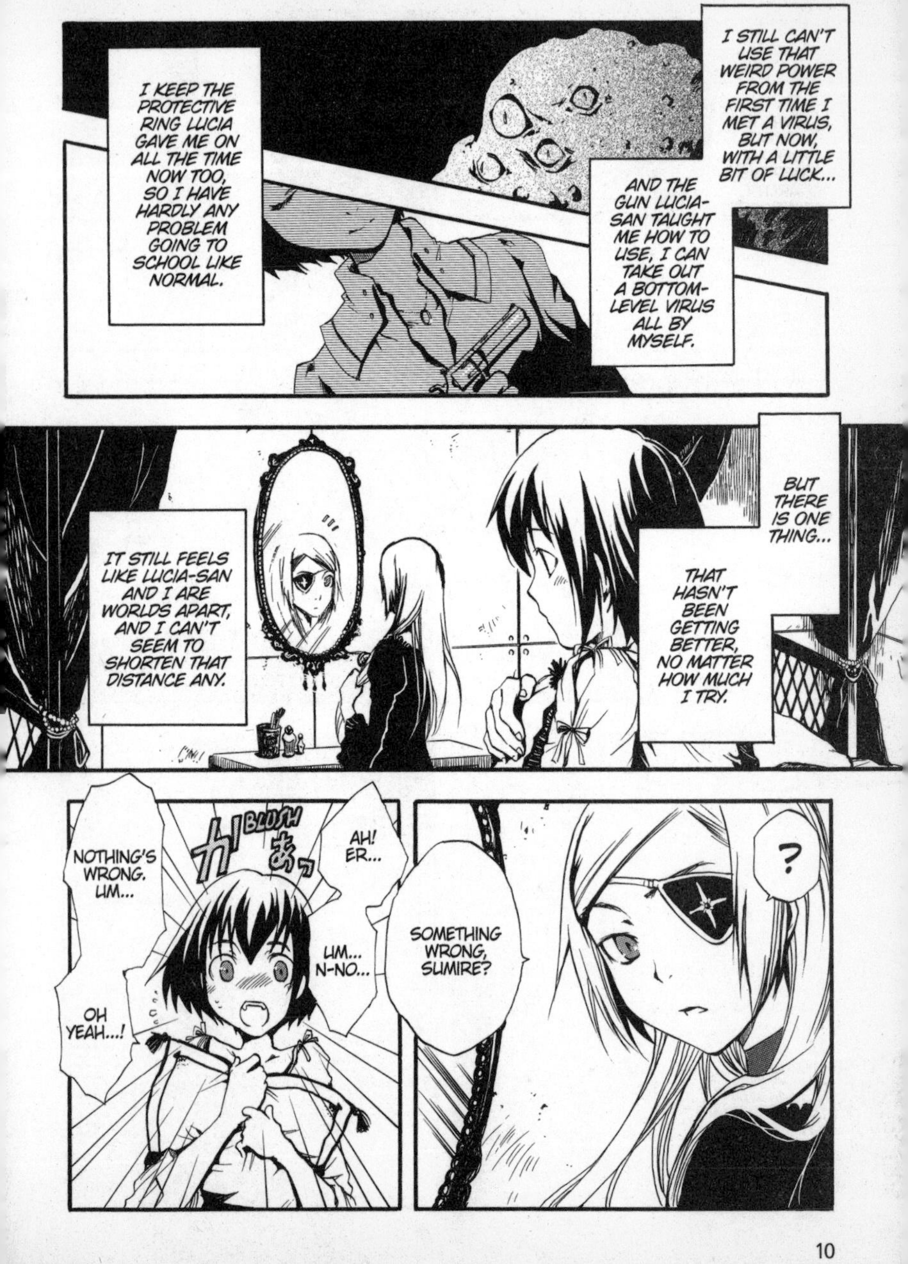
I STILL CAN'T USE THAT WEIRD POWER FROM THE FIRST TIME I MET A VIRUS, BUT NOW, WITH A LITTLE BIT OF LUCK...
AND THE GUN LUCIA-SAN TAUGHT ME HOW TO USE, I CAN TAKE OUT A BOTTOM-LEVEL VIRUS ALL BY MYSELF.
I KEEP THE PROTECTIVE RING LUCIA GAVE ME ON ALL THE TIME NOW TOO, SO I HAVE HARDLY ANY PROBLEM GOING TO SCHOOL LIKE NORMAL.
BUT THERE IS ONE THING...
THAT HASN'T BEEN GETTING BETTER, NO MATTER HOW MUCH I TRY.
IT STILL FEELS LIKE LUCIA-SAN AND I ARE WORLDS APART, AND I CAN'T SEEM TO SHORTEN THAT DISTANCE ANY.
?
SOMETHING WRONG, SUMIRE?
AH! ER...
BLUSH
UM... N-NO...
NOTHING'S WRONG. UM...
OH YEAH...!

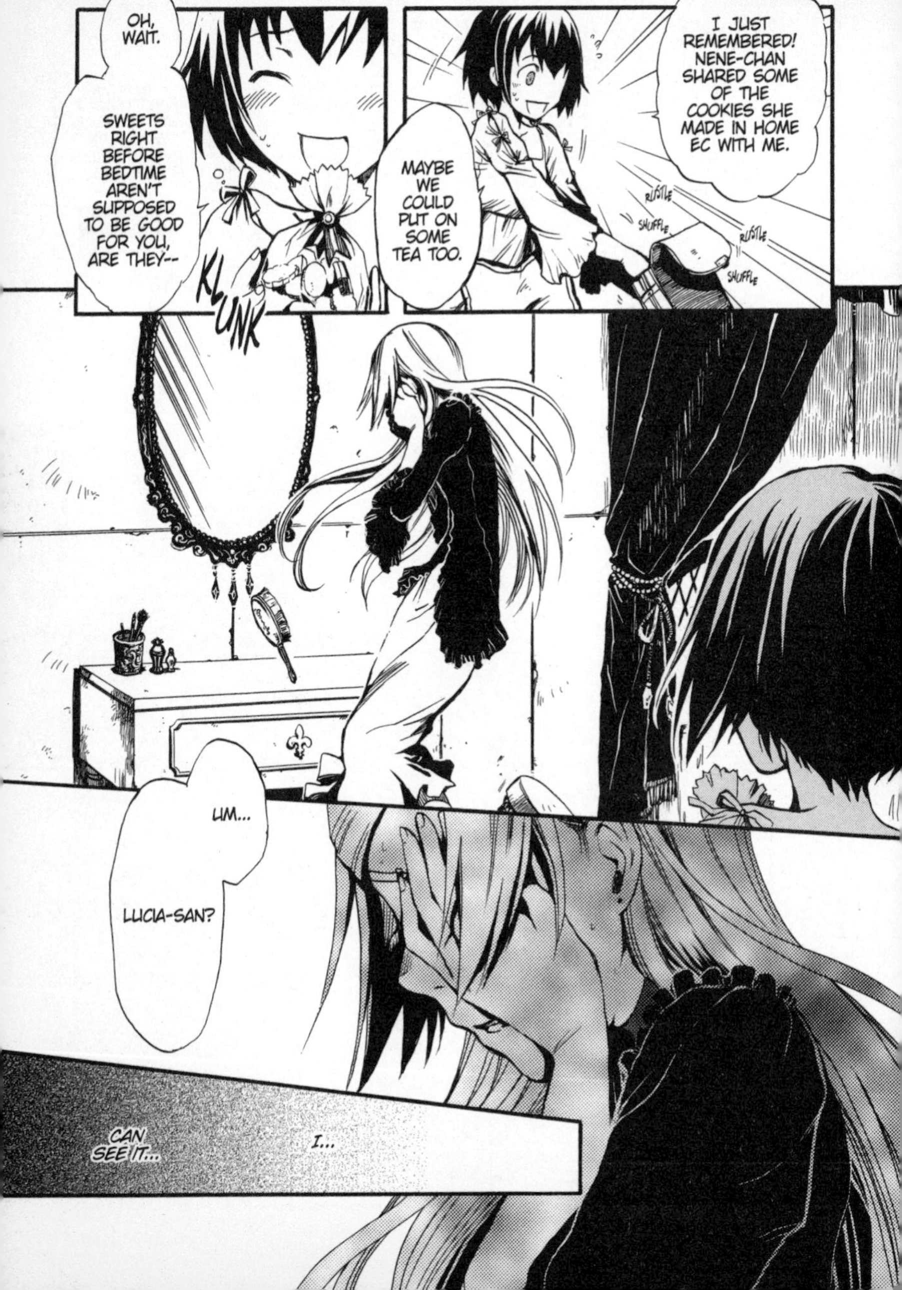
I JUST REMEMBERED! NENE-CHAN SHARED SOME OF THE COOKIES SHE MADE IN HOME EC WITH ME.
RUSTLE
SHUFFLE
RUSTLE
SHUFFLE
MAYBE WE COULD PUT ON SOME TEA TOO.
OH, WAIT.
SWEETS RIGHT BEFORE BEDTIME AREN'T SUPPOSED TO BE GOOD FOR YOU, ARE THEY--
KLUNK
UM...
LUCIA-SAN?
I...
CAN SEE IT...

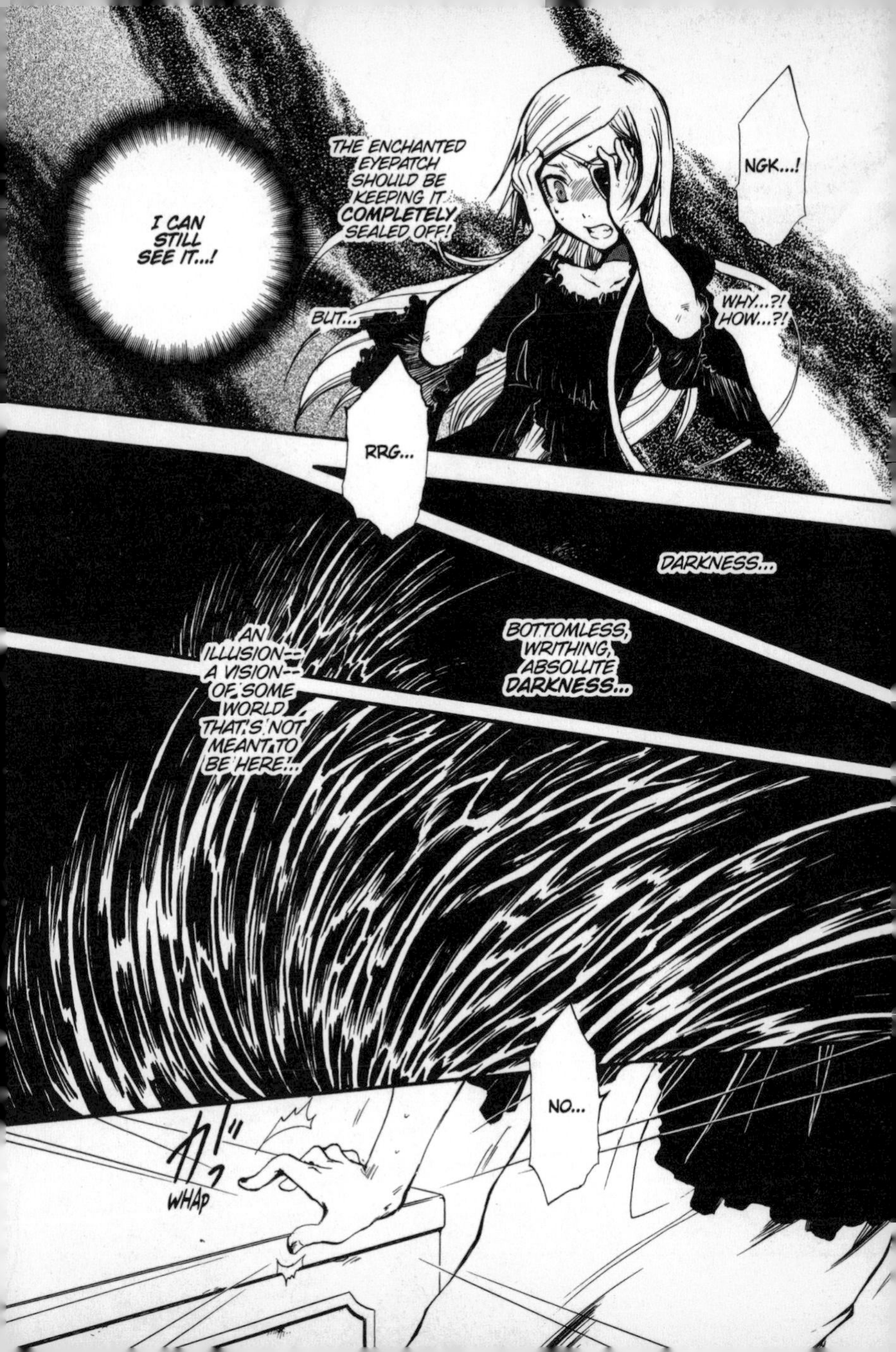
NGK...!
WHY...?! HOW...?!
THE ENCHANTED EYEPATCH SHOULD BE KEEPING IT COMPLETELY SEALED OFF!
I CAN STILL SEE IT...!
BUT...
RRG...
DARKNESS...
BOTTOMLESS, WRITHING, ABSOLUTE DARKNESS...
AN ILLUSION-- A VISION-- OF SOME WORLD THAT'S NOT MEANT TO BE HERE...
NO...
WHAP

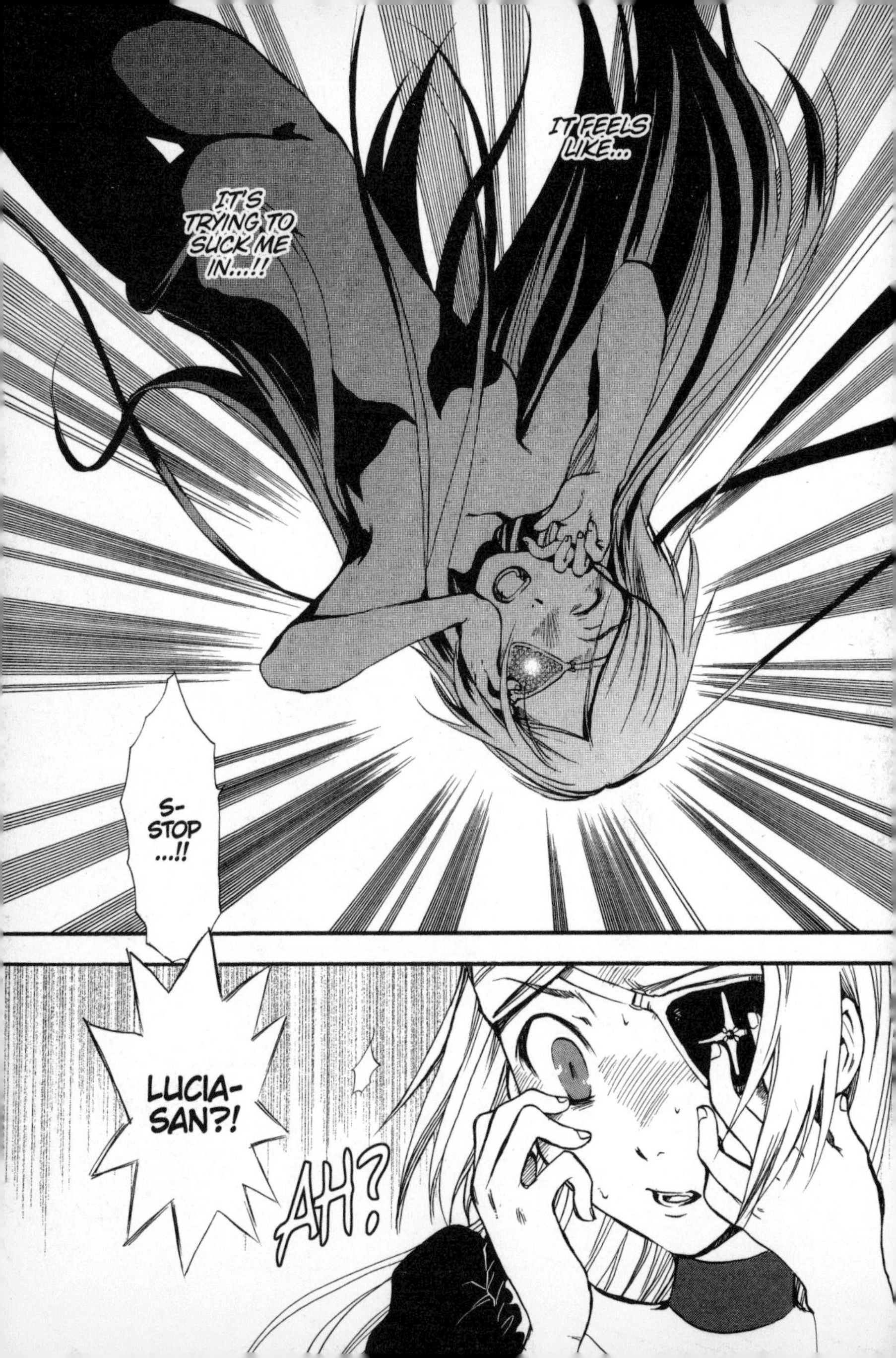
IT FEELS LIKE...
IT'S TRYING TO SUCK ME IN...!!
S-STOP ...!!
LUCIA-SAN?!
AH?

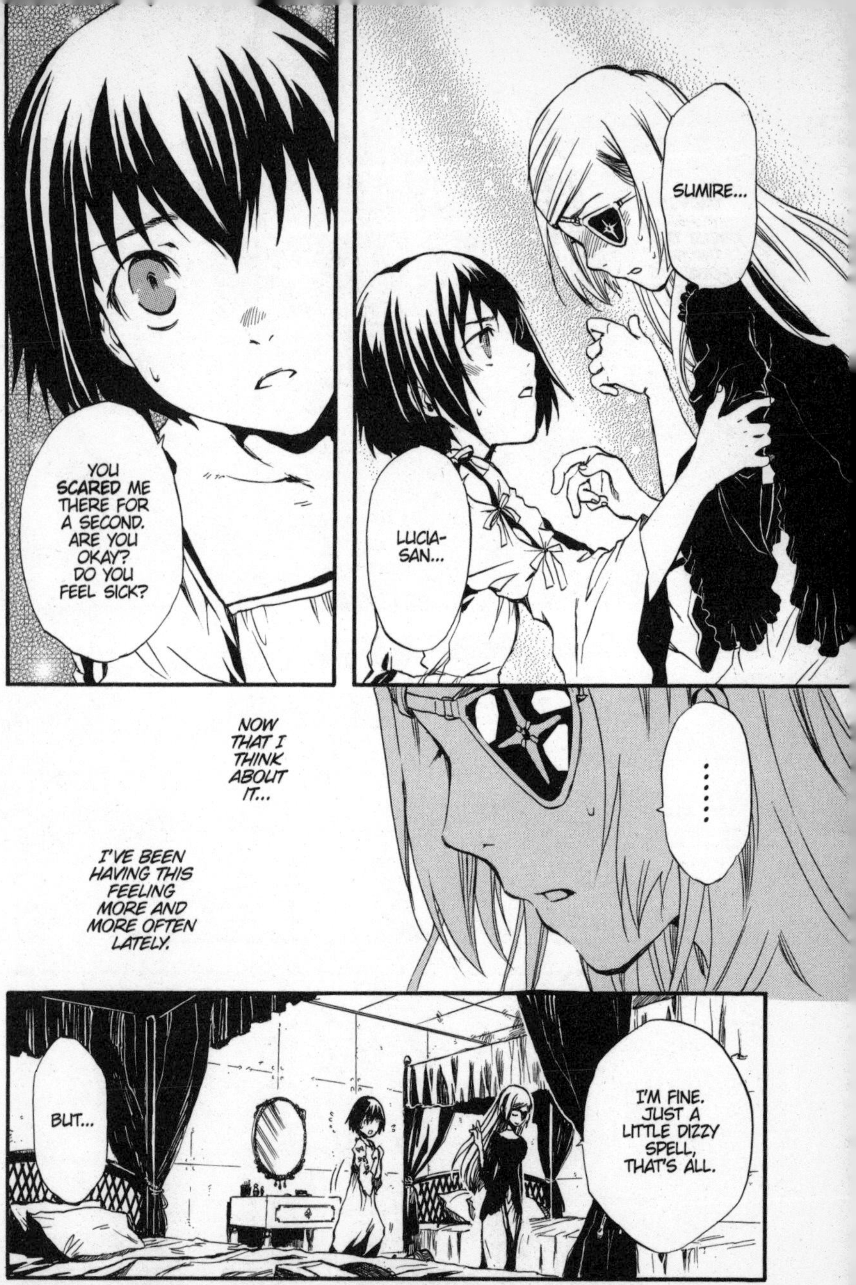
SUMIRE...
LUCIA-SAN...
YOU SCARED ME THERE FOR A SECOND. ARE YOU OKAY? DO YOU FEEL SICK?
......
NOW THAT I THINK ABOUT IT...
I'VE BEEN HAVING THIS FEELING MORE AND MORE OFTEN LATELY.
I'M FINE. JUST A LITTLE DIZZY SPELL, THAT'S ALL.
BUT...

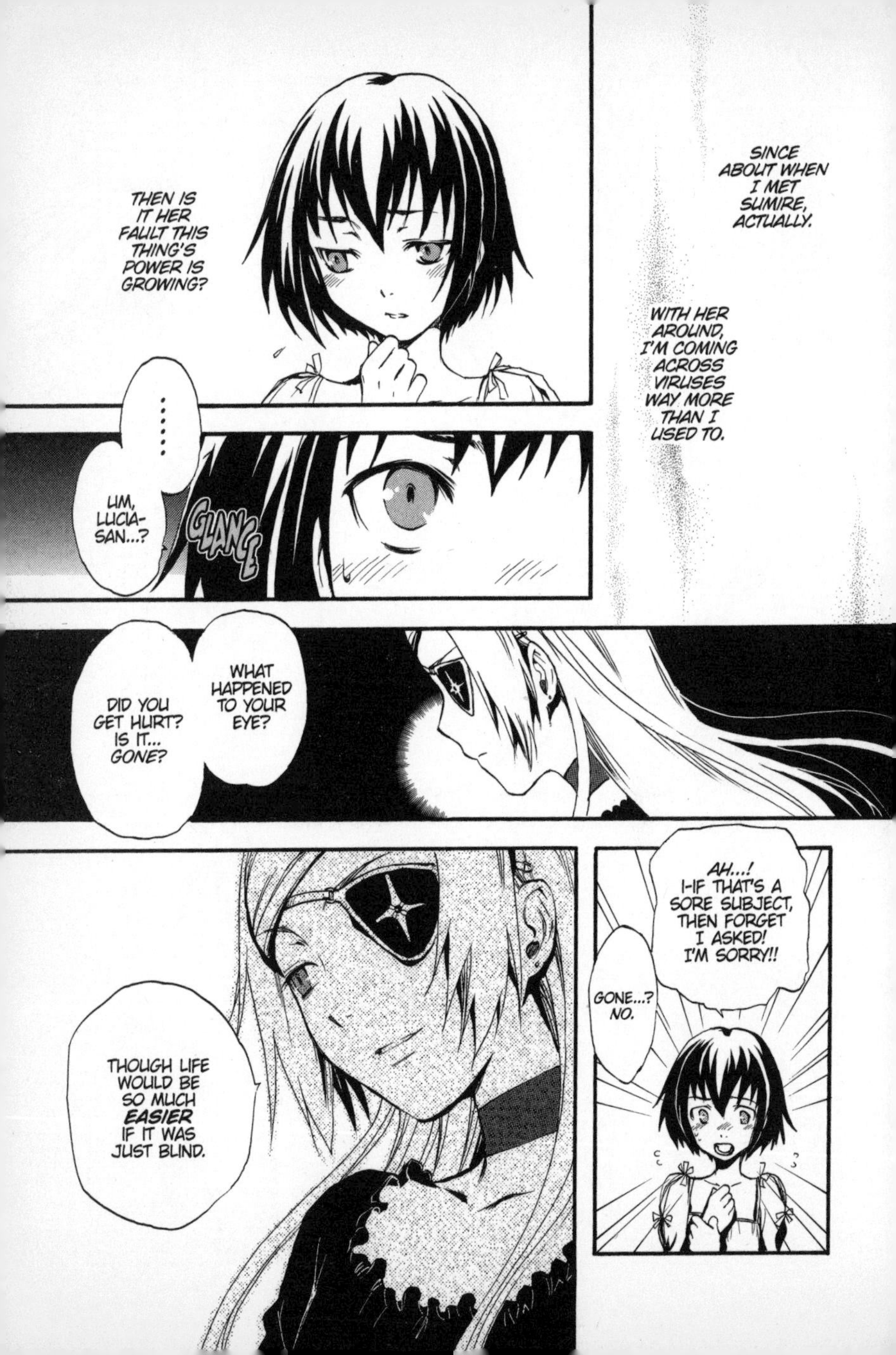

SINCE ABOUT WHEN I MET SUMIRE, ACTUALLY.
WITH HER AROUND, I'M COMING ACROSS VIRUSES WAY MORE THAN I USED TO.
THEN IS IT HER FAULT THIS THING'S POWER IS GROWING?
......
UM, LUCIA-SAN...?
GLANCE
WHAT HAPPENED TO YOUR EYE?
DID YOU GET HURT? IS IT... GONE?
AH...! I-IF THAT'S A SORE SUBJECT, THEN FORGET I ASKED! I'M SORRY!!
GONE...? NO.
THOUGH LIFE WOULD BE SO MUCH *EASIER* IF IT WAS JUST BLIND.

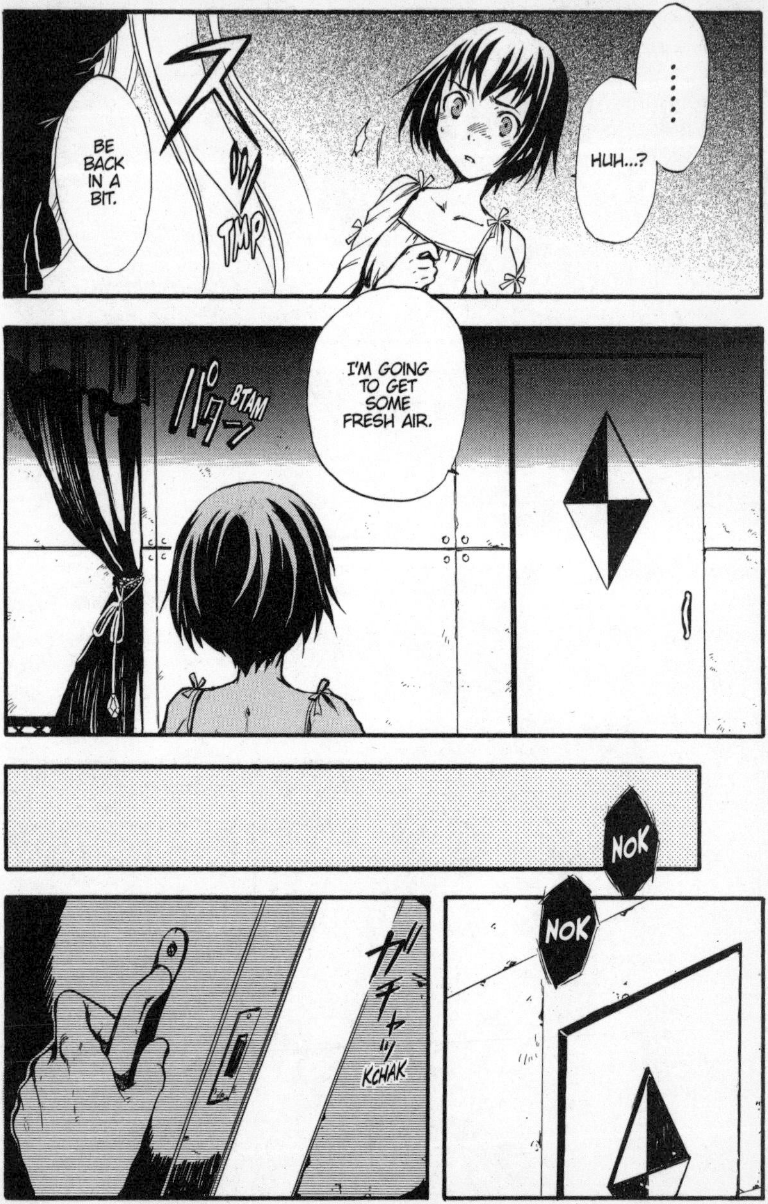
......
HUH...?
BE BACK IN A BIT.
TMP
I'M GOING TO GET SOME FRESH AIR.
BTAM
NOK
NOK
KCHAK

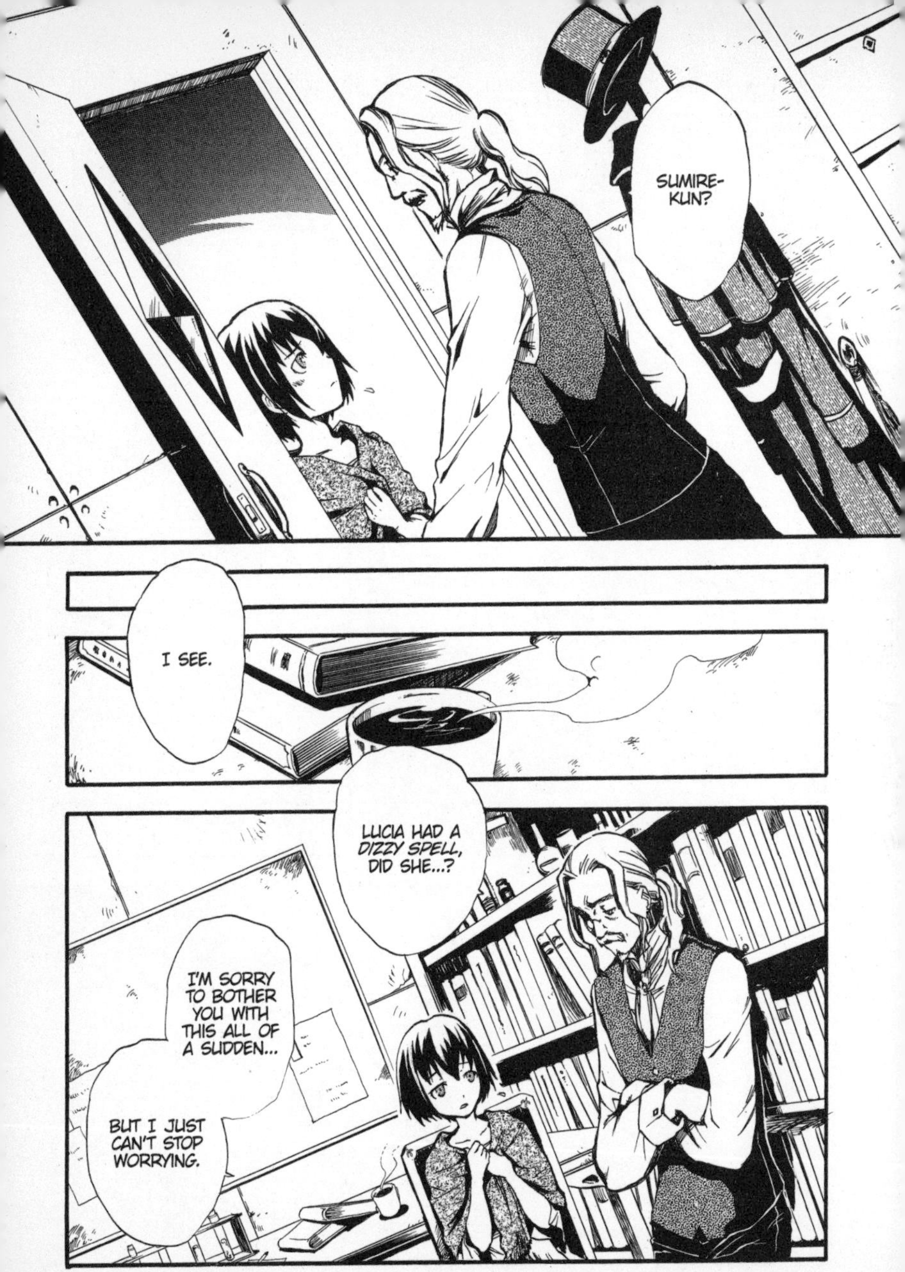
SUMIRE-KUN?
I SEE.
LUCIA HAD A DIZZY SPELL, DID SHE...?
I'M SORRY TO BOTHER YOU WITH THIS ALL OF A SUDDEN...
BUT I JUST CAN'T STOP WORRYING.

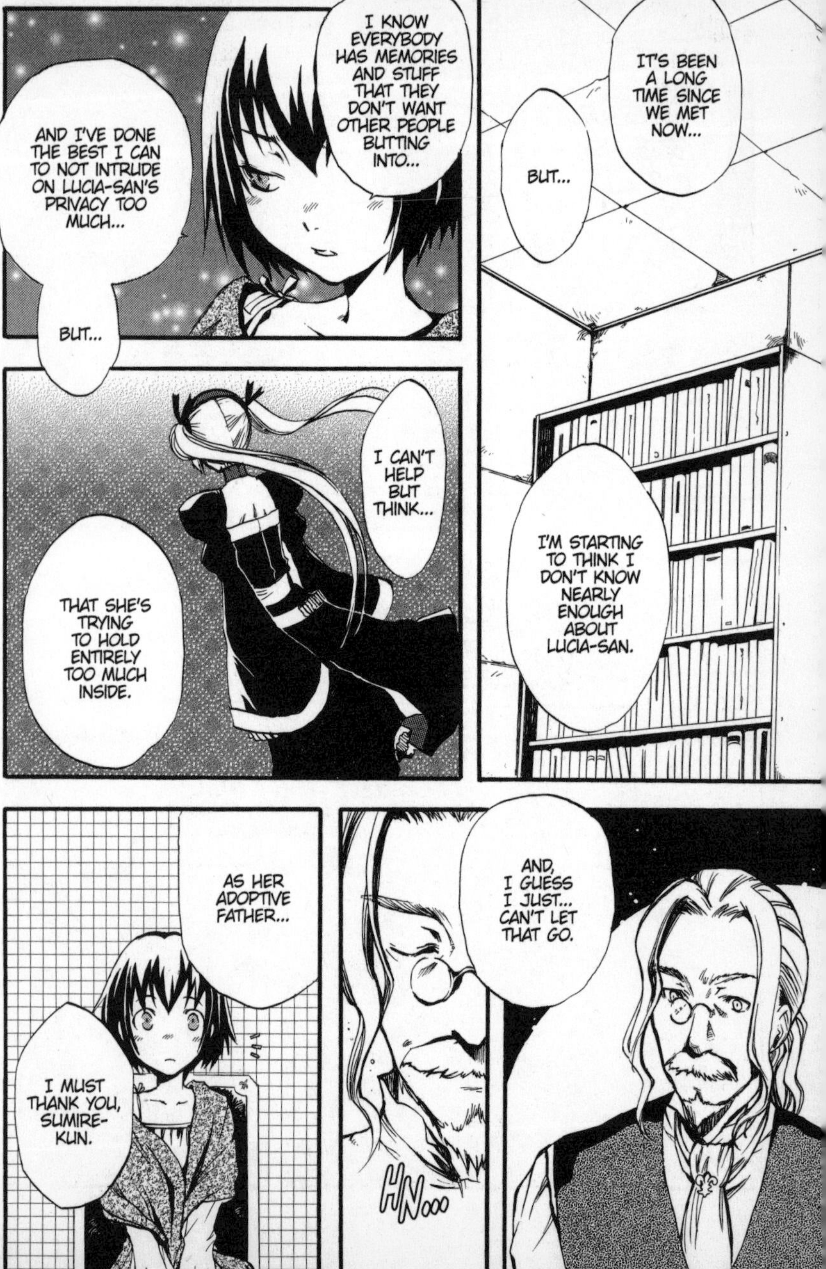
IT'S BEEN A LONG TIME SINCE WE MET NOW...
BUT...
I'M STARTING TO THINK I DON'T KNOW NEARLY ENOUGH ABOUT LUCIA-SAN.
I KNOW EVERYBODY HAS MEMORIES AND STUFF THAT THEY DON'T WANT OTHER PEOPLE BUTTING INTO...
AND I'VE DONE THE BEST I CAN TO NOT INTRUDE ON LUCIA-SAN'S PRIVACY TOO MUCH...
BUT...
I CAN'T HELP BUT THINK...
THAT SHE'S TRYING TO HOLD ENTIRELY TOO MUCH INSIDE.
AND, I GUESS I JUST... CAN'T LET THAT GO.
HNooo
AS HER ADOPTIVE FATHER...
I MUST THANK YOU, SUMIRE-KUN.

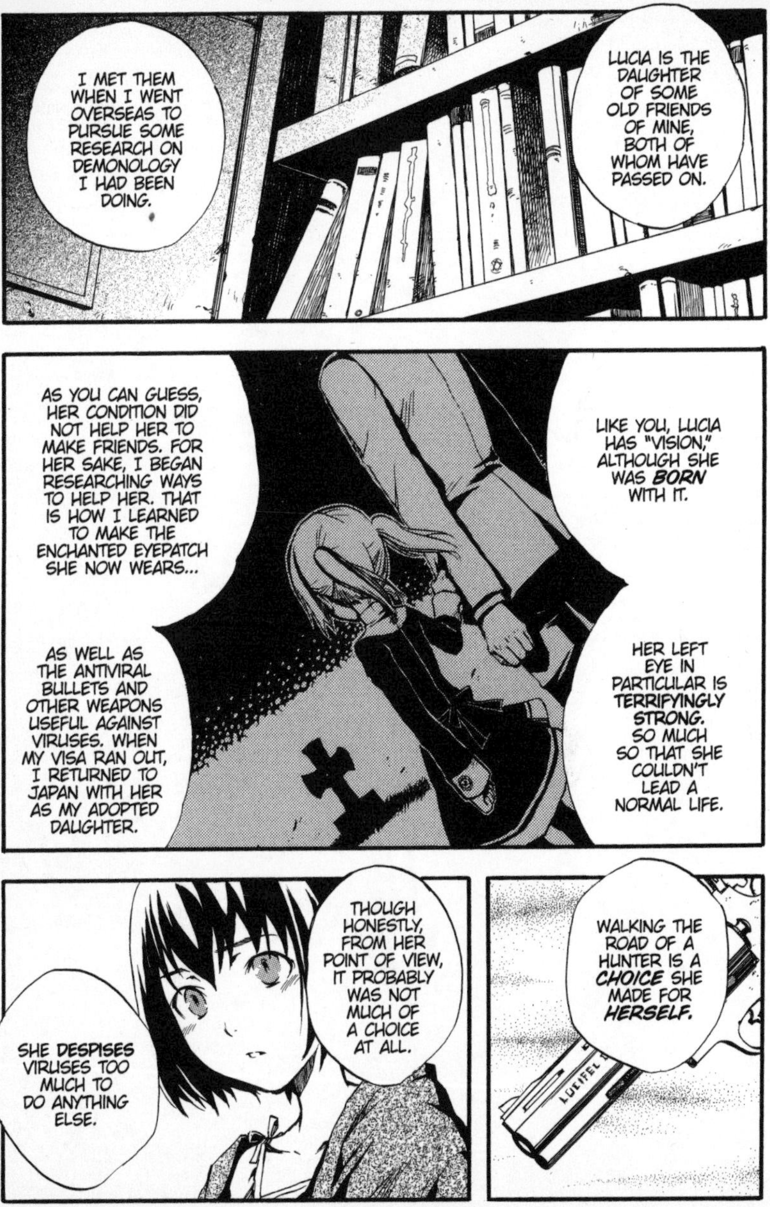
LUCIA IS THE DAUGHTER OF SOME OLD FRIENDS OF MINE, BOTH OF WHOM HAVE PASSED ON.
I MET THEM WHEN I WENT OVERSEAS TO PURSUE SOME RESEARCH ON DEMONOLOGY I HAD BEEN DOING.
LIKE YOU, LUCIA HAS "VISION," ALTHOUGH SHE WAS ***BORN*** WITH IT.
HER LEFT EYE IN PARTICULAR IS **TERRIFYINGLY STRONG.** SO MUCH SO THAT SHE COULDN'T LEAD A NORMAL LIFE.
AS YOU CAN GUESS, HER CONDITION DID NOT HELP HER TO MAKE FRIENDS. FOR HER SAKE, I BEGAN RESEARCHING WAYS TO HELP HER. THAT IS HOW I LEARNED TO MAKE THE ENCHANTED EYEPATCH SHE NOW WEARS...
AS WELL AS THE ANTIVIRAL BULLETS AND OTHER WEAPONS USEFUL AGAINST VIRUSES. WHEN MY VISA RAN OUT, I RETURNED TO JAPAN WITH HER AS MY ADOPTED DAUGHTER.
WALKING THE ROAD OF A HUNTER IS A ***CHOICE*** SHE MADE FOR ***HERSELF.***
THOUGH HONESTLY, FROM HER POINT OF VIEW, IT PROBABLY WAS NOT MUCH OF A CHOICE AT ALL.
SHE **DESPISES** VIRUSES TOO MUCH TO DO ANYTHING ELSE.

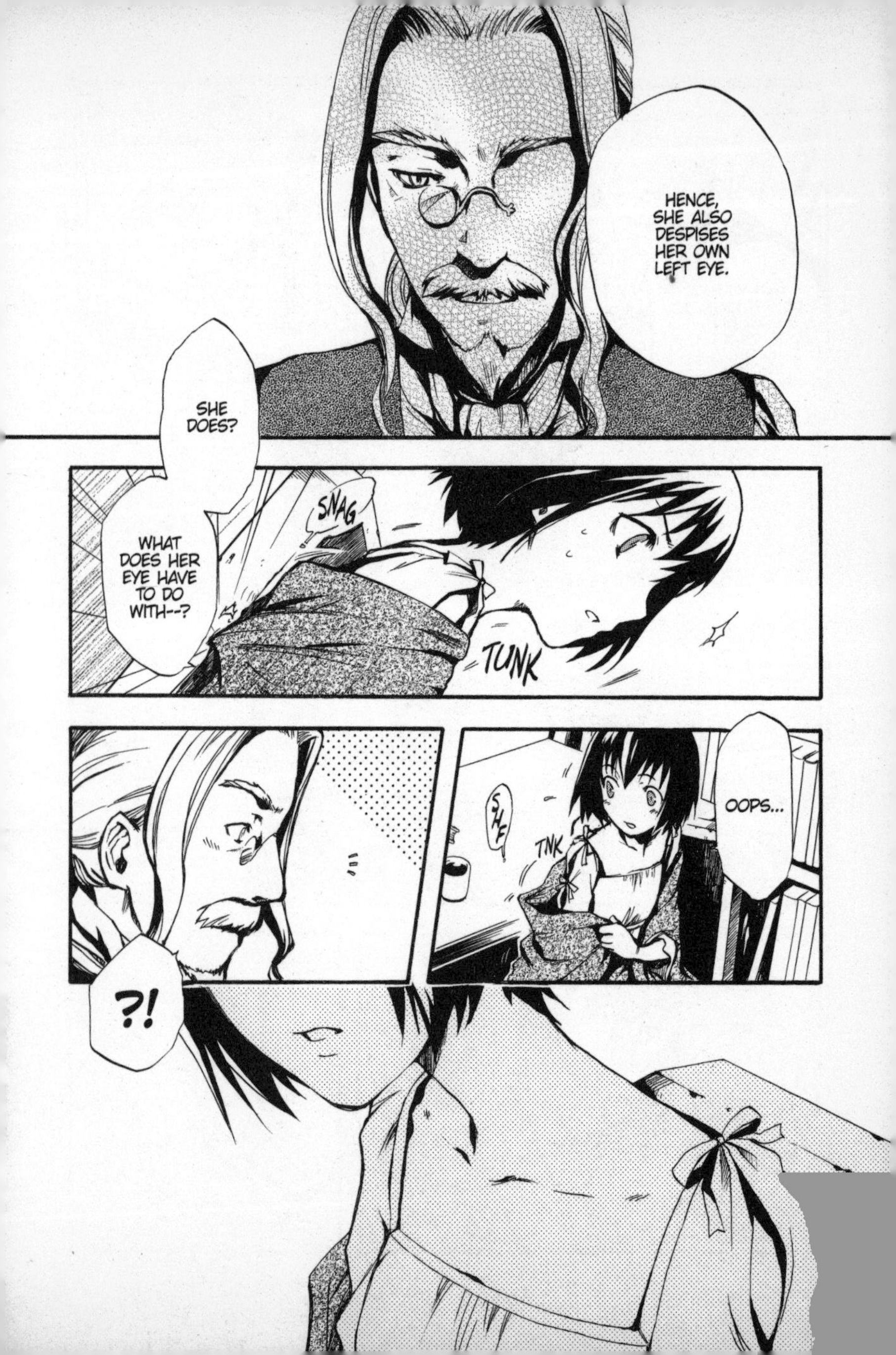
HENCE, SHE ALSO DESPISES HER OWN LEFT EYE.
SHE DOES?
SNAG
WHAT DOES HER EYE HAVE TO DO WITH--?
TUNK
OOPS...
SHF
TNK
?!

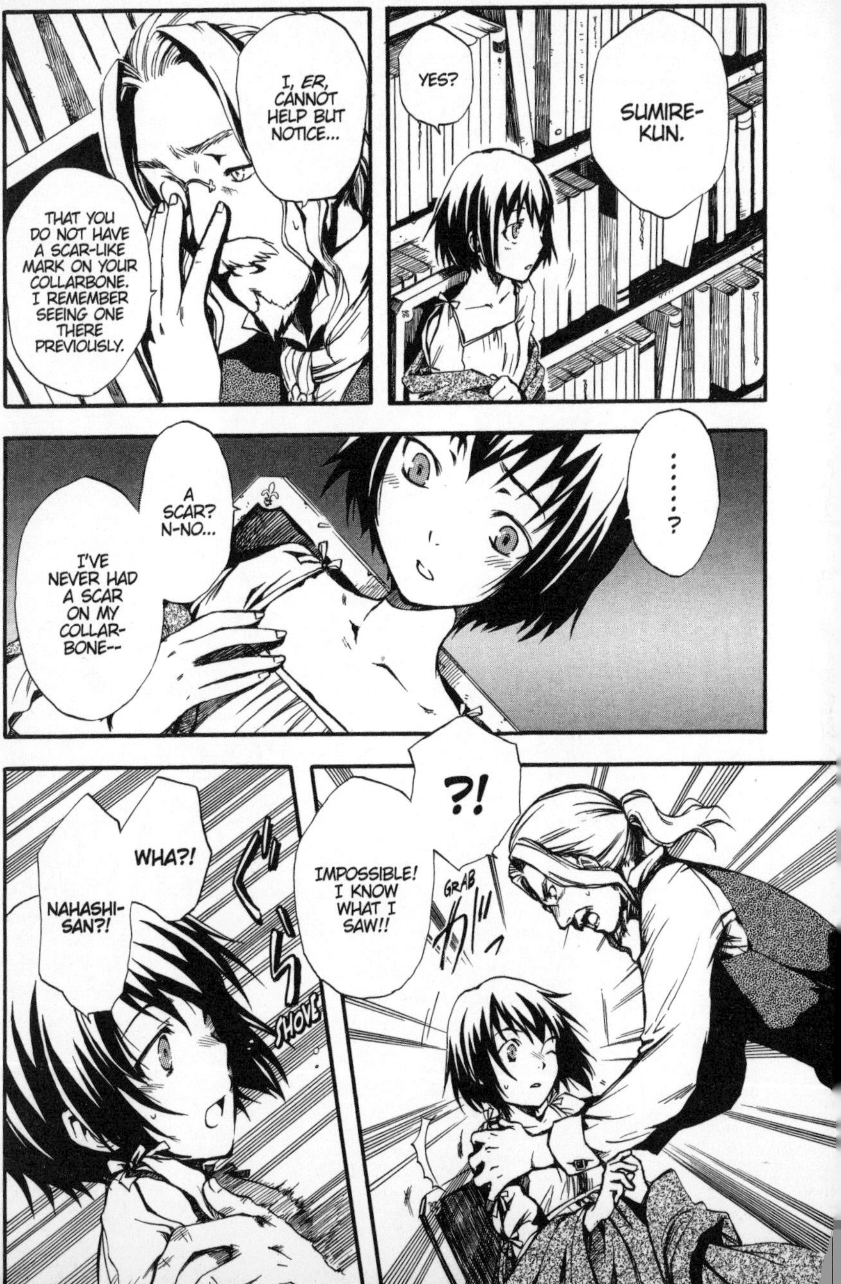
SUMIRE-KUN.
YES?
I, ER, CANNOT HELP BUT NOTICE...
THAT YOU DO NOT HAVE A SCAR-LIKE MARK ON YOUR COLLARBONE. I REMEMBER SEEING ONE THERE PREVIOUSLY.
......?
A SCAR? N-NO...
I'VE NEVER HAD A SCAR ON MY COLLAR-BONE--
?!
IMPOSSIBLE! I KNOW WHAT I SAW!!
GRAB
WHA?!
NAHASHI-SAN?!
SHOVE

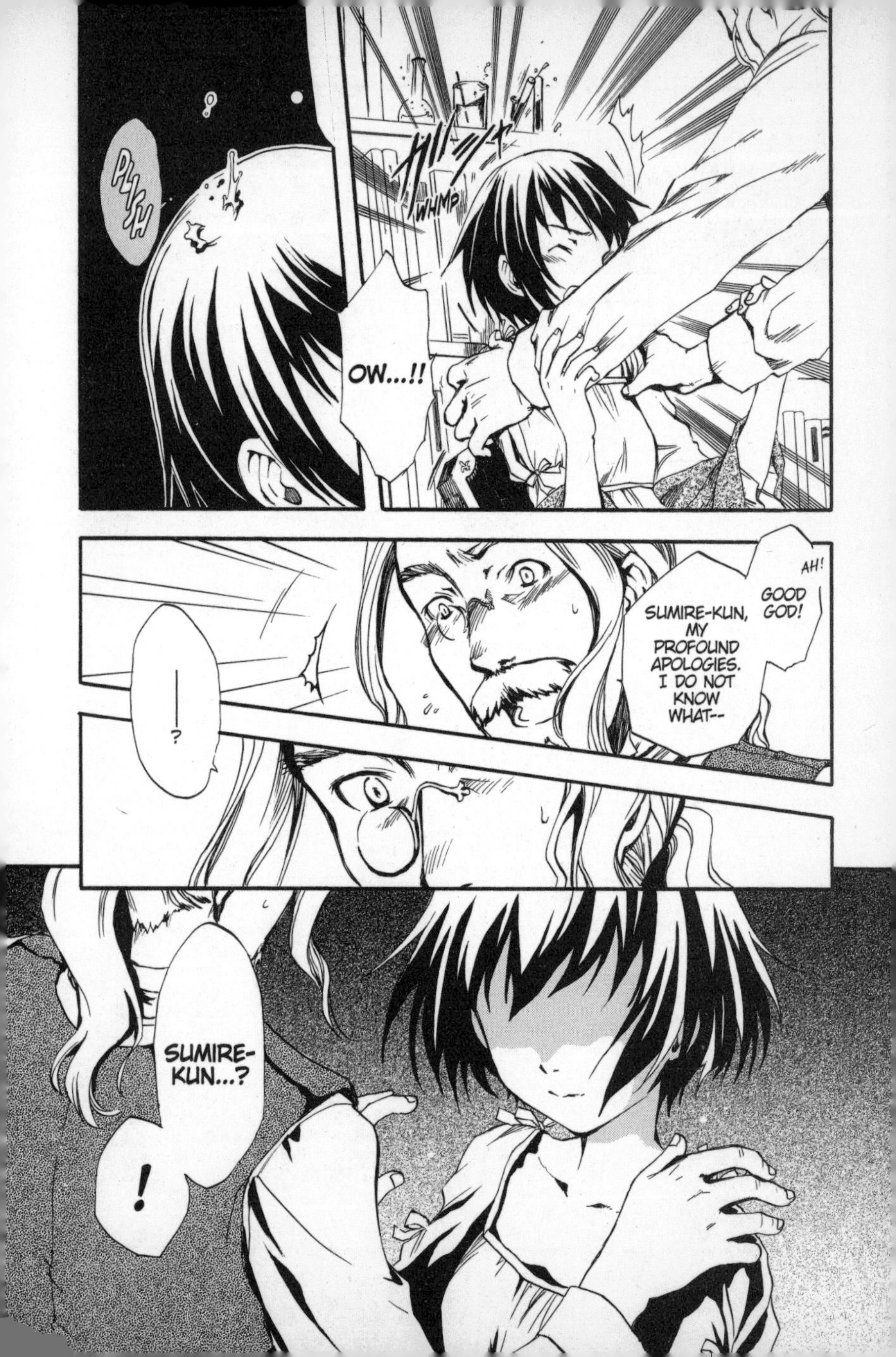
WHMP
OW...!!
PLISH
AH!
GOOD GOD!
SUMIRE-KUN, MY PROFOUND APOLOGIES. I DO NOT KNOW WHAT--
—?
SUMIRE-KUN...?
!

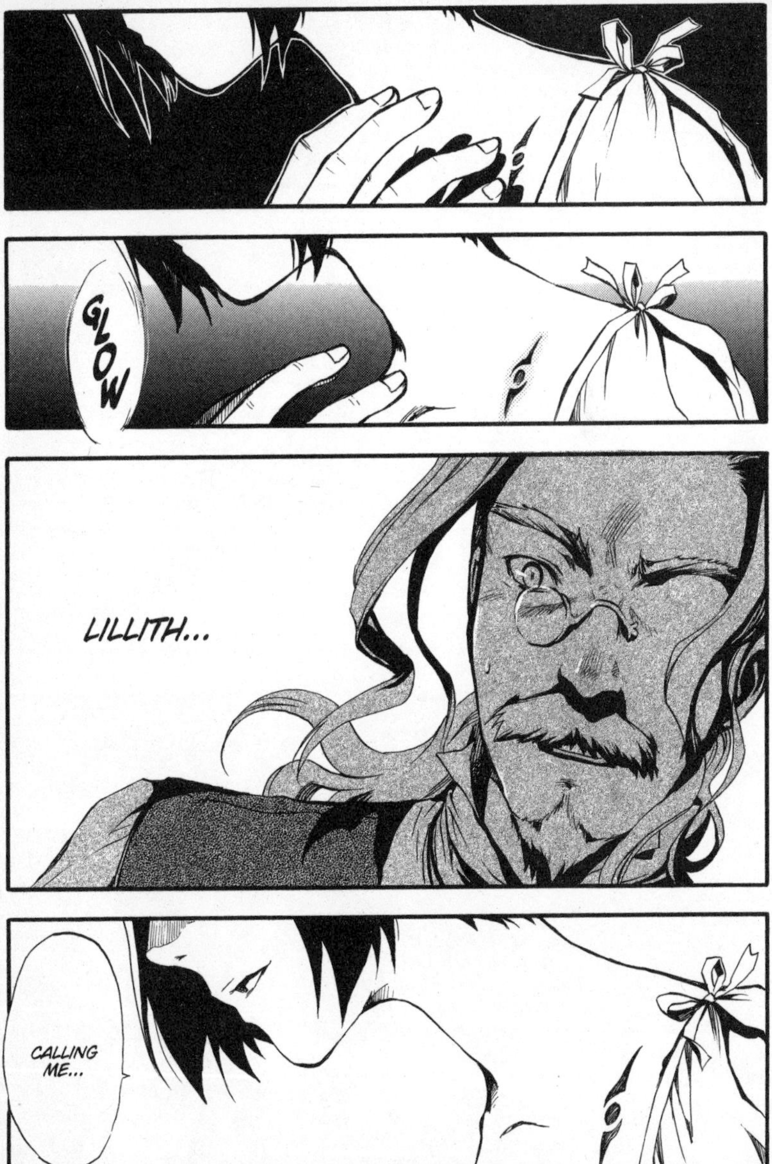
GLOW
LILLITH...
CALLING ME...

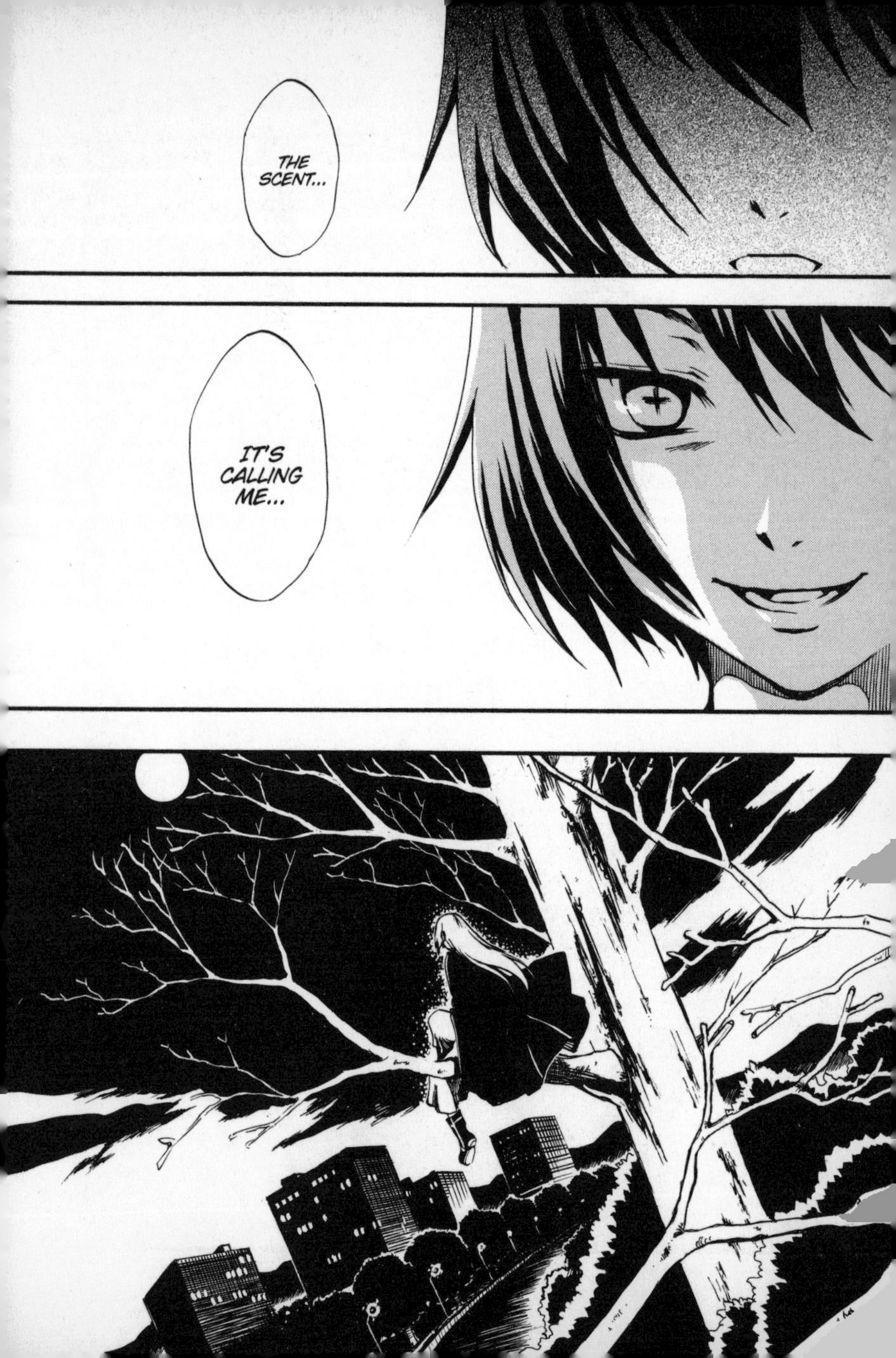
THE SCENT...
IT'S CALLING ME...

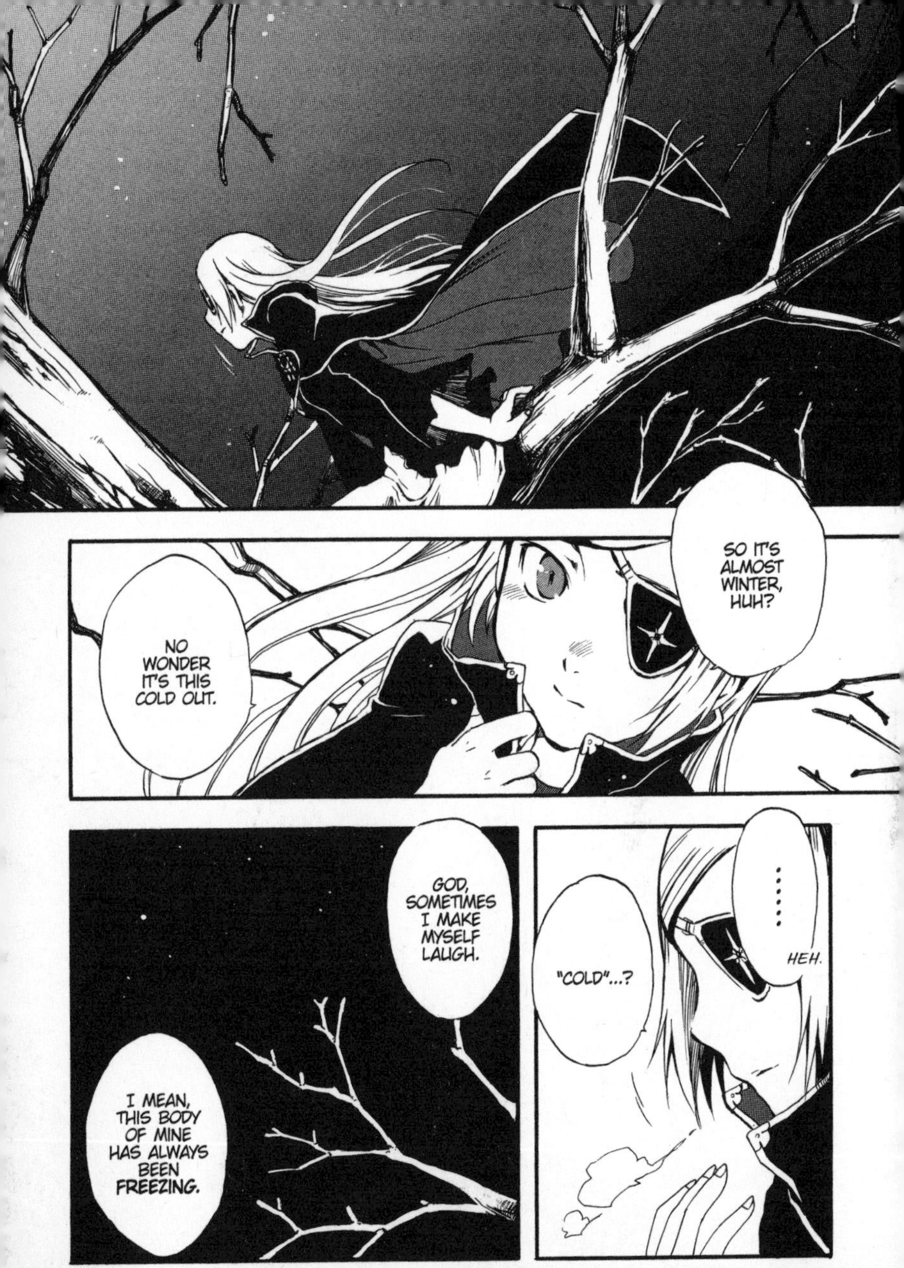
SO IT'S ALMOST WINTER, HUH?
NO WONDER IT'S THIS COLD OUT.
......
HEH.
"COLD"...?
GOD, SOMETIMES I MAKE MYSELF LAUGH.
I MEAN, THIS BODY OF MINE HAS ALWAYS BEEN FREEZING.

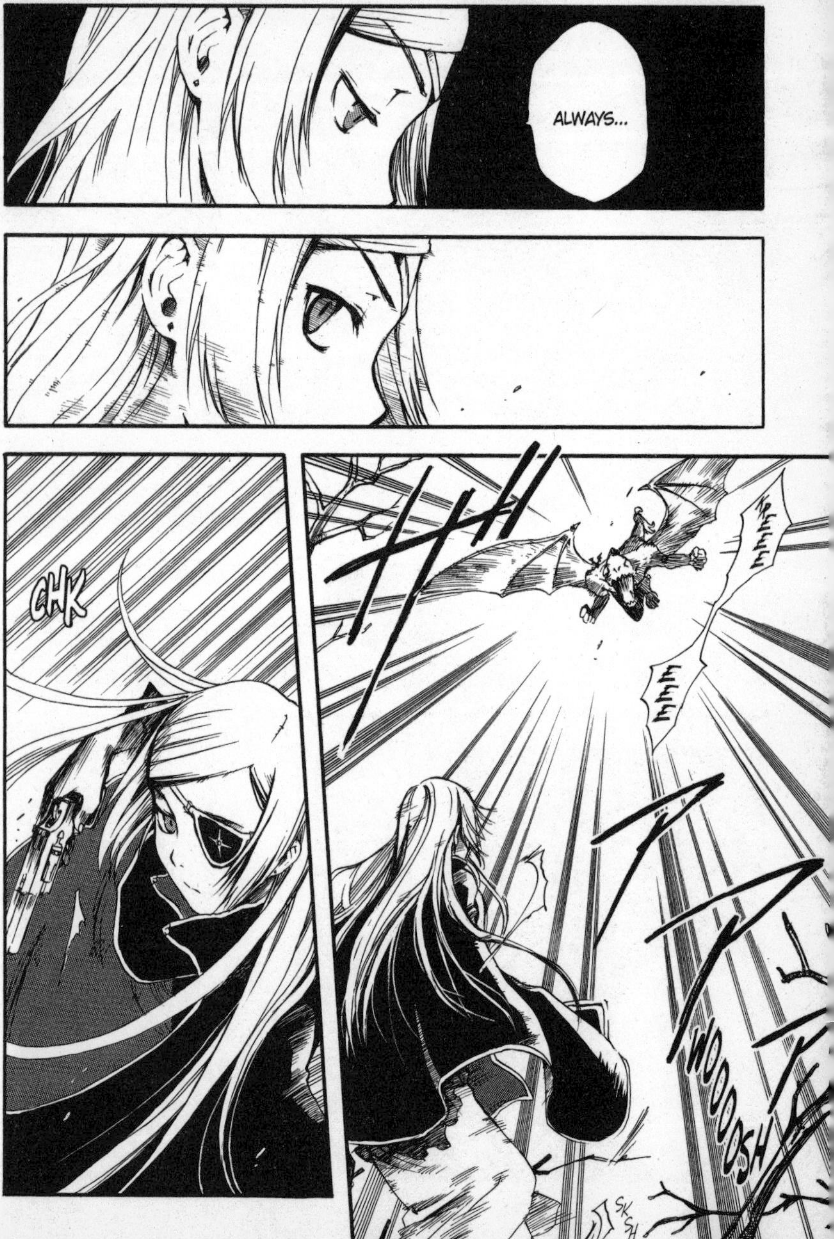
ALWAYS...
KREEEEE
EEEE
WOOOOSH
SKSH
CHK

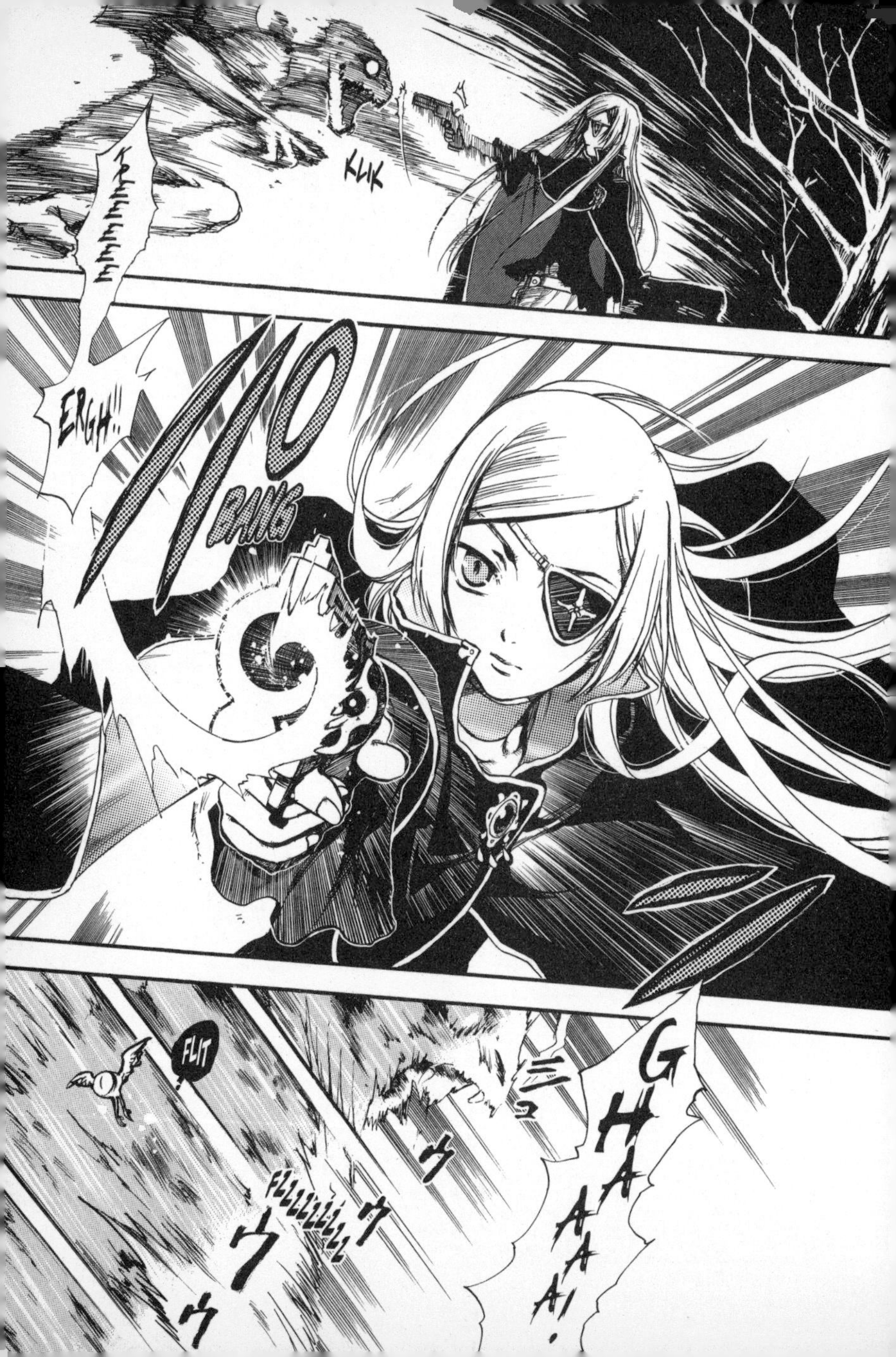
KLIK
KREEEEEEEE
BANG
ERGH!!
GHAAAAA!
ミュ
ウウ
FZZZZZZZZZZ
ウウ
FLIT

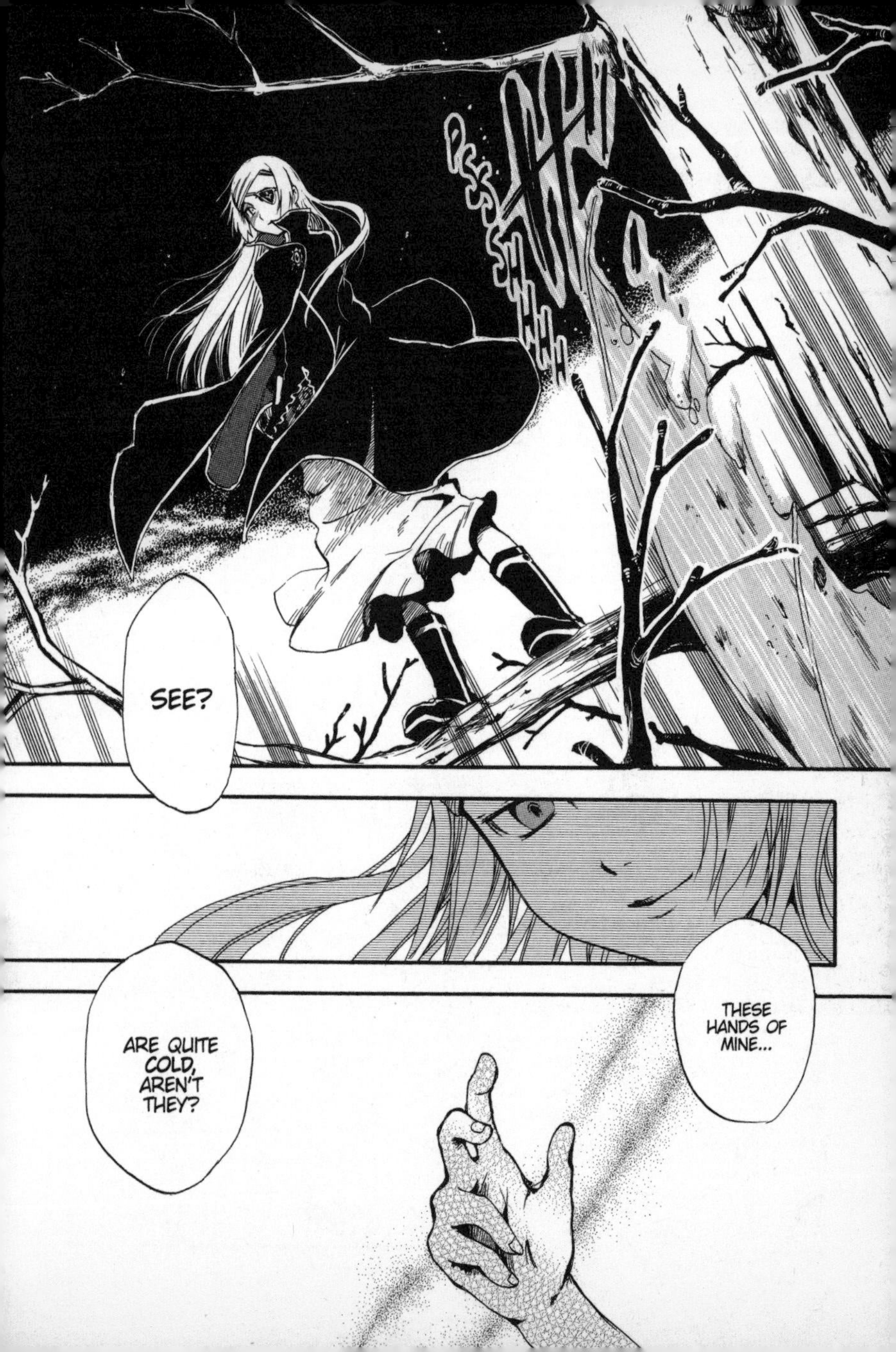
PSSSHHHH
SEE?
THESE HANDS OF MINE...
ARE QUITE COLD, AREN'T THEY?

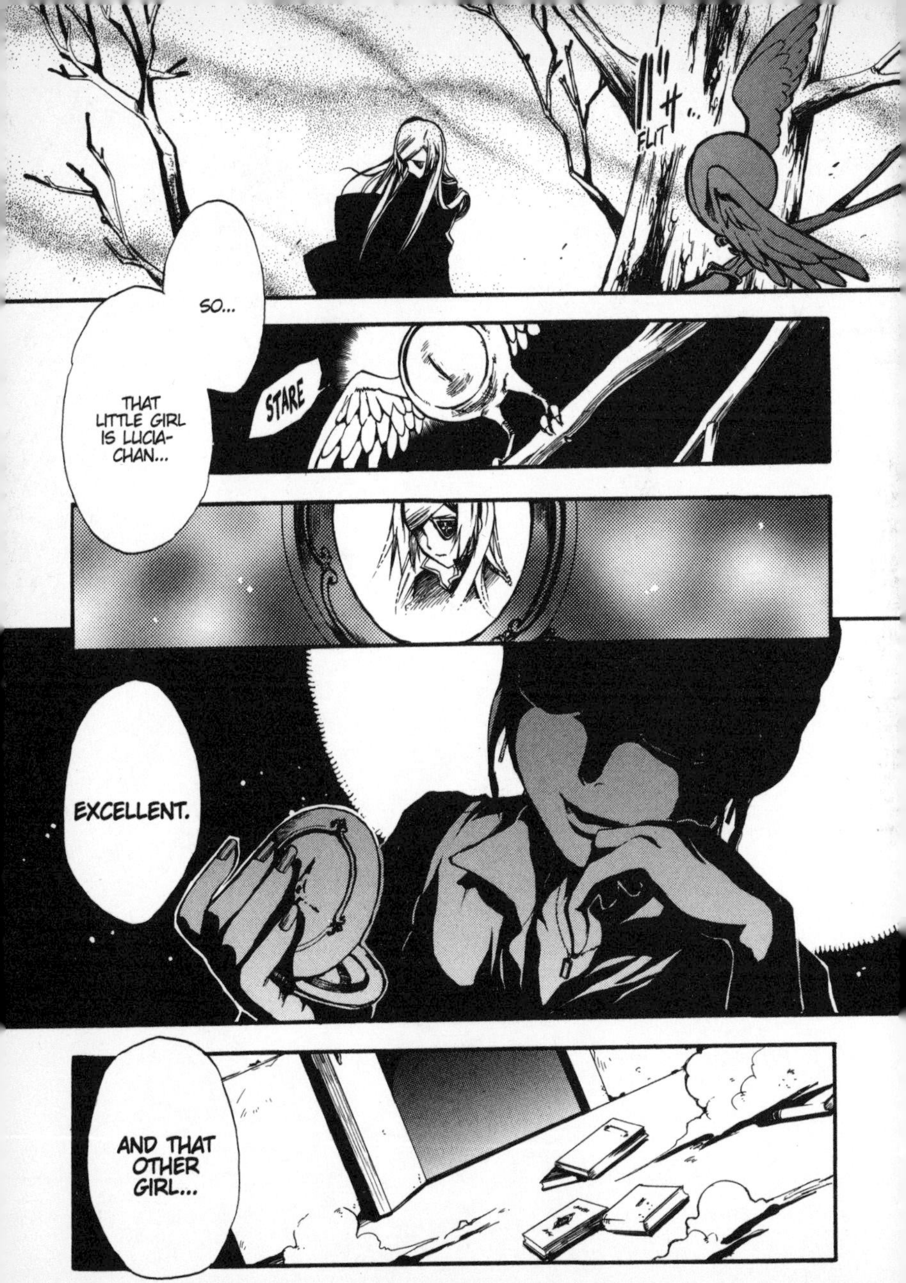
FLIT
SO... THAT LITTLE GIRL IS LUCIA-CHAN...
STARE
EXCELLENT.
AND THAT OTHER GIRL...

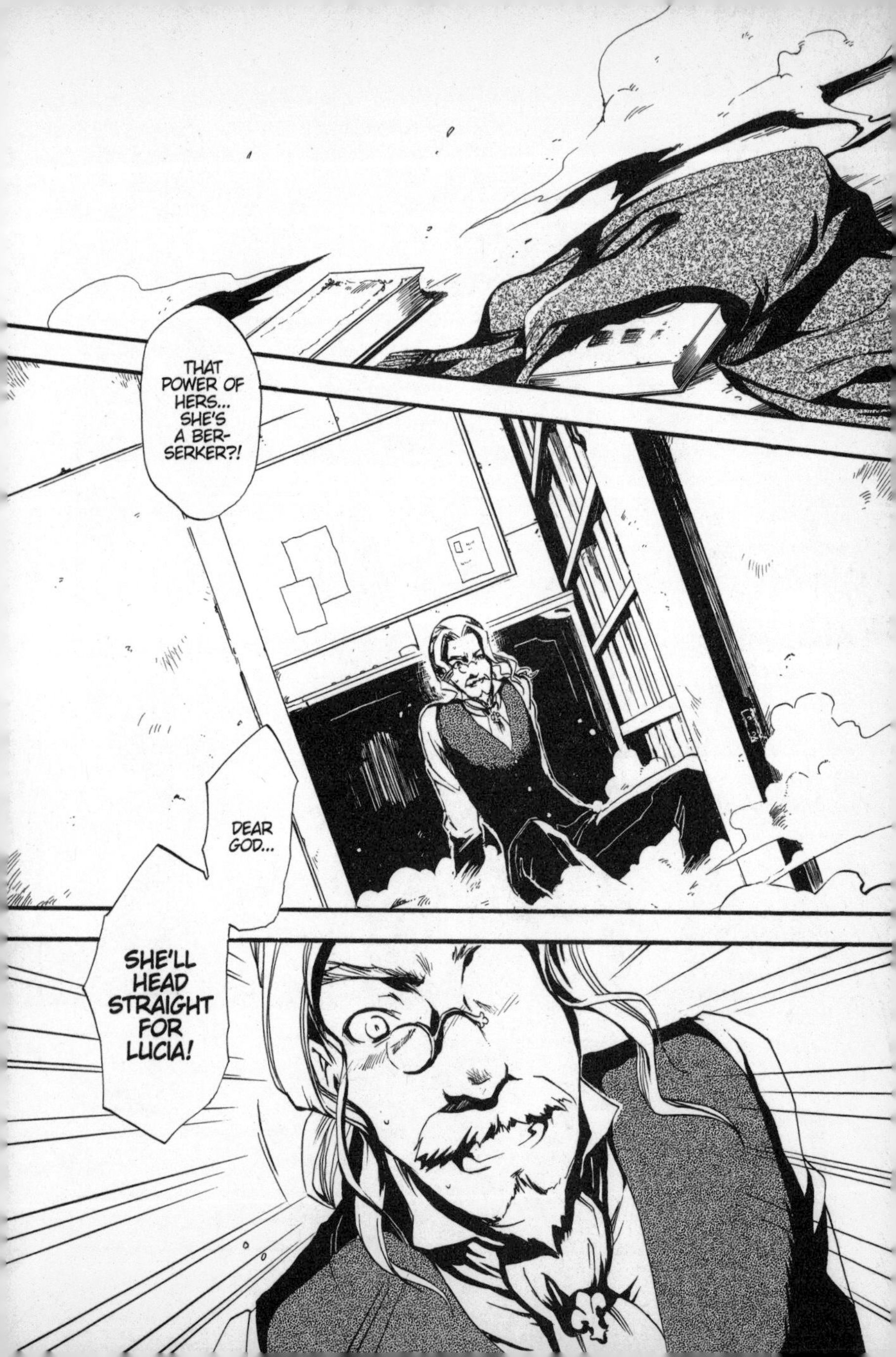
THAT POWER OF HERS... SHE'S A BER-SERKER?!
DEAR GOD...
SHE'LL HEAD STRAIGHT FOR LUCIA!

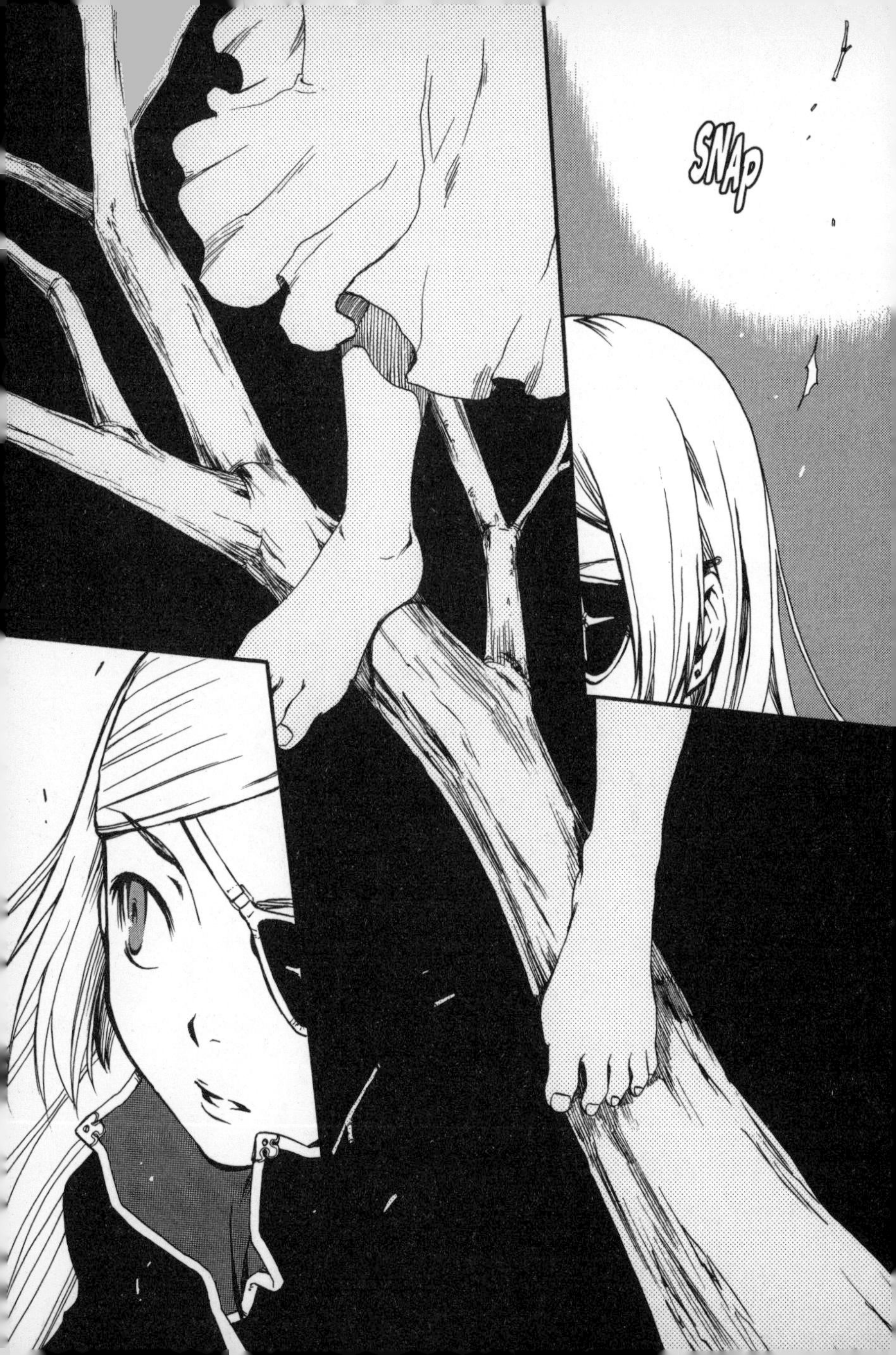
SNAP

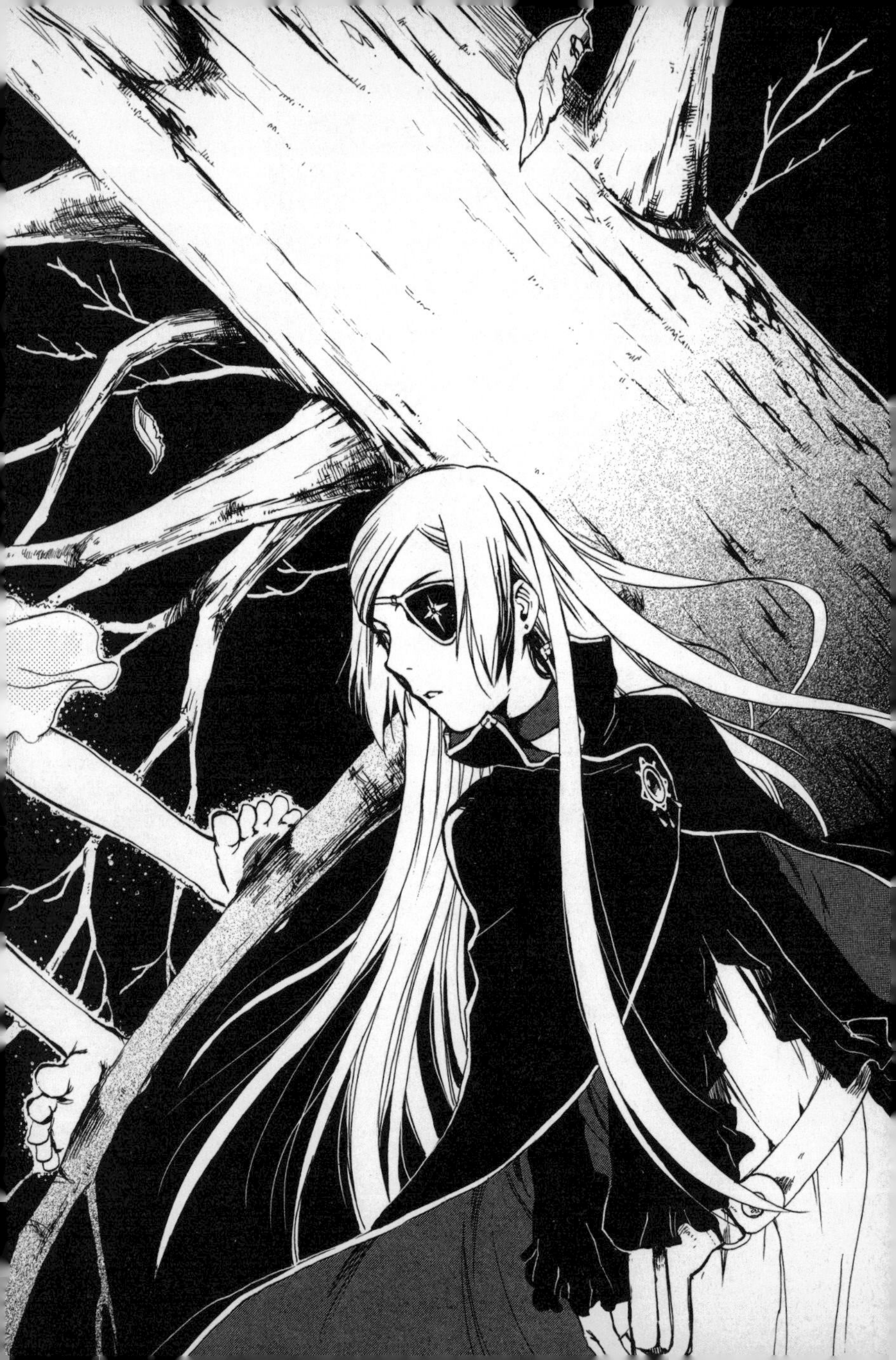

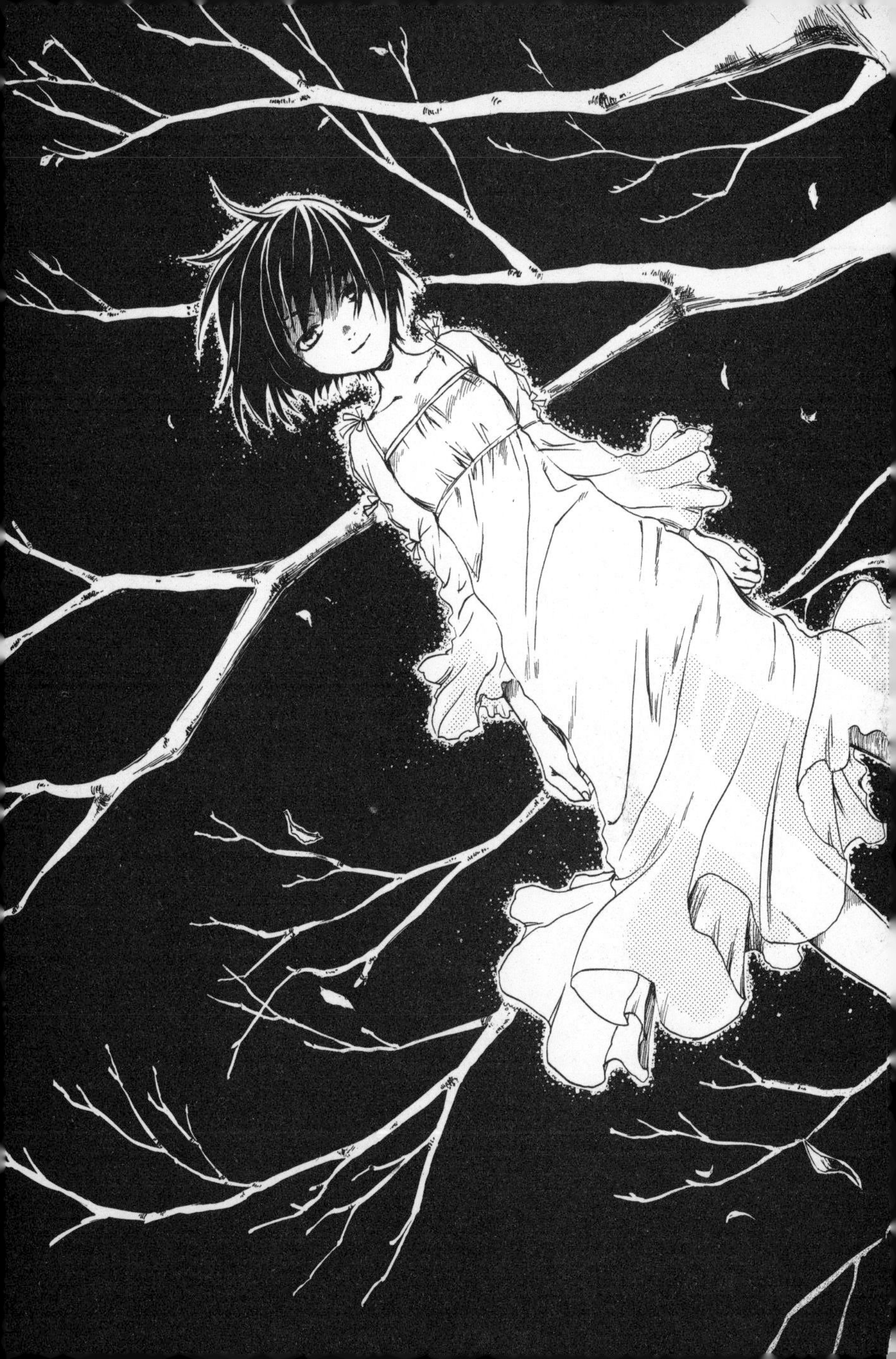

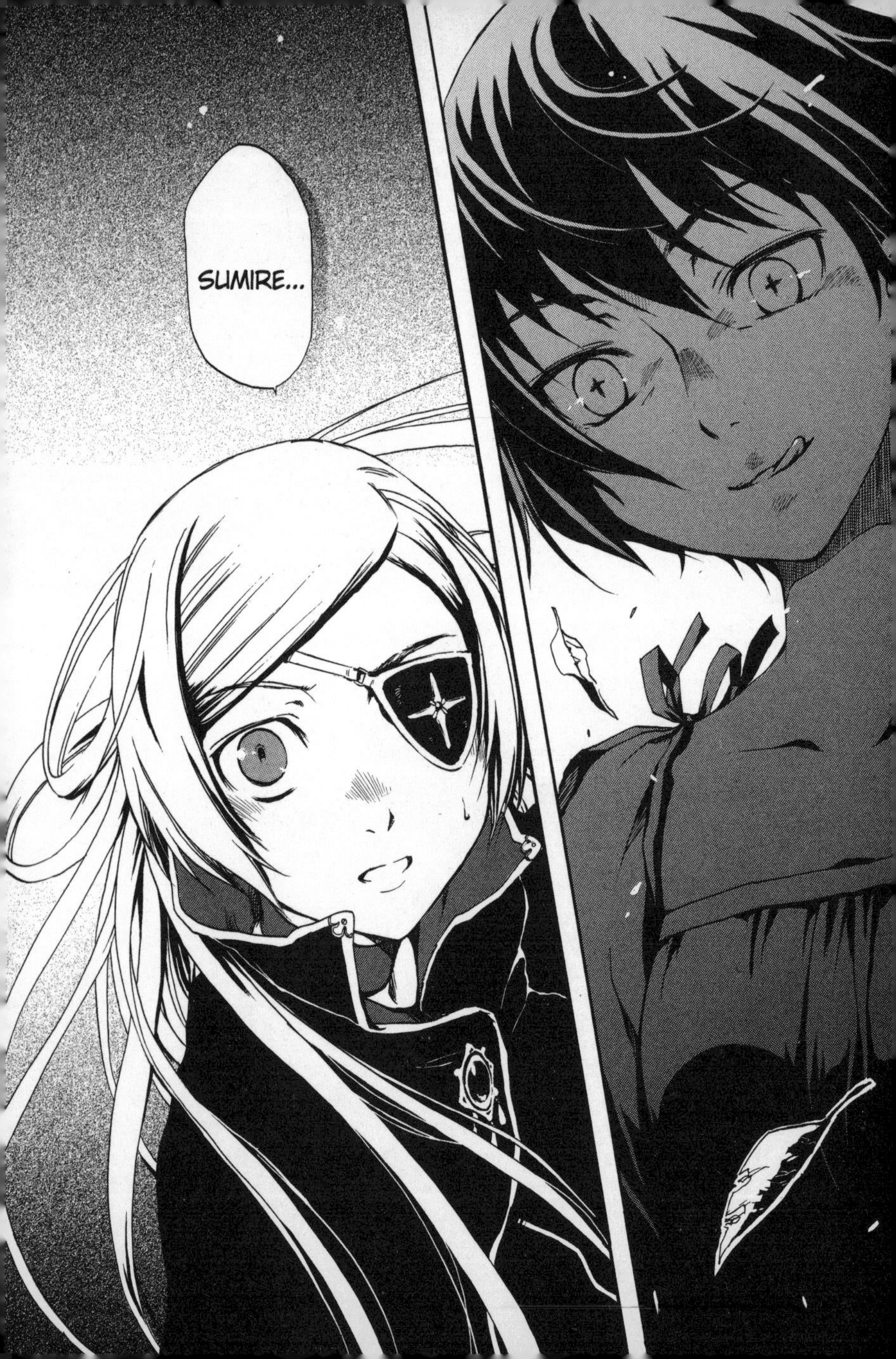
SUMIRE...

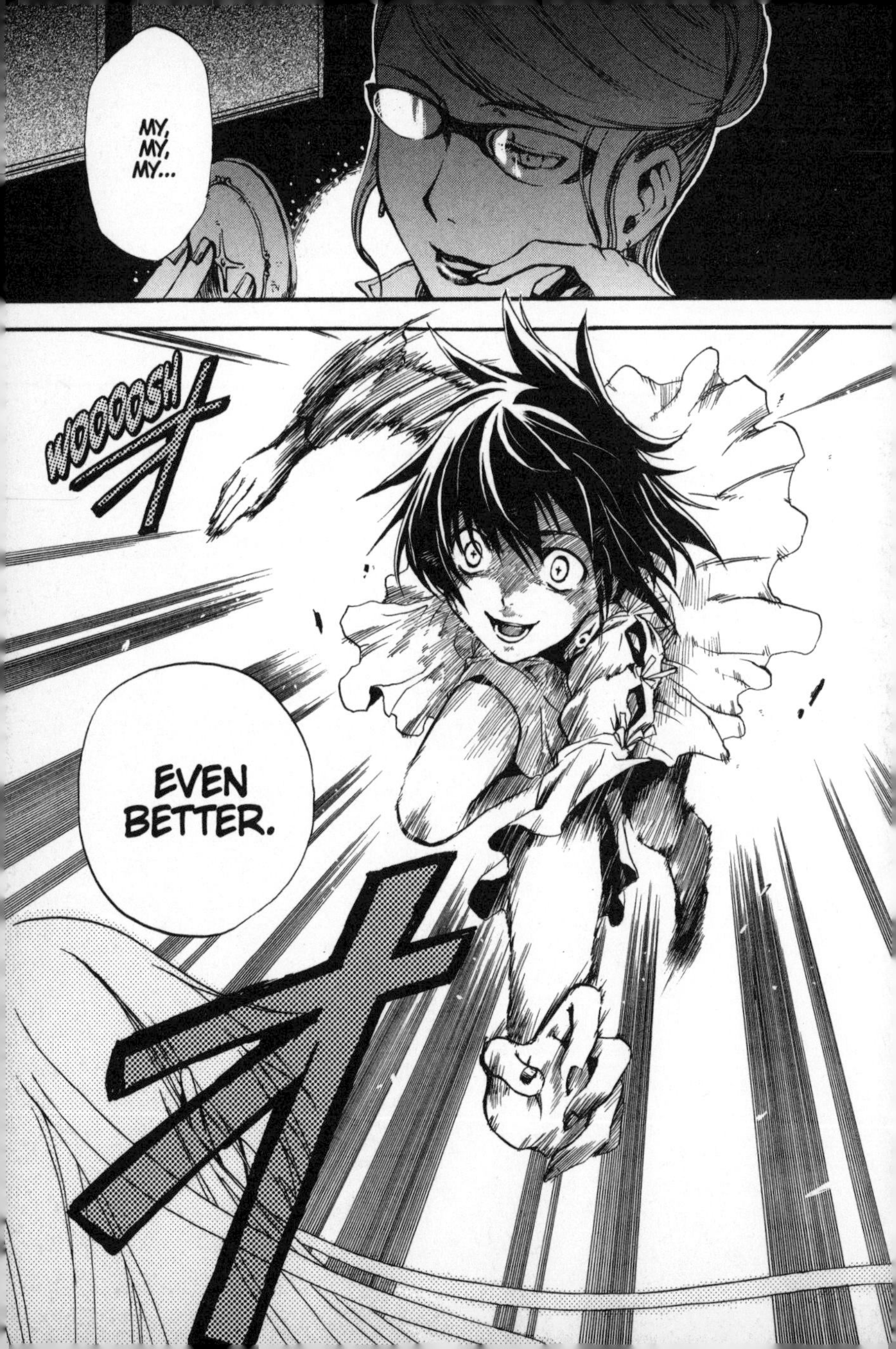
MY, MY, MY...
WOOOOSH
EVEN BETTER.

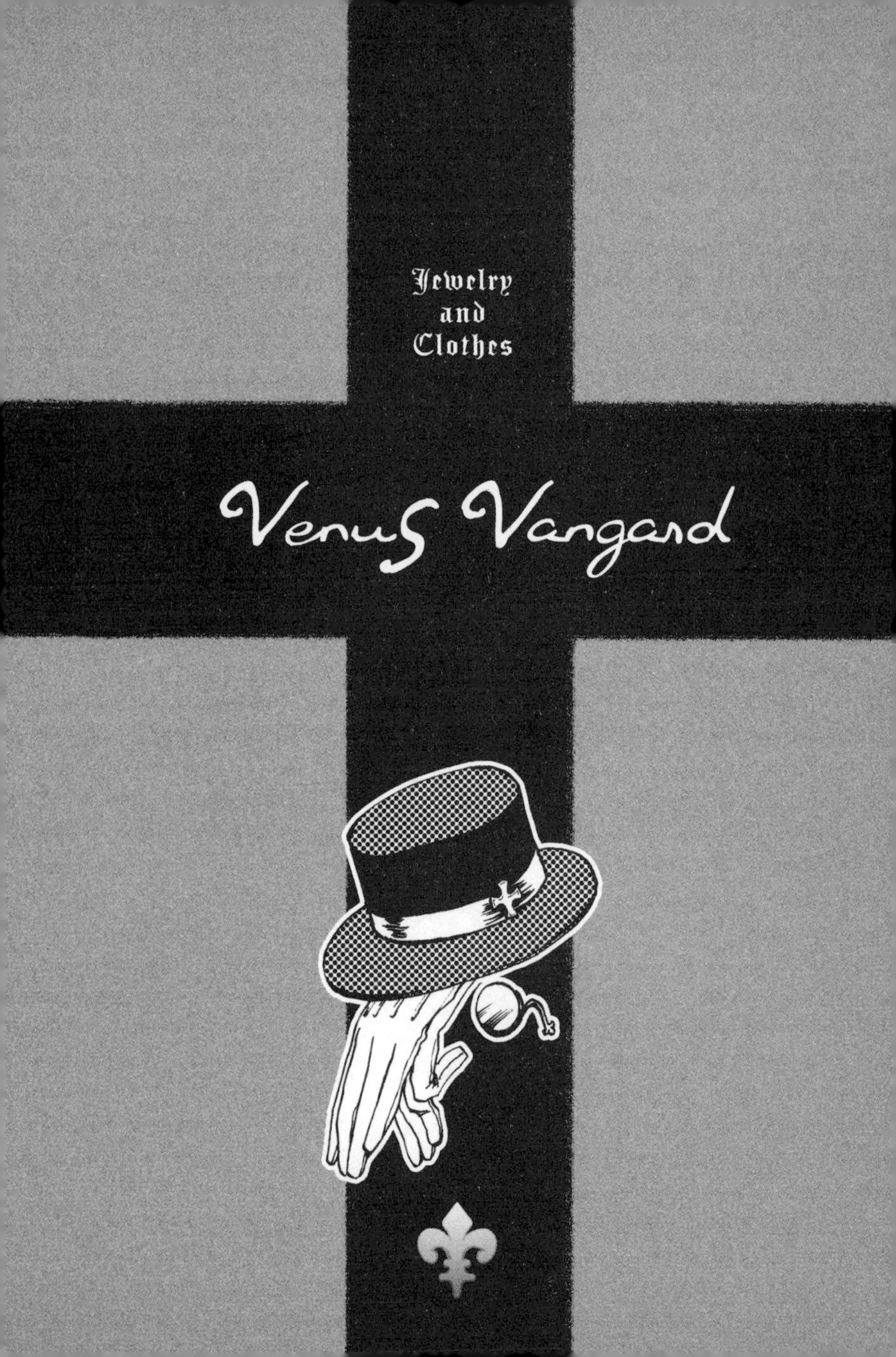
Jewelry
and
Clothes
Venus Vangard

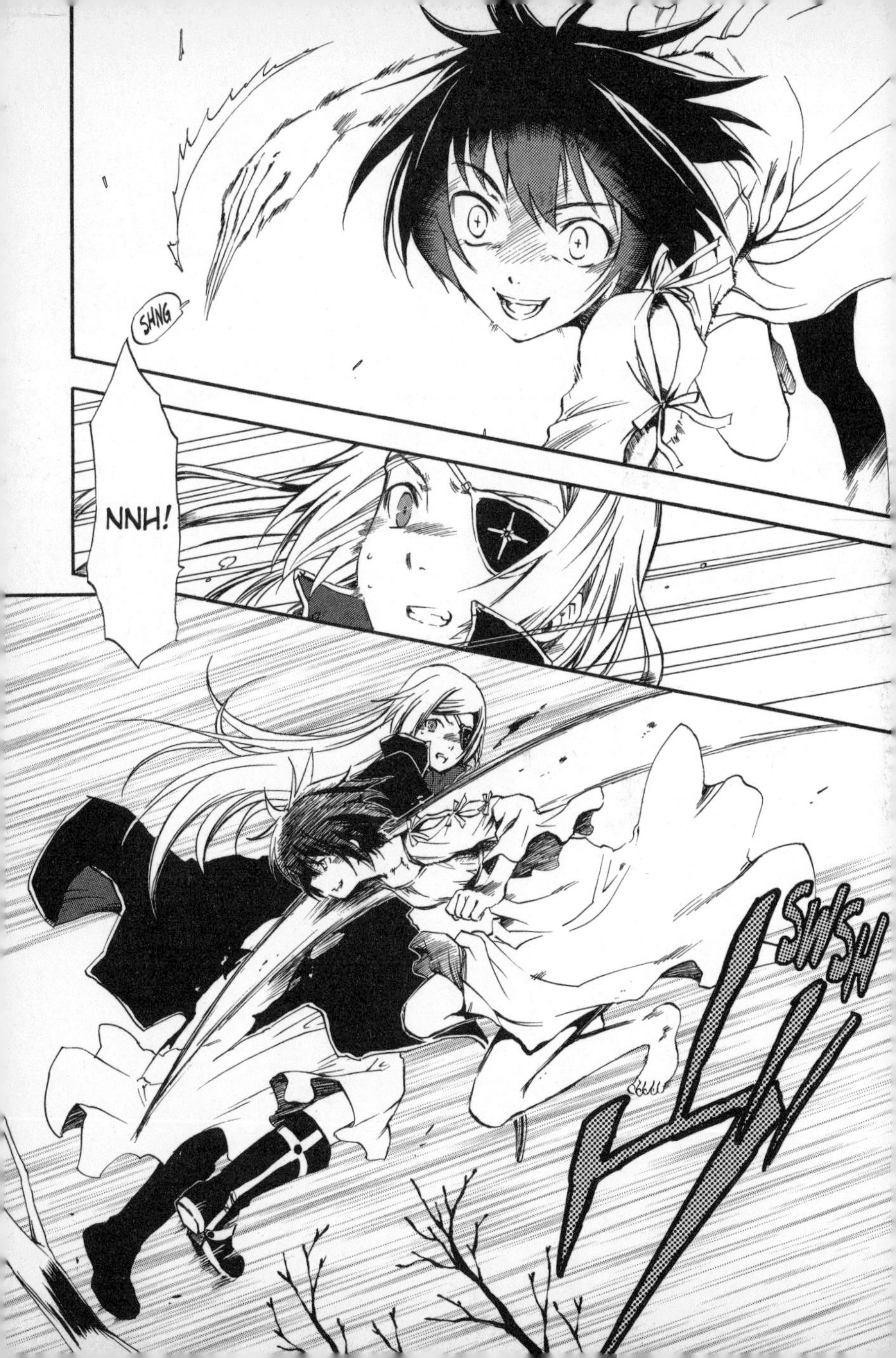
SHNG
NNH!
SWISH

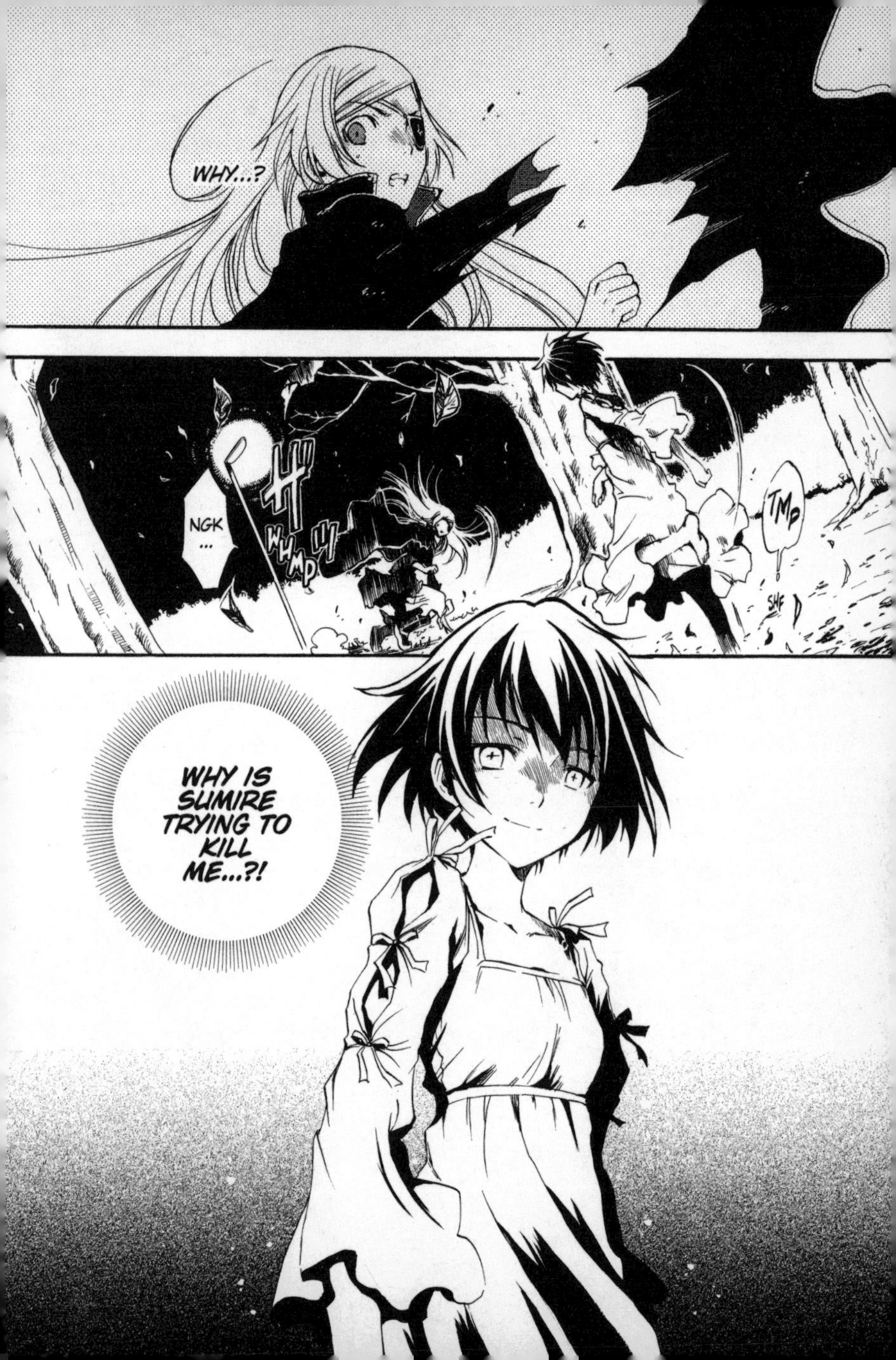
WHY...?
TMP
SHF
WHMP
NGK ...
WHY IS SUMIRE TRYING TO KILL ME...?!

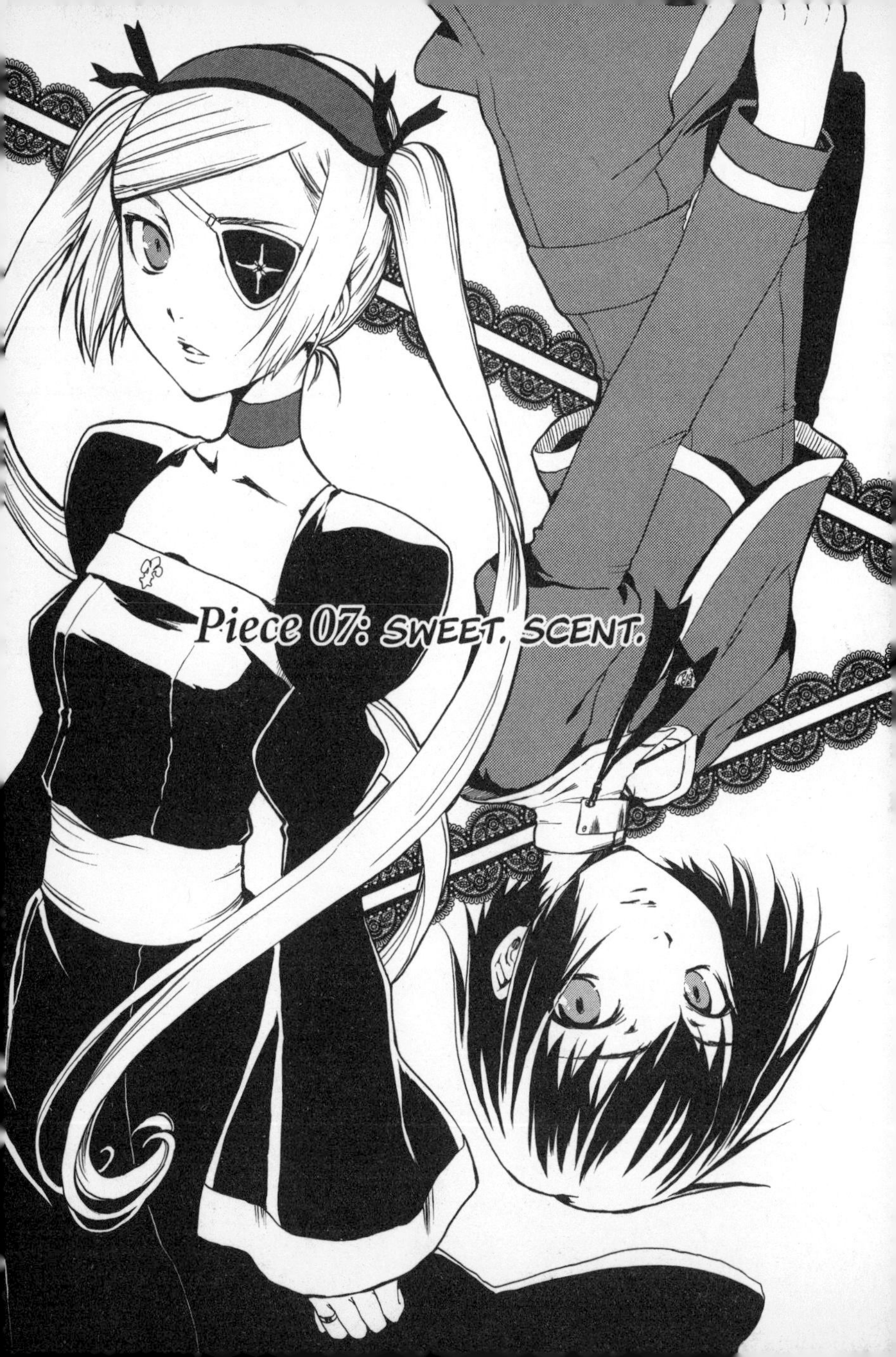
Piece 07: SWEET. SCENT.

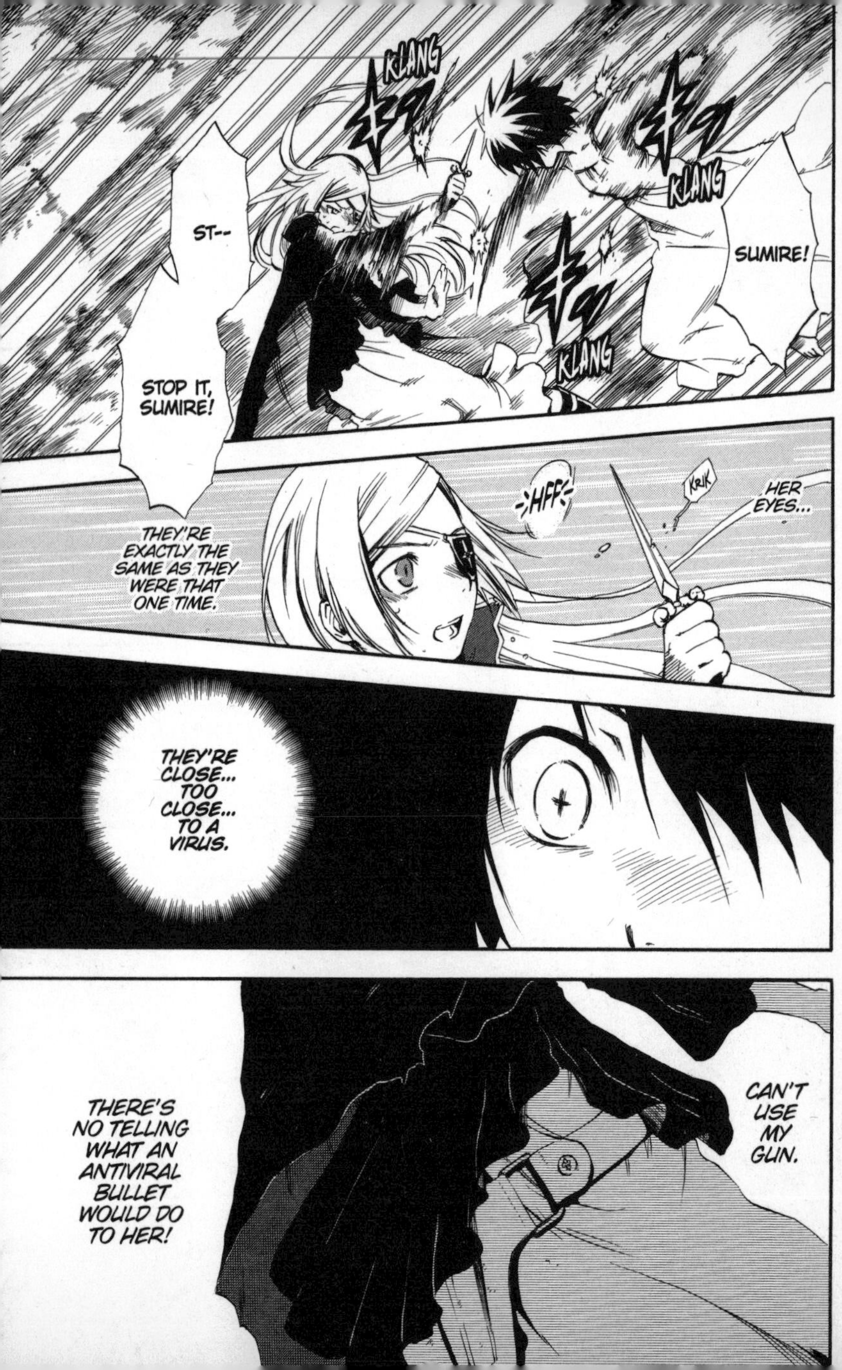
SUMIRE!
KLANG
KLANG
KLANG
ST--
STOP IT, SUMIRE!
HER EYES...
KRIK
HFF
THEY'RE EXACTLY THE SAME AS THEY WERE THAT ONE TIME.
THEY'RE CLOSE... TOO CLOSE... TO A VIRUS.
CAN'T USE MY GUN.
THERE'S NO TELLING WHAT AN ANTIVIRAL BULLET WOULD DO TO HER!

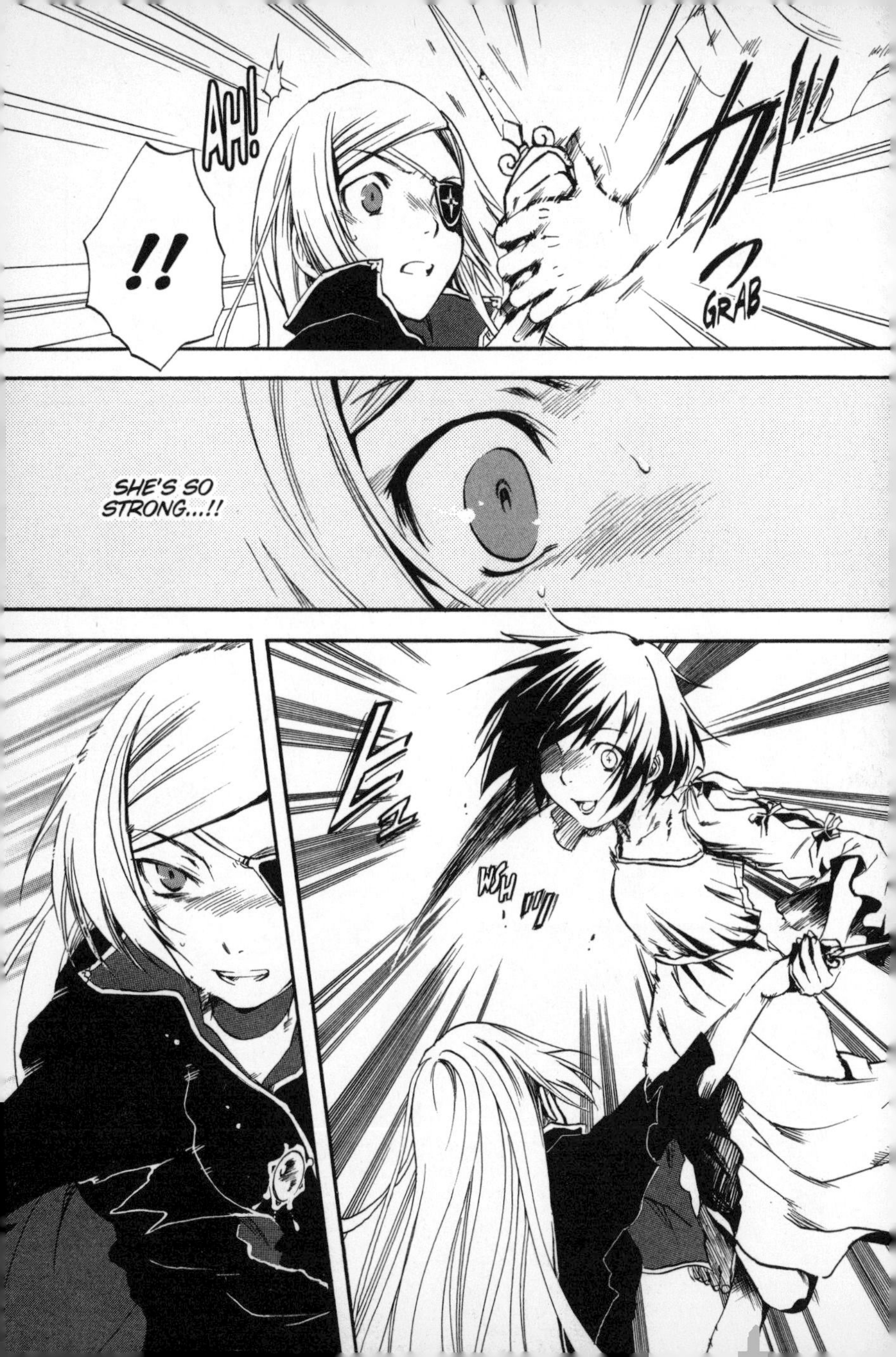
GRAB
AH!
!!
SHE'S SO STRONG...!!

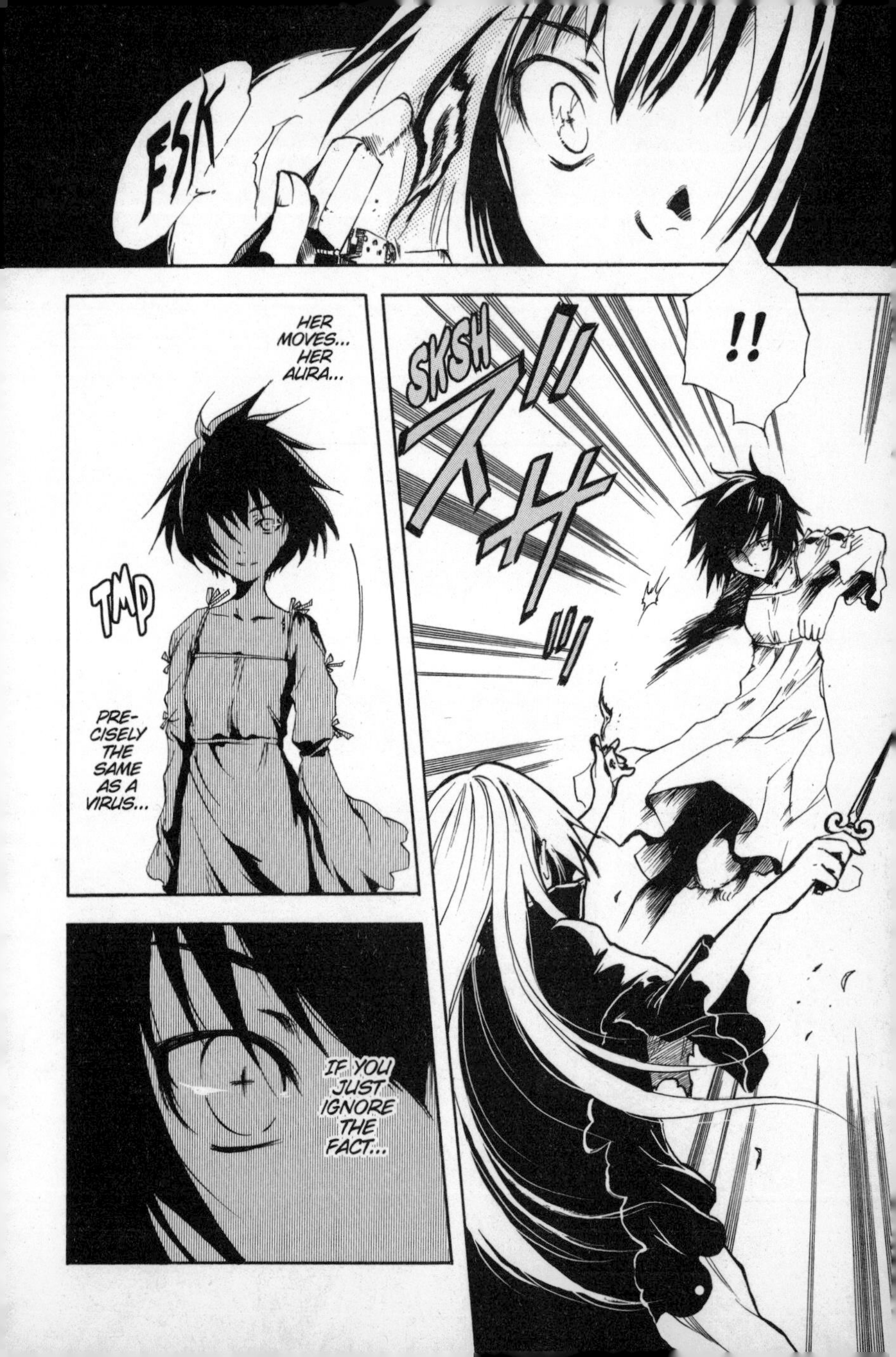
FSK
!!
SKSH
HER MOVES... HER AURA...
TMD
PRE-CISELY THE SAME AS A VIRUS...
IF YOU JUST IGNORE THE FACT...

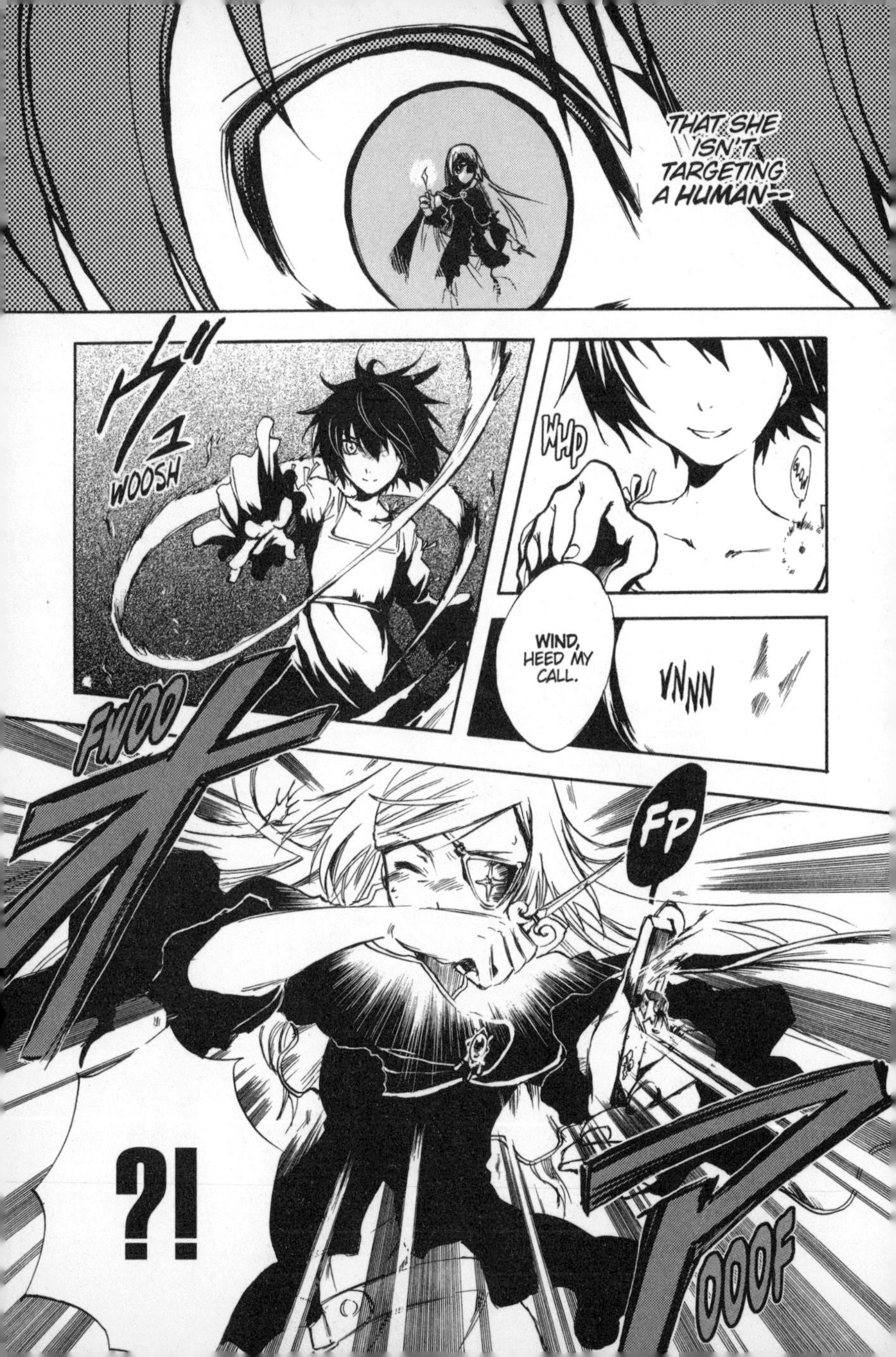
THAT SHE ISN'T TARGETING A HUMAN--
WHP
GLOW
WIND, HEED MY CALL.
VNNN
ジュ
WOOSH
FP
FWOO
OOOF
?!

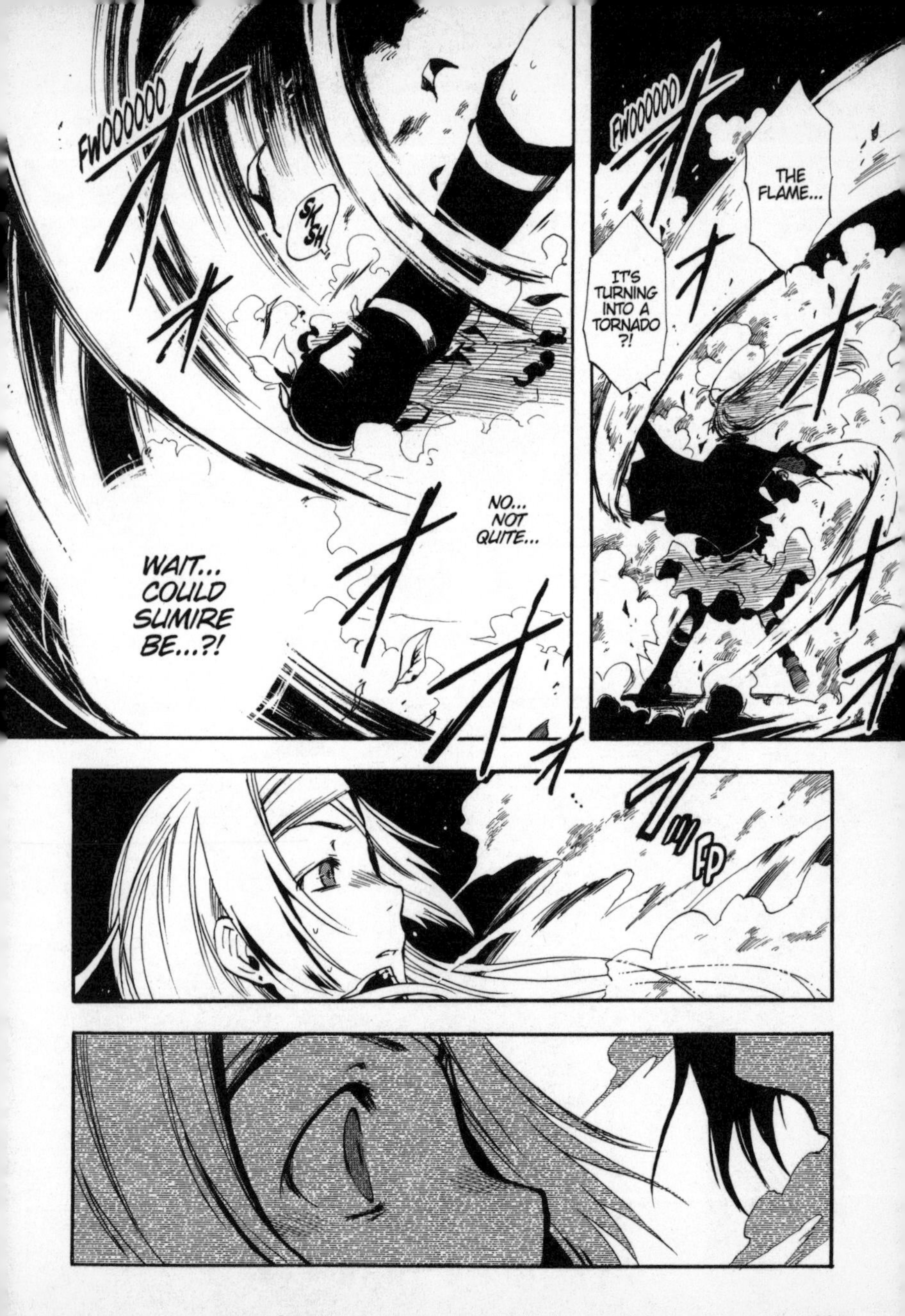
FWOOOOOO
THE FLAME...
IT'S TURNING INTO A TORNADO?!
FWOOOOOO
SH SH
NO... NOT QUITE...
WAIT... COULD SUMIRE BE...?!

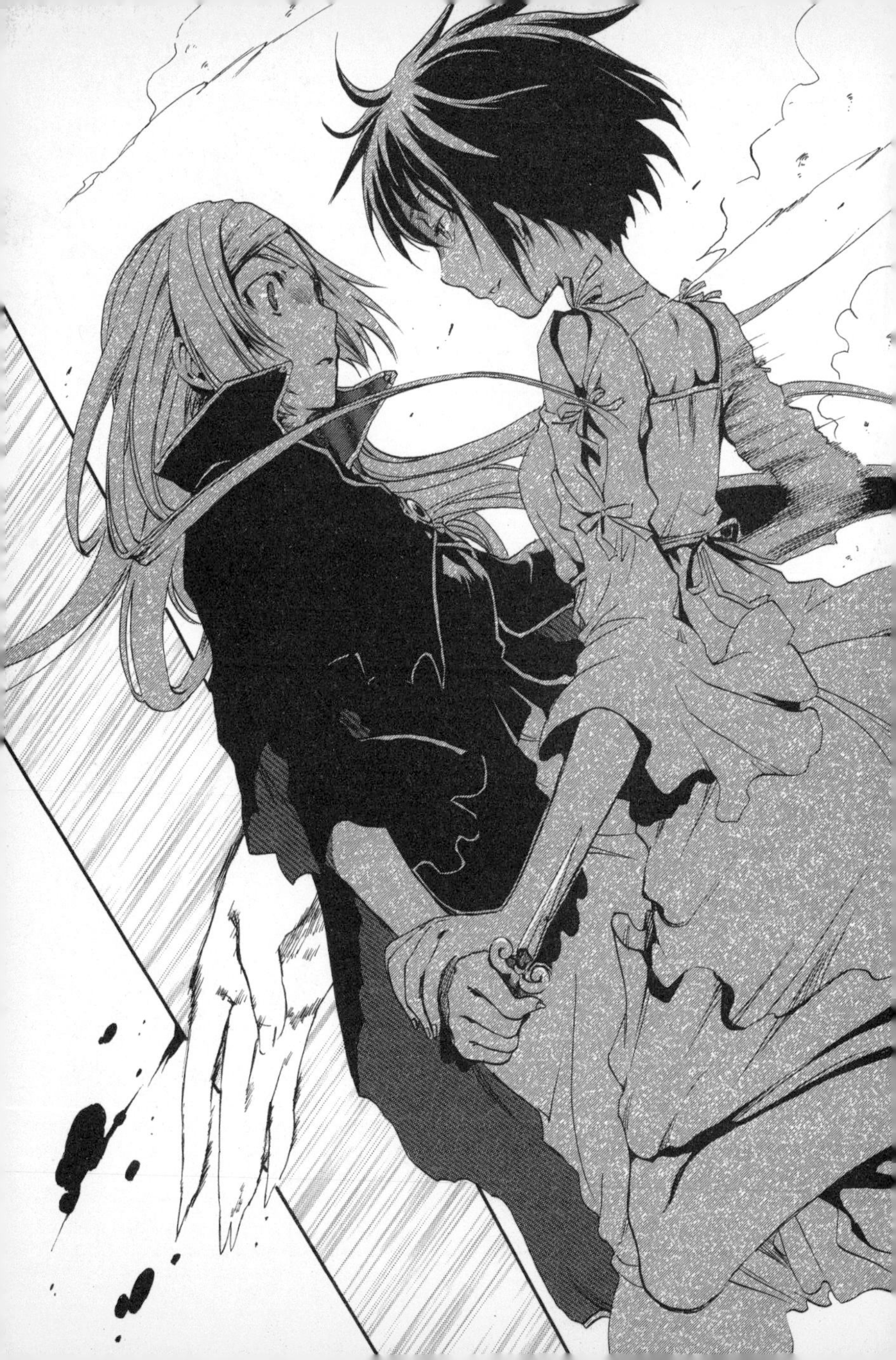

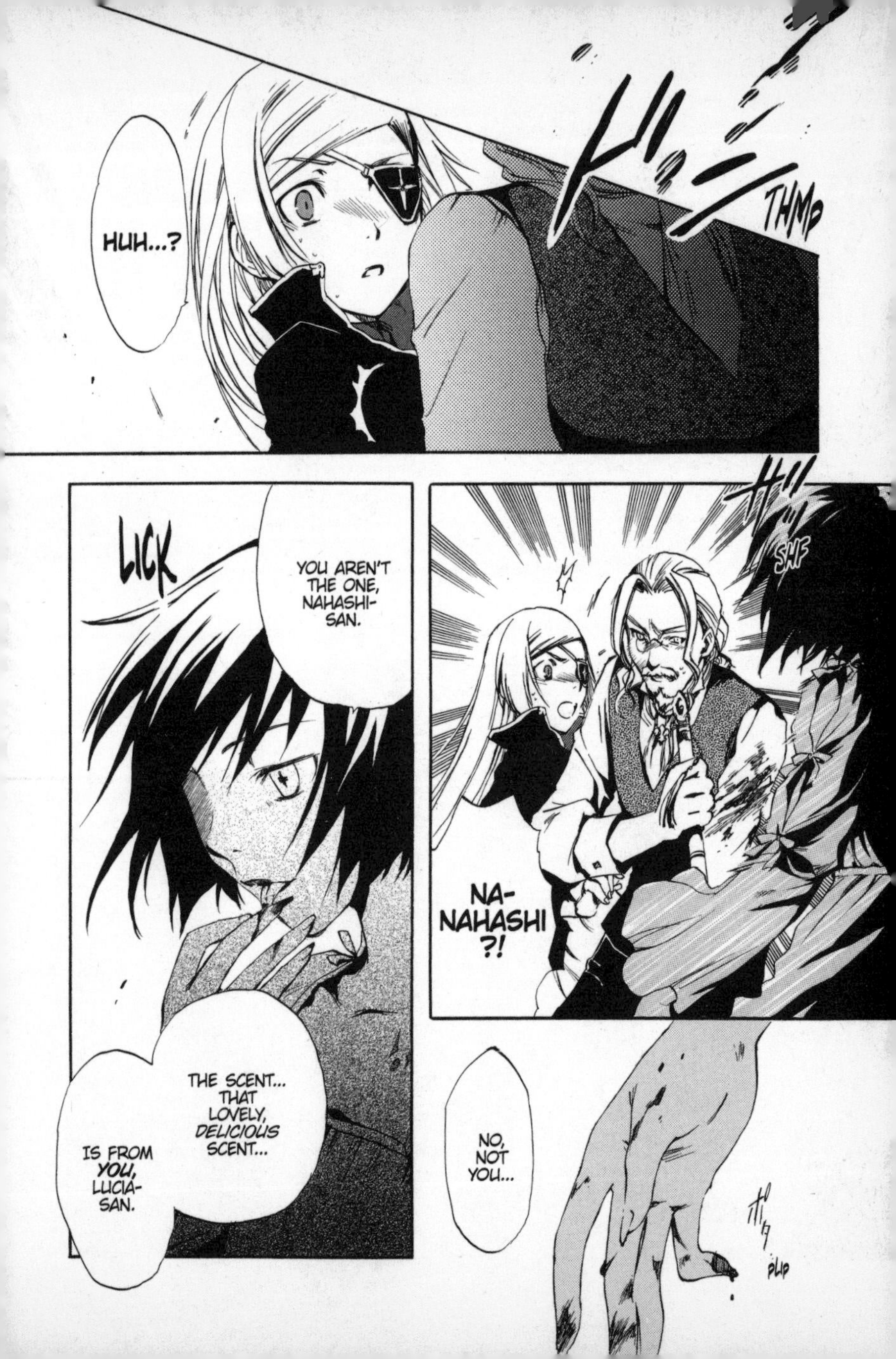
THMP
HUH...?
SHF
NA-NAHASHI?!
NO, NOT YOU...
plip
LICK
YOU AREN'T THE ONE, NAHASHI-SAN.
THE SCENT... THAT LOVELY, DELICIOUS SCENT...
IS FROM YOU, LUCIA-SAN.

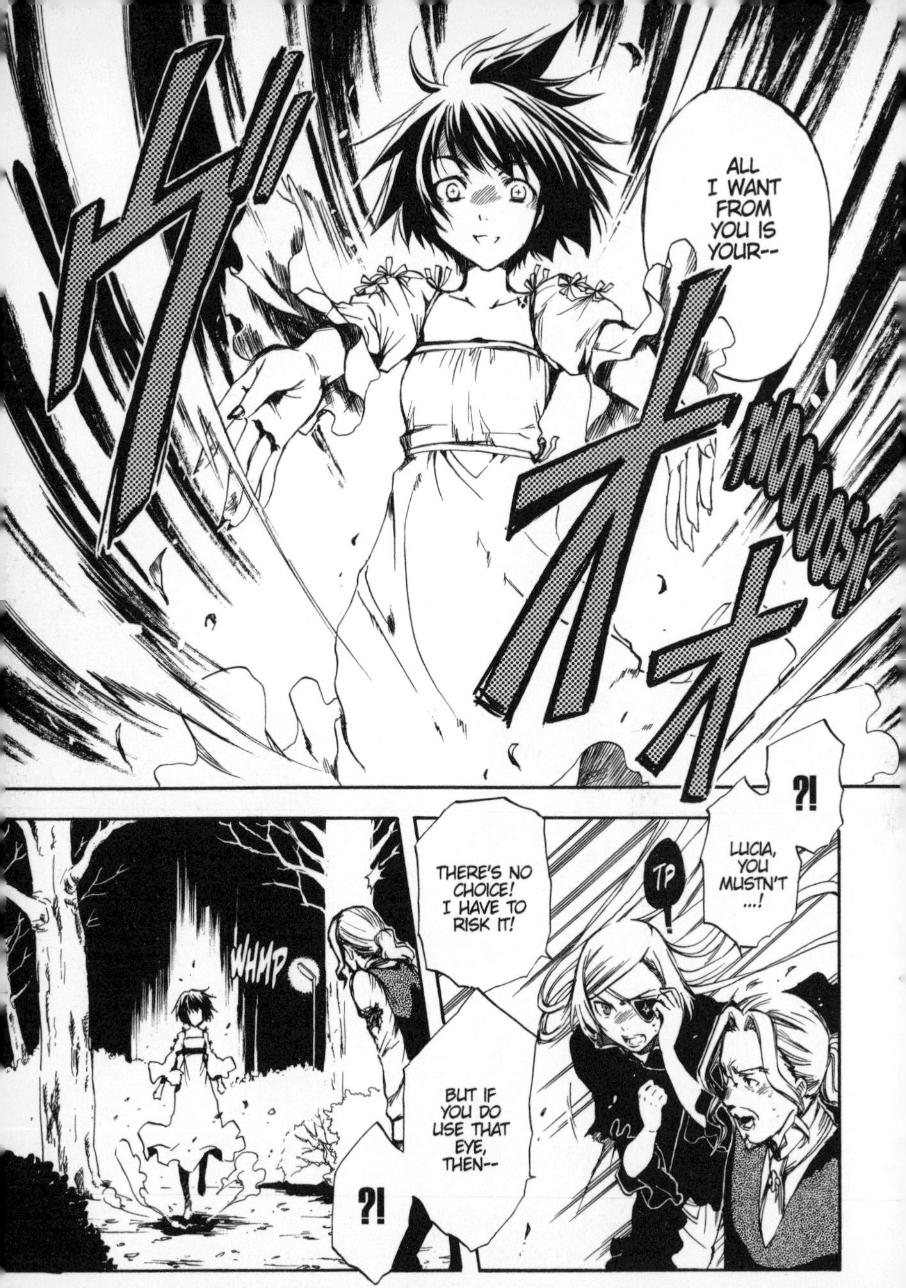
ALL I WANT FROM YOU IS YOUR--
FWOOOOSH!
?!
LUCIA, YOU MUSTN'T ...!
TP
THERE'S NO CHOICE! I HAVE TO RISK IT!
BUT IF YOU DO USE THAT EYE, THEN--
?!
WHMP

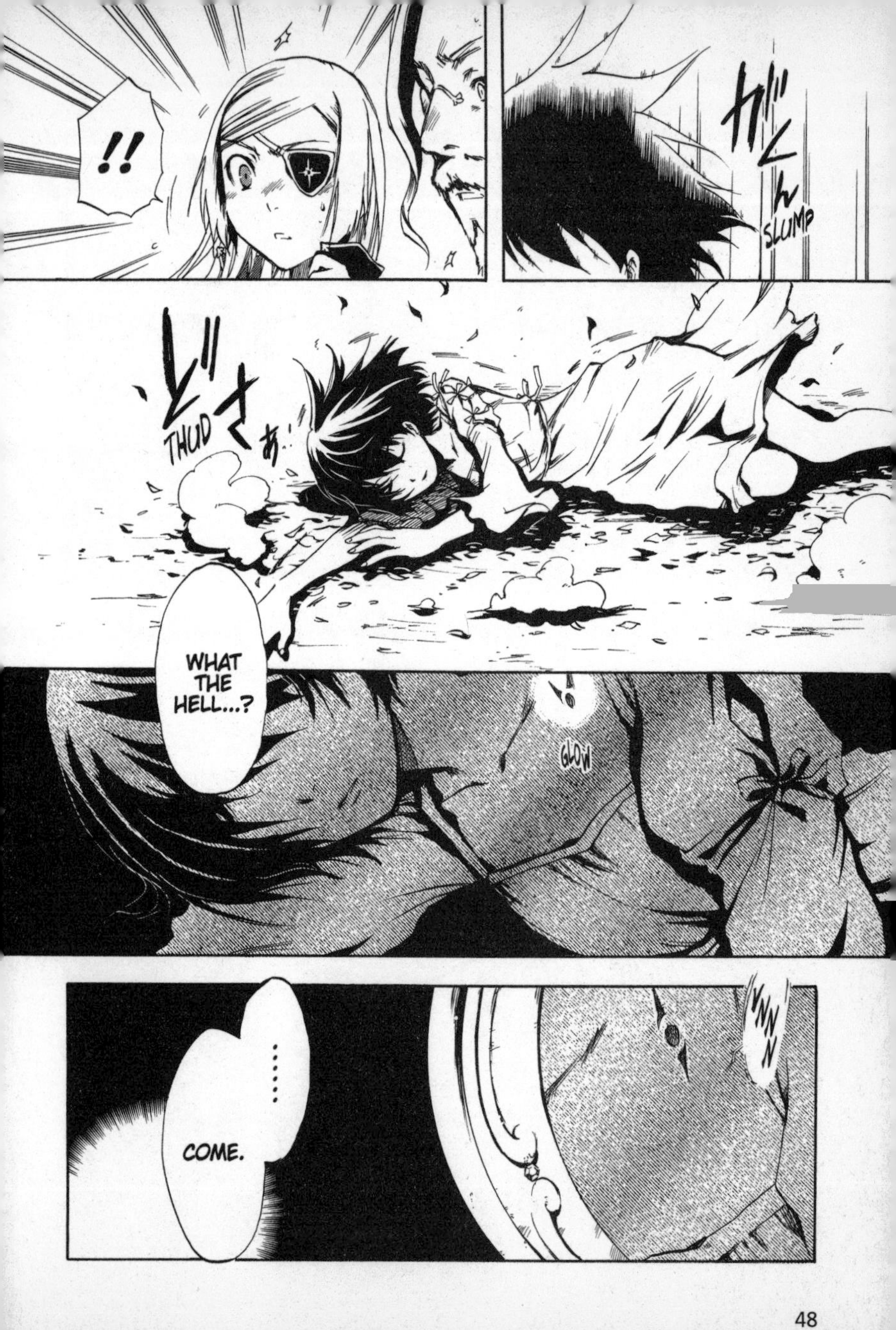
がくん
SLUMP
!!
どさ
THUD
WHAT THE HELL...?
GLOW
VNNN
......
COME.

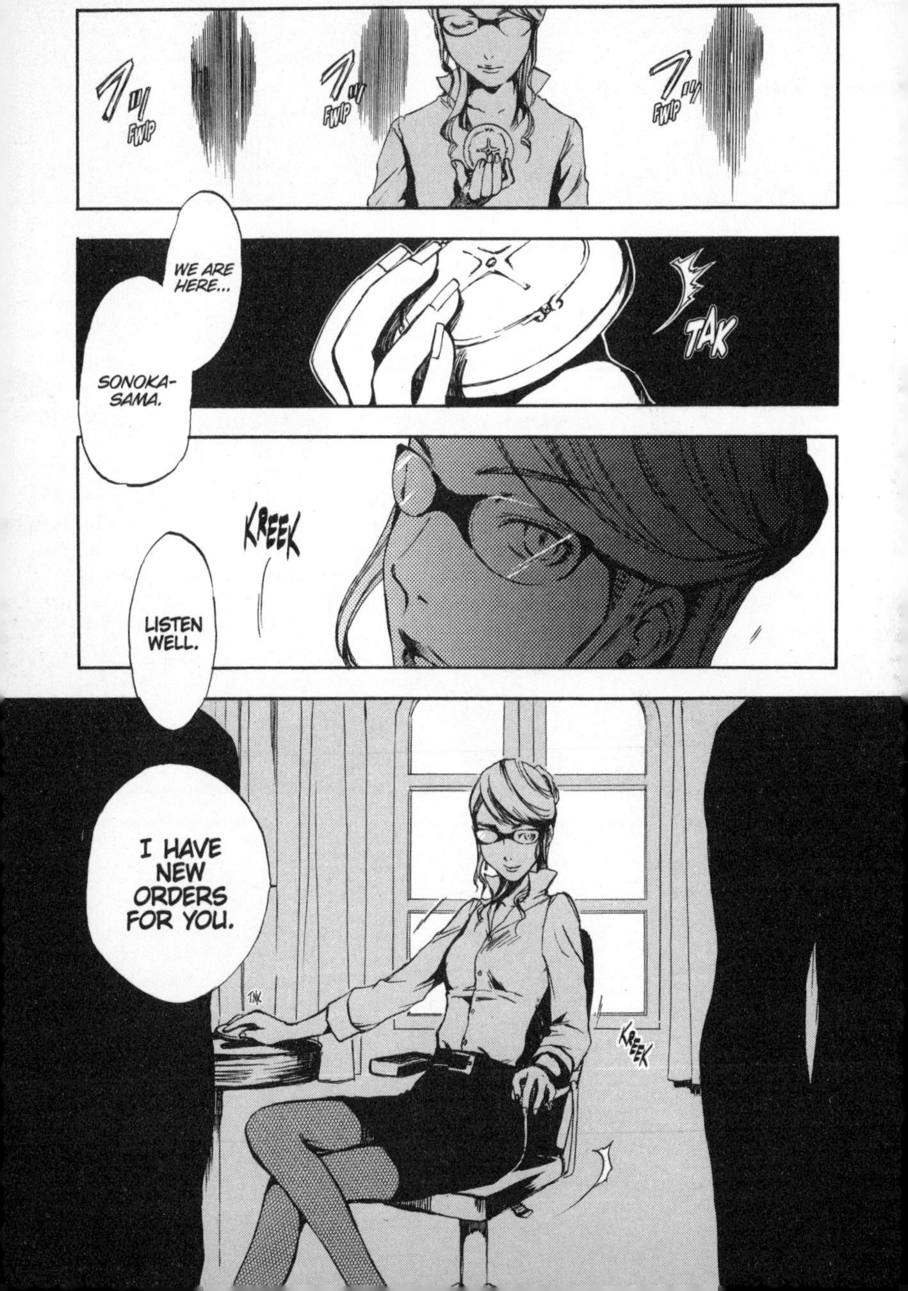
FWIP
FWIP
FWIP
TAK
WE ARE HERE...
SONOKA-SAMA.
KREEK
LISTEN WELL.
KREEK
I HAVE NEW ORDERS FOR YOU.
TINK

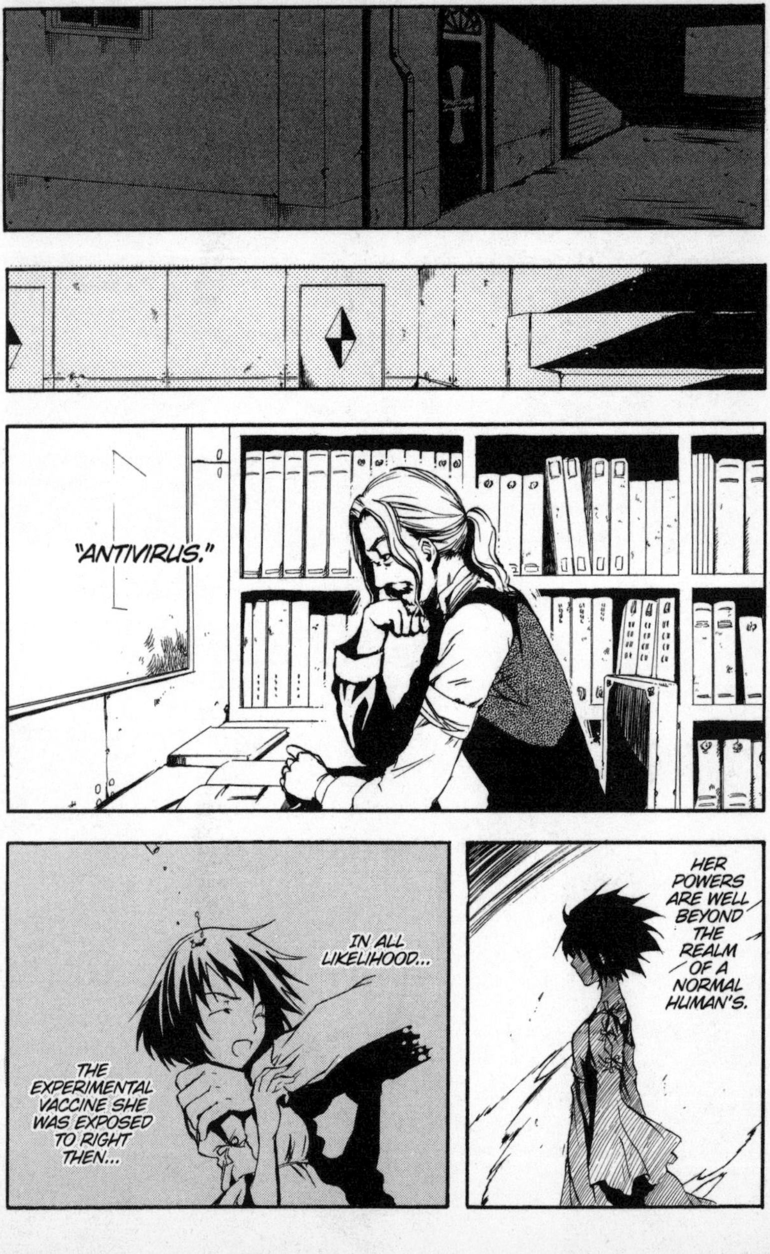
"ANTIVIRUS."
HER POWERS ARE WELL BEYOND THE REALM OF A NORMAL HUMAN'S.
IN ALL LIKELIHOOD...
THE EXPERIMENTAL VACCINE SHE WAS EXPOSED TO RIGHT THEN...

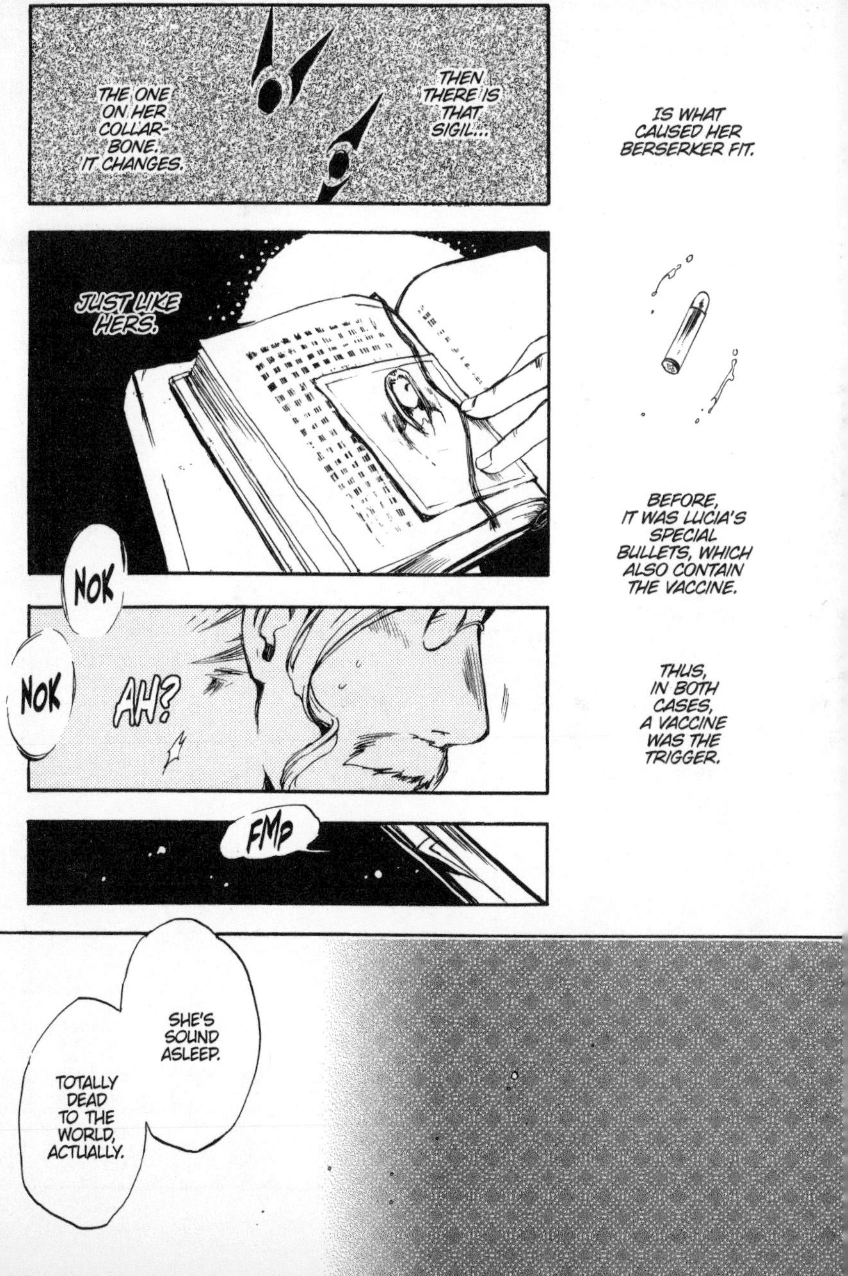
IS WHAT CAUSED HER BERSERKER FIT.
BEFORE, IT WAS LUCIA'S SPECIAL BULLETS, WHICH ALSO CONTAIN THE VACCINE.
THUS, IN BOTH CASES, A VACCINE WAS THE TRIGGER.
THEN THERE IS THAT SIGIL...
THE ONE ON HER COLLAR-BONE. IT CHANGES.
JUST LIKE HERS.
NOK
NOK
AH?
FMP
SHE'S SOUND ASLEEP.
TOTALLY DEAD TO THE WORLD, ACTUALLY.

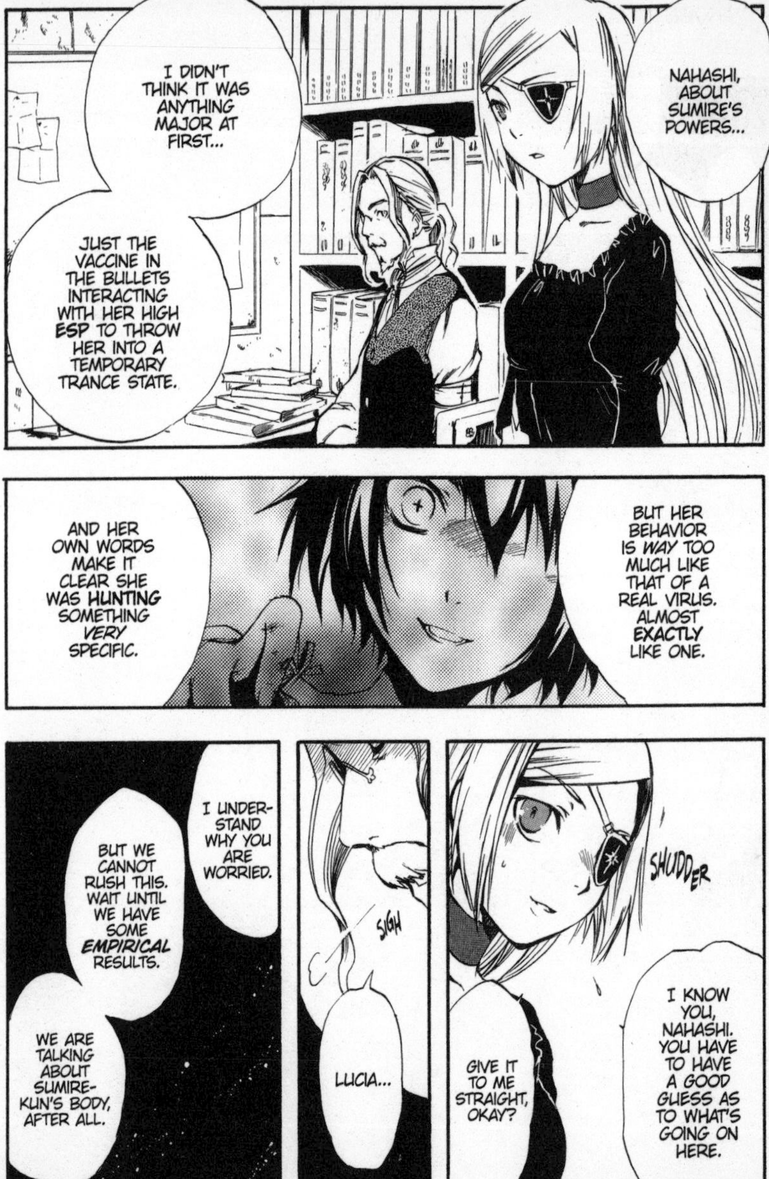
NAHASHI, ABOUT SUMIRE'S POWERS...
I DIDN'T THINK IT WAS ANYTHING MAJOR AT FIRST...
JUST THE VACCINE IN THE BULLETS INTERACTING WITH HER HIGH ESP TO THROW HER INTO A TEMPORARY TRANCE STATE.
BUT HER BEHAVIOR IS WAY TOO MUCH LIKE THAT OF A REAL VIRUS. ALMOST EXACTLY LIKE ONE.
AND HER OWN WORDS MAKE IT CLEAR SHE WAS HUNTING SOMETHING VERY SPECIFIC.
SHUDDER
I KNOW YOU, NAHASHI. YOU HAVE TO HAVE A GOOD GUESS AS TO WHAT'S GOING ON HERE.
GIVE IT TO ME STRAIGHT, OKAY?
I UNDER-STAND WHY YOU ARE WORRIED.
SIGH
LUCIA...
BUT WE CANNOT RUSH THIS. WAIT UNTIL WE HAVE SOME EMPIRICAL RESULTS.
WE ARE TALKING ABOUT SUMIRE-KUN'S BODY, AFTER ALL.

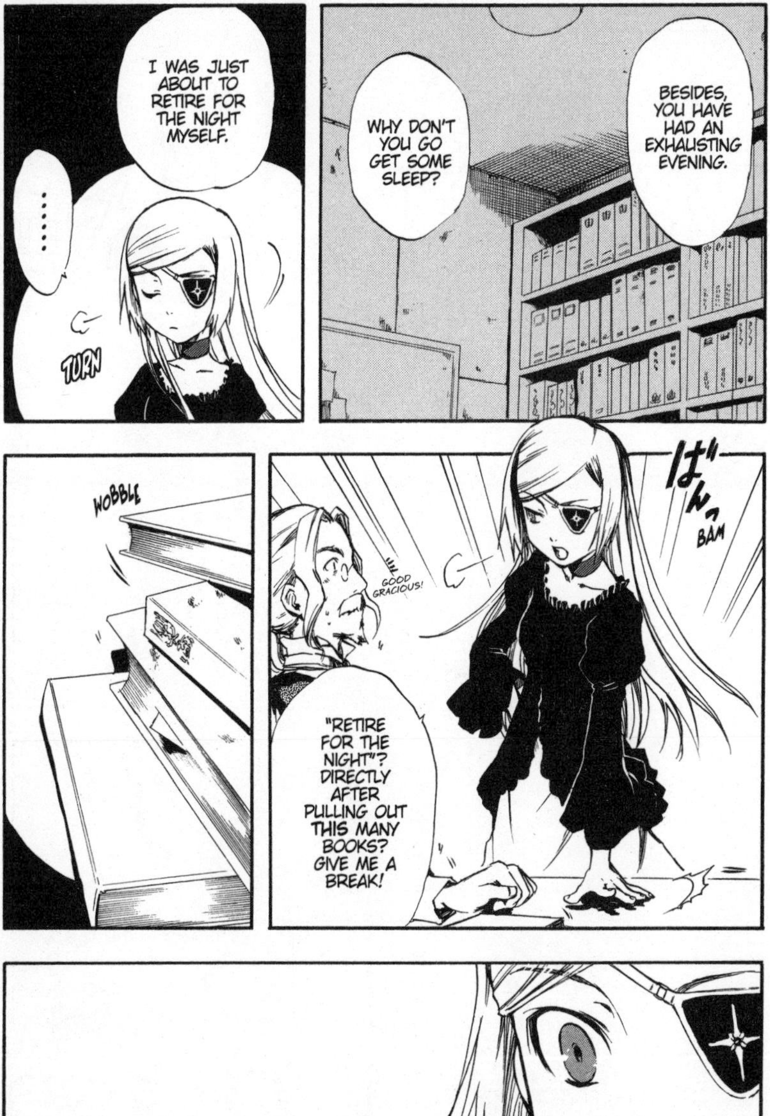
BESIDES, YOU HAVE HAD AN EXHAUSTING EVENING.
WHY DON'T YOU GO GET SOME SLEEP?
I WAS JUST ABOUT TO RETIRE FOR THE NIGHT MYSELF.
......
TURN
ばんっ
BAM
GOOD GRACIOUS!
"RETIRE FOR THE NIGHT"? DIRECTLY AFTER PULLING OUT THIS MANY BOOKS? GIVE ME A BREAK!
WOBBLE

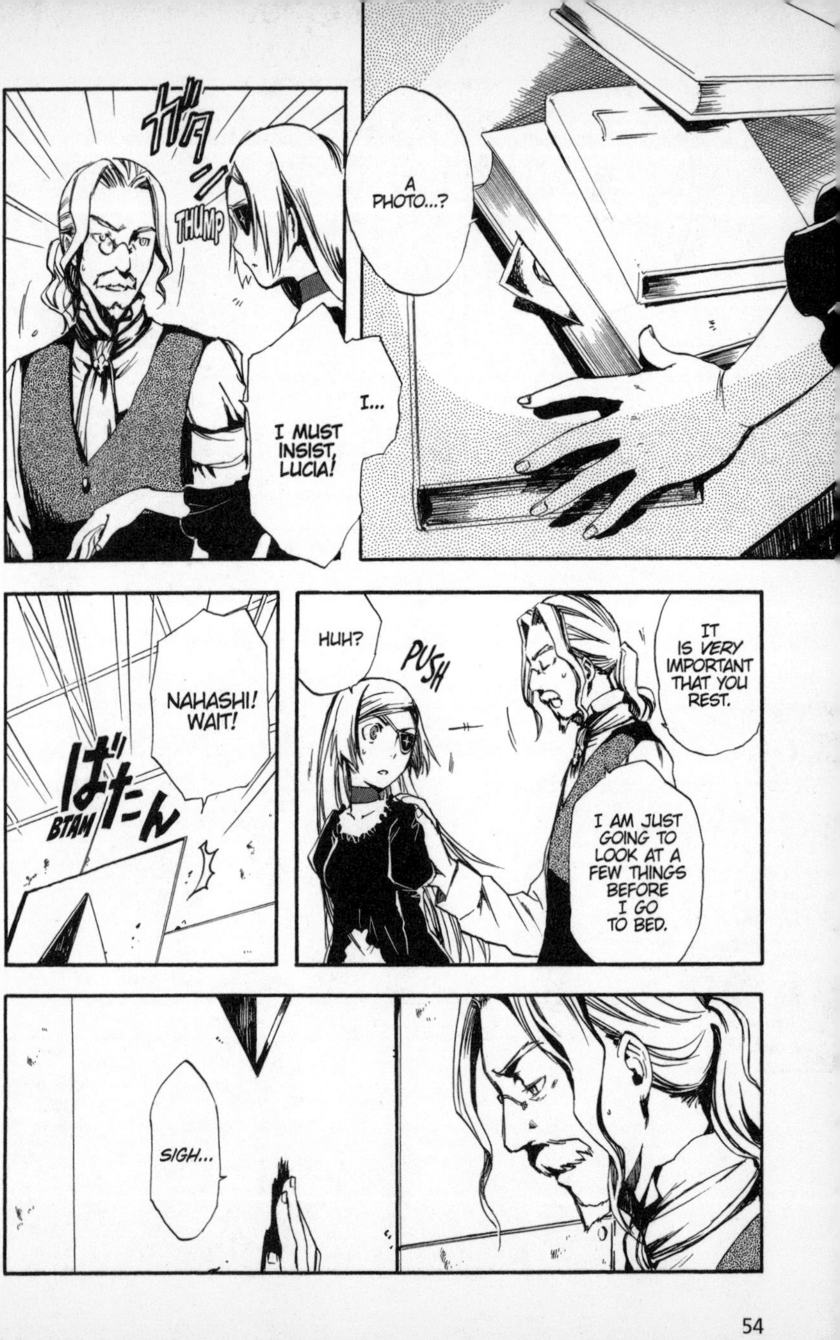
A PHOTO...?
ガタン
THUMP
I...
I MUST INSIST, LUCIA!
IT IS VERY IMPORTANT THAT YOU REST.
HUH?
PUSH
I AM JUST GOING TO LOOK AT A FEW THINGS BEFORE I GO TO BED.
NAHASHI! WAIT!
ばたん
BTAM
SIGH...

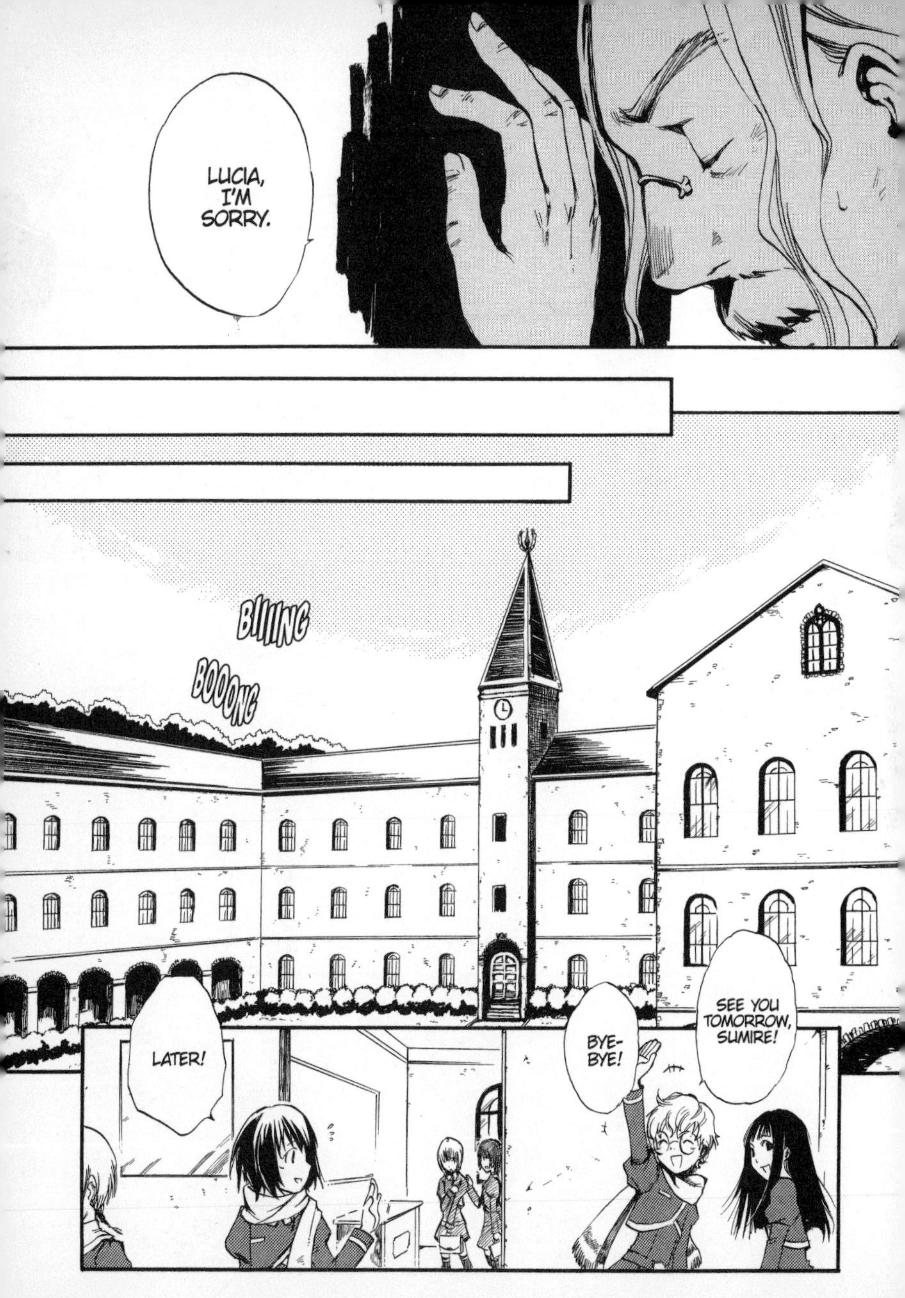
LUCIA, I'M SORRY.
BIIIING
BOOONG
SEE YOU TOMORROW, SUMIRE!
BYE-BYE!
LATER!

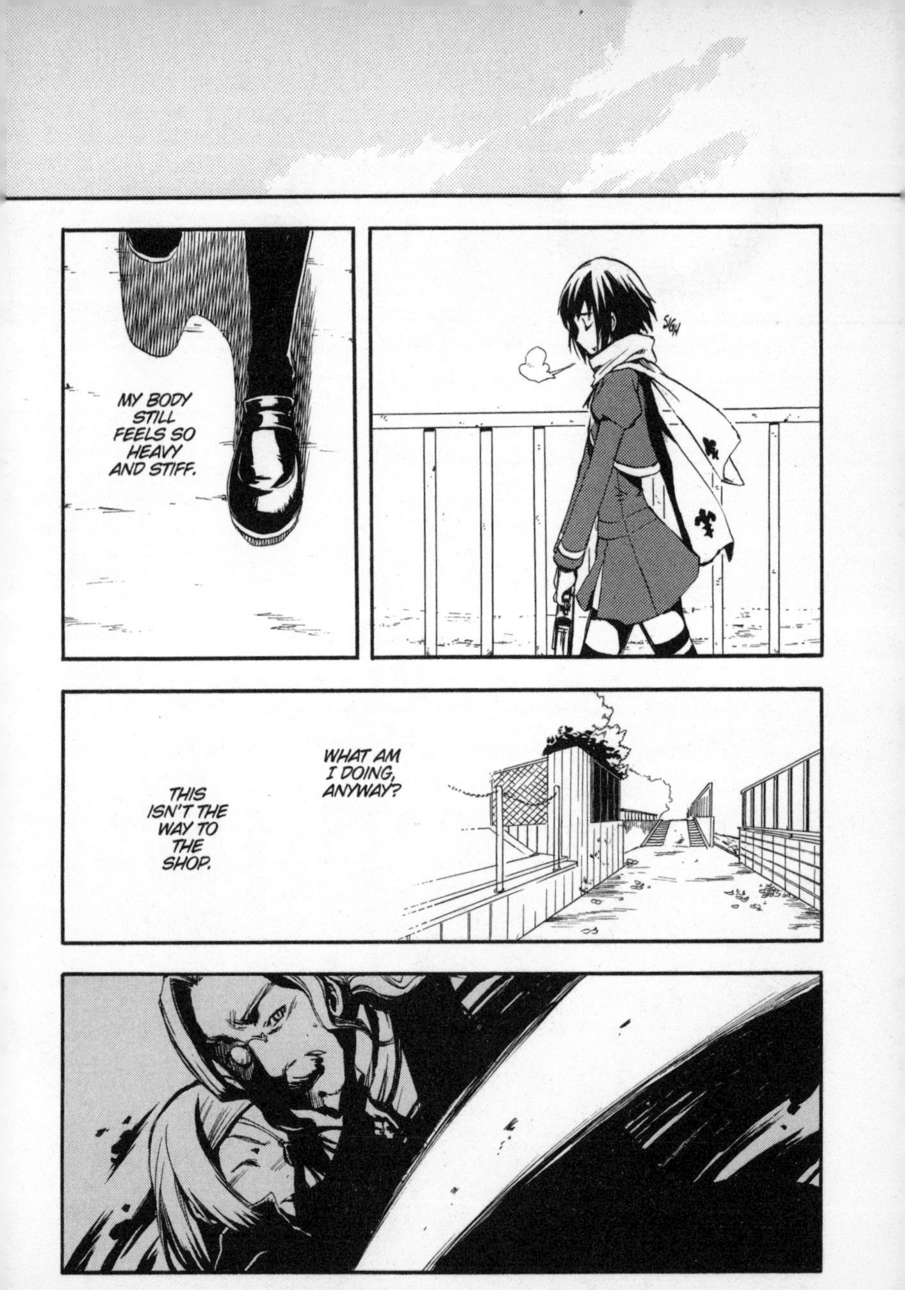
SIGH
MY BODY STILL FEELS SO HEAVY AND STIFF.
WHAT AM I DOING, ANYWAY?
THIS ISN'T THE WAY TO THE SHOP.

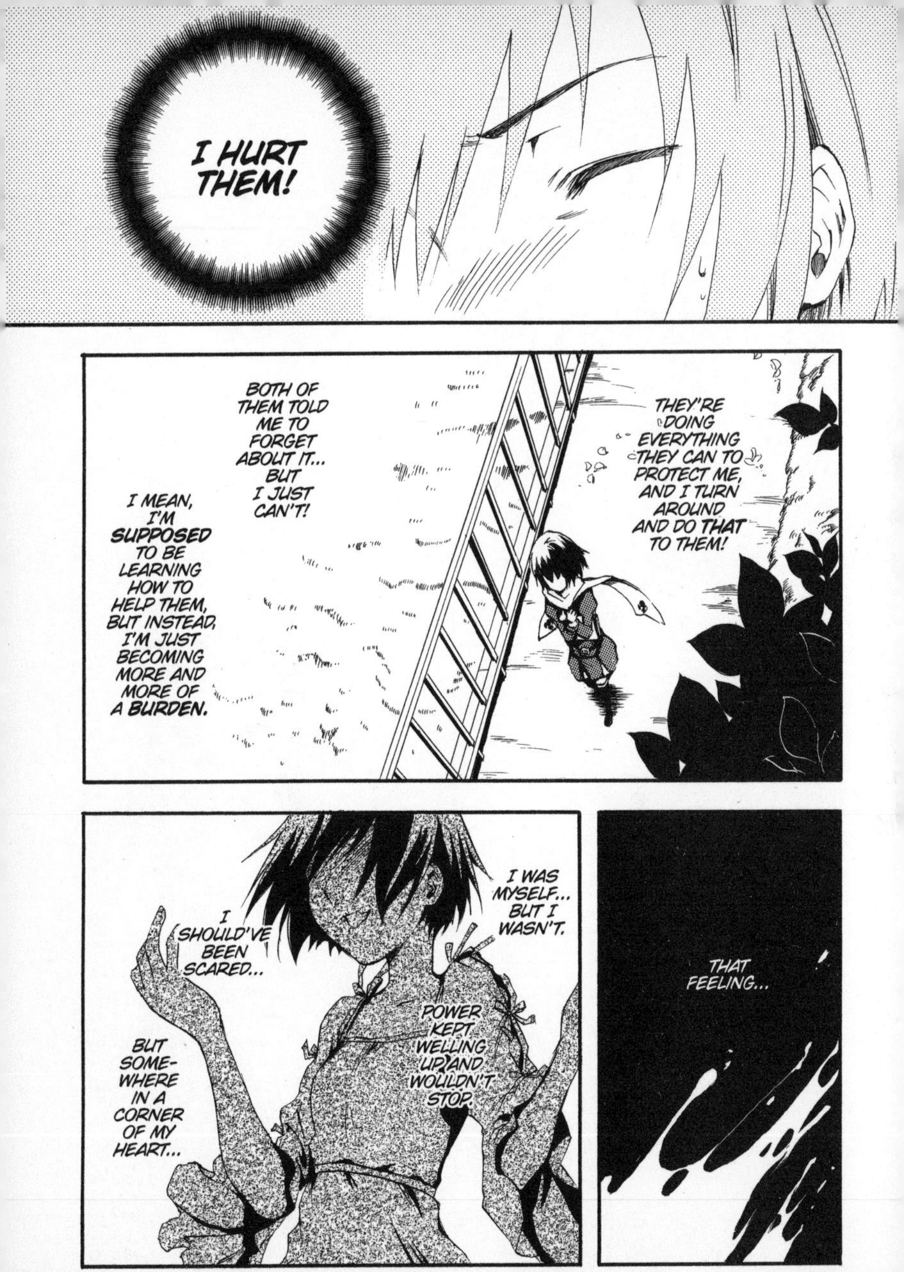
I HURT THEM!
THEY'RE DOING EVERYTHING THEY CAN TO PROTECT ME, AND I TURN AROUND AND DO THAT TO THEM!
BOTH OF THEM TOLD ME TO FORGET ABOUT IT... BUT I JUST CAN'T!
I MEAN, I'M SUPPOSED TO BE LEARNING HOW TO HELP THEM, BUT INSTEAD, I'M JUST BECOMING MORE AND MORE OF A BURDEN.
THAT FEELING...
I WAS MYSELF... BUT I WASN'T.
I SHOULD'VE BEEN SCARED...
POWER KEPT WELLING UP AND WOULDN'T STOP.
BUT SOME-WHERE IN A CORNER OF MY HEART...

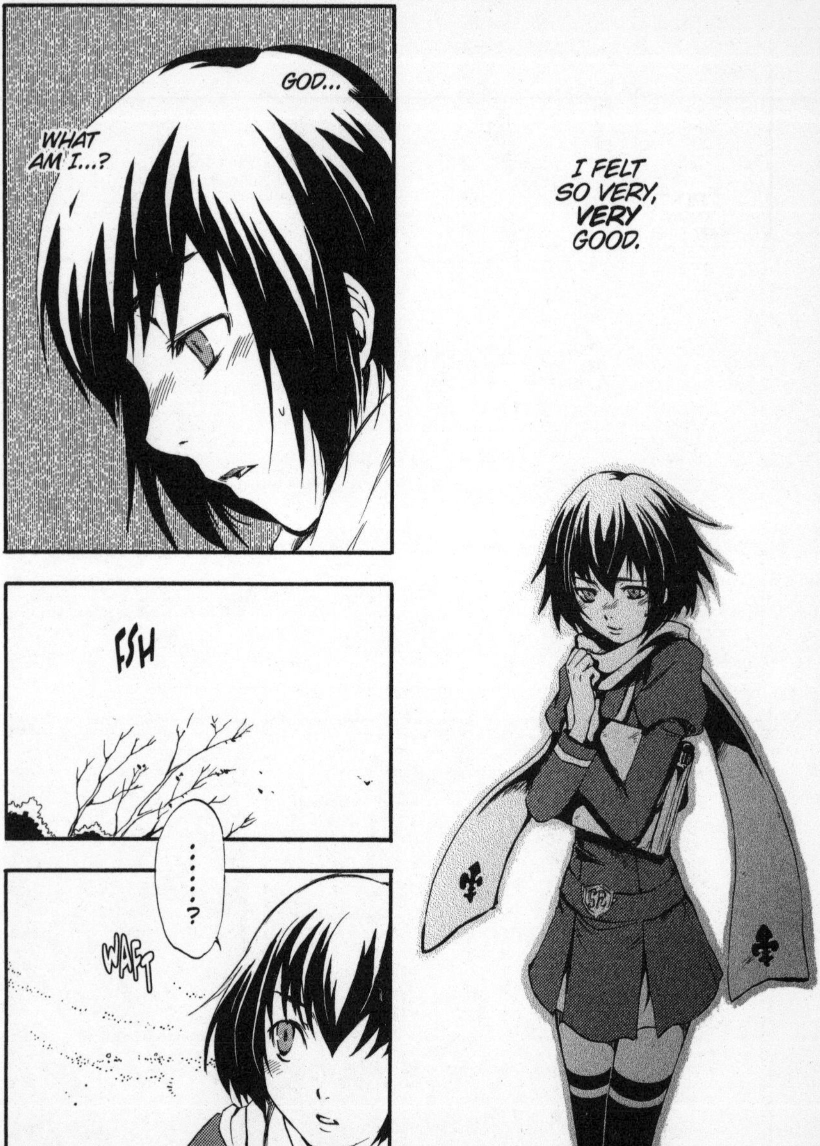
I FELT SO VERY, VERY GOOD.
GOD...
WHAT AM I...?
FSH
......?
WAFT

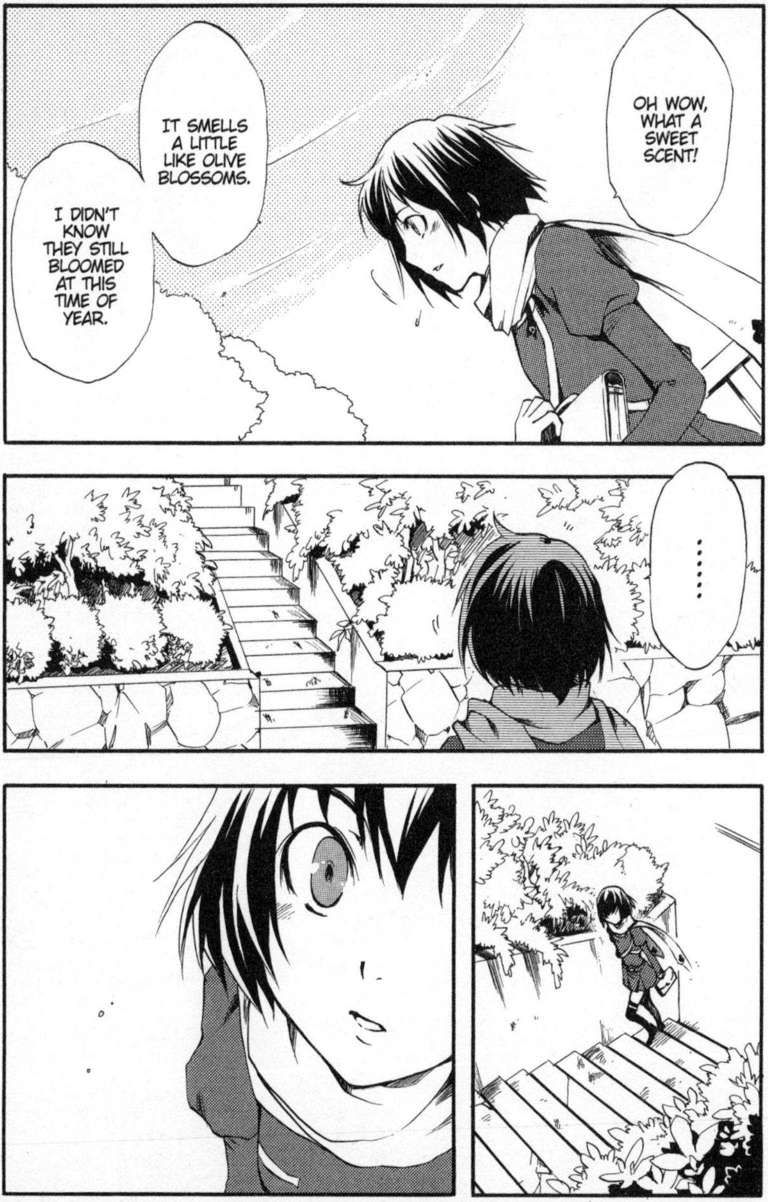
OH WOW, WHAT A SWEET SCENT!
IT SMELLS A LITTLE LIKE OLIVE BLOSSOMS.
I DIDN'T KNOW THEY STILL BLOOMED AT THIS TIME OF YEAR.
……

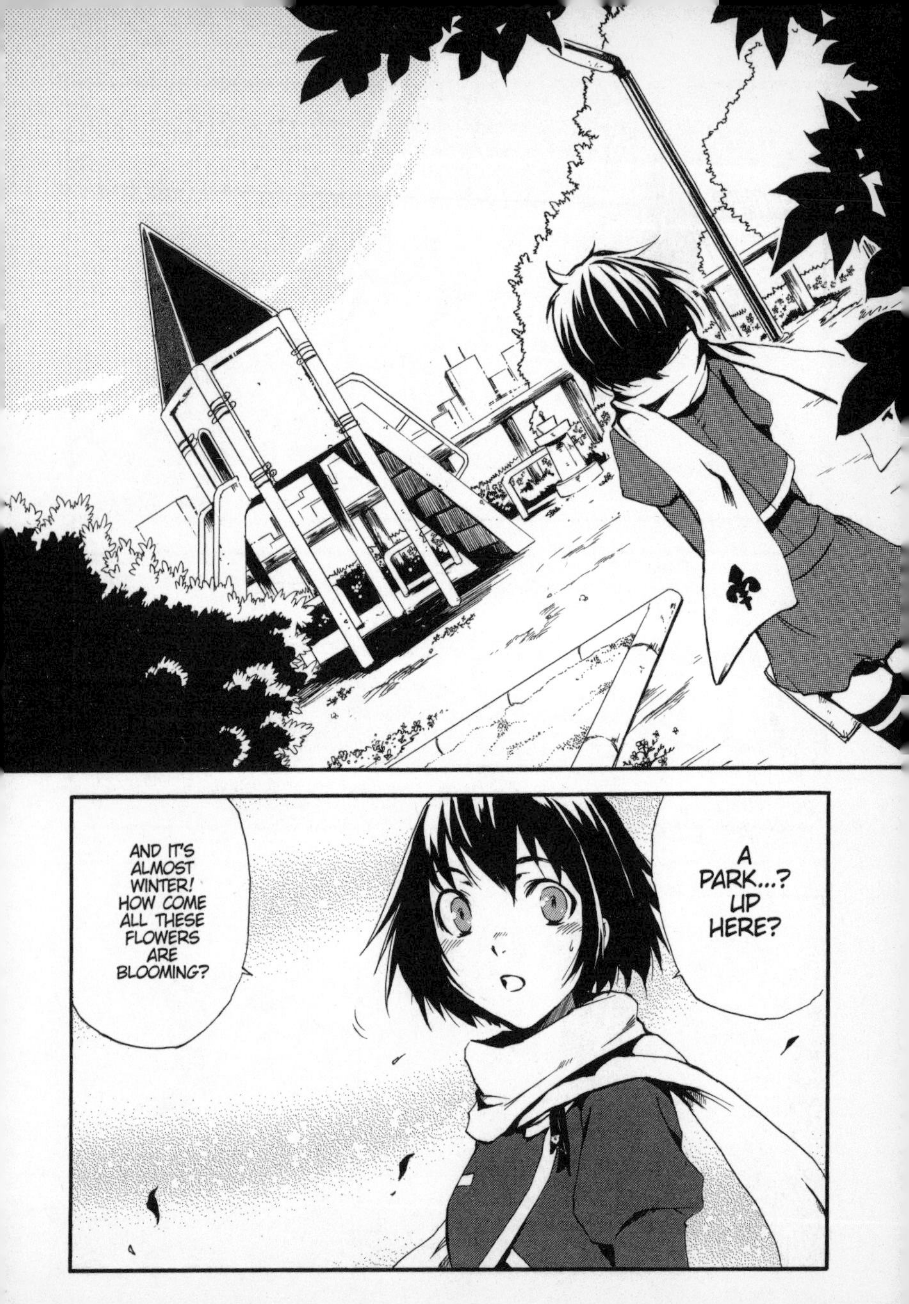
A PARK...? UP HERE?
AND IT'S ALMOST WINTER! HOW COME ALL THESE FLOWERS ARE BLOOMING?

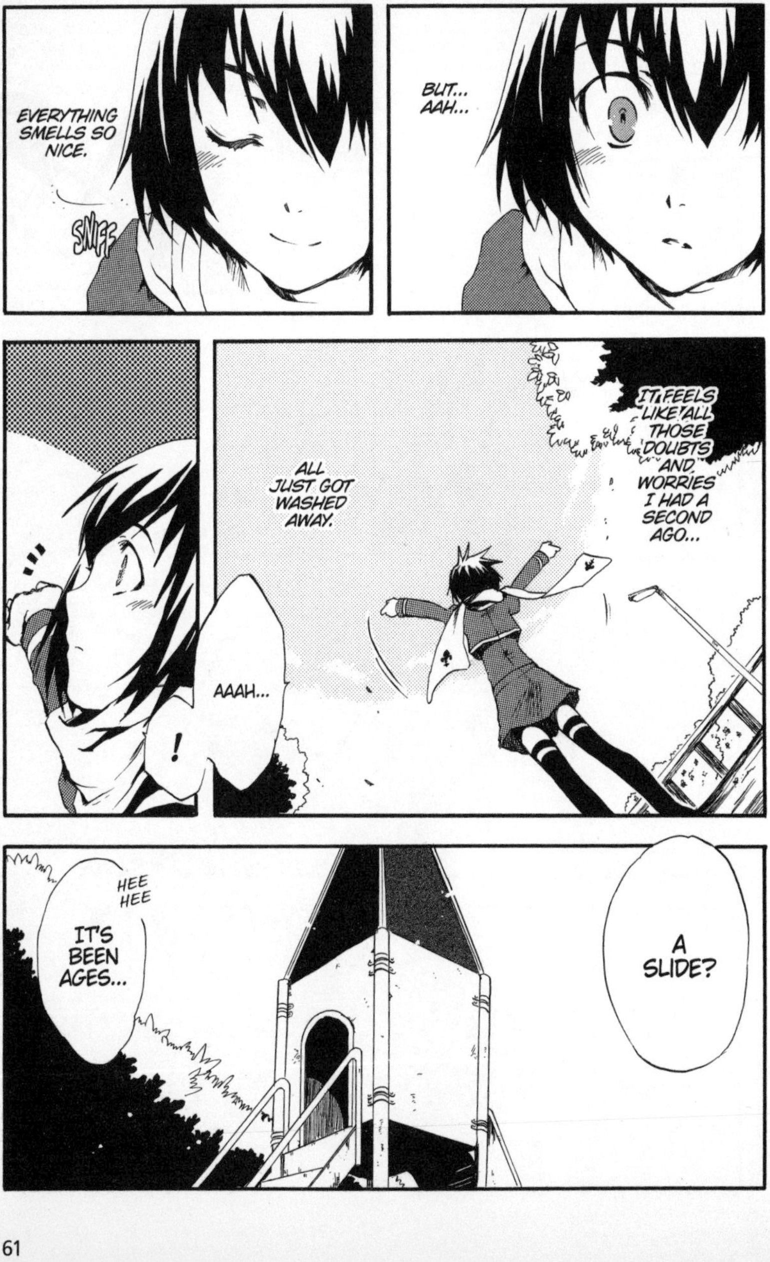
BUT... AAH...
EVERYTHING SMELLS SO NICE.
SNIFF
IT FEELS LIKE ALL THOSE DOUBTS AND WORRIES I HAD A SECOND AGO...
ALL JUST GOT WASHED AWAY.
AAAH...
!
A SLIDE?
HEE HEE
IT'S BEEN AGES...

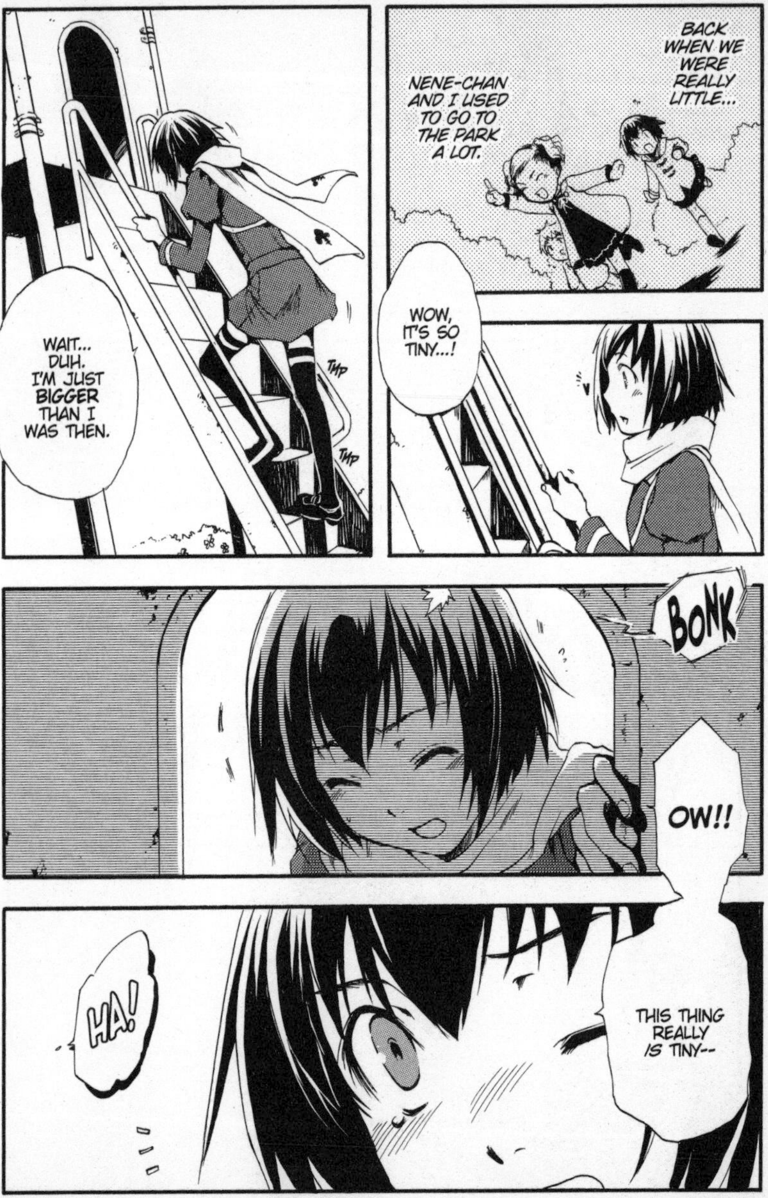
BACK WHEN WE WERE REALLY LITTLE...
NENE-CHAN AND I USED TO GO TO THE PARK A LOT.
WOW, IT'S SO TINY...!
WAIT... DUH. I'M JUST BIGGER THAN I WAS THEN.
TMP
TMP
BONK
OW!!
THIS THING REALLY IS TINY--
HA!

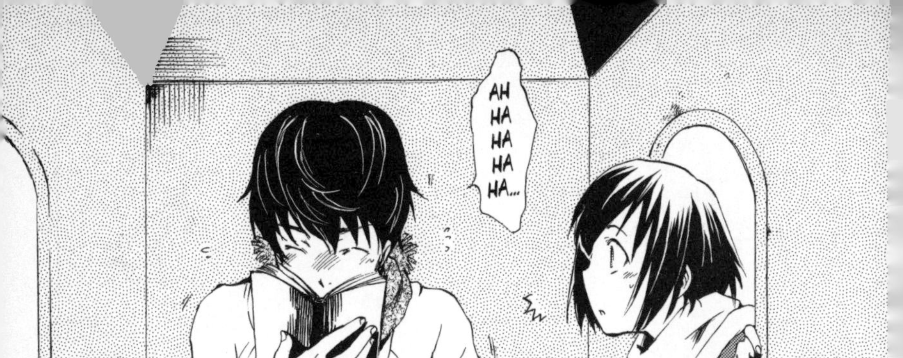
AH HA HA HA HA...
HA HA!
S-SORRY...

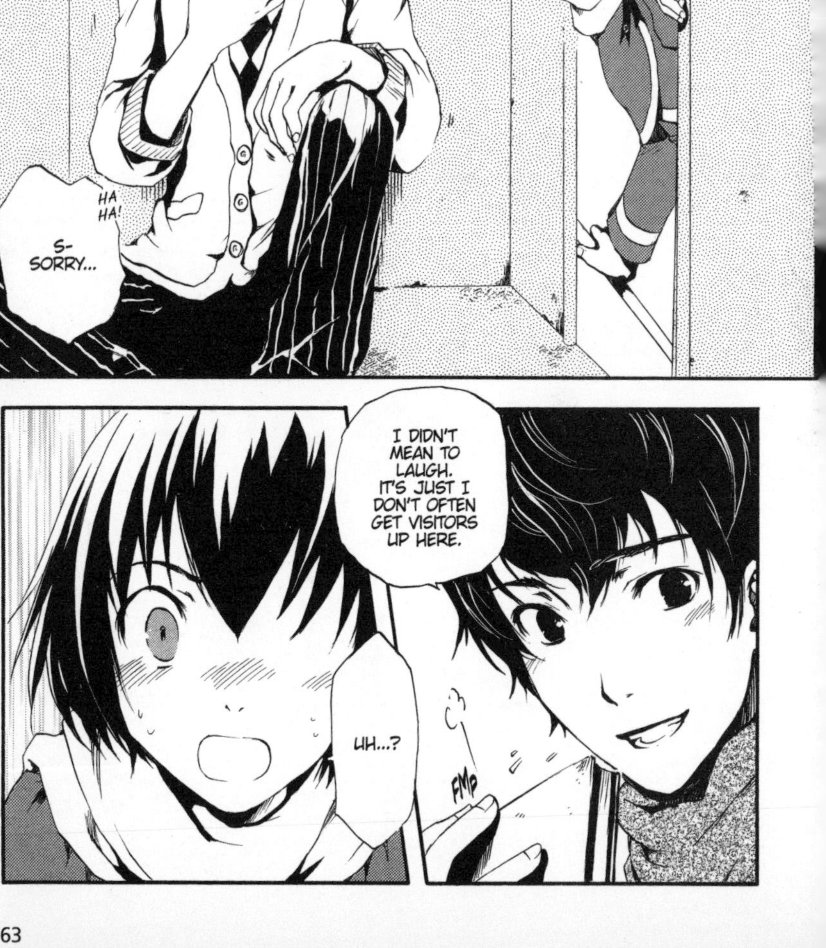
I DIDN'T MEAN TO LAUGH. IT'S JUST I DON'T OFTEN GET VISITORS UP HERE.
FMP
UH...?

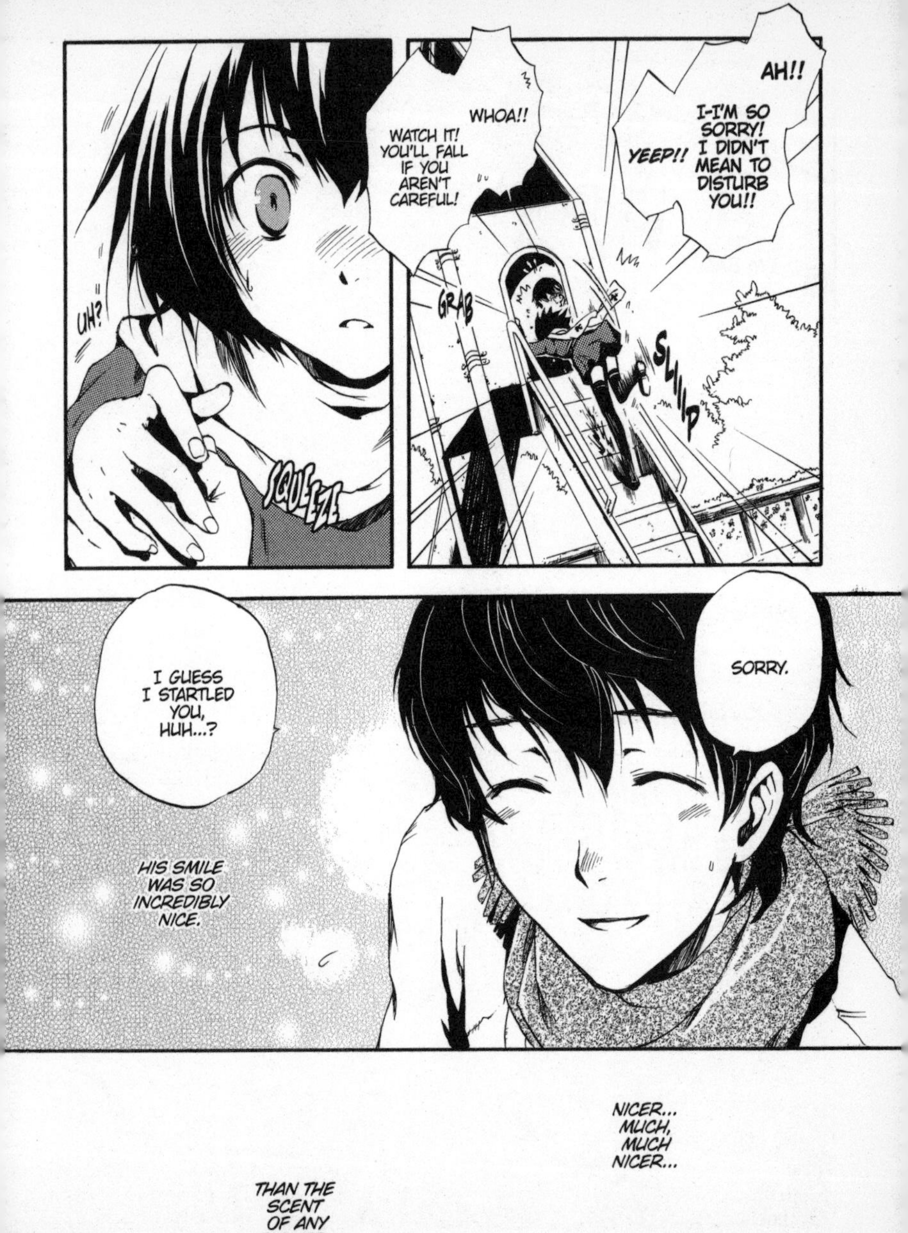
AH!!
I-I'M SO SORRY! I DIDN'T MEAN TO DISTURB YOU!!
YEEP!!
WHOA!!
WATCH IT! YOU'LL FALL IF YOU AREN'T CAREFUL!
SLIIIP
GRAB
SQUEEZE
UH?
SORRY.
I GUESS I STARTLED YOU, HUH...?
HIS SMILE WAS SO INCREDIBLY NICE.
NICER... MUCH, MUCH NICER...
THAN THE SCENT OF ANY FLOWER.

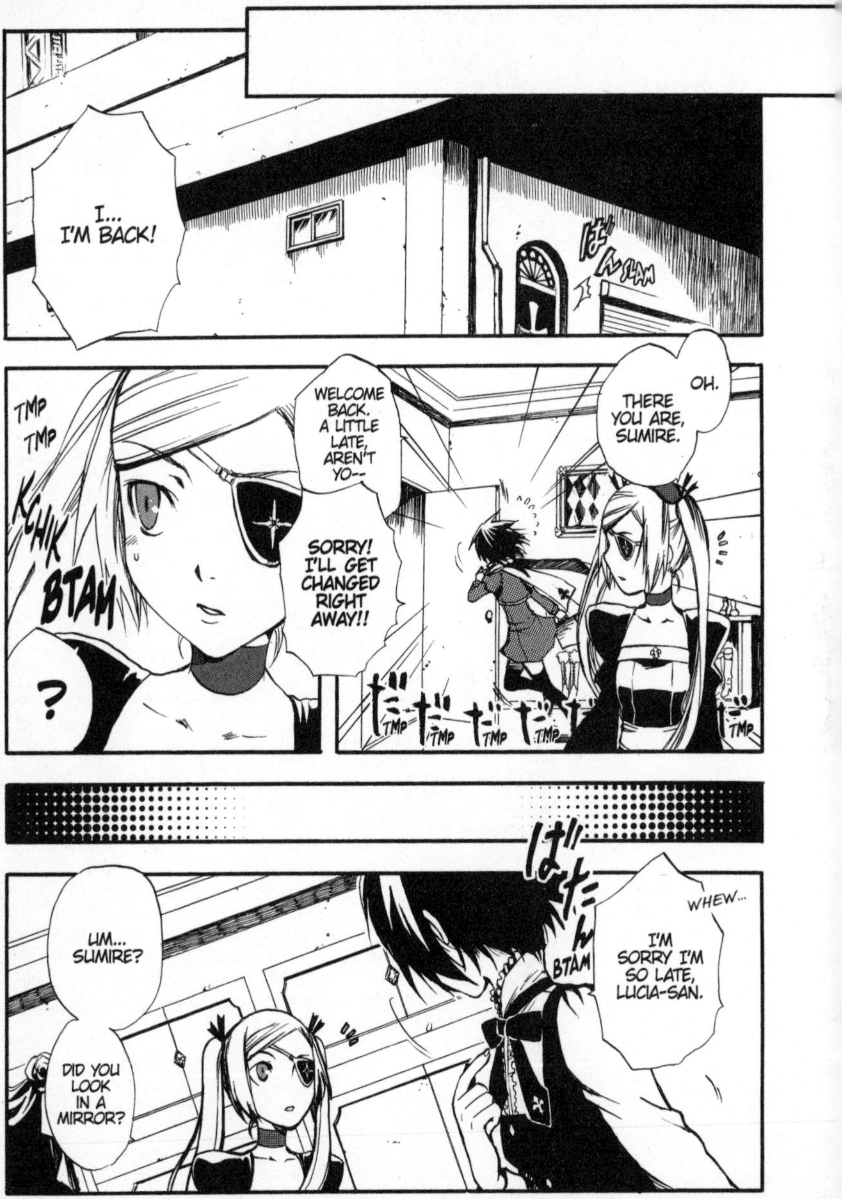
ばん SLAM
I... I'M BACK!
OH. THERE YOU ARE, SUMIRE.
WELCOME BACK. A LITTLE LATE, AREN'T YO--
SORRY! I'LL GET CHANGED RIGHT AWAY!!
だ TMP だ TMP だ TMP だ TMP TMP
TMP TMP
KCHIK
BTAM
?
ばたん BTAM
WHEW...
I'M SORRY I'M SO LATE, LUCIA-SAN.
UM... SUMIRE?
DID YOU LOOK IN A MIRROR?

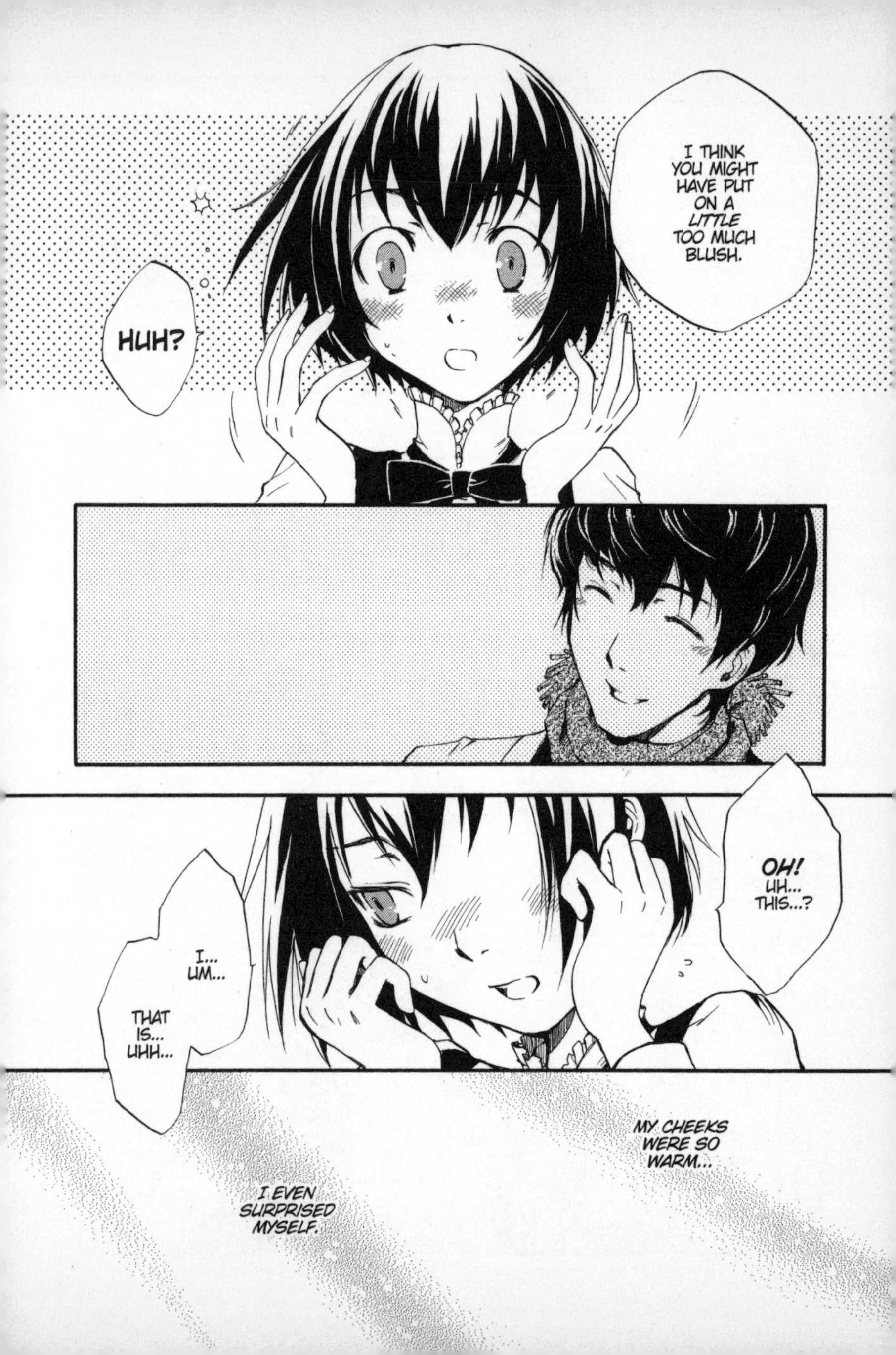
I THINK YOU MIGHT HAVE PUT ON A *LITTLE* TOO MUCH BLUSH.
HUH?
OH! UH... THIS...?
I... UM... THAT IS... UHH...
MY CHEEKS WERE SO WARM...
I EVEN SURPRISED MYSELF.

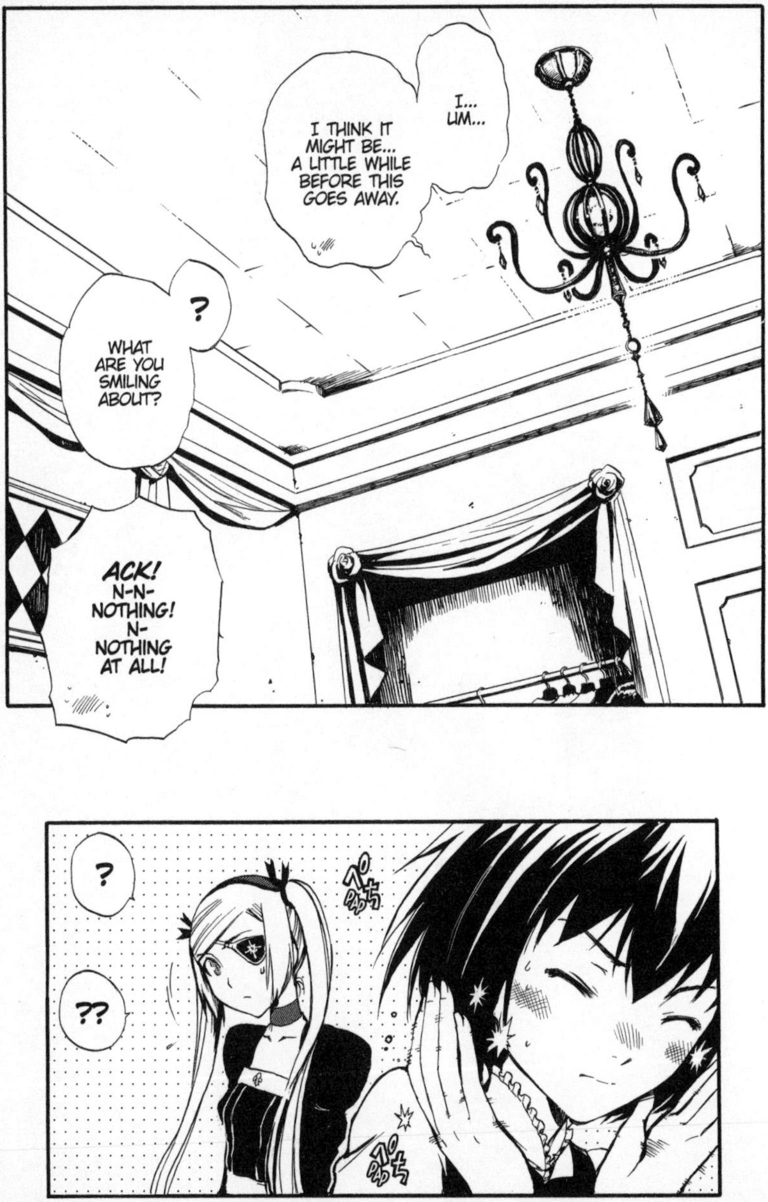

I... UM...
I THINK IT MIGHT BE... A LITTLE WHILE BEFORE THIS GOES AWAY.
?
WHAT ARE YOU SMILING ABOUT?
ACK! N-N-NOTHING! N-NOTHING AT ALL!
PAD
PAD
?
??

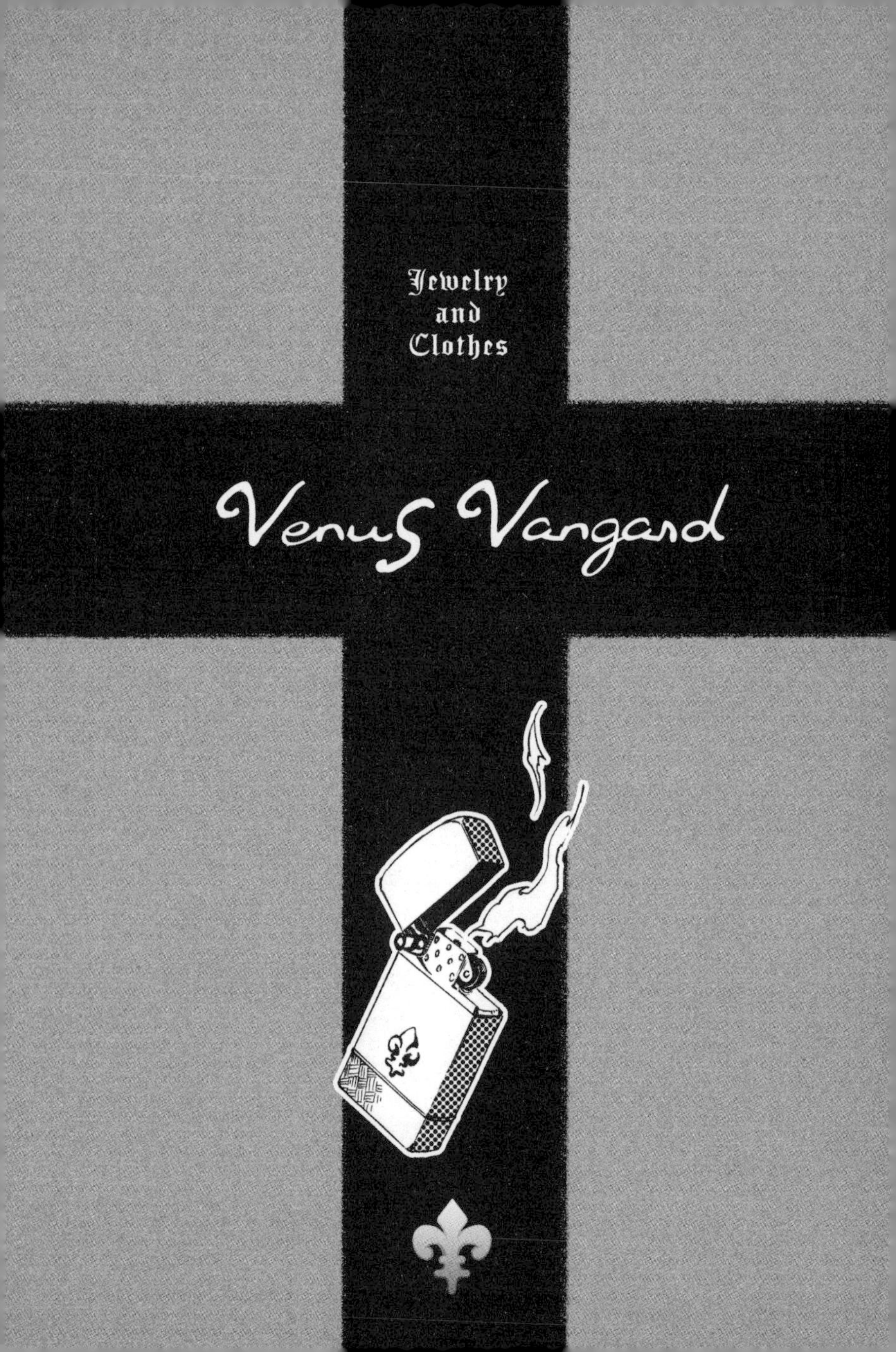
Jewelry
and
Clothes
Venus Vangard

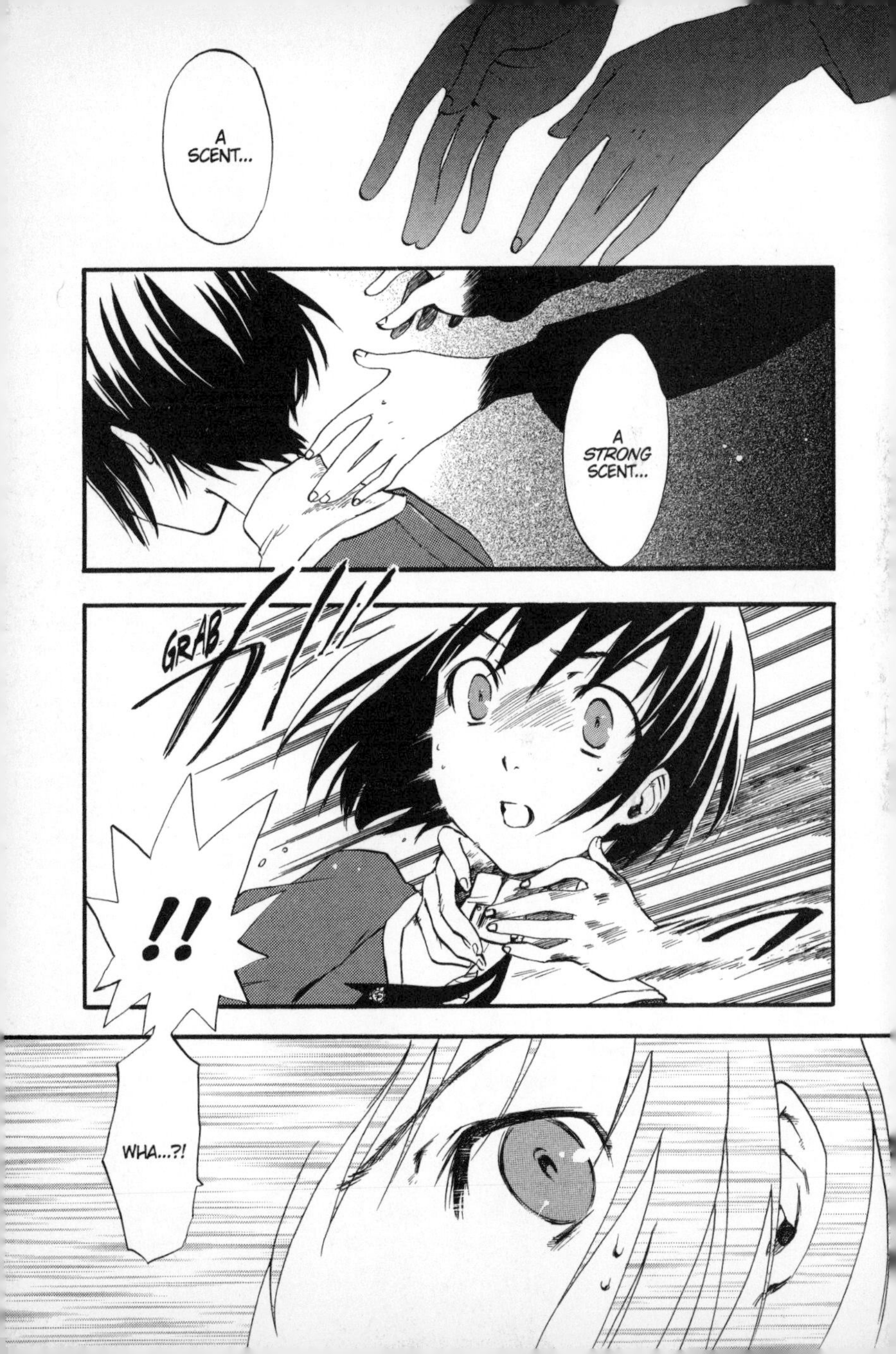
A SCENT...
A STRONG SCENT...
GRAB
!!
WHA...?!

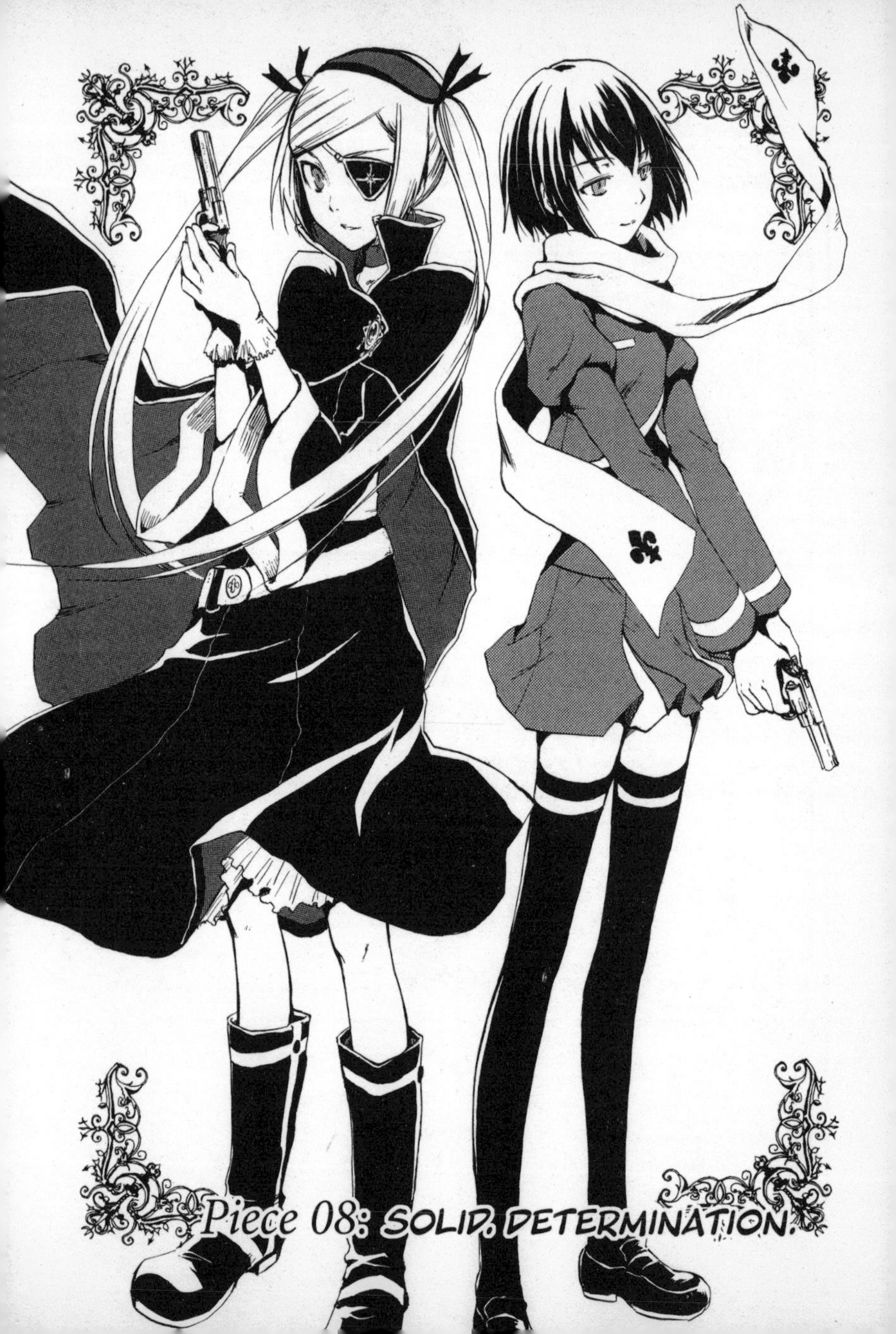
Piece 08: SOLID. DETERMINATION.

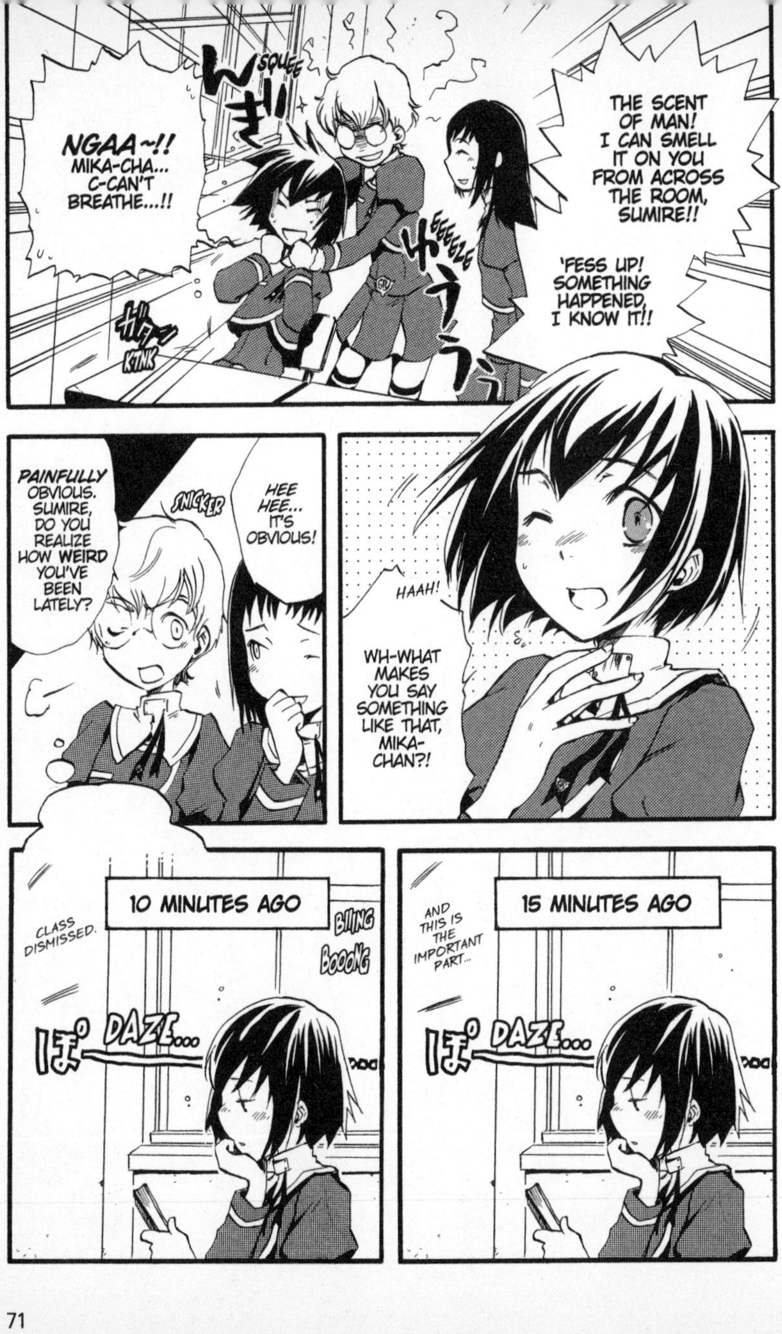
THE SCENT OF MAN! I CAN SMELL IT ON YOU FROM ACROSS THE ROOM, SUMIRE!!
'FESS UP! SOMETHING HAPPENED, I KNOW IT!!
SQUEE
EEEEZE
NGAA~!! MIKA-CHA... C-CAN'T BREATHE...!!
KTINK
HAAH!
WH-WHAT MAKES YOU SAY SOMETHING LIKE THAT, MIKA-CHAN?!
HEE HEE... IT'S OBVIOUS!
SNICKER
PAINFULLY OBVIOUS. SUMIRE, DO YOU REALIZE HOW WEIRD YOU'VE BEEN LATELY?
15 MINUTES AGO
AND THIS IS THE IMPORTANT PART...
DAZE...
10 MINUTES AGO
BIIING
BOOONG
CLASS DISMISSED.
DAZE...

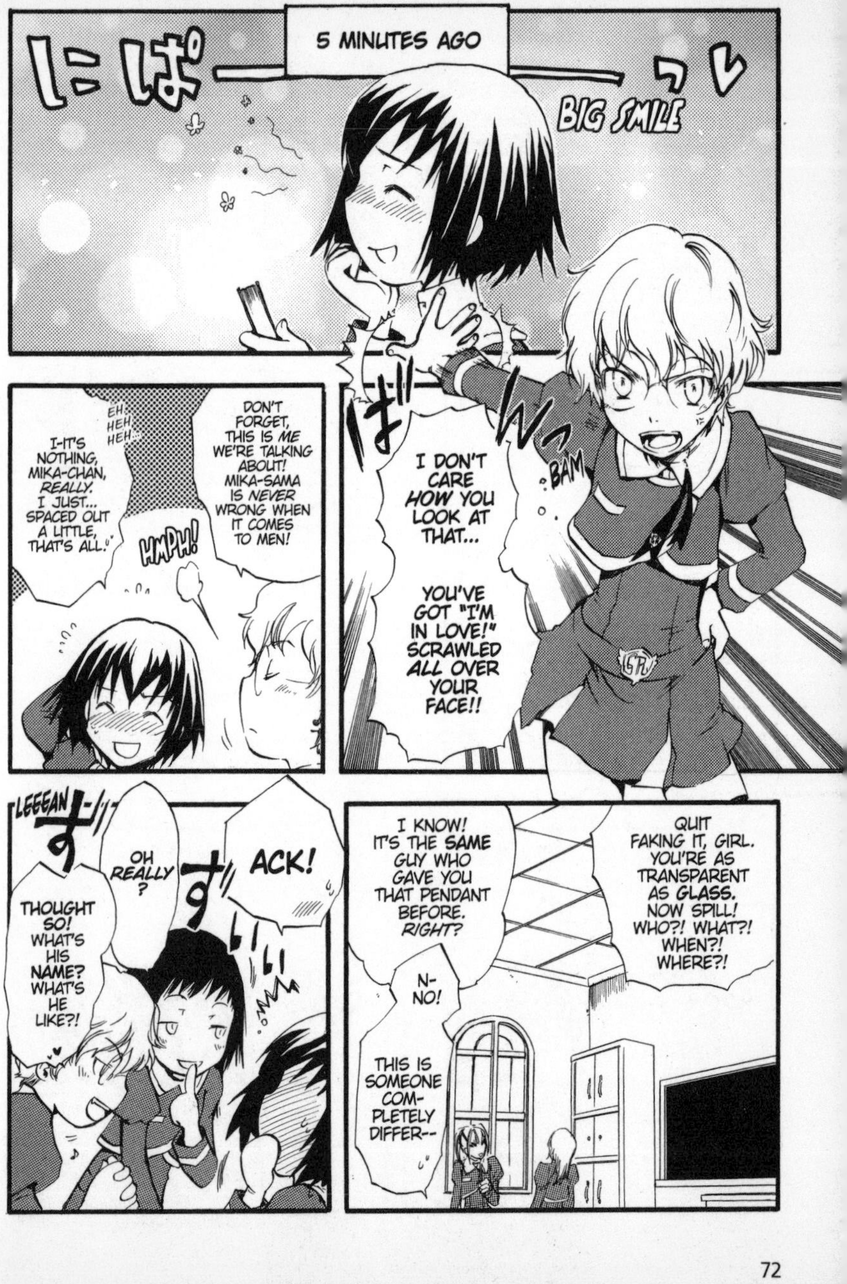
5 MINUTES AGO
BIG SMILE
BAM
I DON'T CARE *HOW* YOU LOOK AT THAT...
YOU'VE GOT "I'M IN LOVE!" SCRAWLED *ALL* OVER YOUR FACE!!
DON'T FORGET, THIS IS *ME* WE'RE TALKING ABOUT! MIKA-SAMA IS *NEVER* WRONG WHEN IT COMES TO MEN!
HMPH!
EH, HEH, HEH...
I-IT'S NOTHING, MIKA-CHAN, *REALLY.* I JUST... SPACED OUT A LITTLE, THAT'S ALL.
QUIT FAKING IT, GIRL. YOU'RE AS TRANSPARENT AS GLASS. NOW SPILL! WHO?! WHAT?! WHEN?! WHERE?!
I KNOW! IT'S THE SAME GUY WHO GAVE YOU THAT PENDANT BEFORE. *RIGHT?*
N-NO!
THIS IS SOMEONE COMPLETELY DIFFER--
ACK!
OH *REALLY* ?
LEEEAN
THOUGHT SO! WHAT'S HIS NAME? WHAT'S HE LIKE?!

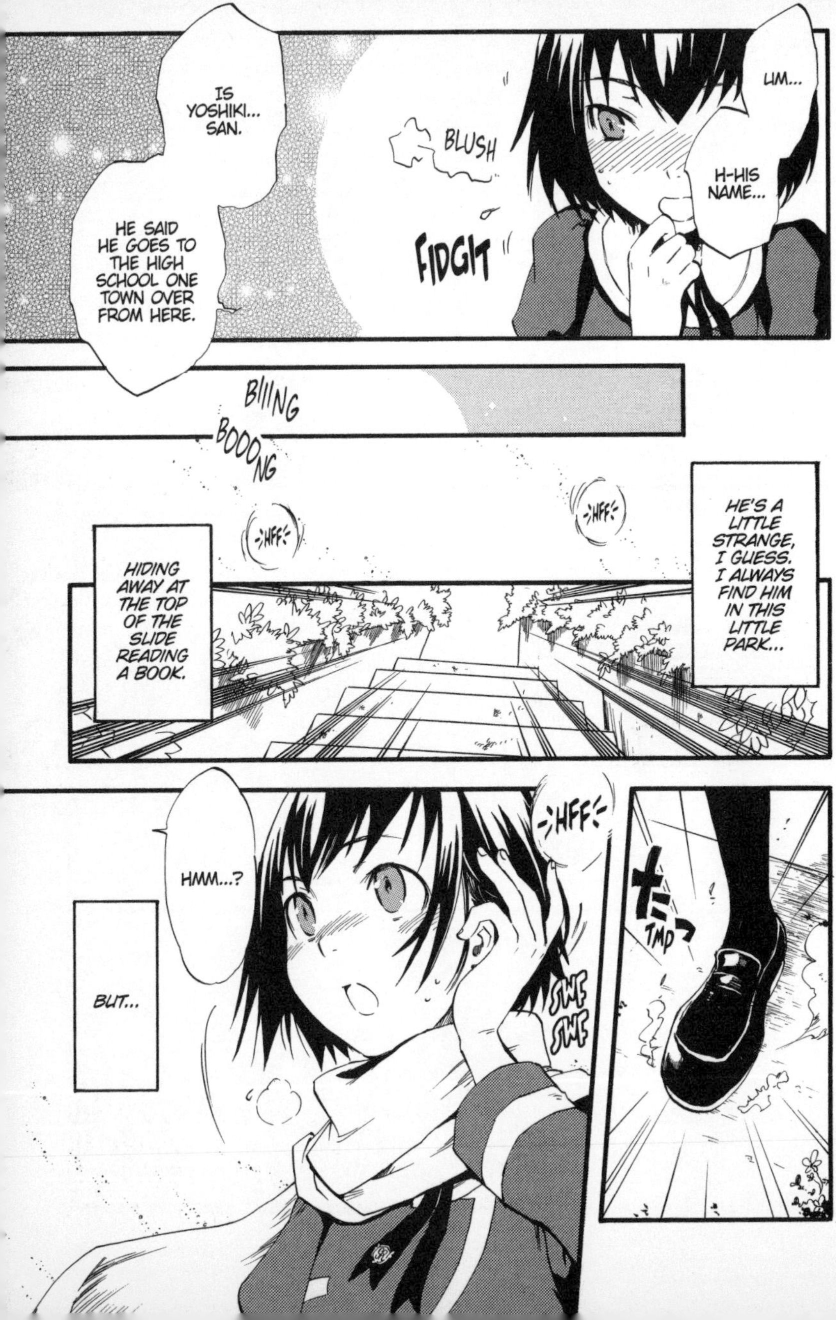
UM...
H-HIS NAME...
BLUSH
IS YOSHIKI... SAN.
FIDGIT
HE SAID HE GOES TO THE HIGH SCHOOL ONE TOWN OVER FROM HERE.
BIIING
BOOONG
HFF
HE'S A LITTLE STRANGE, I GUESS. I ALWAYS FIND HIM IN THIS LITTLE PARK...
HFF
HIDING AWAY AT THE TOP OF THE SLIDE READING A BOOK.
TMP
HFF
HMM...?
SWF SWF
BUT...

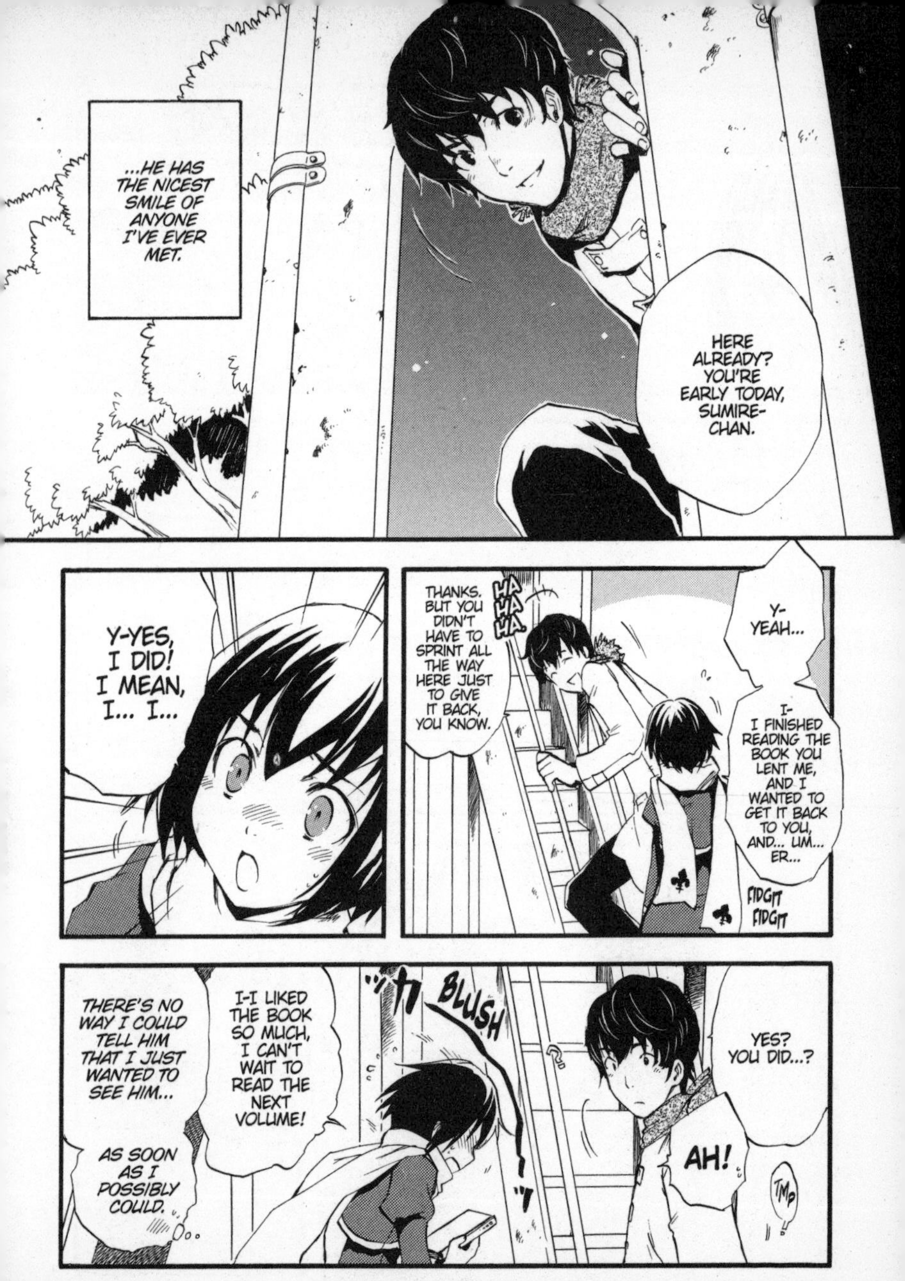
HERE ALREADY? YOU'RE EARLY TODAY, SUMIRE-CHAN.
...HE HAS THE NICEST SMILE OF ANYONE I'VE EVER MET.
Y- YEAH...
I- I FINISHED READING THE BOOK YOU LENT ME, AND I WANTED TO GET IT BACK TO YOU, AND... UM... ER...
FIDGIT FIDGIT
HA HA HA.
THANKS. BUT YOU DIDN'T HAVE TO SPRINT ALL THE WAY HERE JUST TO GIVE IT BACK, YOU KNOW.
Y-YES, I DID! I MEAN, I... I...
YES? YOU DID...?
AH!
TMP
BLUSH
I-I LIKED THE BOOK SO MUCH, I CAN'T WAIT TO READ THE NEXT VOLUME!
THERE'S NO WAY I COULD TELL HIM THAT I JUST WANTED TO SEE HIM...
AS SOON AS I POSSIBLY COULD.

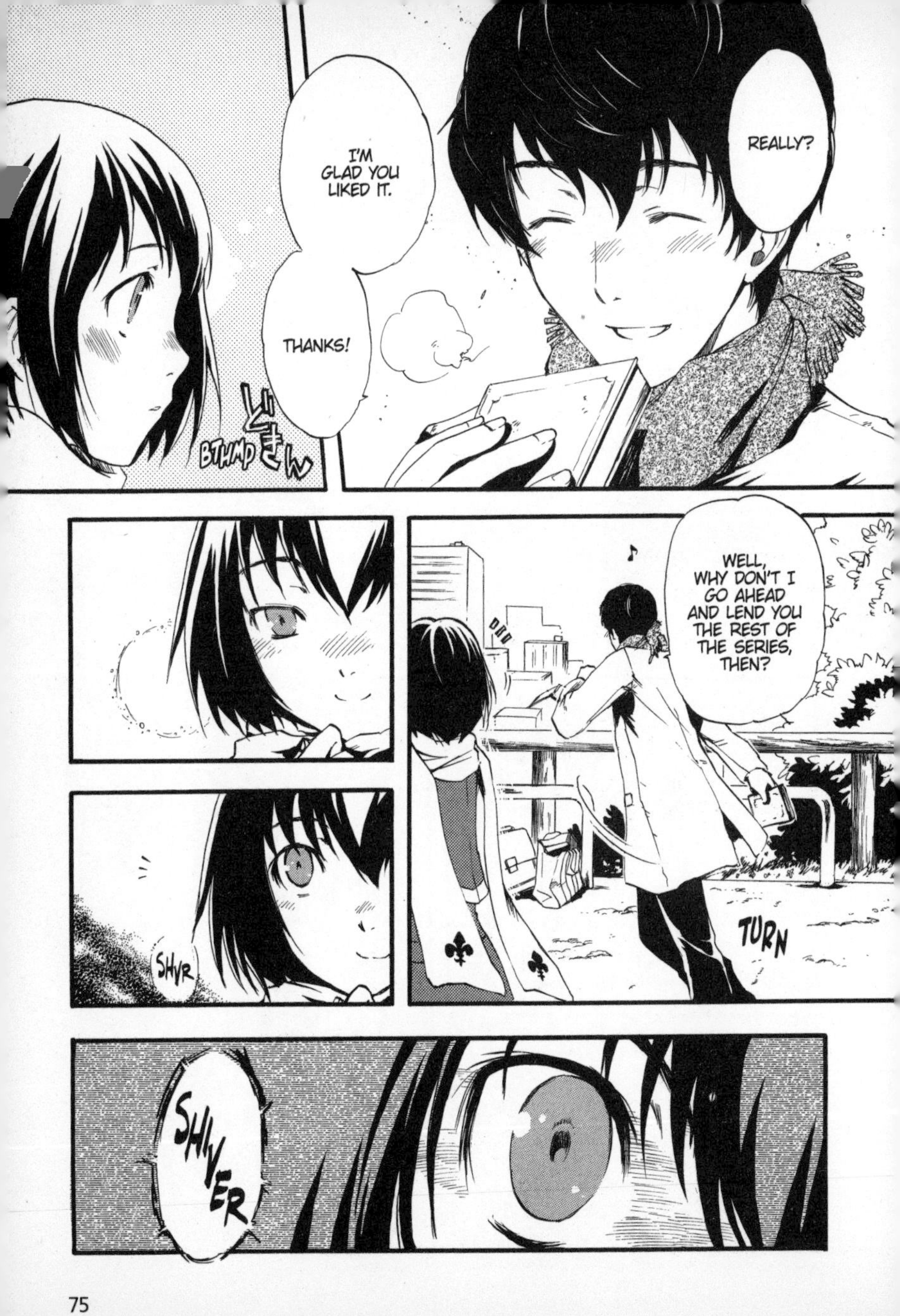
REALLY?
I'M GLAD YOU LIKED IT.
THANKS!
BTHMP どきん
WELL, WHY DON'T I GO AHEAD AND LEND YOU THE REST OF THE SERIES, THEN?
TURN
SHVR
SHIVER

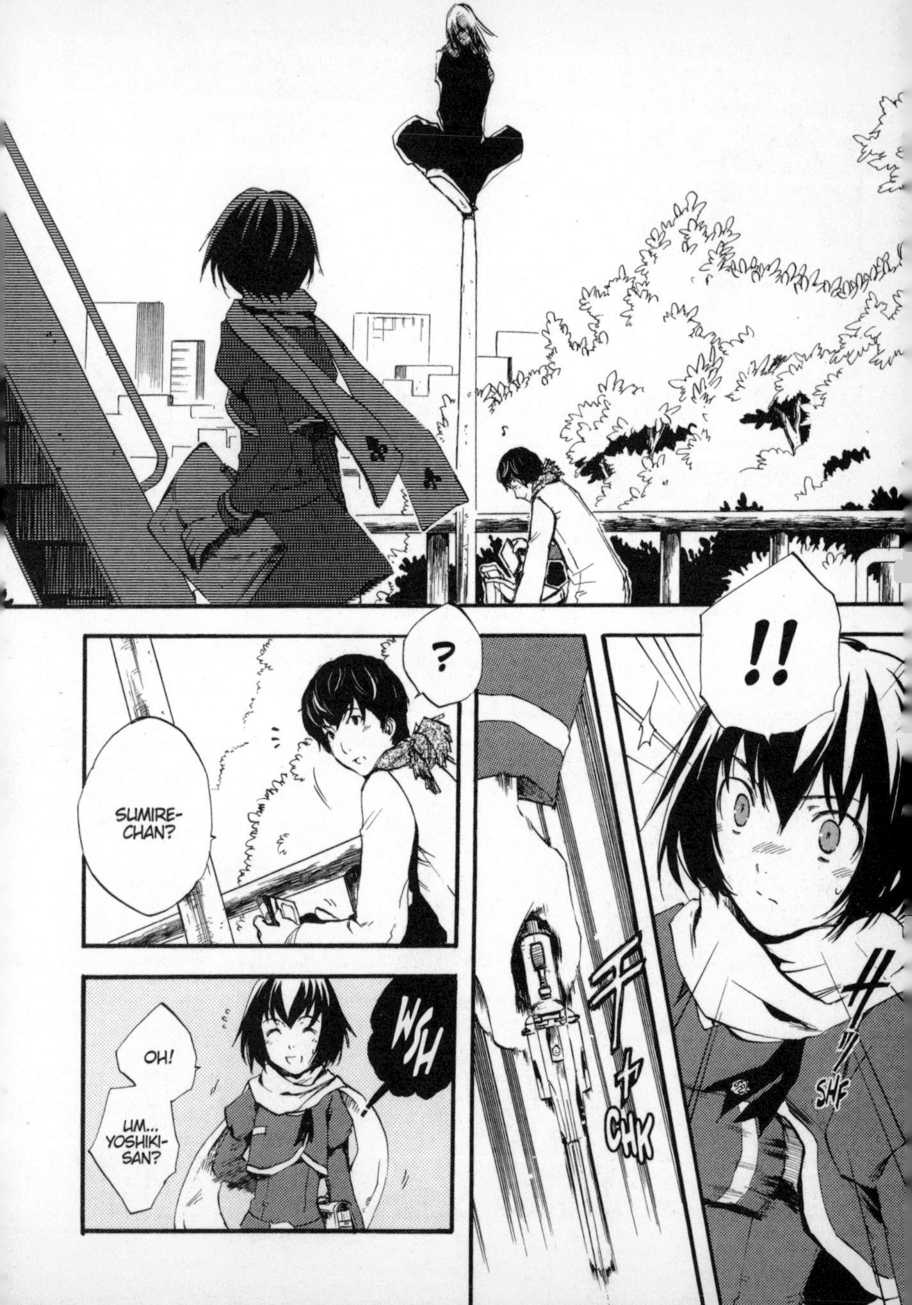

!!
SHF
CHK
?
SUMIRE-CHAN?
WSH
OH!
UM... YOSHIKI-SAN?

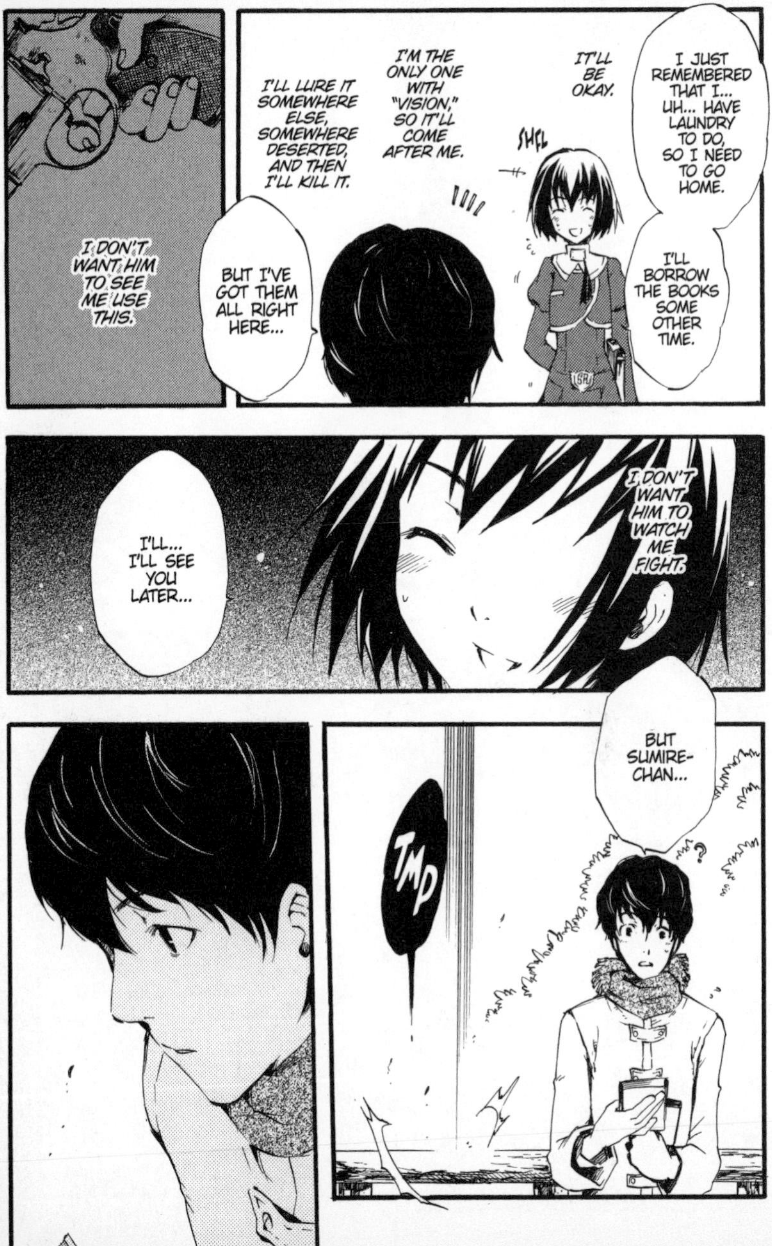
I JUST REMEMBERED THAT I... UH... HAVE LAUNDRY TO DO, SO I NEED TO GO HOME.
IT'LL BE OKAY.
I'M THE ONLY ONE WITH "VISION," SO IT'LL COME AFTER ME.
I'LL LURE IT SOMEWHERE ELSE, SOMEWHERE DESERTED, AND THEN I'LL KILL IT.
SHFL
I'LL BORROW THE BOOKS SOME OTHER TIME.
BUT I'VE GOT THEM ALL RIGHT HERE...
I DON'T WANT HIM TO SEE ME USE THIS.
I DON'T WANT HIM TO WATCH ME FIGHT.
I'LL... I'LL SEE YOU LATER...
BUT SUMIRE-CHAN...
TMP

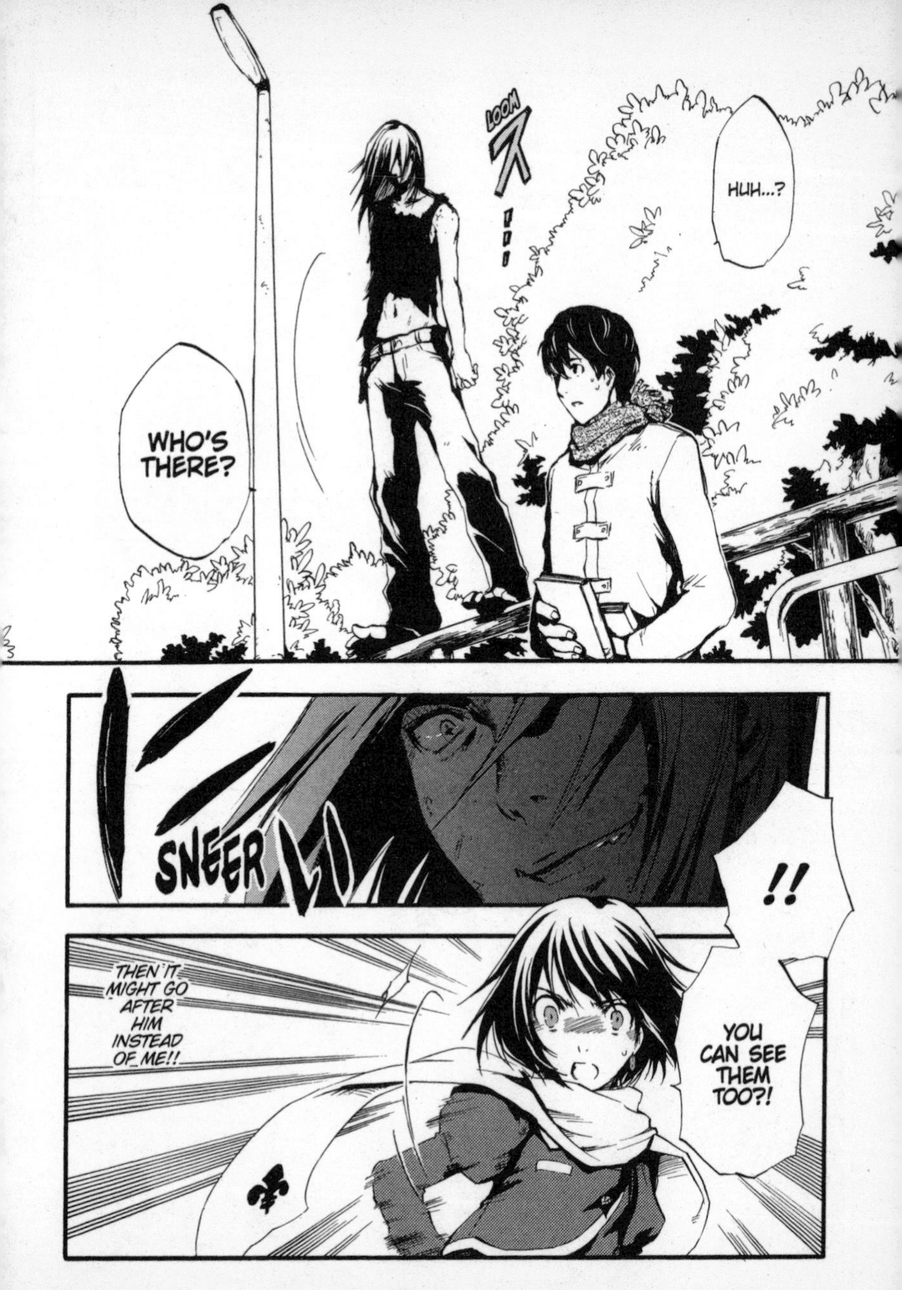
HUH...?
LOOM
WHO'S THERE?
SNEER
!!
YOU CAN SEE THEM TOO?!
THEN IT MIGHT GO AFTER HIM INSTEAD OF ME!!

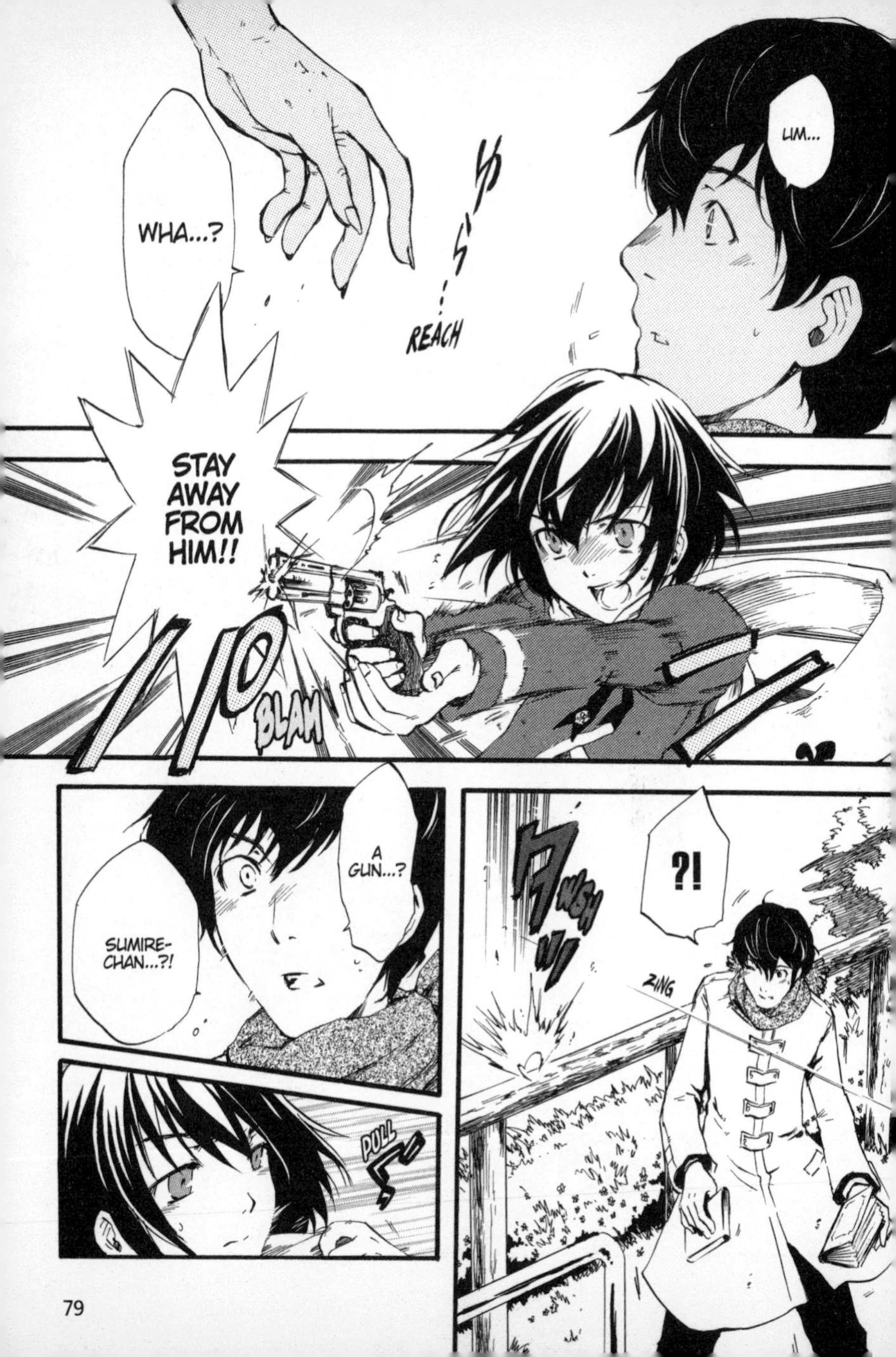
UM...
REACH
WHA...?
STAY AWAY FROM HIM!!
BLAM
?!
ZING
A GUN...?
SUMIRE-CHAN...?!
PULL

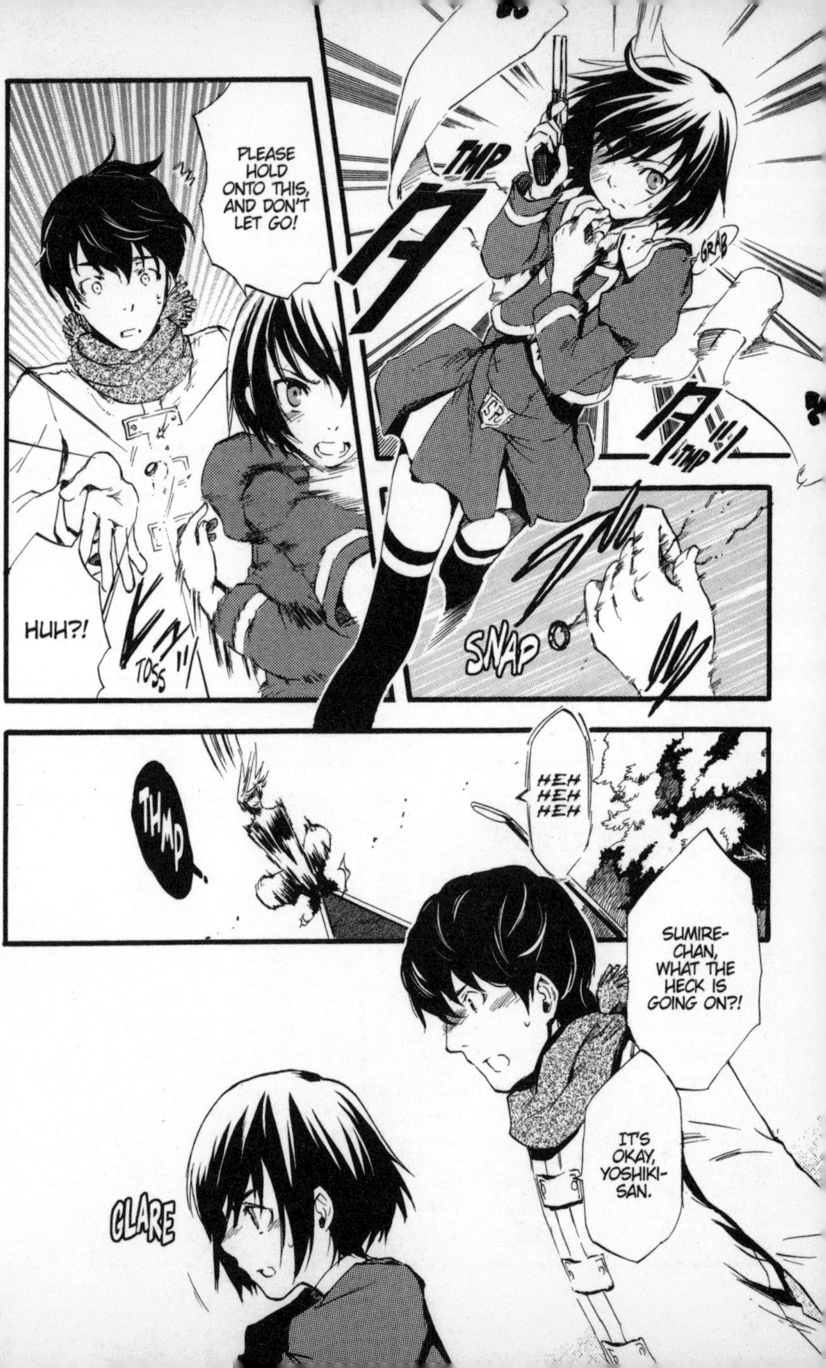
TMP
GRAB
TMP
SNAP
PLEASE HOLD ONTO THIS, AND DON'T LET GO!
HUH?!
TOSS
HEH HEH HEH
THMP
SUMIRE-CHAN, WHAT THE HECK IS GOING ON?!
IT'S OKAY, YOSHIKI-SAN.
GLARE

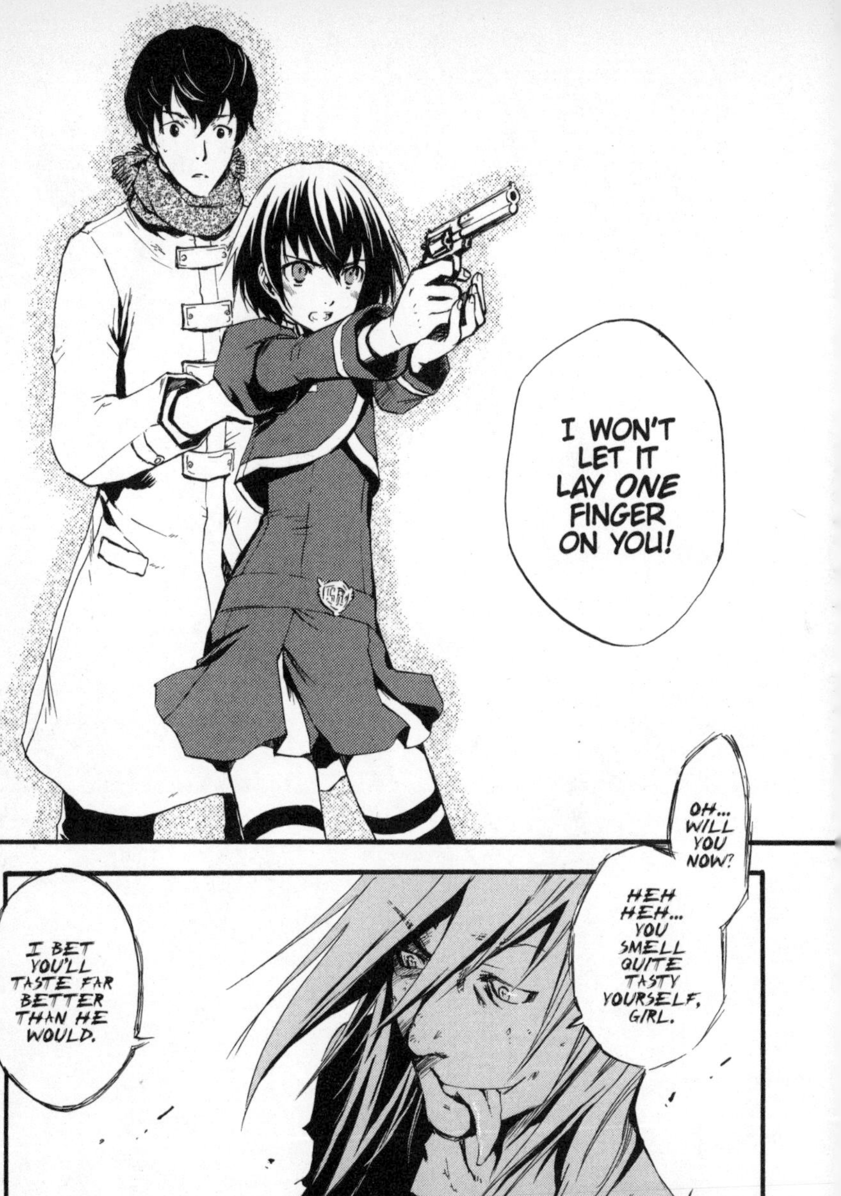
I WON'T LET IT LAY *ONE* FINGER ON YOU!
OH... WILL YOU NOW?
HEH HEH... YOU SMELL QUITE TASTY YOURSELF, GIRL.
I BET YOU'LL TASTE FAR BETTER THAN HE WOULD.

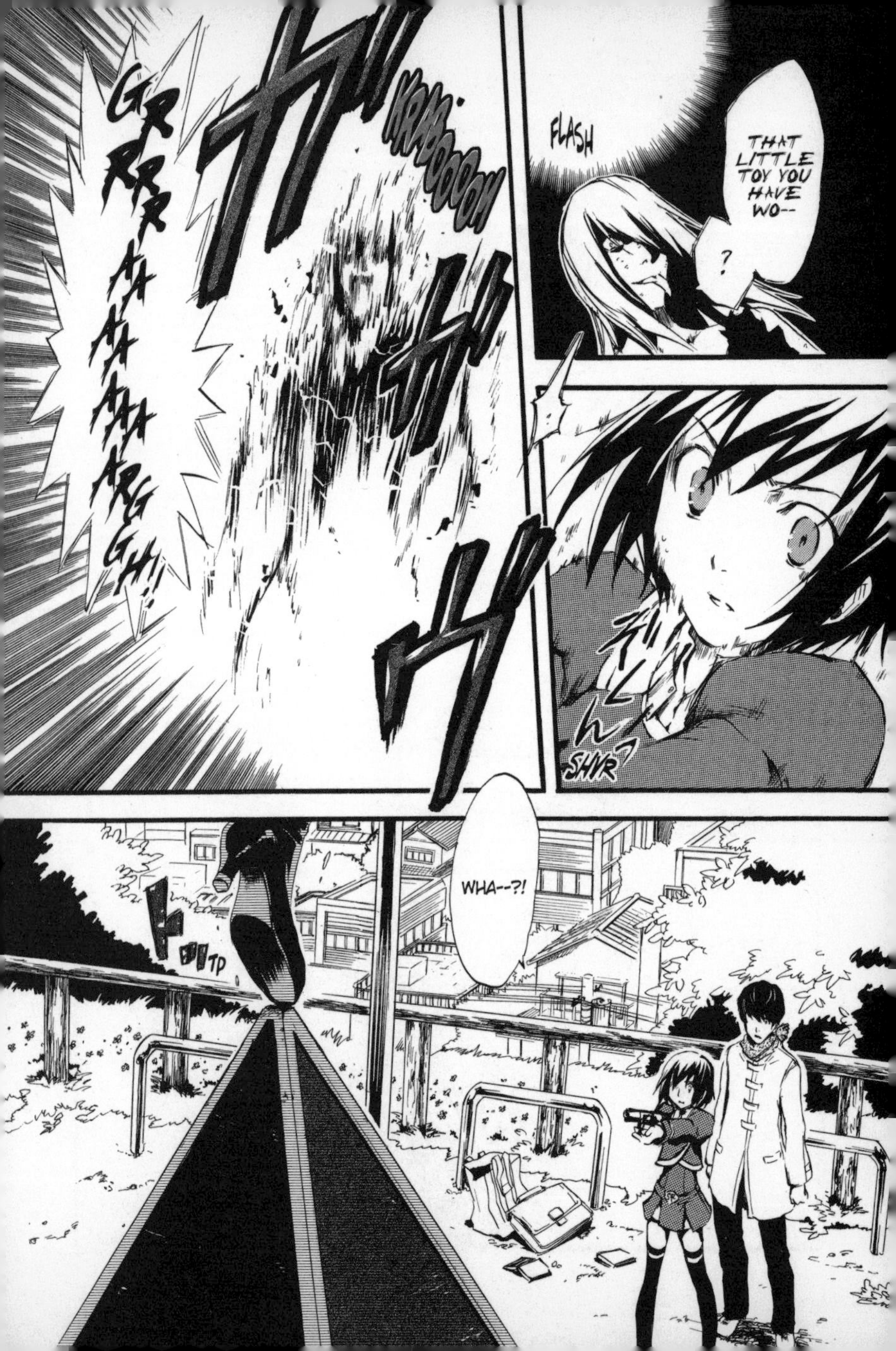
FLASH
THAT LITTLE TOY YOU HAVE WO--
?
SHVR
KRABOOOOOM
GRRRRAAAAAAAAAARGGH!!
TP
WHA--?!

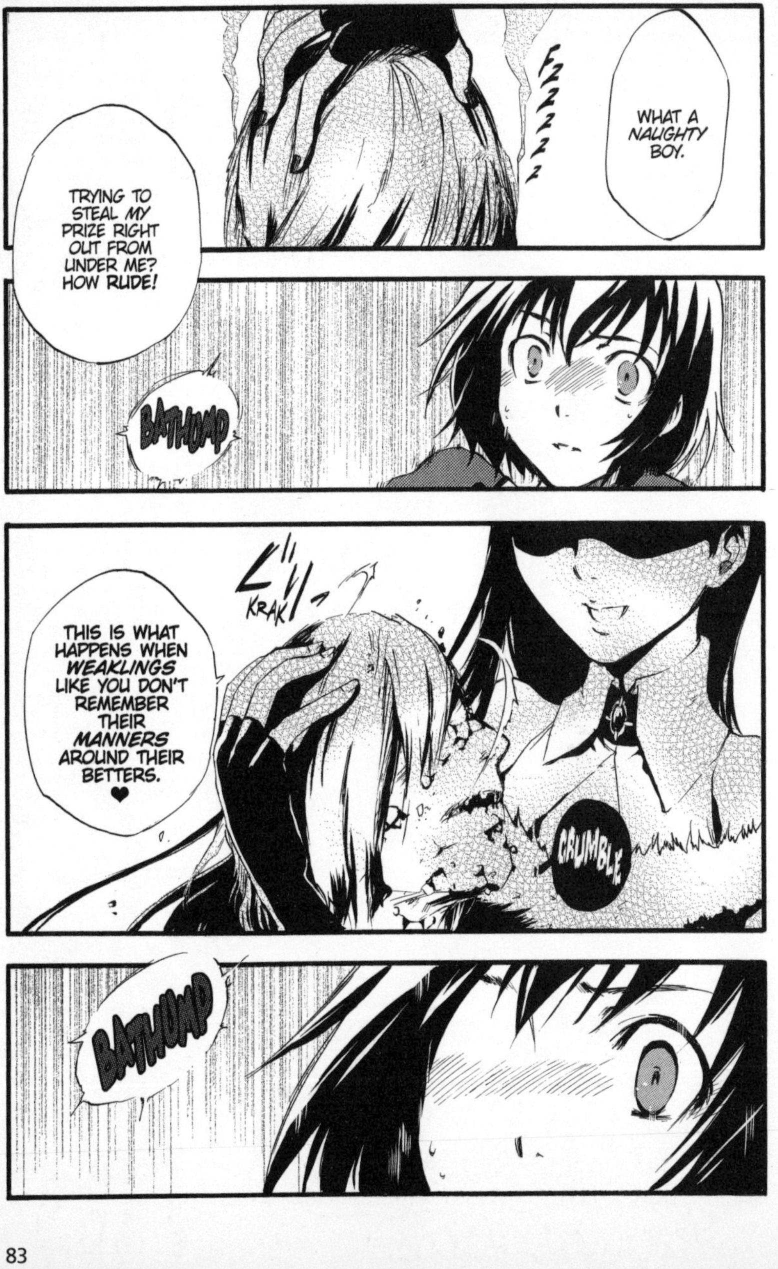
WHAT A NAUGHTY BOY.
FZZZZZZZ
TRYING TO STEAL MY PRIZE RIGHT OUT FROM UNDER ME? HOW RUDE!
BATHUMP
KRAK
THIS IS WHAT HAPPENS WHEN WEAKLINGS LIKE YOU DON'T REMEMBER THEIR MANNERS AROUND THEIR BETTERS. ❤
CRUMBLE
BATHUMP

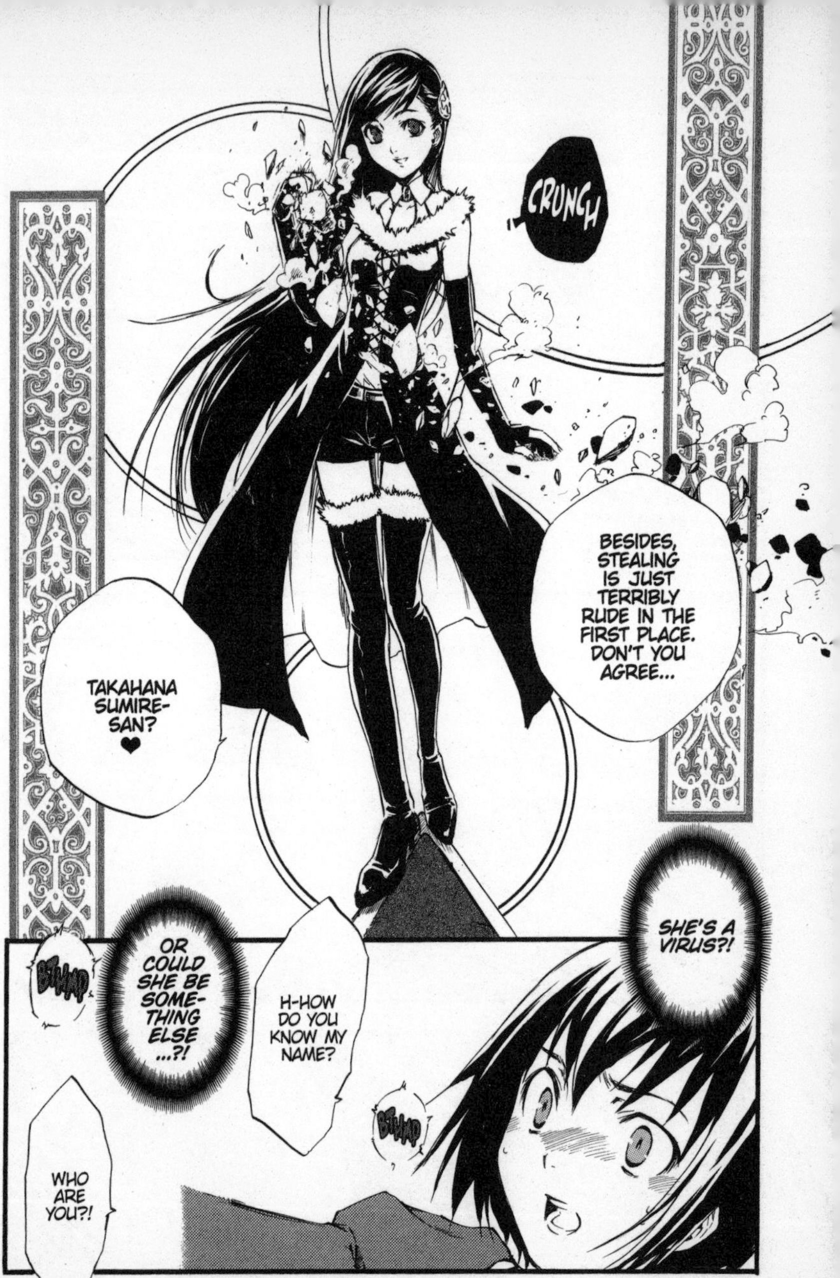
CRUNCH
BESIDES, STEALING IS JUST TERRIBLY RUDE IN THE FIRST PLACE. DON'T YOU AGREE...
TAKAHANA SUMIRE-SAN? ♥
SHE'S A VIRUS?!
BTHAP
OR COULD SHE BE SOME-THING ELSE ...?!
H-HOW DO YOU KNOW MY NAME?
BTHAP
WHO ARE YOU?!

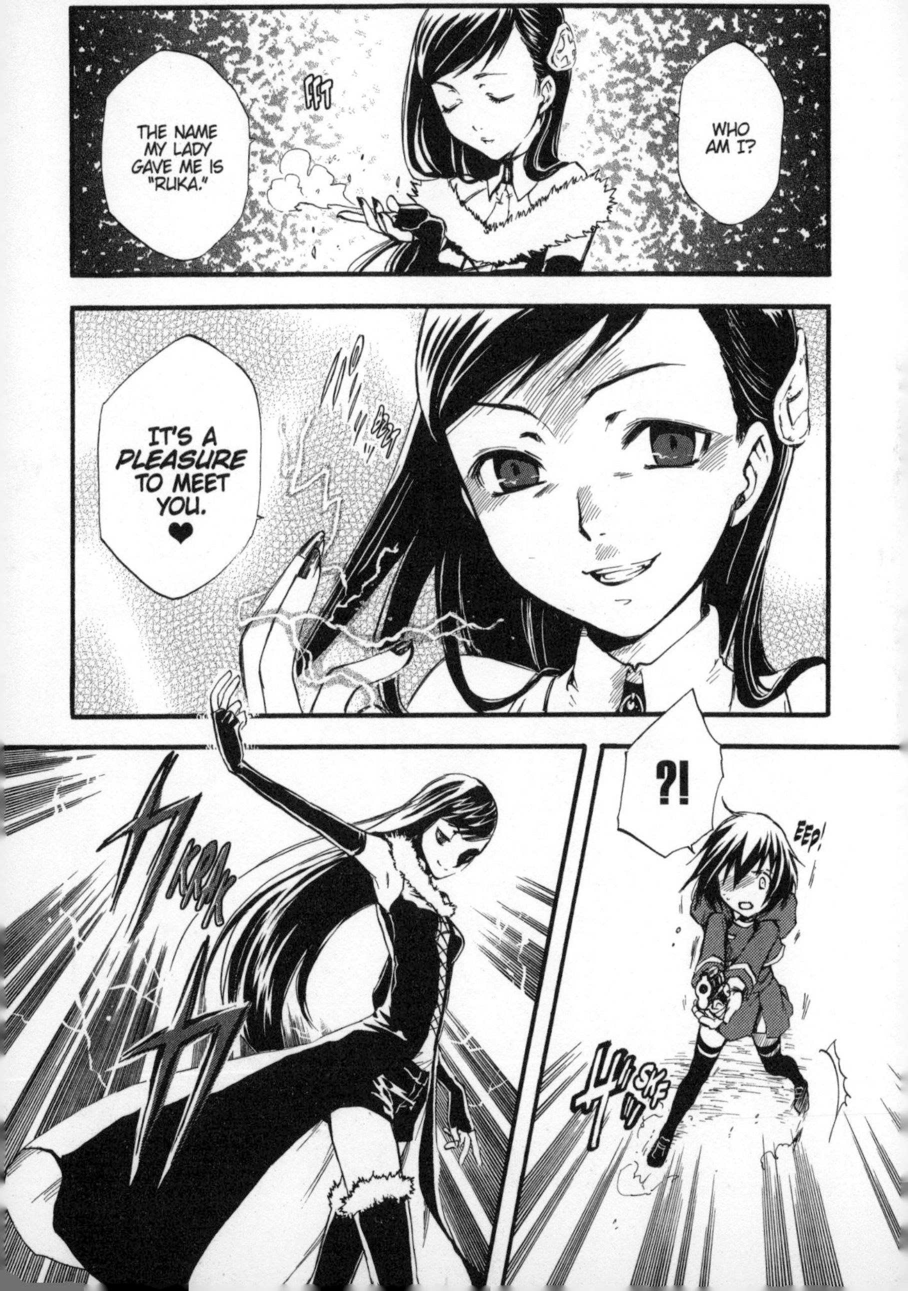
WHO AM I?
FFT
THE NAME MY LADY GAVE ME IS "RUKA."
IT'S A *PLEASURE* TO MEET YOU. ❤
?!
EEP!
SKF
KRAK

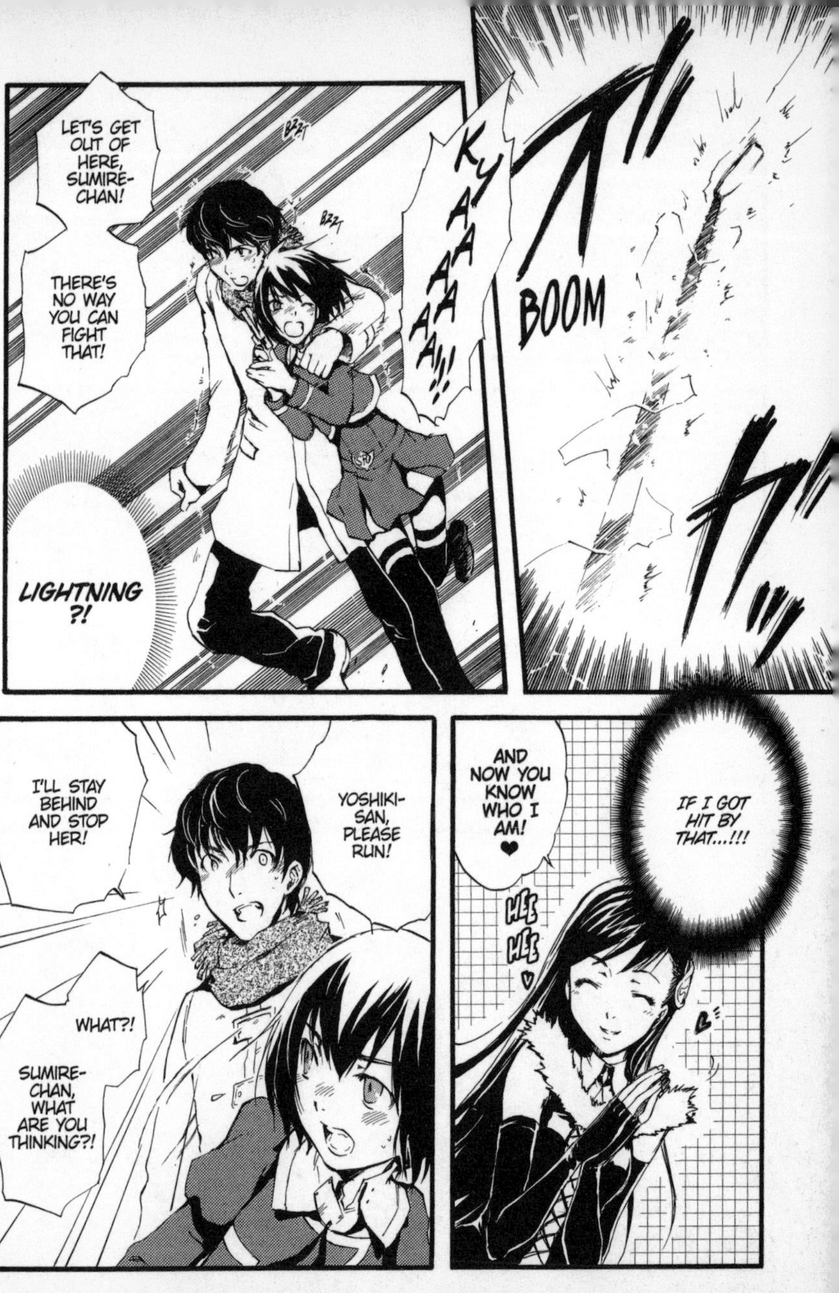
BOOM
KYAAAAAA!!!
LET'S GET OUT OF HERE, SUMIRE-CHAN!
BZZT
BZZT
THERE'S NO WAY YOU CAN FIGHT THAT!
LIGHTNING ?!
IF I GOT HIT BY THAT...!!!
AND NOW YOU KNOW WHO I AM! ❤
HEE HEE
YOSHIKI-SAN, PLEASE RUN!
I'LL STAY BEHIND AND STOP HER!
WHAT?!
SUMIRE-CHAN, WHAT ARE YOU THINKING?!

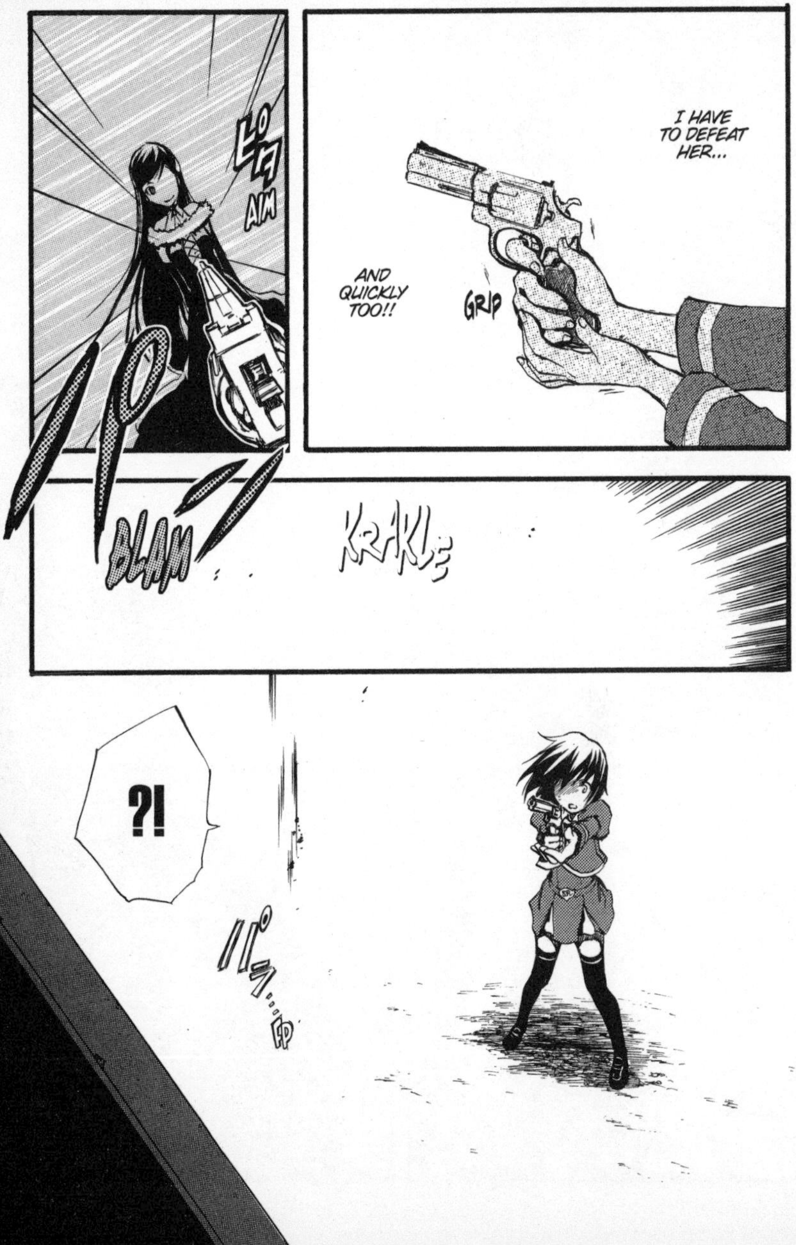
I HAVE TO DEFEAT HER...
AND QUICKLY TOO!!
GRIP
AIM
BLAM
KRAKLE
?!
FP

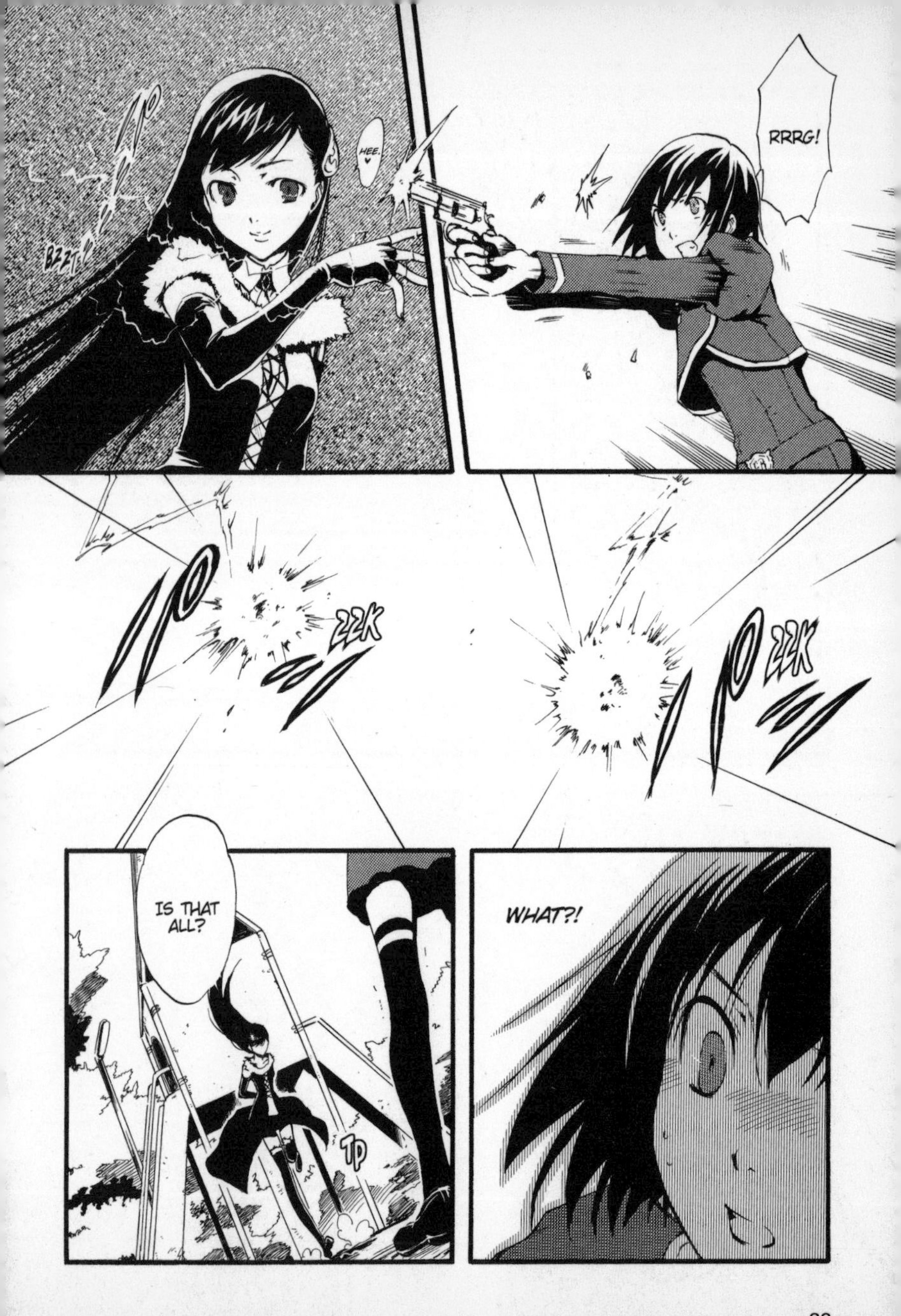

RRRG!
HEE. ♥
BZZT
ZZK
ZZK
WHAT?!
IS THAT ALL?
TP

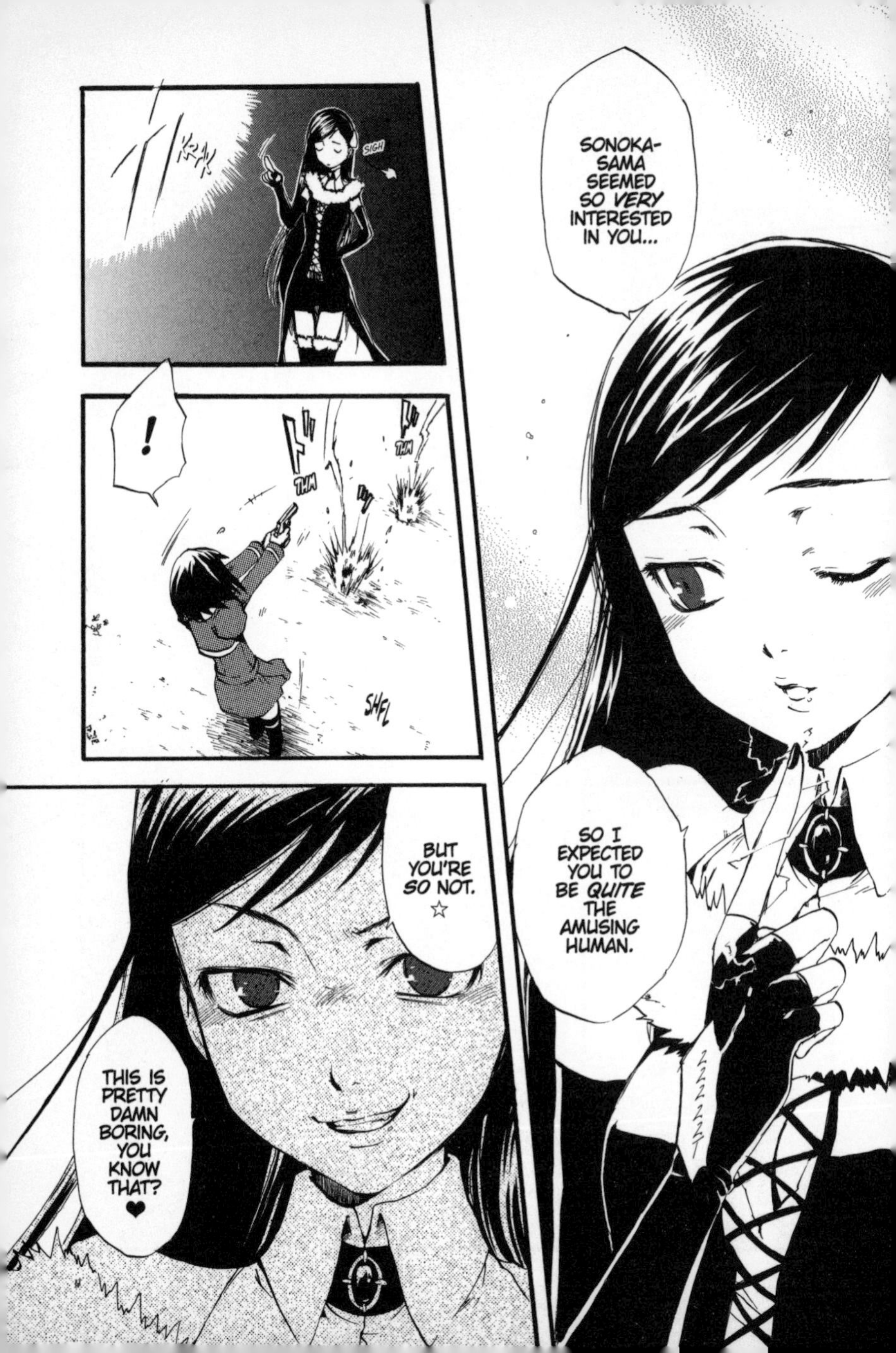
SONOKA-SAMA SEEMED SO VERY INTERESTED IN YOU...
SO I EXPECTED YOU TO BE QUITE THE AMUSING HUMAN.
SIGH
!
THM
THM
SHFL
BUT YOU'RE SO NOT. ☆
THIS IS PRETTY DAMN BORING, YOU KNOW THAT? ❤

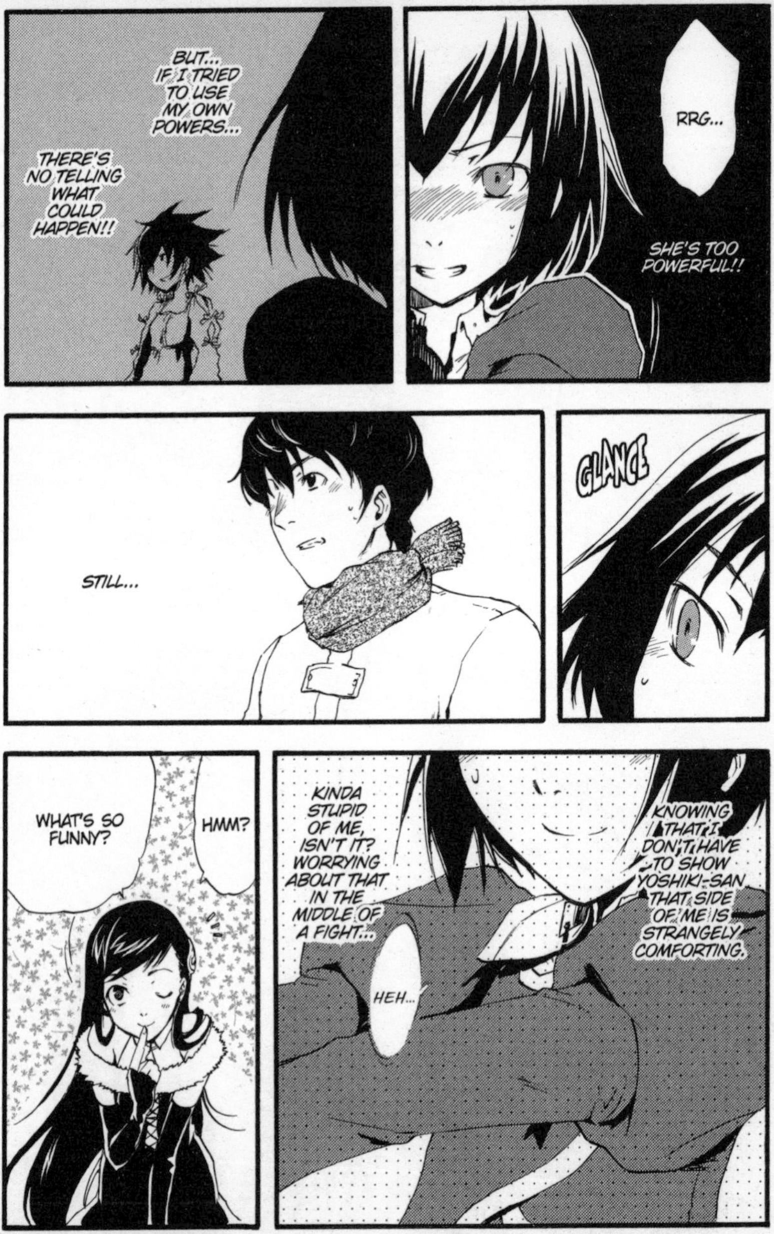
RRG...
SHE'S TOO POWERFUL!!
BUT... IF I TRIED TO USE MY OWN POWERS...
THERE'S NO TELLING WHAT COULD HAPPEN!!
GLANCE
STILL...
KNOWING THAT I DON'T HAVE TO SHOW YOSHIKI-SAN THAT SIDE OF ME IS STRANGELY COMFORTING.
KINDA STUPID OF ME, ISN'T IT? WORRYING ABOUT THAT IN THE MIDDLE OF A FIGHT...
HEH...
HMM?
WHAT'S SO FUNNY?

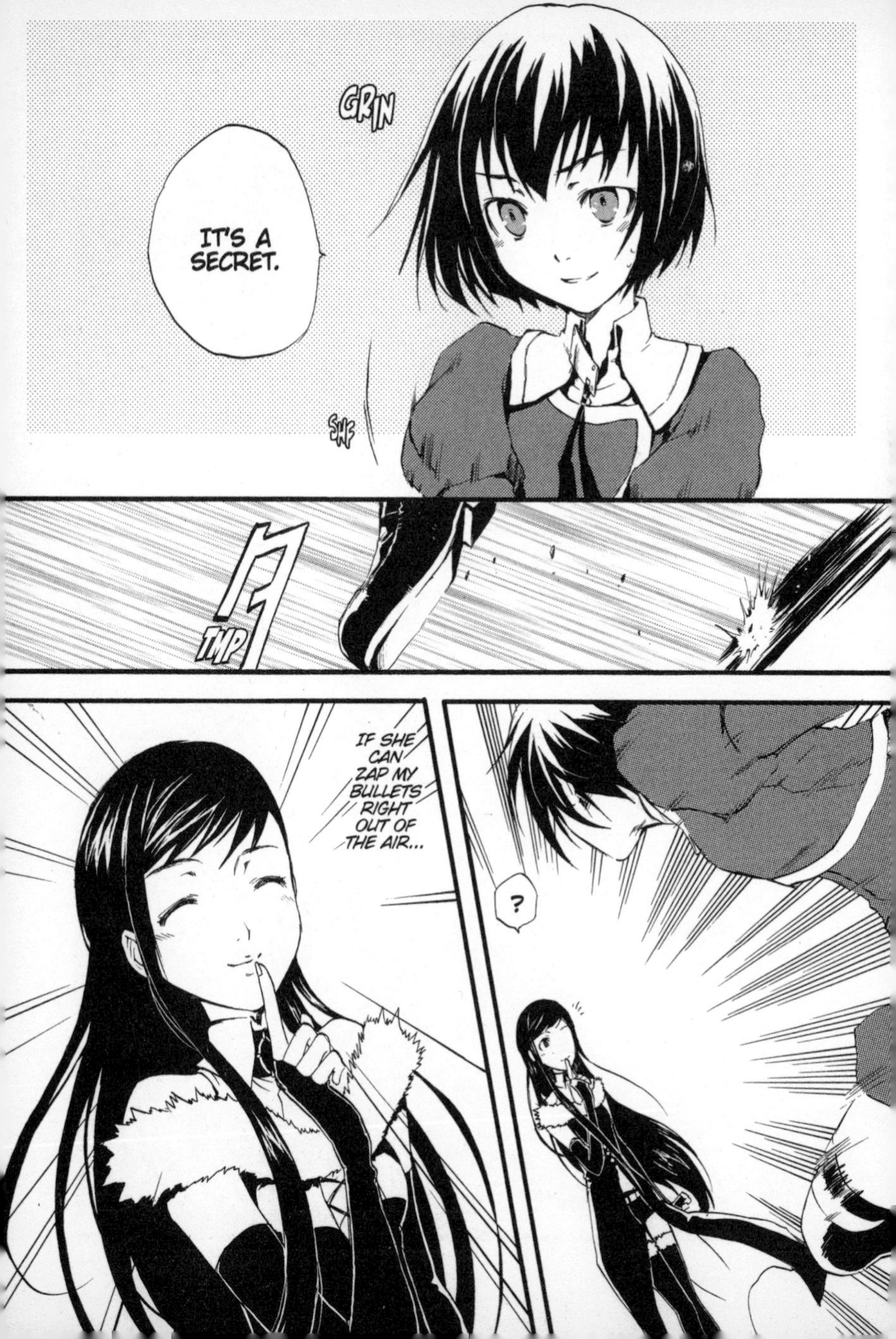
GRIN
IT'S A SECRET.
SHF
TMP
IF SHE CAN ZAP MY BULLETS RIGHT OUT OF THE AIR...
?

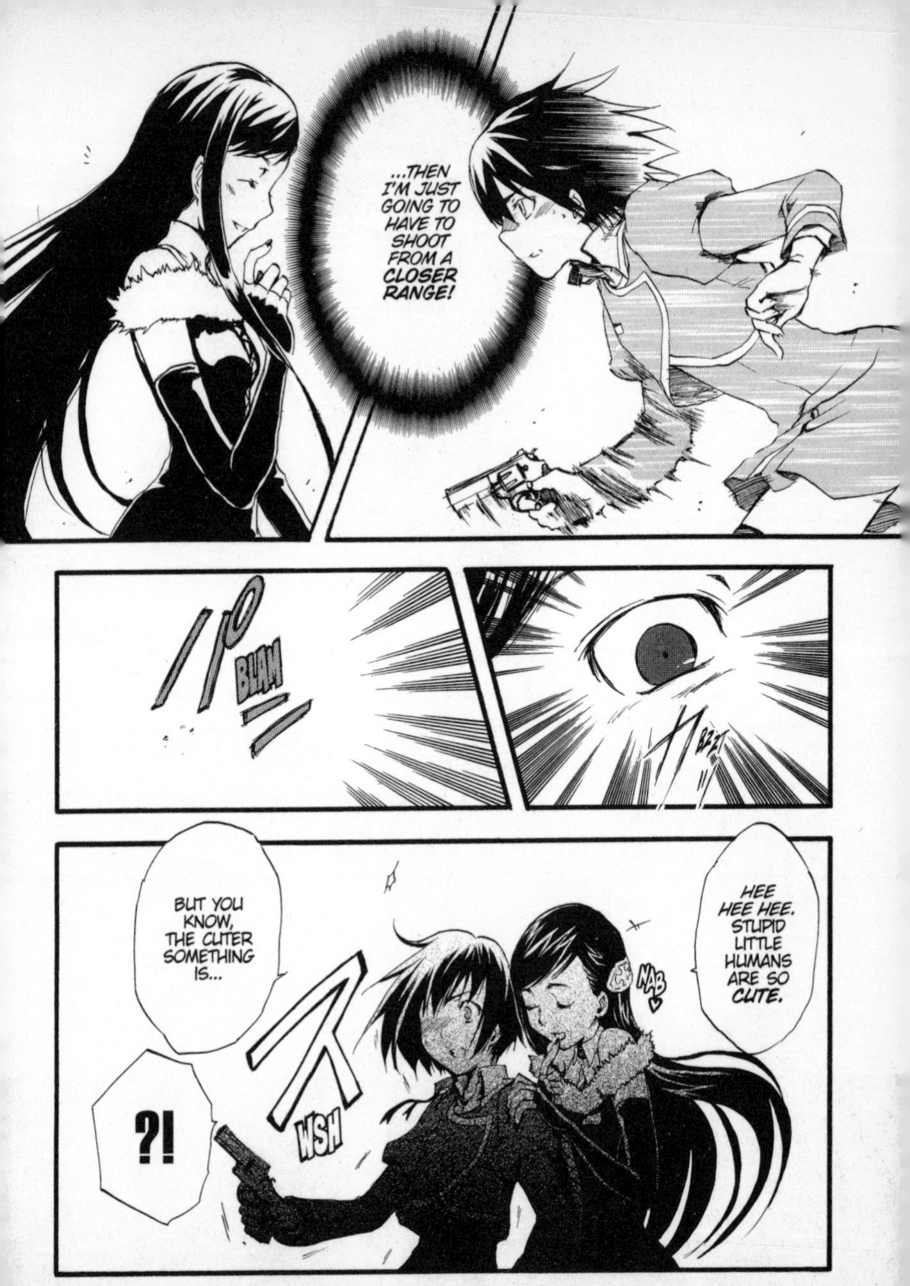
...THEN I'M JUST GOING TO HAVE TO SHOOT FROM A CLOSER RANGE!
BZZT
BLAM
HEE HEE HEE. STUPID LITTLE HUMANS ARE SO CUTE.
NAB
BUT YOU KNOW, THE CUTER SOMETHING IS...
WSH
?!

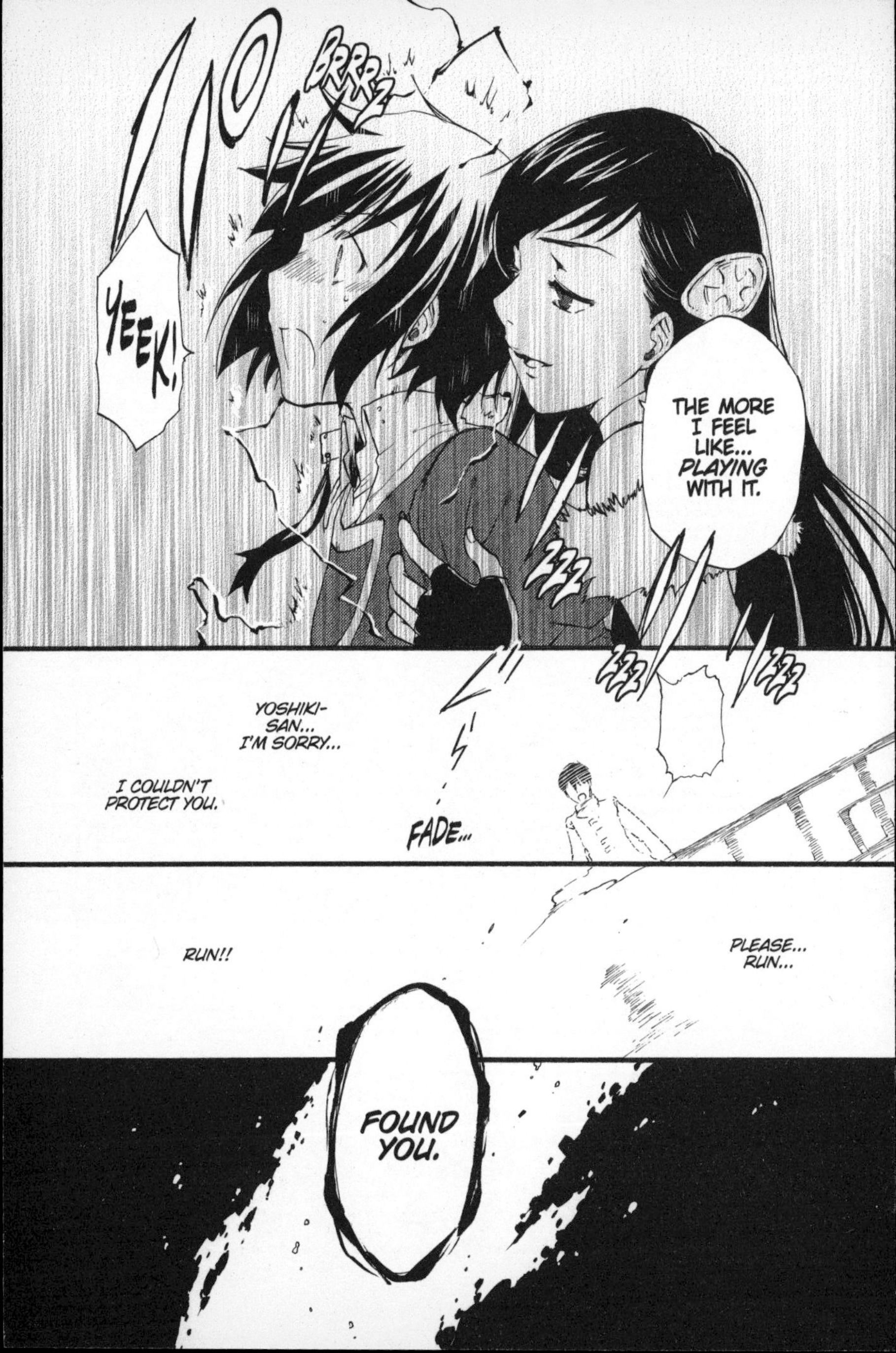
THE MORE I FEEL LIKE... PLAYING WITH IT.
YEEK!
NO
FADE...
YOSHIKI-SAN... I'M SORRY...
I COULDN'T PROTECT YOU.
PLEASE... RUN...
RUN!!
FOUND YOU.

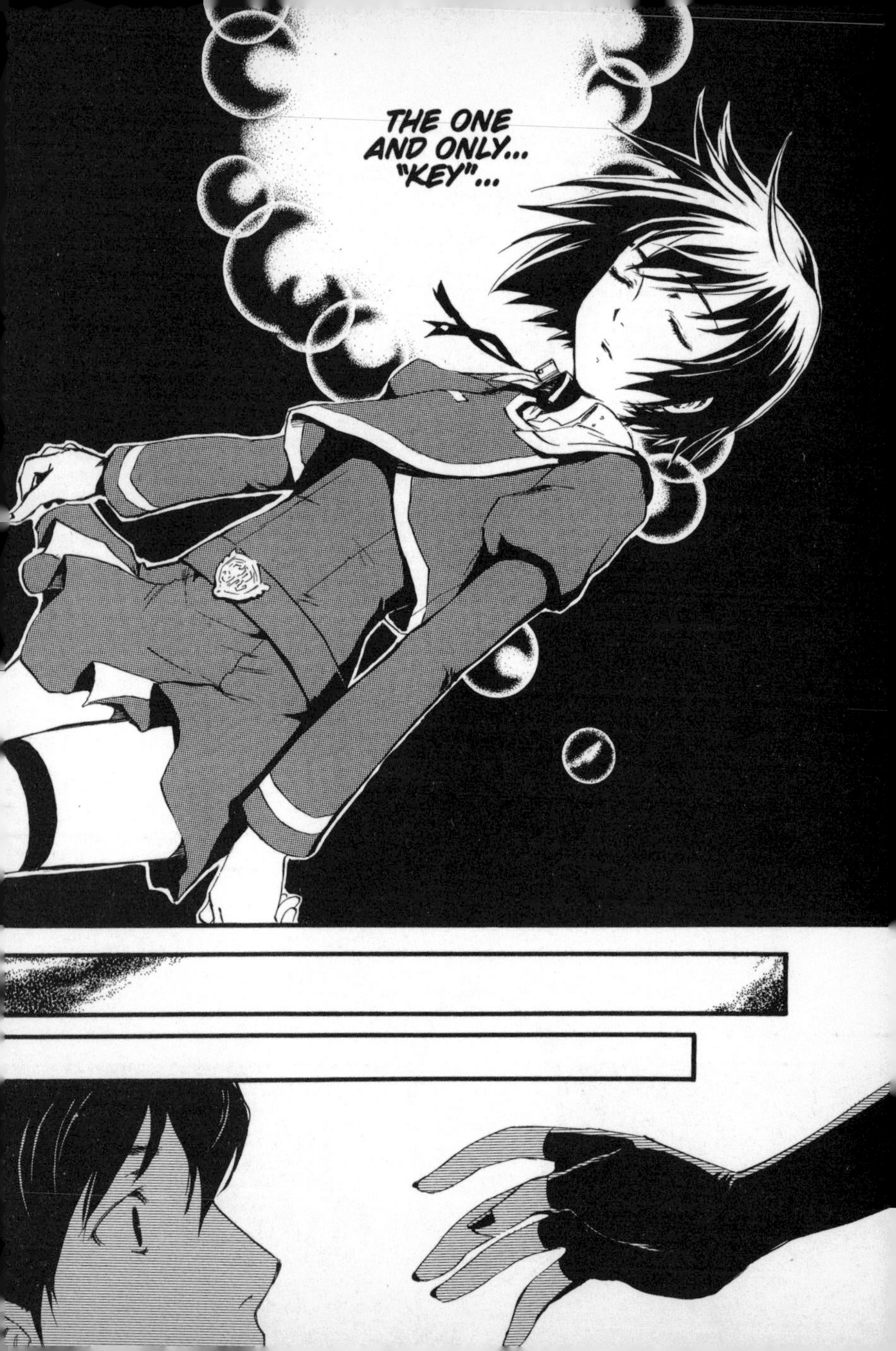
THE ONE AND ONLY... "KEY"...

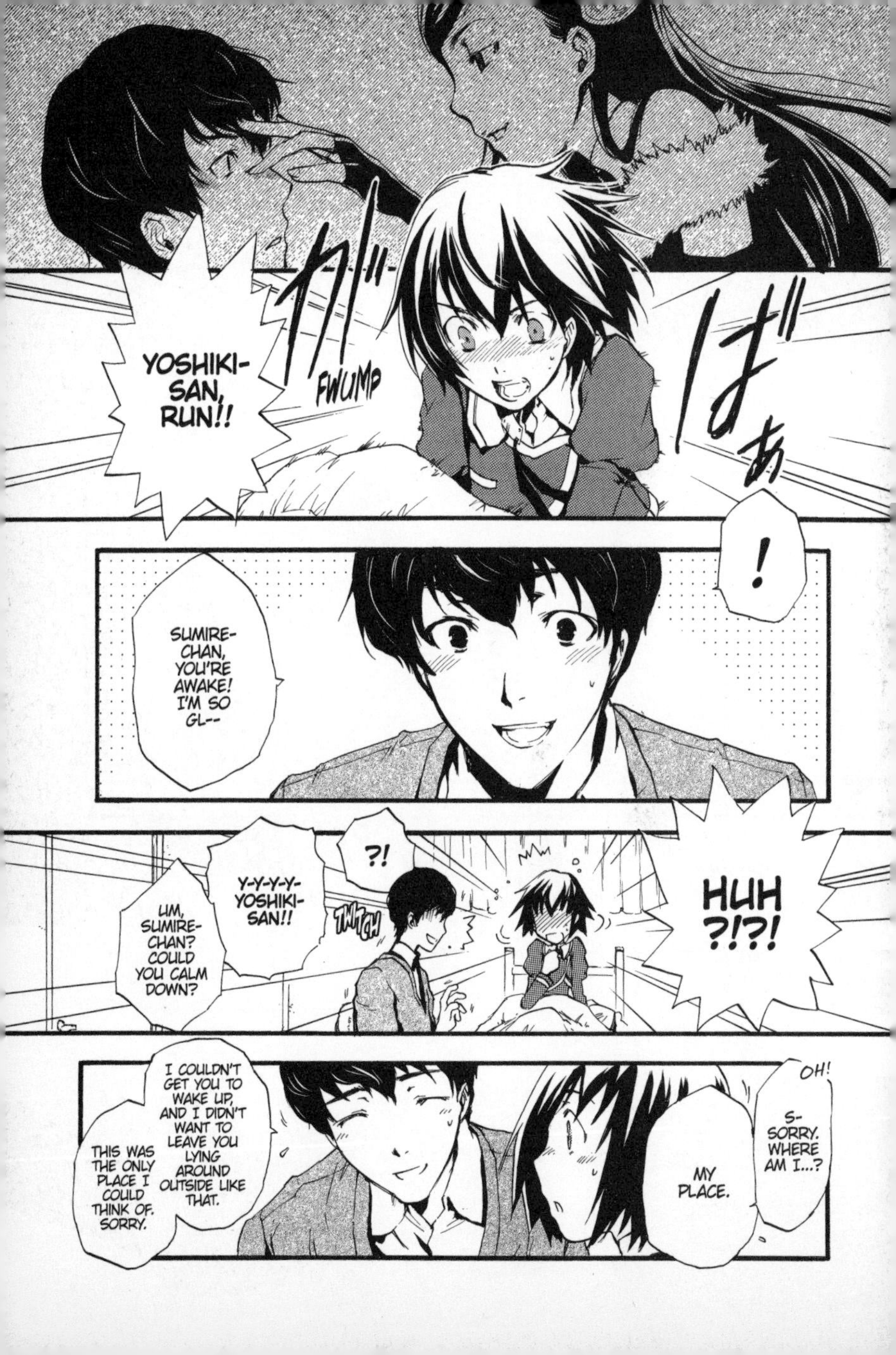
ばぁ
!
FWUMP
YOSHIKI-SAN, RUN!!
SUMIRE-CHAN, YOU'RE AWAKE! I'M SO GL--
HUH?!?!
?!
Y-Y-Y-Y-YOSHIKI-SAN!!
TWITCH
UM, SUMIRE-CHAN? COULD YOU CALM DOWN?
OH!
S-SORRY. WHERE AM I...?
MY PLACE.
I COULDN'T GET YOU TO WAKE UP, AND I DIDN'T WANT TO LEAVE YOU LYING AROUND OUTSIDE LIKE THAT.
THIS WAS THE ONLY PLACE I COULD THINK OF. SORRY.

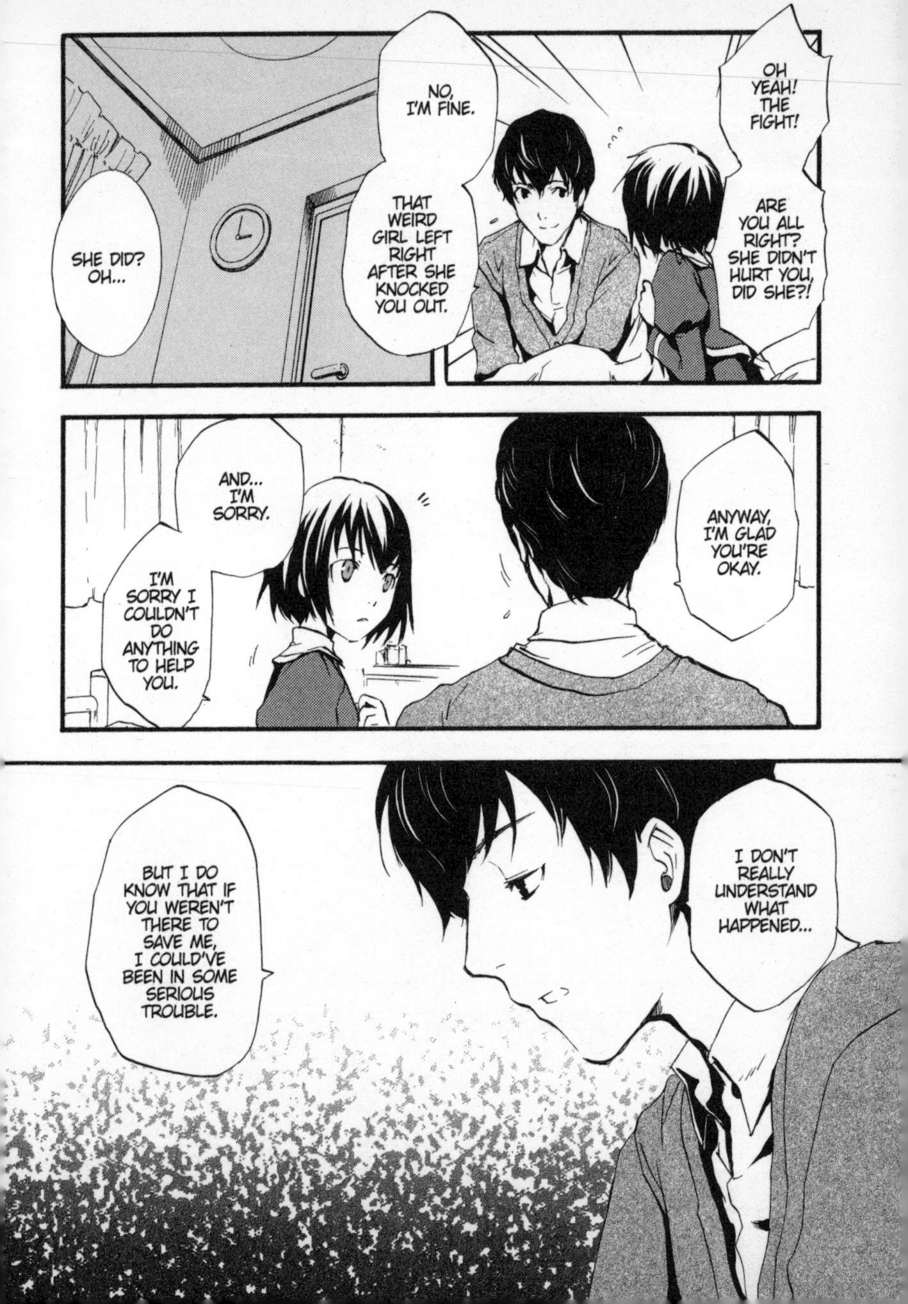
OH YEAH! THE FIGHT!
ARE YOU ALL RIGHT? SHE DIDN'T HURT YOU, DID SHE?!
NO, I'M FINE.
THAT WEIRD GIRL LEFT RIGHT AFTER SHE KNOCKED YOU OUT.
SHE DID? OH...
ANYWAY, I'M GLAD YOU'RE OKAY.
AND... I'M SORRY.
I'M SORRY I COULDN'T DO ANYTHING TO HELP YOU.
I DON'T REALLY UNDERSTAND WHAT HAPPENED...
BUT I DO KNOW THAT IF YOU WEREN'T THERE TO SAVE ME, I COULD'VE BEEN IN SOME SERIOUS TROUBLE.

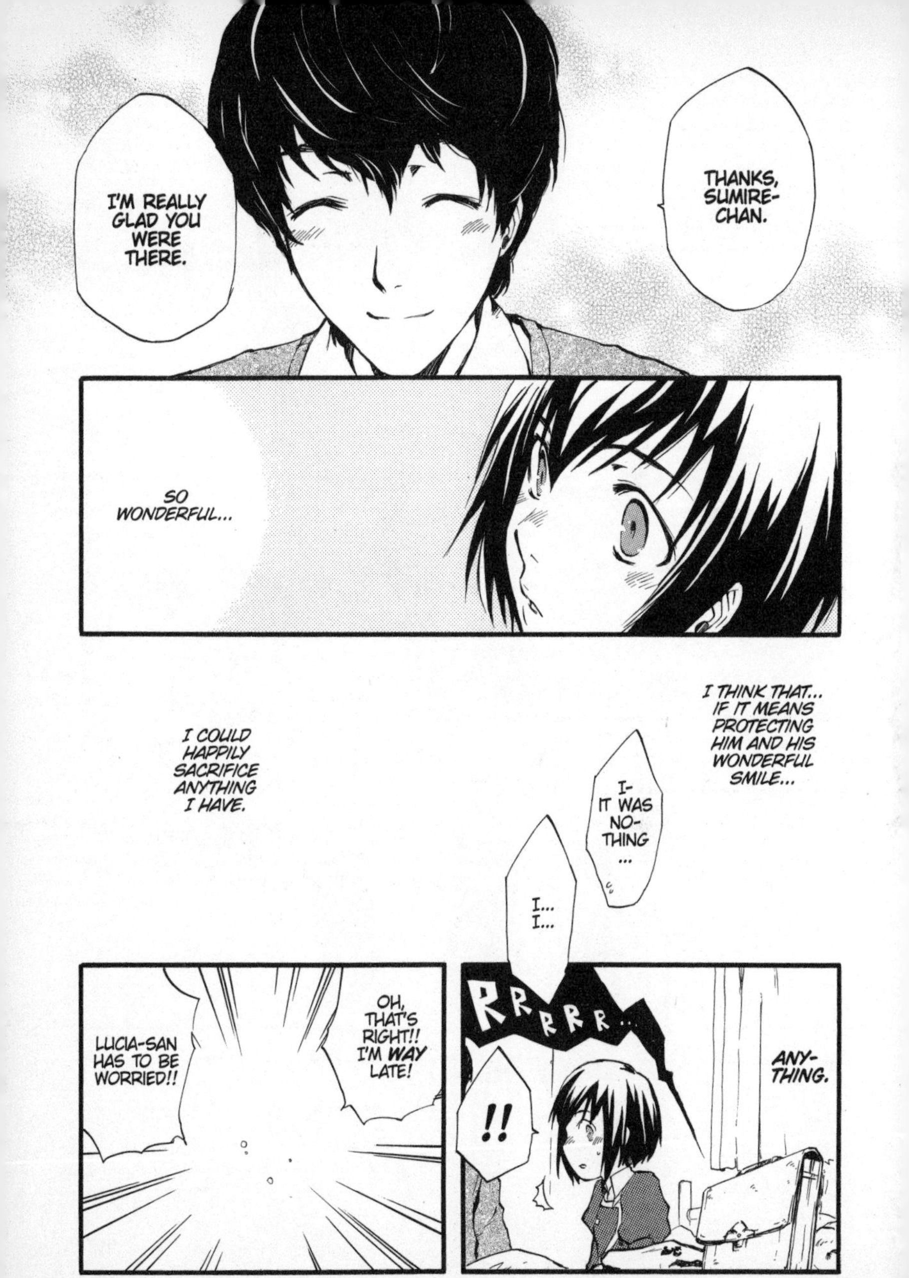
THANKS, SUMIRE-CHAN.
I'M REALLY GLAD YOU WERE THERE.
SO WONDERFUL...
I THINK THAT... IF IT MEANS PROTECTING HIM AND HIS WONDERFUL SMILE...
I- IT WAS NO-THING ...
I... I...
I COULD HAPPILY SACRIFICE ANYTHING I HAVE.
ANY-THING.
RRRRR...
!!
OH, THAT'S RIGHT!! I'M **WAY** LATE!
LUCIA-SAN HAS TO BE WORRIED!!

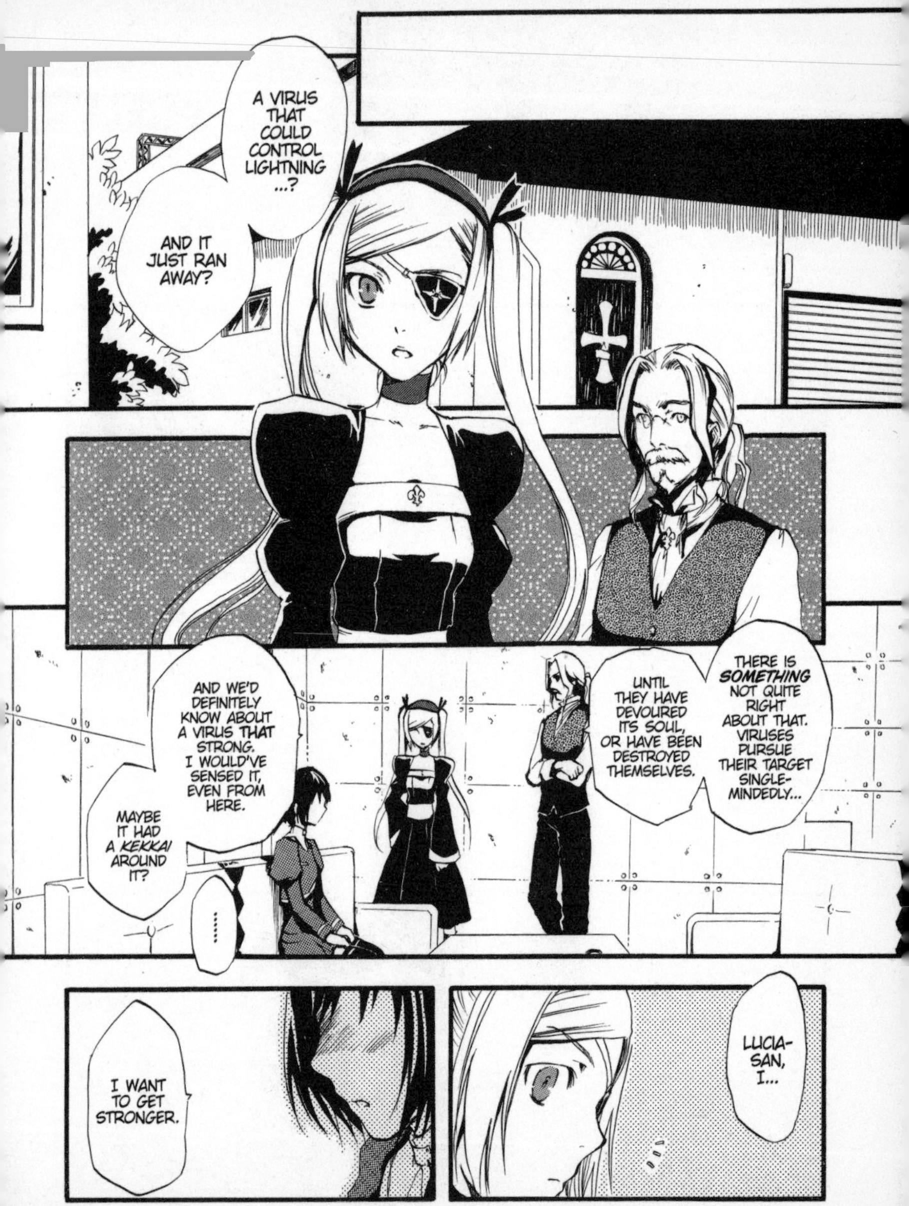
A VIRUS THAT COULD CONTROL LIGHTNING ...?
AND IT JUST RAN AWAY?
THERE IS *SOMETHING* NOT QUITE RIGHT ABOUT THAT. VIRUSES PURSUE THEIR TARGET SINGLE-MINDEDLY...
UNTIL THEY HAVE DEVOURED ITS SOUL, OR HAVE BEEN DESTROYED THEMSELVES.
AND WE'D DEFINITELY KNOW ABOUT A VIRUS THAT STRONG. I WOULD'VE SENSED IT, EVEN FROM HERE.
MAYBE IT HAD A *KEKKAI* AROUND IT?
......
LUCIA-SAN, I...
I WANT TO GET STRONGER.

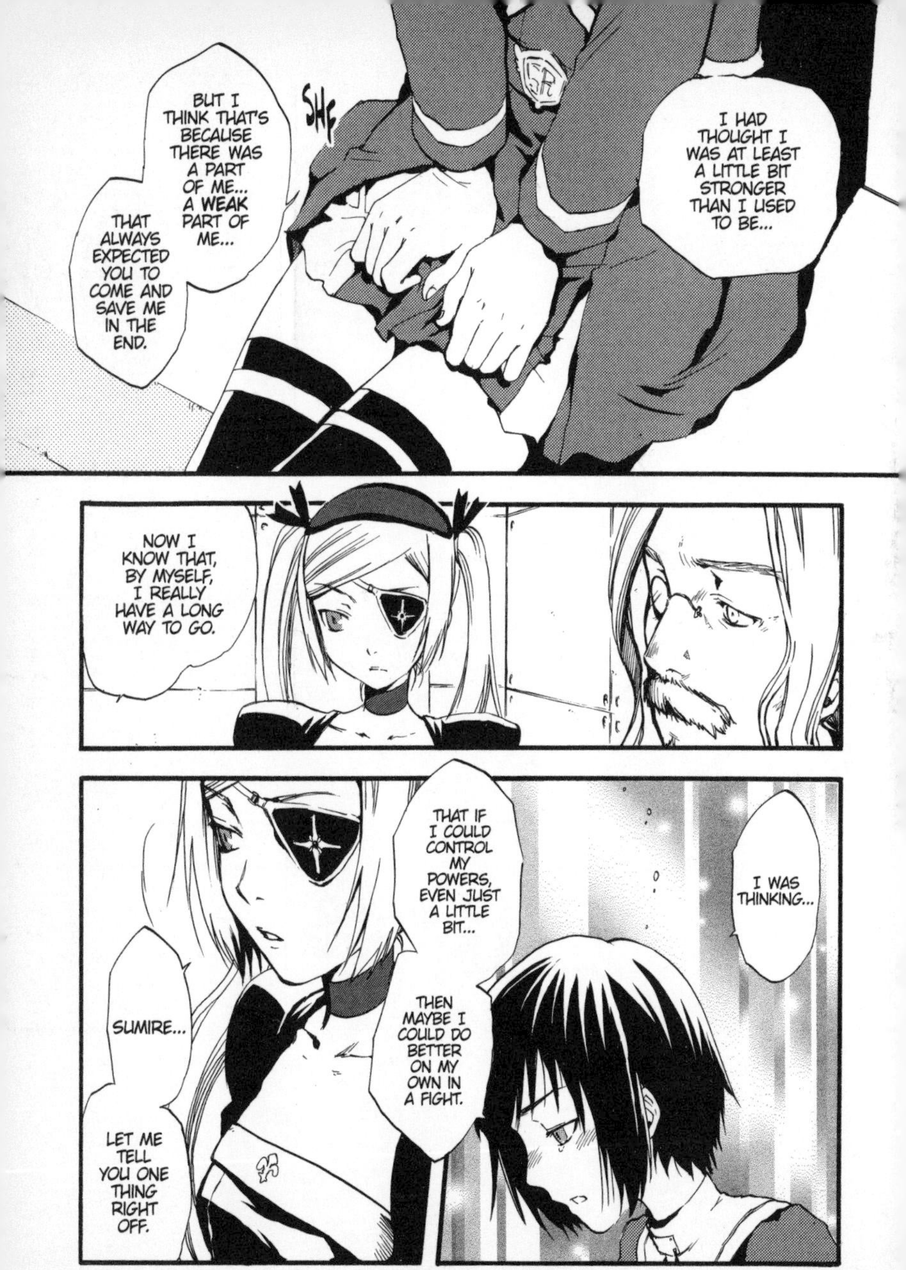

I HAD THOUGHT I WAS AT LEAST A LITTLE BIT STRONGER THAN I USED TO BE...
SHF
BUT I THINK THAT'S BECAUSE THERE WAS A PART OF ME... A **WEAK** PART OF ME...
THAT ALWAYS EXPECTED YOU TO COME AND SAVE ME IN THE END.
NOW I KNOW THAT, BY MYSELF, I REALLY HAVE A LONG WAY TO GO.
I WAS THINKING...
THAT IF I COULD CONTROL MY POWERS, EVEN JUST A LITTLE BIT...
THEN MAYBE I COULD DO BETTER ON MY OWN IN A FIGHT.
SUMIRE...
LET ME TELL YOU ONE THING RIGHT OFF.

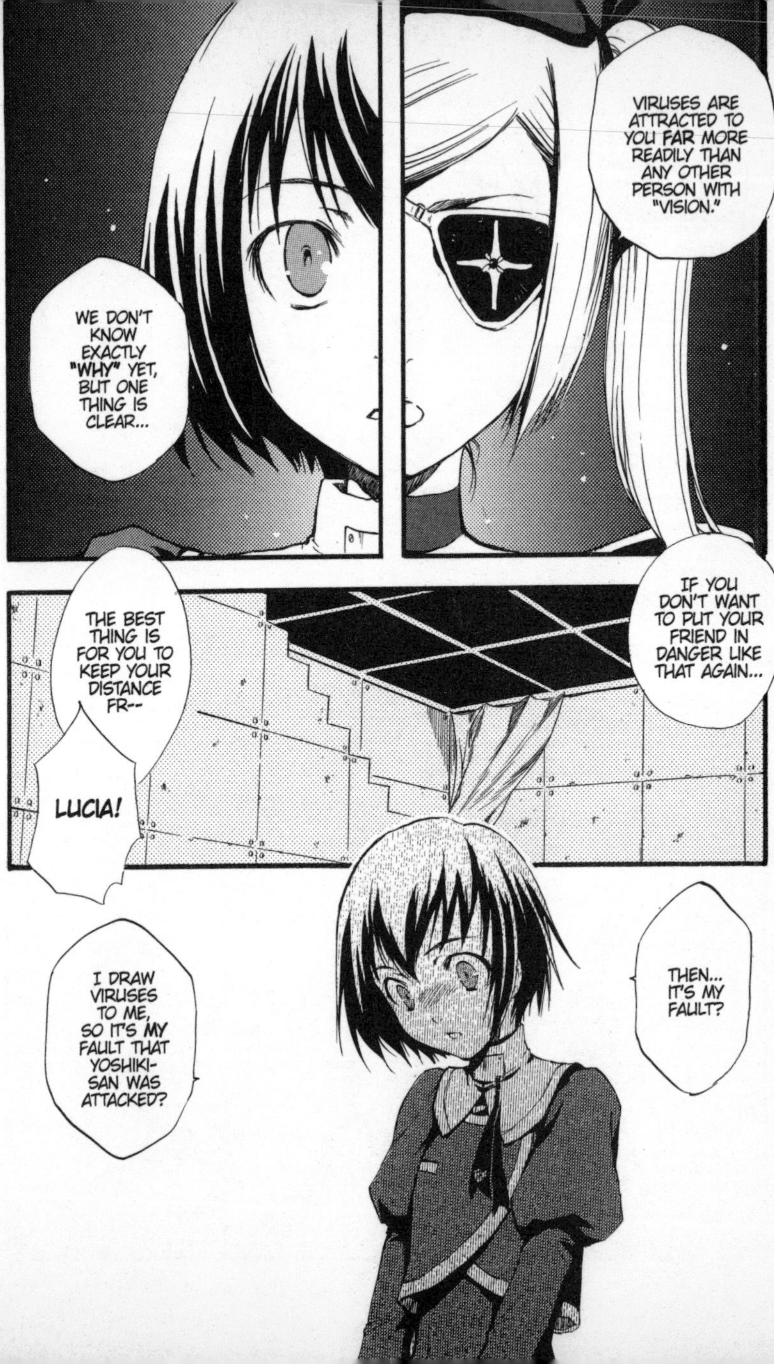
VIRUSES ARE ATTRACTED TO YOU FAR MORE READILY THAN ANY OTHER PERSON WITH "VISION."
WE DON'T KNOW EXACTLY "WHY" YET, BUT ONE THING IS CLEAR...
IF YOU DON'T WANT TO PUT YOUR FRIEND IN DANGER LIKE THAT AGAIN...
THE BEST THING IS FOR YOU TO KEEP YOUR DISTANCE FR--
LUCIA!
THEN... IT'S MY FAULT?
I DRAW VIRUSES TO ME, SO IT'S MY FAULT THAT YOSHIKI-SAN WAS ATTACKED?

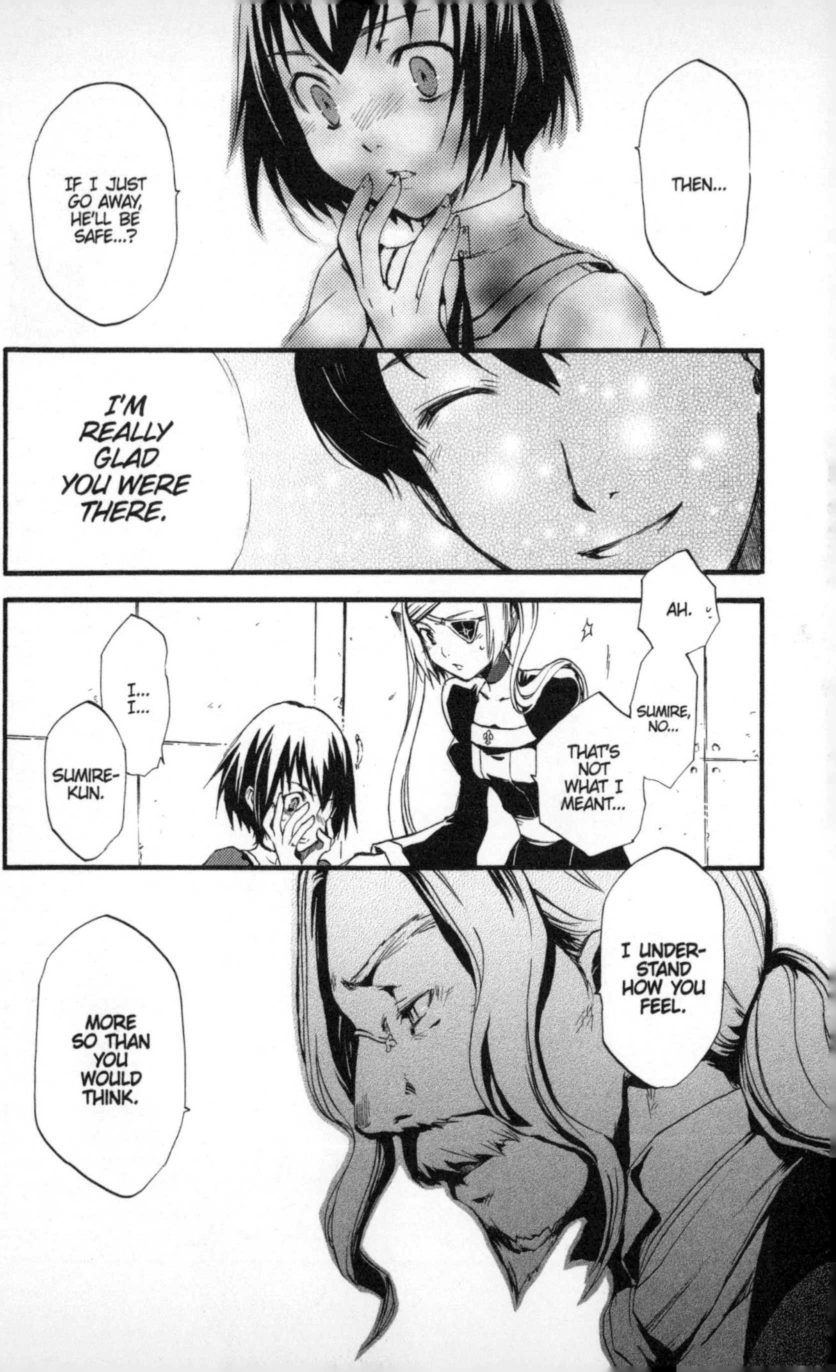
THEN...
IF I JUST GO AWAY, HE'LL BE SAFE...?
I'M REALLY GLAD YOU WERE THERE.
AH.
SUMIRE, NO...
THAT'S NOT WHAT I MEANT...
I... I...
SUMIRE-KUN.
I UNDER-STAND HOW YOU FEEL.
MORE SO THAN YOU WOULD THINK.

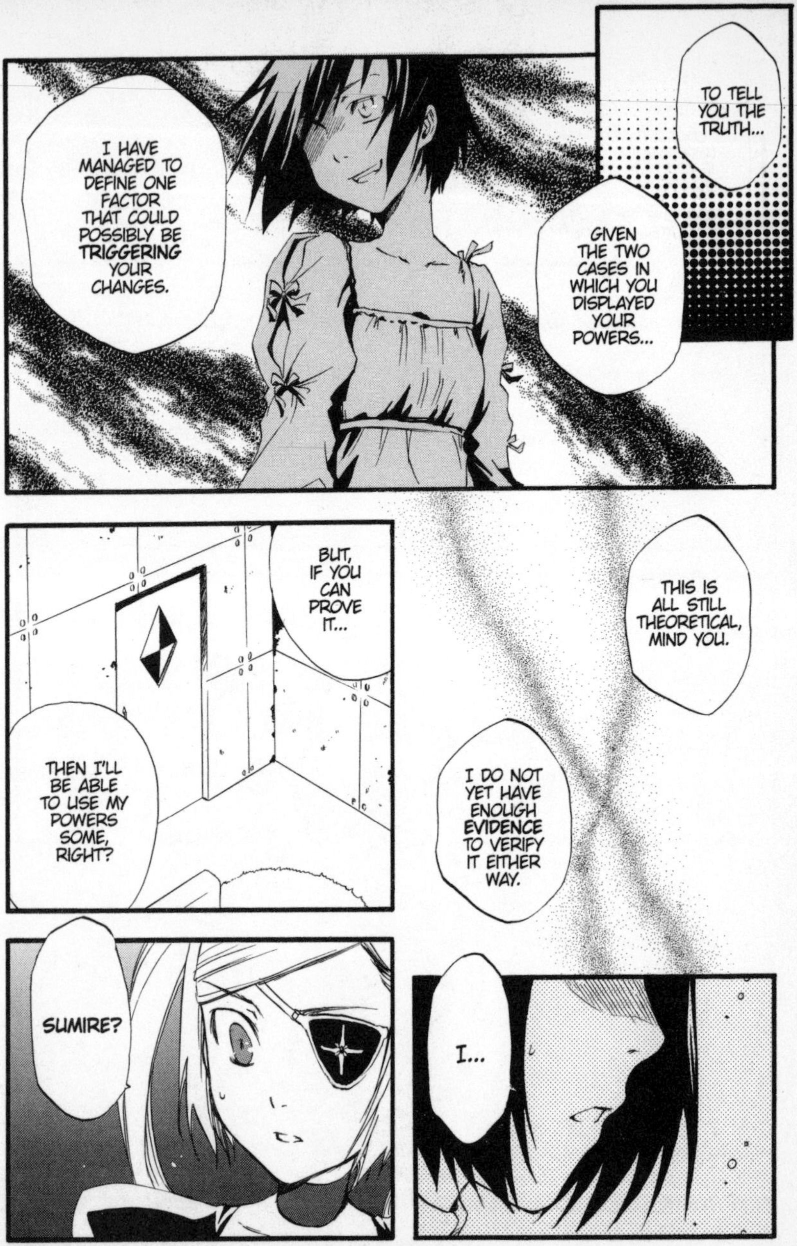
TO TELL YOU THE TRUTH...
GIVEN THE TWO CASES IN WHICH YOU DISPLAYED YOUR POWERS...
I HAVE MANAGED TO DEFINE ONE FACTOR THAT COULD POSSIBLY BE **TRIGGERING** YOUR CHANGES.
THIS IS ALL STILL THEORETICAL, MIND YOU.
I DO NOT YET HAVE ENOUGH **EVIDENCE** TO VERIFY IT EITHER WAY.
BUT, IF YOU CAN PROVE IT...
THEN I'LL BE ABLE TO USE MY POWERS SOME, RIGHT?
I...
SUMIRE?

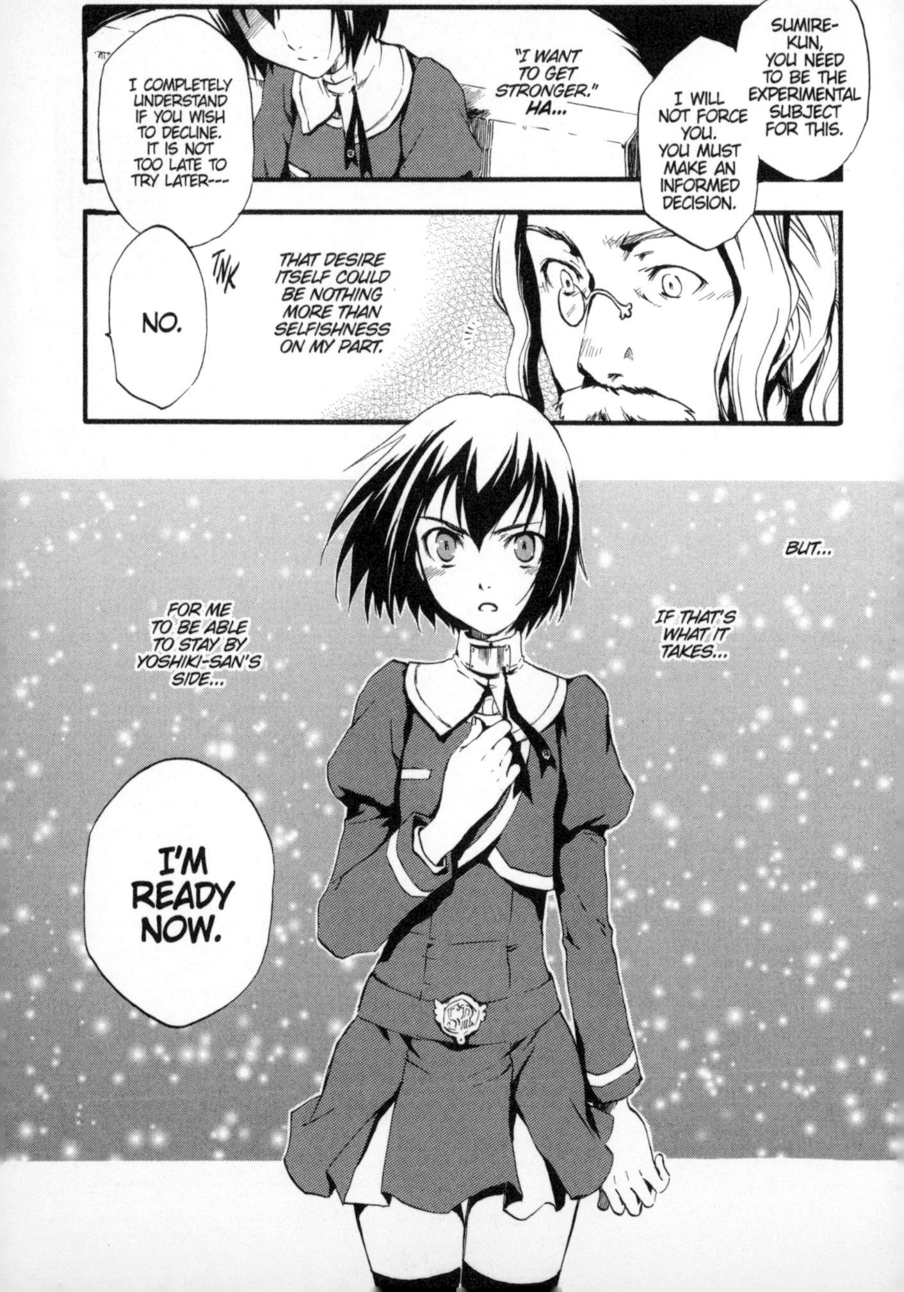
SUMIRE-KUN, YOU NEED TO BE THE EXPERIMENTAL SUBJECT FOR THIS.
I WILL NOT FORCE YOU. YOU MUST MAKE AN INFORMED DECISION.
"I WANT TO GET STRONGER." HA...
I COMPLETELY UNDERSTAND IF YOU WISH TO DECLINE. IT IS NOT TOO LATE TO TRY LATER---
THAT DESIRE ITSELF COULD BE NOTHING MORE THAN SELFISHNESS ON MY PART.
TNK
NO.
BUT...
IF THAT'S WHAT IT TAKES...
FOR ME TO BE ABLE TO STAY BY YOSHIKI-SAN'S SIDE...
I'M READY NOW.

Jewelry
and
Clothes

Venus Vangard

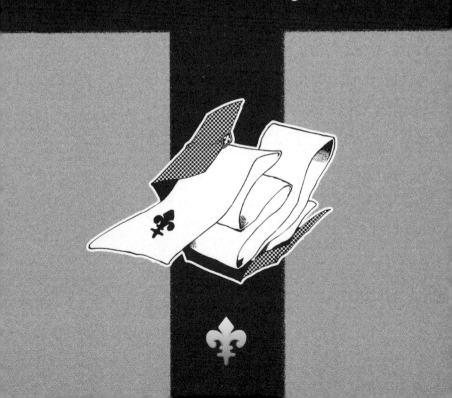

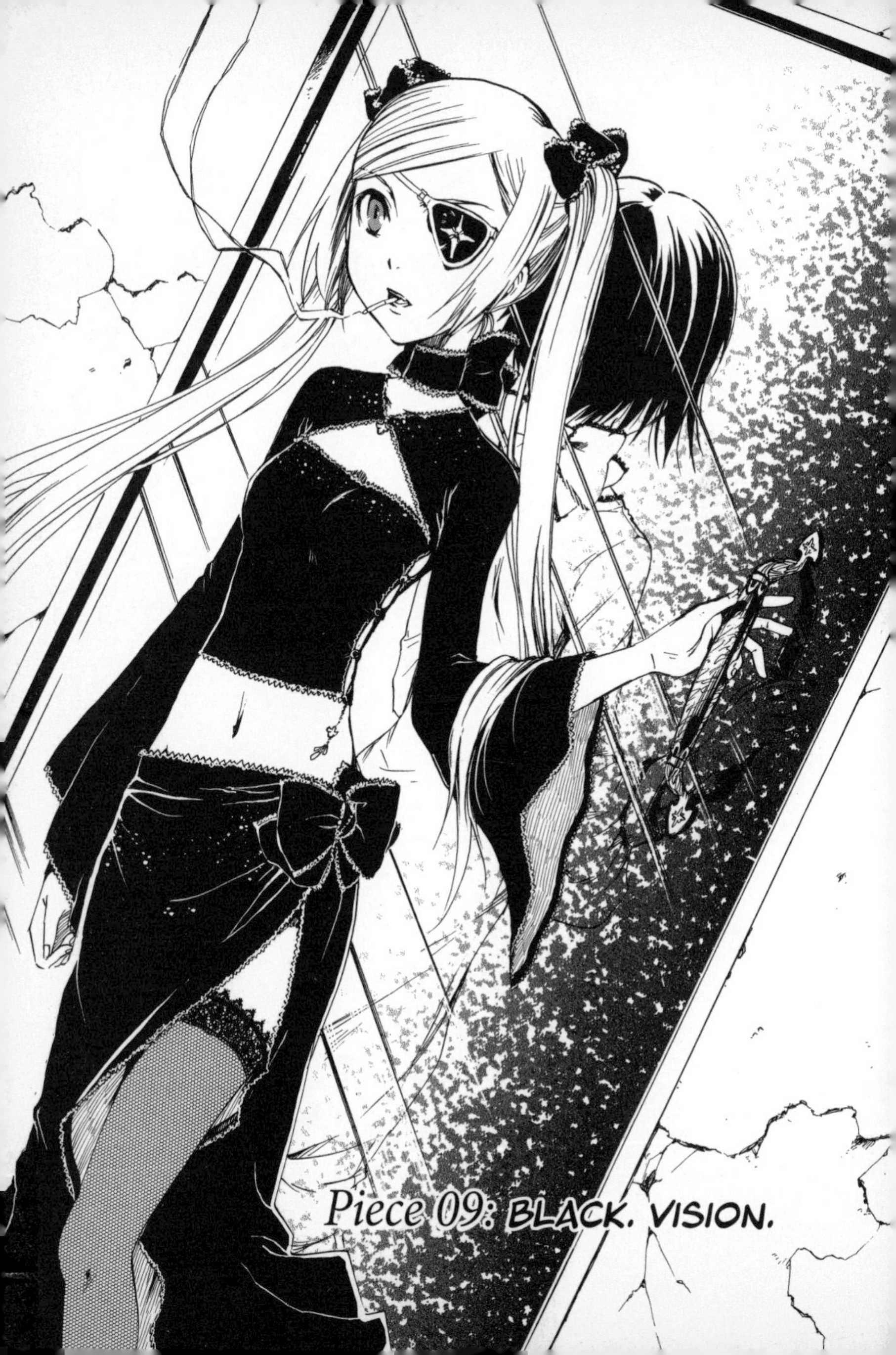
Piece 09: BLACK. VISION.

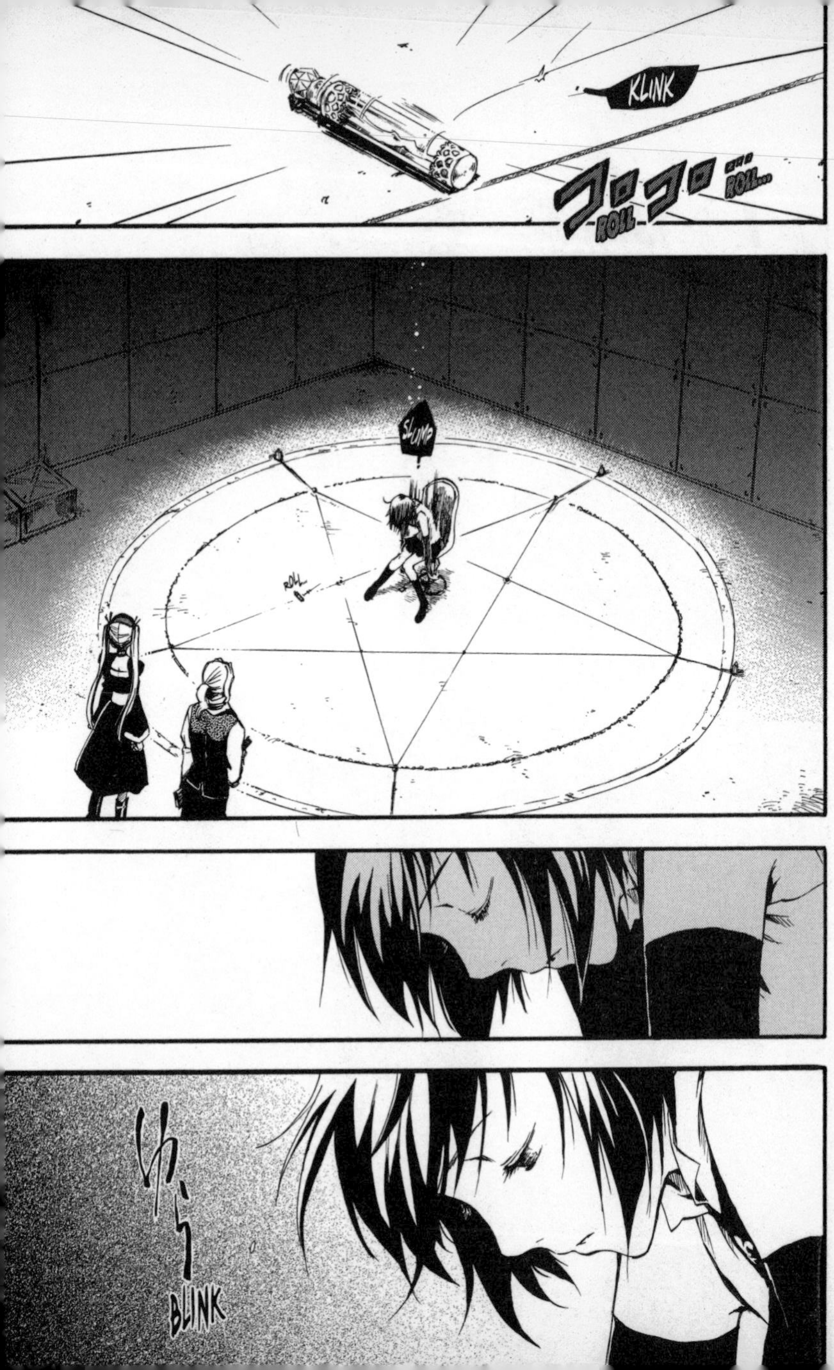
KLINK
コロコロ
ROLL ROLL...
SLUMP
ROLL
ゆら
BLINK

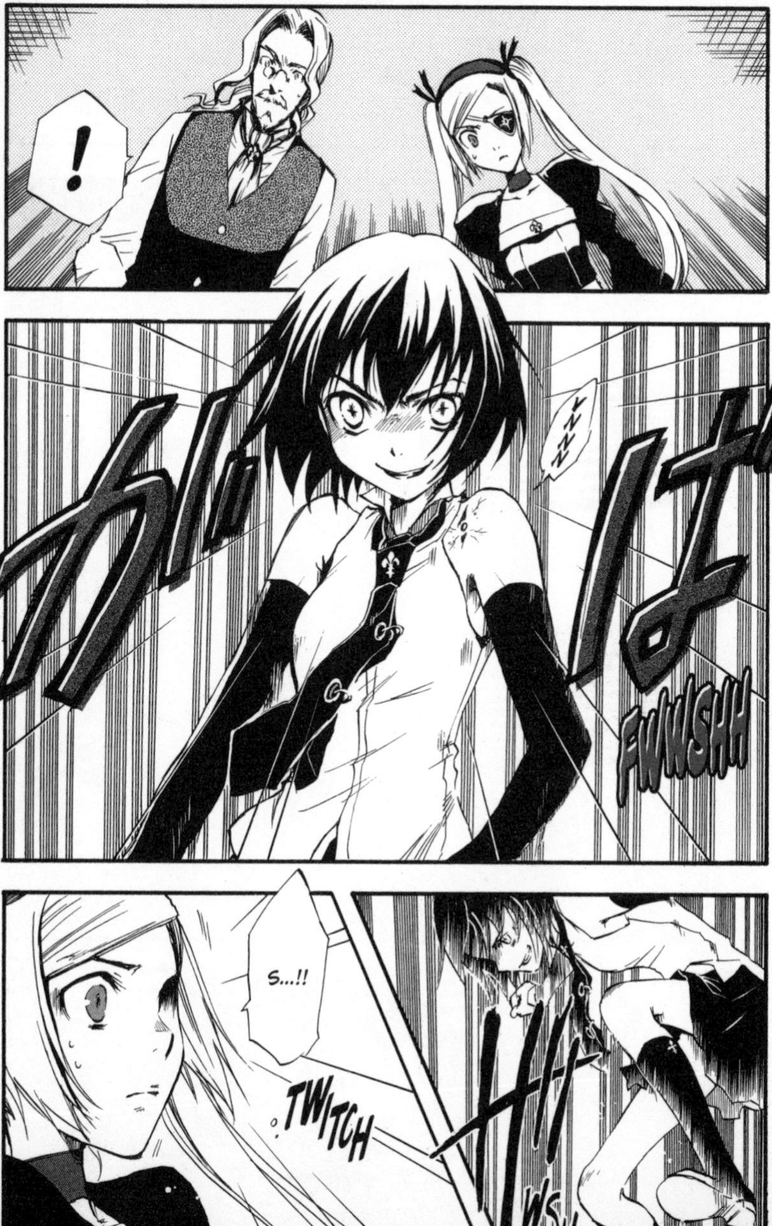
!
FWNSHH
WSH
S...!!
TWITCH

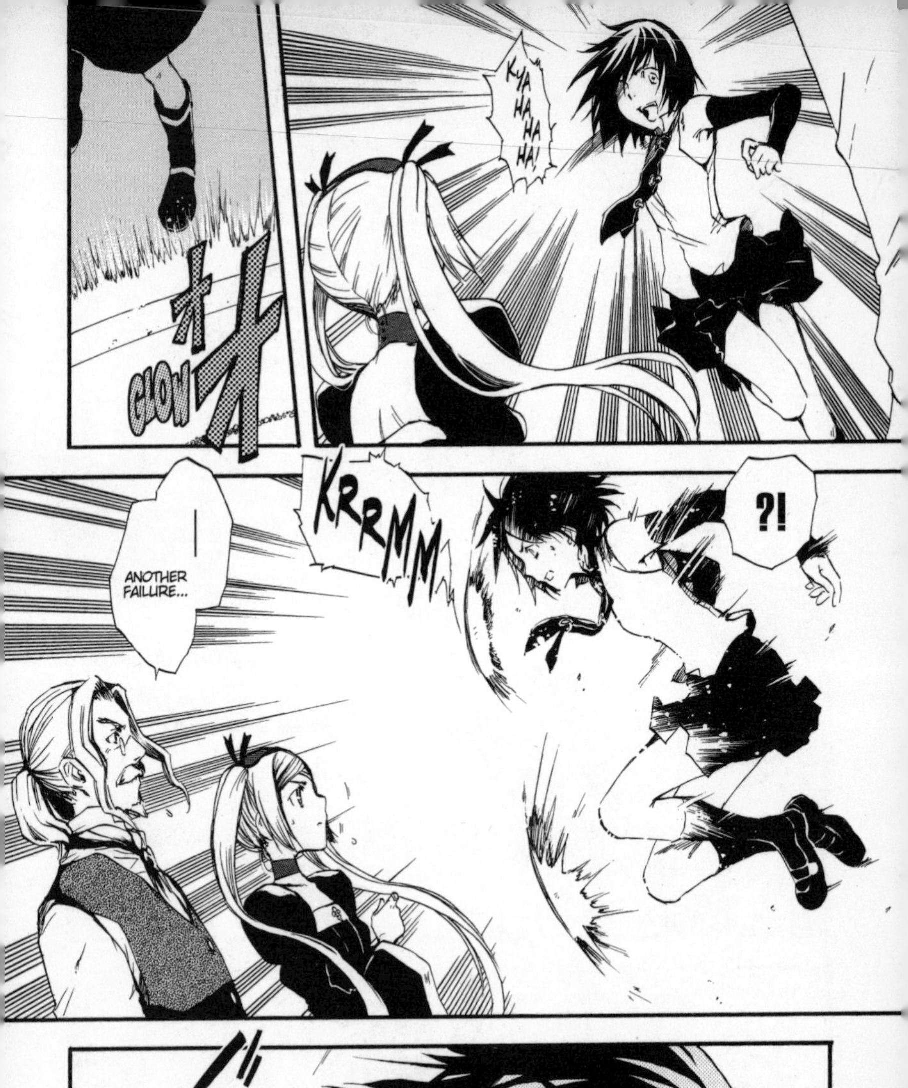
KYA HA HA HA HA!
GLOW
?!
KRRMMM
ANOTHER FAILURE...
SLUMP

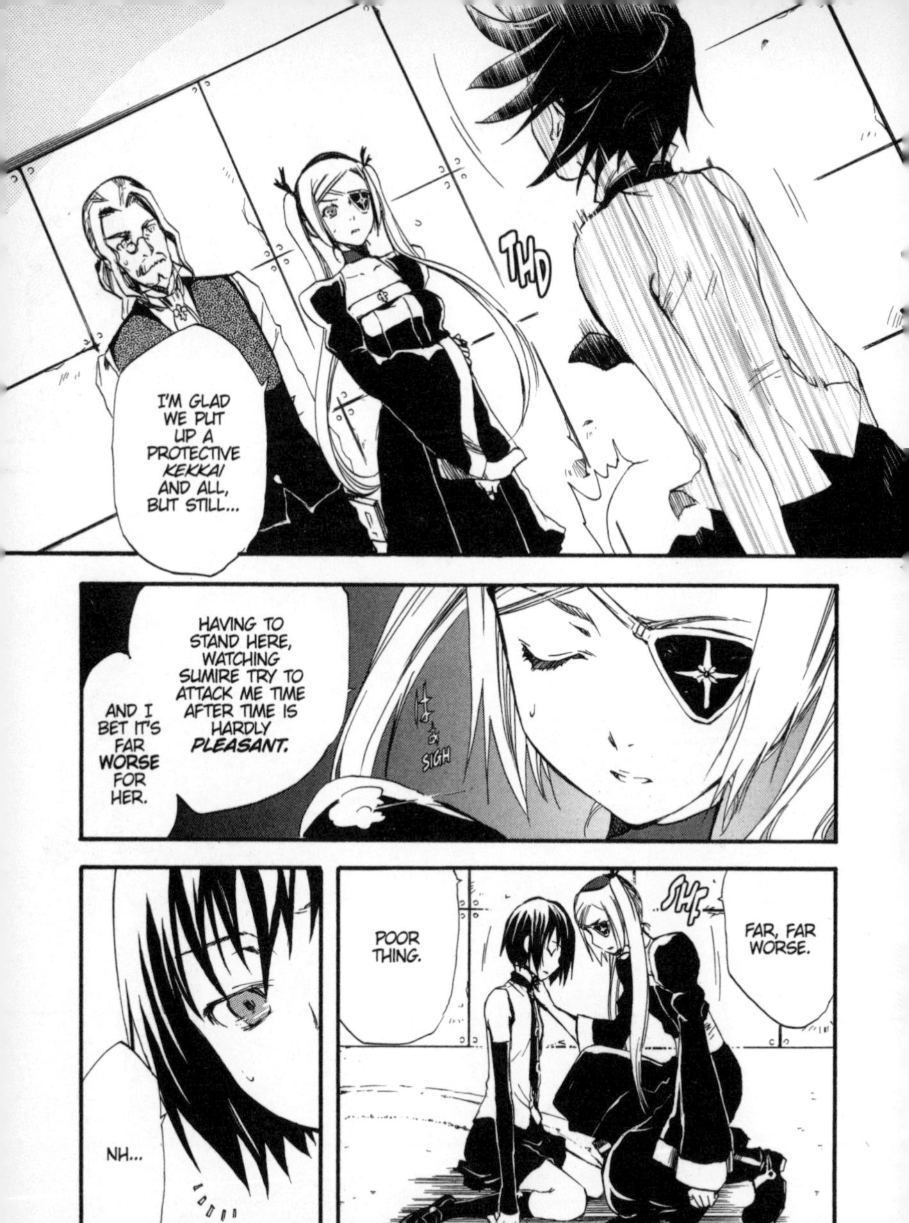
THD
I'M GLAD WE PUT UP A PROTECTIVE *KEKKAI* AND ALL, BUT STILL...
SIGH
HAVING TO STAND HERE, WATCHING SUMIRE TRY TO ATTACK ME TIME AFTER TIME IS HARDLY ***PLEASANT.***
AND I BET IT'S FAR **WORSE** FOR HER.
SHF
FAR, FAR WORSE.
POOR THING.
NH...

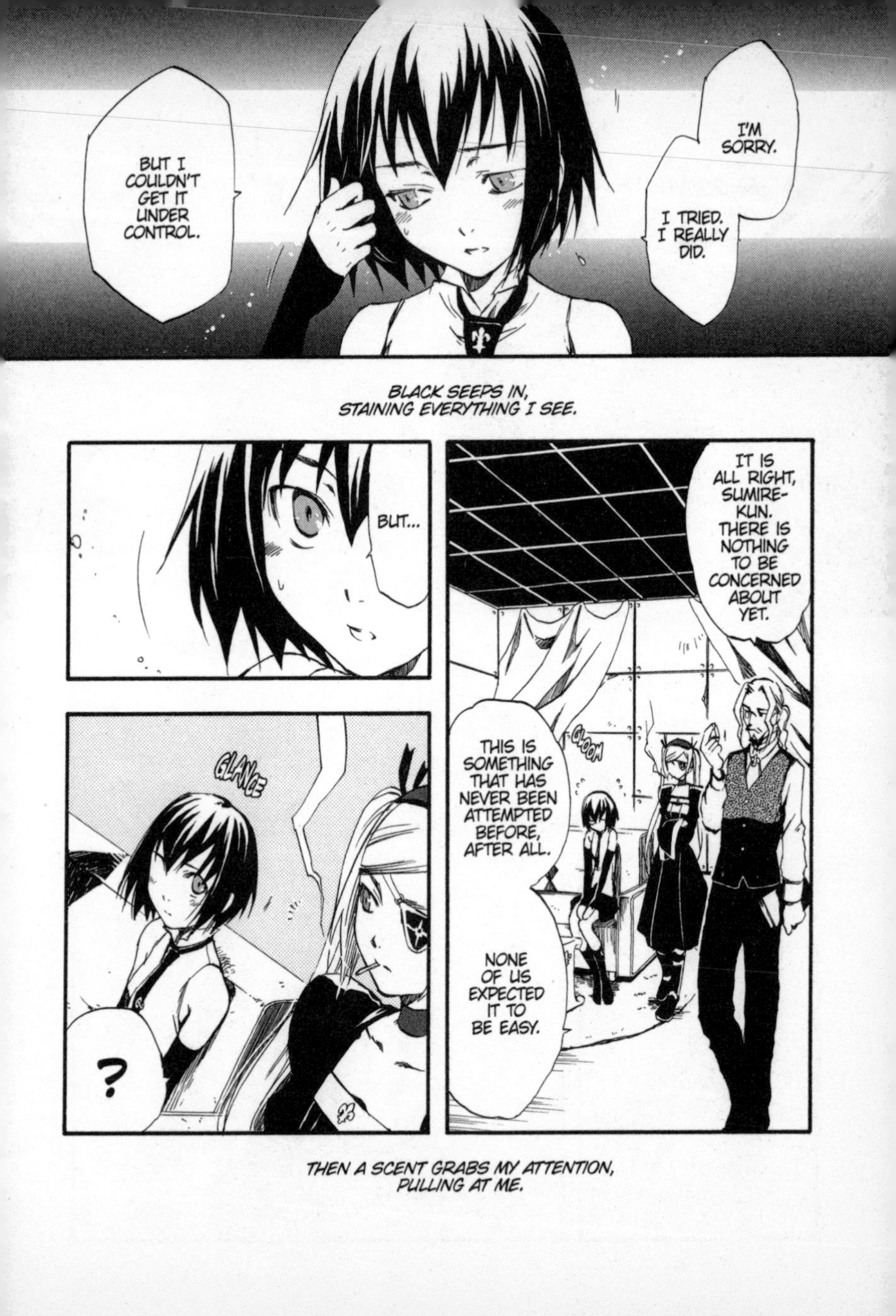
I'M SORRY.
I TRIED. I REALLY DID.
BUT I COULDN'T GET IT UNDER CONTROL.
BLACK SEEPS IN, STAINING EVERYTHING I SEE.
IT IS ALL RIGHT, SUMIRE-KUN. THERE IS NOTHING TO BE CONCERNED ABOUT YET.
GLOOM
THIS IS SOMETHING THAT HAS NEVER BEEN ATTEMPTED BEFORE, AFTER ALL.
NONE OF US EXPECTED IT TO BE EASY.
BUT...
GLANCE
?
THEN A SCENT GRABS MY ATTENTION, PULLING AT ME.

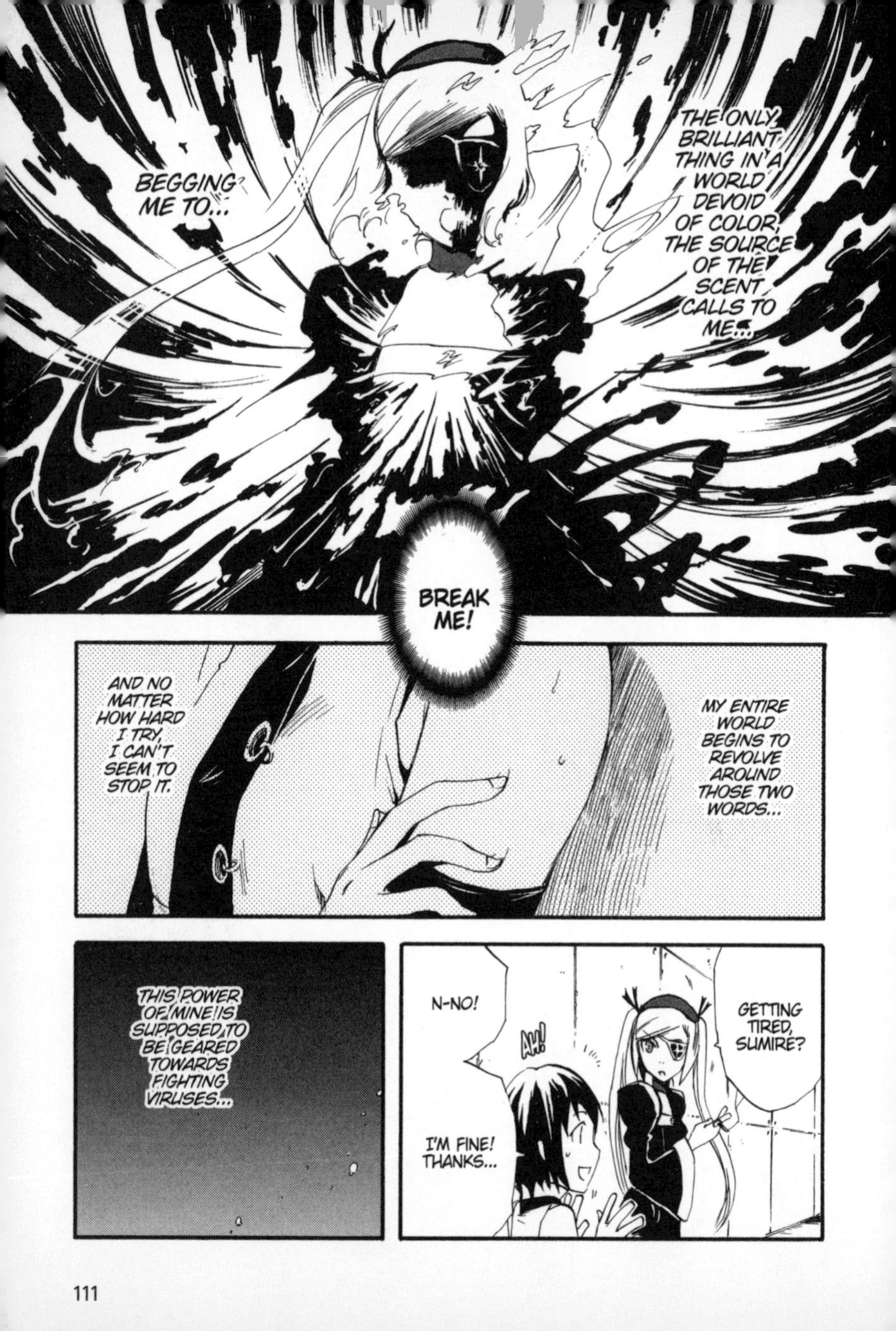
THE ONLY BRILLIANT THING IN A WORLD DEVOID OF COLOR, THE SOURCE OF THE SCENT CALLS TO ME...
BEGGING ME TO...
BREAK ME!
MY ENTIRE WORLD BEGINS TO REVOLVE AROUND THOSE TWO WORDS...
AND NO MATTER HOW HARD I TRY, I CAN'T SEEM TO STOP IT.
GETTING TIRED, SUMIRE?
N-NO!
AH!
I'M FINE! THANKS...
THIS POWER OF MINE IS SUPPOSED TO BE GEARED TOWARDS FIGHTING VIRUSES...

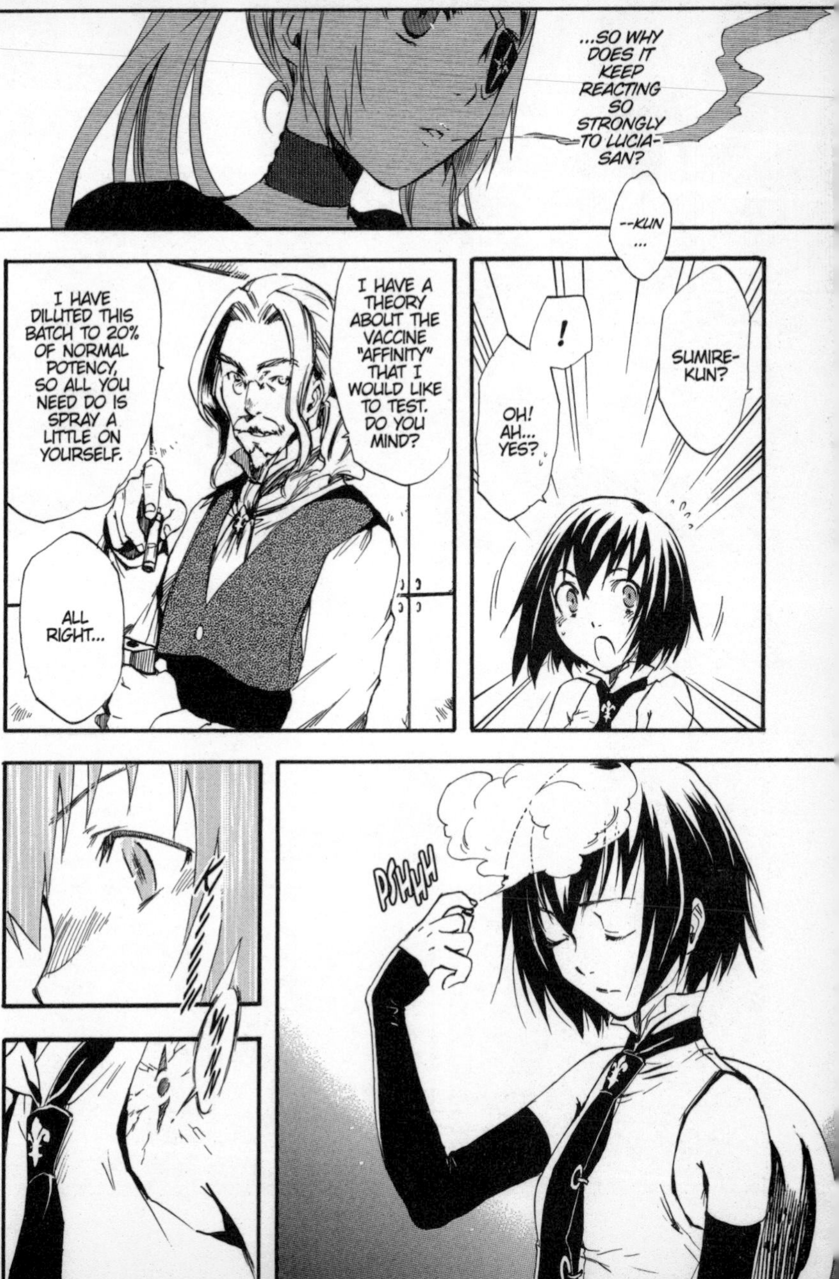
...SO WHY DOES IT KEEP REACTING SO STRONGLY TO LUCIA-SAN?
--KUN ...
SUMIRE-KUN?
!
OH! AH... YES?
I HAVE A THEORY ABOUT THE VACCINE "AFFINITY" THAT I WOULD LIKE TO TEST. DO YOU MIND?
I HAVE DILUTED THIS BATCH TO 20% OF NORMAL POTENCY, SO ALL YOU NEED DO IS SPRAY A LITTLE ON YOURSELF.
ALL RIGHT...
PSHHHH

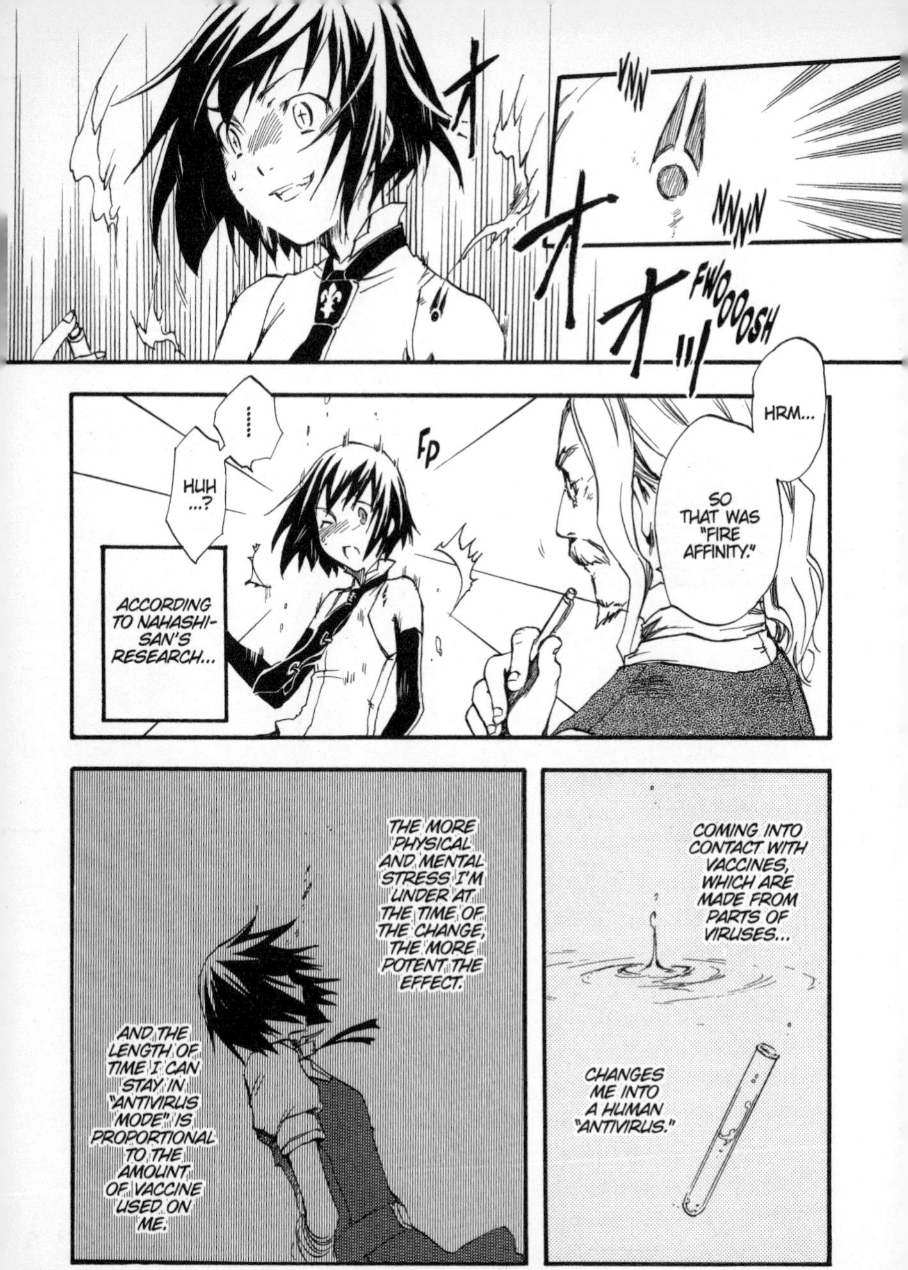
VNN
NNNN
FWOOOOSH
オオオッ
HRM...
SO THAT WAS "FIRE AFFINITY."
FD
......
HUH ...?
ACCORDING TO NAHASHI-SAN'S RESEARCH...
COMING INTO CONTACT WITH VACCINES, WHICH ARE MADE FROM PARTS OF VIRUSES...
CHANGES ME INTO A HUMAN "ANTIVIRUS."
THE MORE PHYSICAL AND MENTAL STRESS I'M UNDER AT THE TIME OF THE CHANGE, THE MORE POTENT THE EFFECT.
AND THE LENGTH OF TIME I CAN STAY IN "ANTIVIRUS MODE" IS PROPORTIONAL TO THE AMOUNT OF VACCINE USED ON ME.

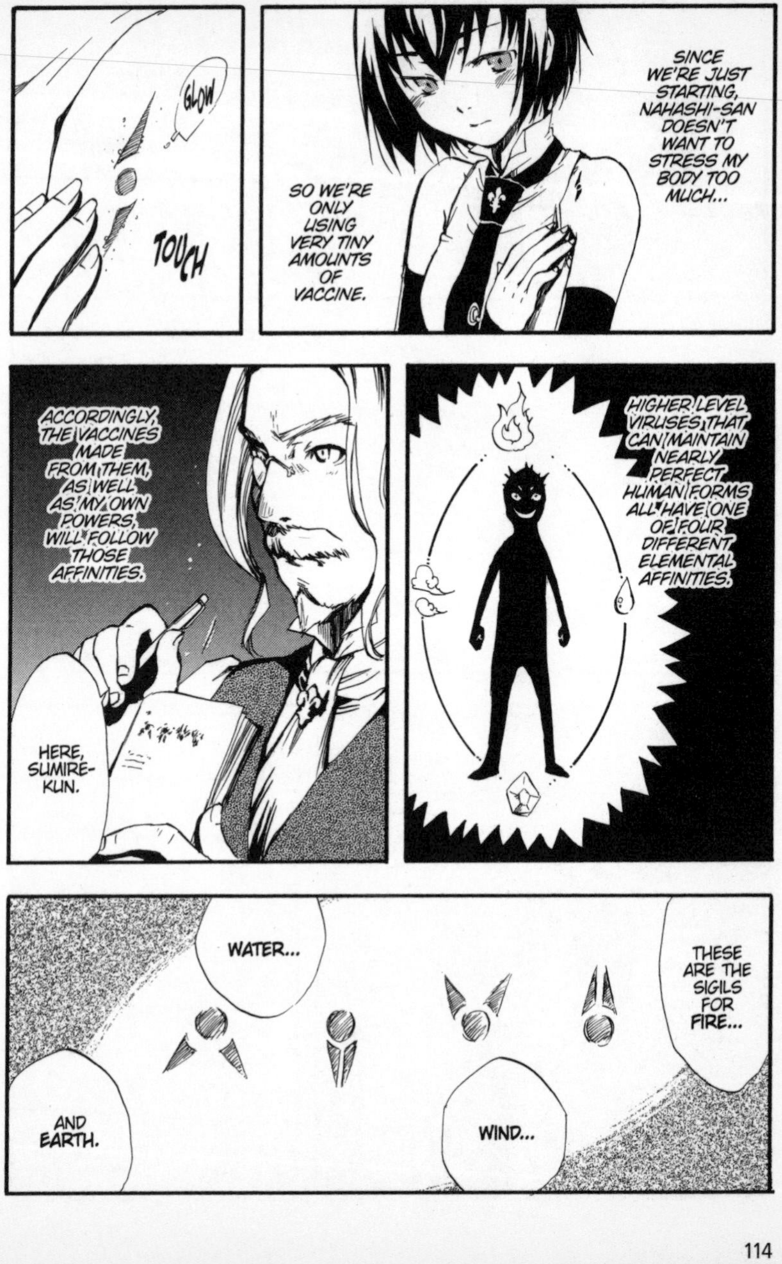
SINCE WE'RE JUST STARTING, NAHASHI-SAN DOESN'T WANT TO STRESS MY BODY TOO MUCH...
SO WE'RE ONLY USING VERY TINY AMOUNTS OF VACCINE.
GLOW
TOUCH
HIGHER LEVEL VIRUSES THAT CAN MAINTAIN NEARLY PERFECT HUMAN FORMS ALL HAVE ONE OF FOUR DIFFERENT ELEMENTAL AFFINITIES.
ACCORDINGLY, THE VACCINES MADE FROM THEM, AS WELL AS MY OWN POWERS, WILL FOLLOW THOSE AFFINITIES.
HERE, SUMIRE-KUN.
THESE ARE THE SIGILS FOR FIRE...
WIND...
WATER...
AND EARTH.

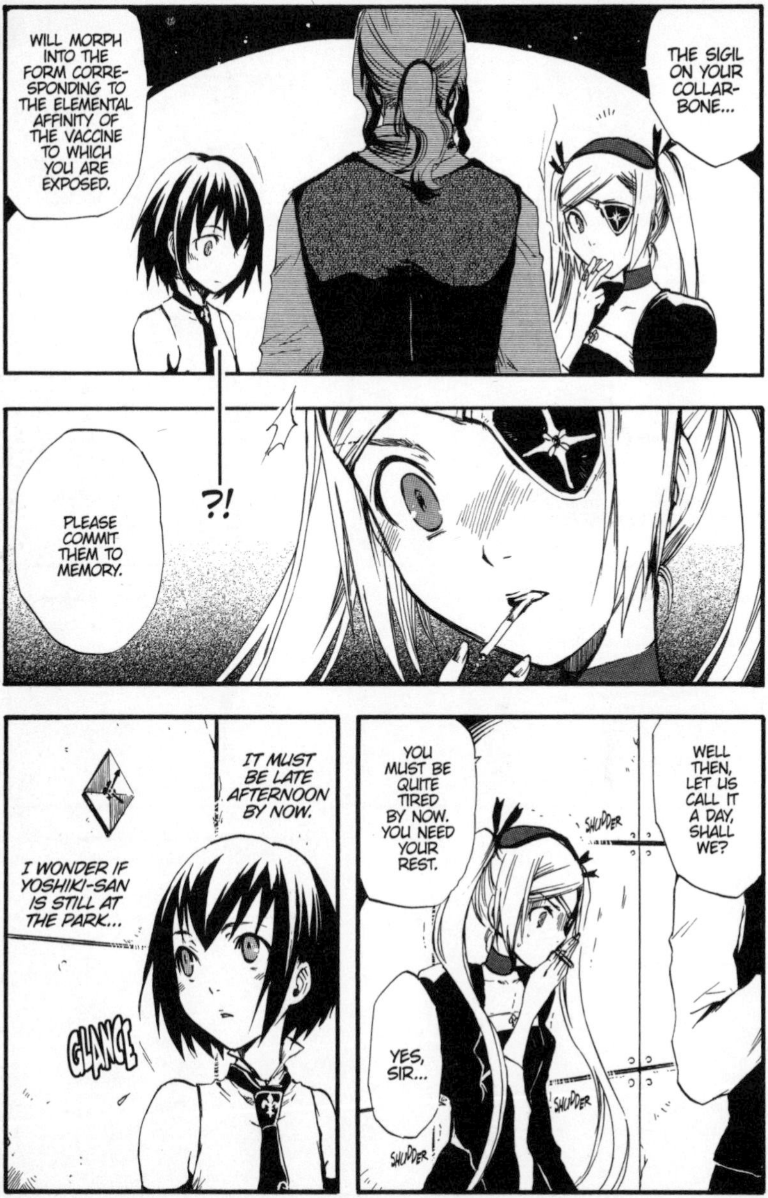
THE SIGIL ON YOUR COLLAR-BONE...
WILL MORPH INTO THE FORM CORRE-SPONDING TO THE ELEMENTAL AFFINITY OF THE VACCINE TO WHICH YOU ARE EXPOSED.
?!
PLEASE COMMIT THEM TO MEMORY.
WELL THEN, LET US CALL IT A DAY, SHALL WE?
YOU MUST BE QUITE TIRED BY NOW. YOU NEED YOUR REST.
SHUDDER
YES, SIR...
SHUDDER
SHUDDER
IT MUST BE LATE AFTERNOON BY NOW.
I WONDER IF YOSHIKI-SAN IS STILL AT THE PARK...
GLANCE

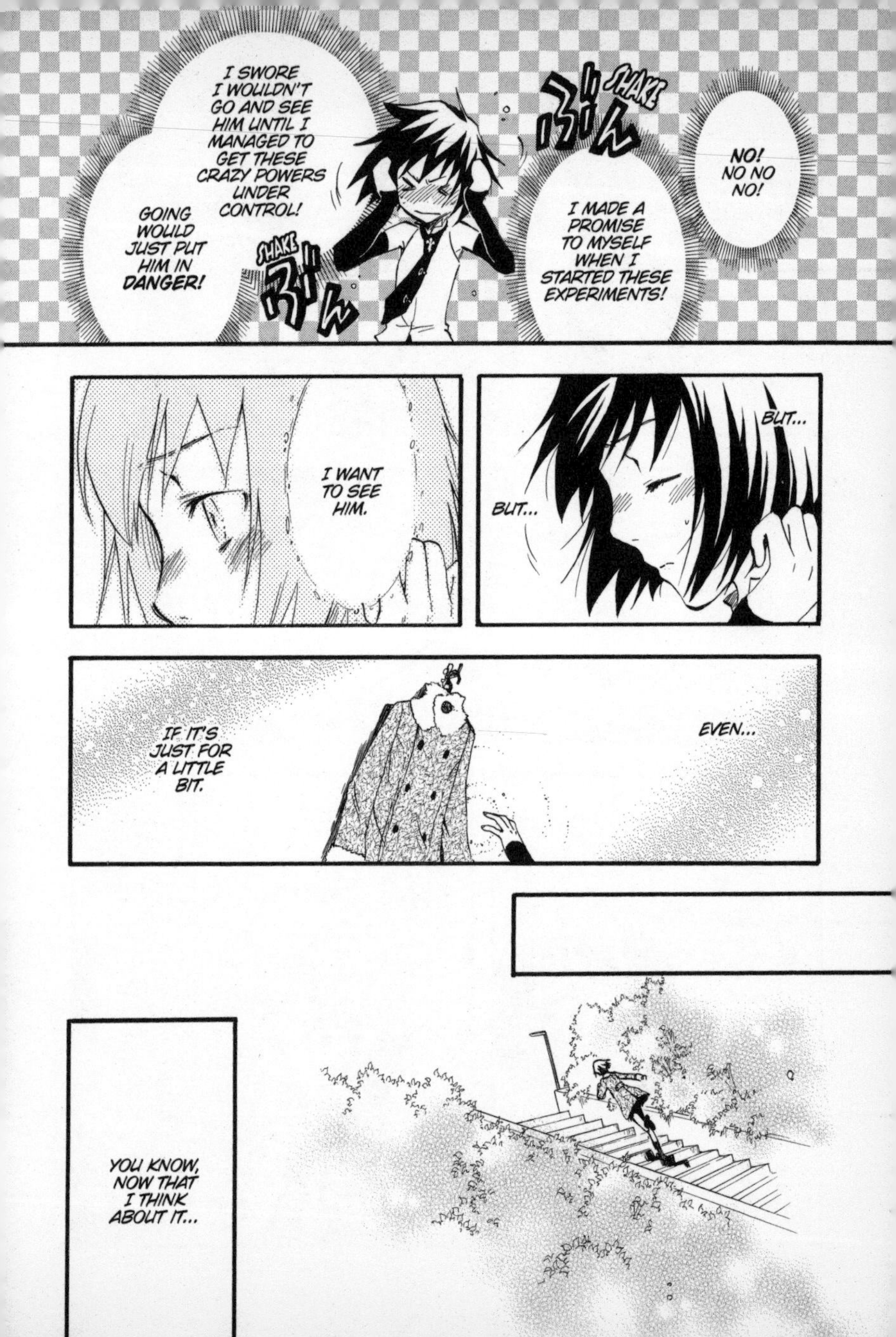
NO! NO NO NO!
I MADE A PROMISE TO MYSELF WHEN I STARTED THESE EXPERIMENTS!
SHAKE
ぶん
I SWORE I WOULDN'T GO AND SEE HIM UNTIL I MANAGED TO GET THESE CRAZY POWERS UNDER CONTROL!
GOING WOULD JUST PUT HIM IN DANGER!
SHAKE
ぶん
BUT...
BUT...
I WANT TO SEE HIM.
EVEN...
IF IT'S JUST FOR A LITTLE BIT.
YOU KNOW, NOW THAT I THINK ABOUT IT...

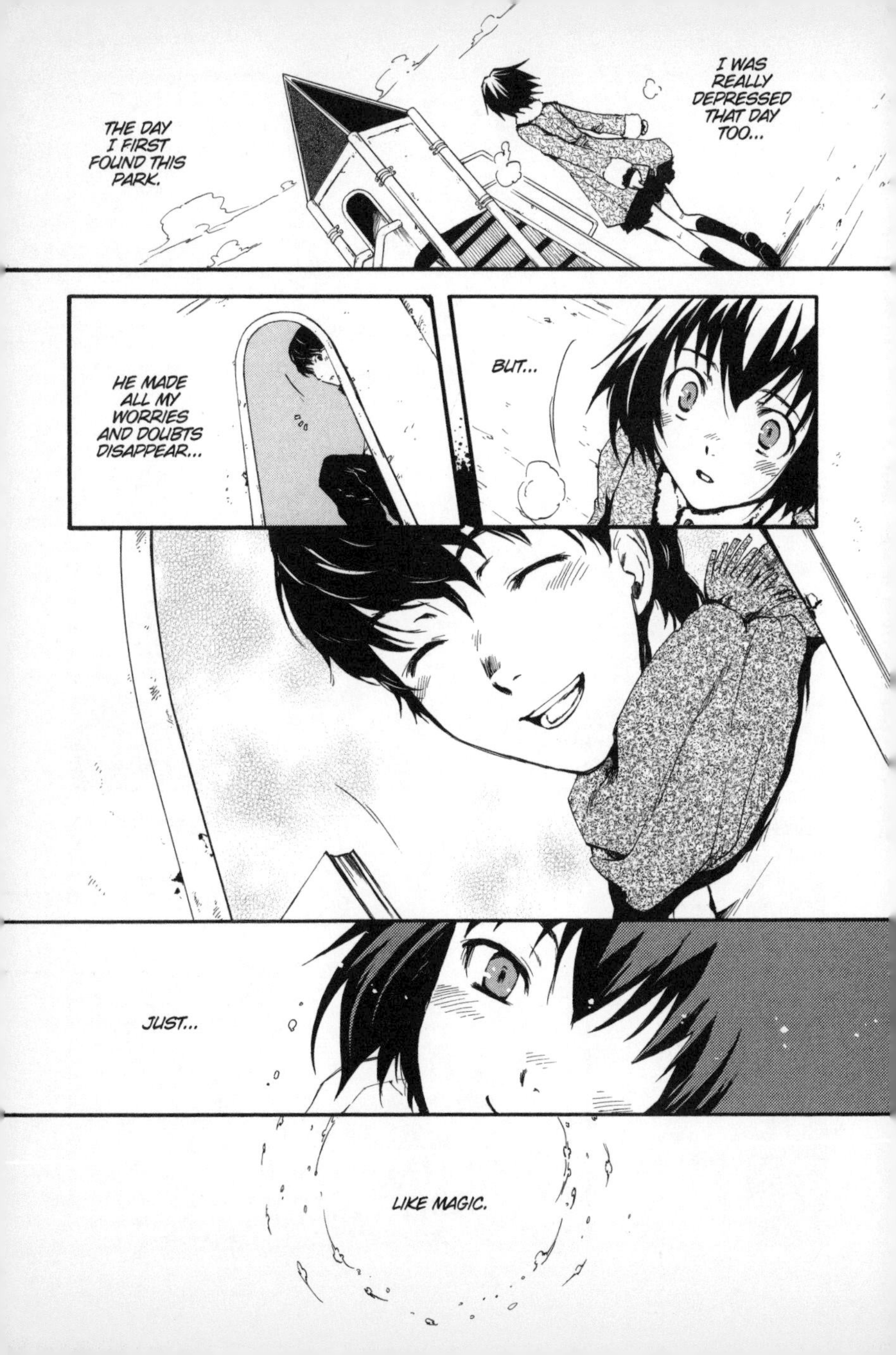
I WAS REALLY DEPRESSED THAT DAY TOO...
THE DAY I FIRST FOUND THIS PARK.
BUT...
HE MADE ALL MY WORRIES AND DOUBTS DISAPPEAR...
JUST...
LIKE MAGIC.

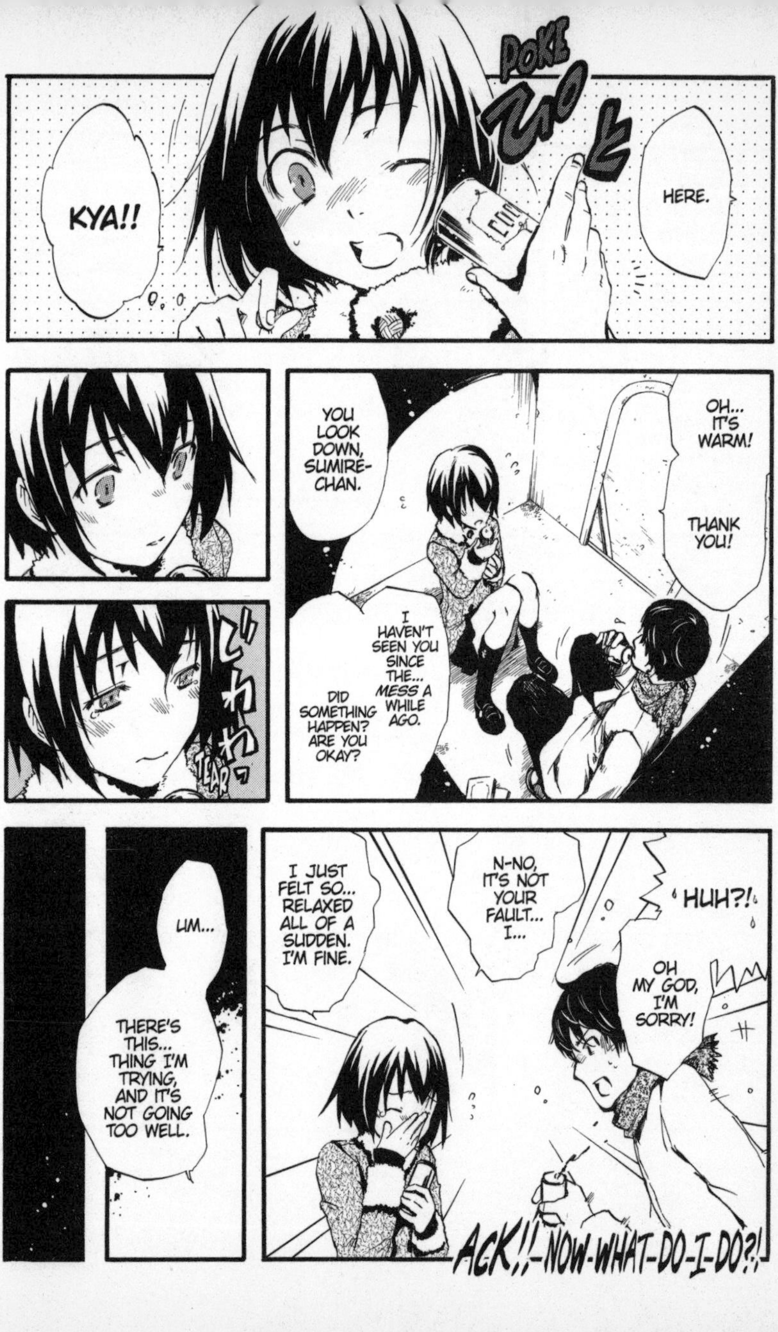
POKE
HERE.
KYA!!
OH... IT'S WARM!
THANK YOU!
YOU LOOK DOWN, SUMIRE-CHAN.
I HAVEN'T SEEN YOU SINCE THE... *MESS* A WHILE AGO.
DID SOMETHING HAPPEN? ARE YOU OKAY?
TEAR
HUH?!
OH MY GOD, I'M SORRY!
N-NO, IT'S NOT YOUR FAULT... I...
I JUST FELT SO... RELAXED ALL OF A SUDDEN. I'M FINE.
ACK!! NOW-WHAT-DO-I-DO?!
UM...
THERE'S THIS... THING I'M TRYING, AND IT'S NOT GOING TOO WELL.

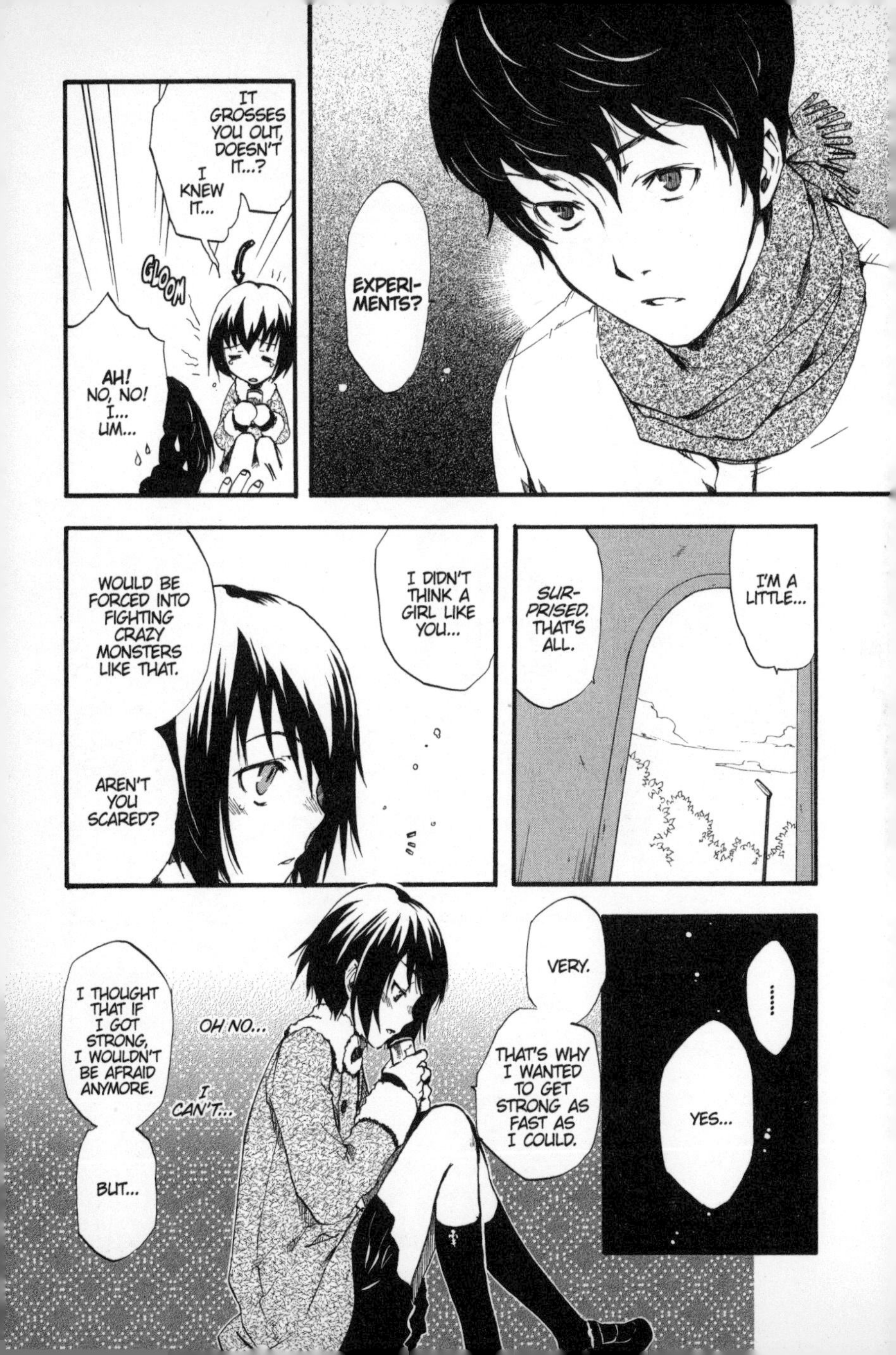
EXPERI-MENTS?
IT GROSSES YOU OUT, DOESN'T IT...?
I KNEW IT...
GLOOM
AH! NO, NO! I... UM...
I'M A LITTLE...
SUR-PRISED. THAT'S ALL.
I DIDN'T THINK A GIRL LIKE YOU...
WOULD BE FORCED INTO FIGHTING CRAZY MONSTERS LIKE THAT.
AREN'T YOU SCARED?
......
YES...
VERY.
THAT'S WHY I WANTED TO GET STRONG AS FAST AS I COULD.
I THOUGHT THAT IF I GOT STRONG, I WOULDN'T BE AFRAID ANYMORE.
OH NO...
I CAN'T...
BUT...

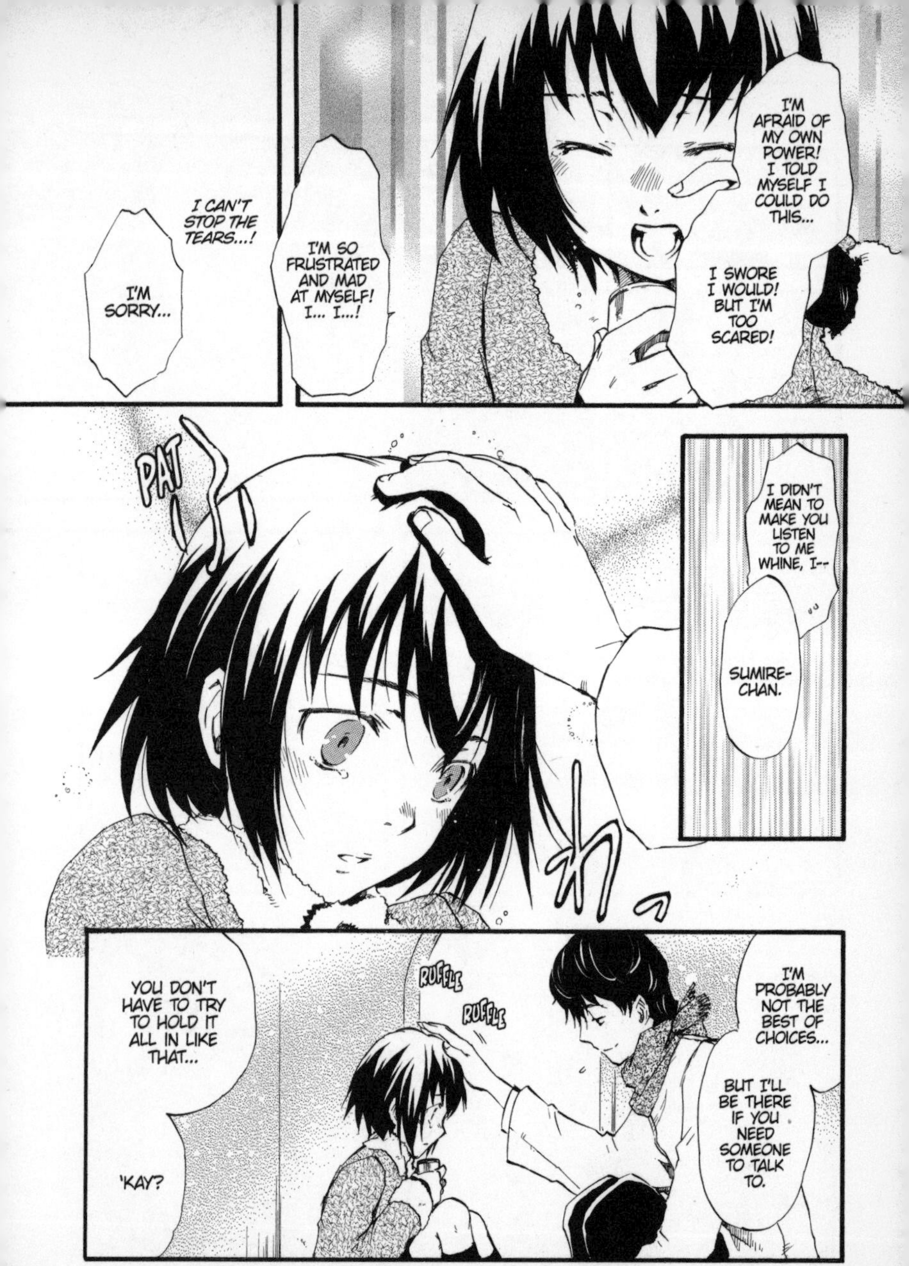
I'M AFRAID OF MY OWN POWER! I TOLD MYSELF I COULD DO THIS...
I SWORE I WOULD! BUT I'M TOO SCARED!
I'M SO FRUSTRATED AND MAD AT MYSELF! I... I...!
I CAN'T STOP THE TEARS...!
I'M SORRY...
I DIDN'T MEAN TO MAKE YOU LISTEN TO ME WHINE, I--
SUMIRE-CHAN.
PAT
I'M PROBABLY NOT THE BEST OF CHOICES...
BUT I'LL BE THERE IF YOU NEED SOMEONE TO TALK TO.
RUFFLE
RUFFLE
YOU DON'T HAVE TO TRY TO HOLD IT ALL IN LIKE THAT...
'KAY?

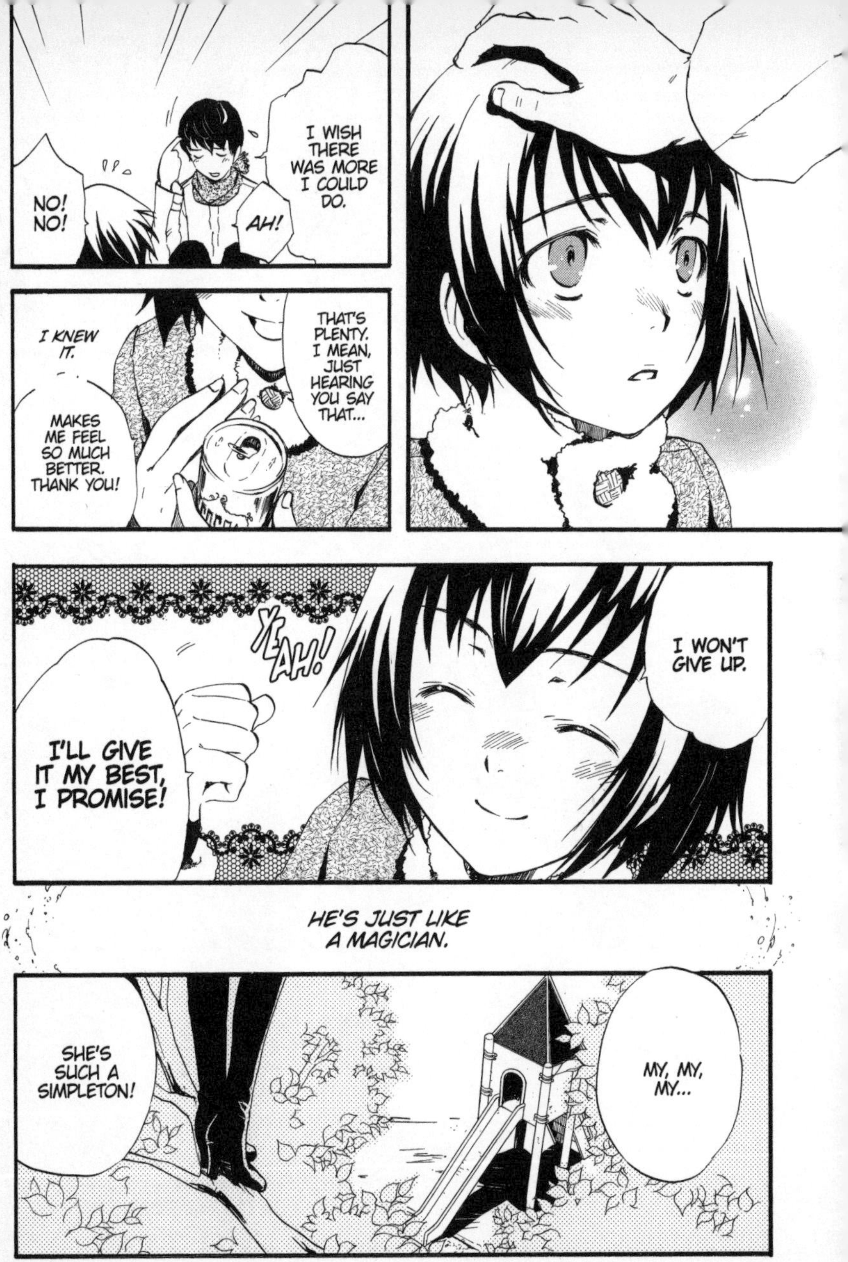
I WISH THERE WAS MORE I COULD DO.
AH!
NO! NO!
THAT'S PLENTY. I MEAN, JUST HEARING YOU SAY THAT...
I KNEW IT.
MAKES ME FEEL SO MUCH BETTER. THANK YOU!
I WON'T GIVE UP.
YEAH!
I'LL GIVE IT MY BEST, I PROMISE!
HE'S JUST LIKE A MAGICIAN.
MY, MY, MY...
SHE'S SUCH A SIMPLETON!

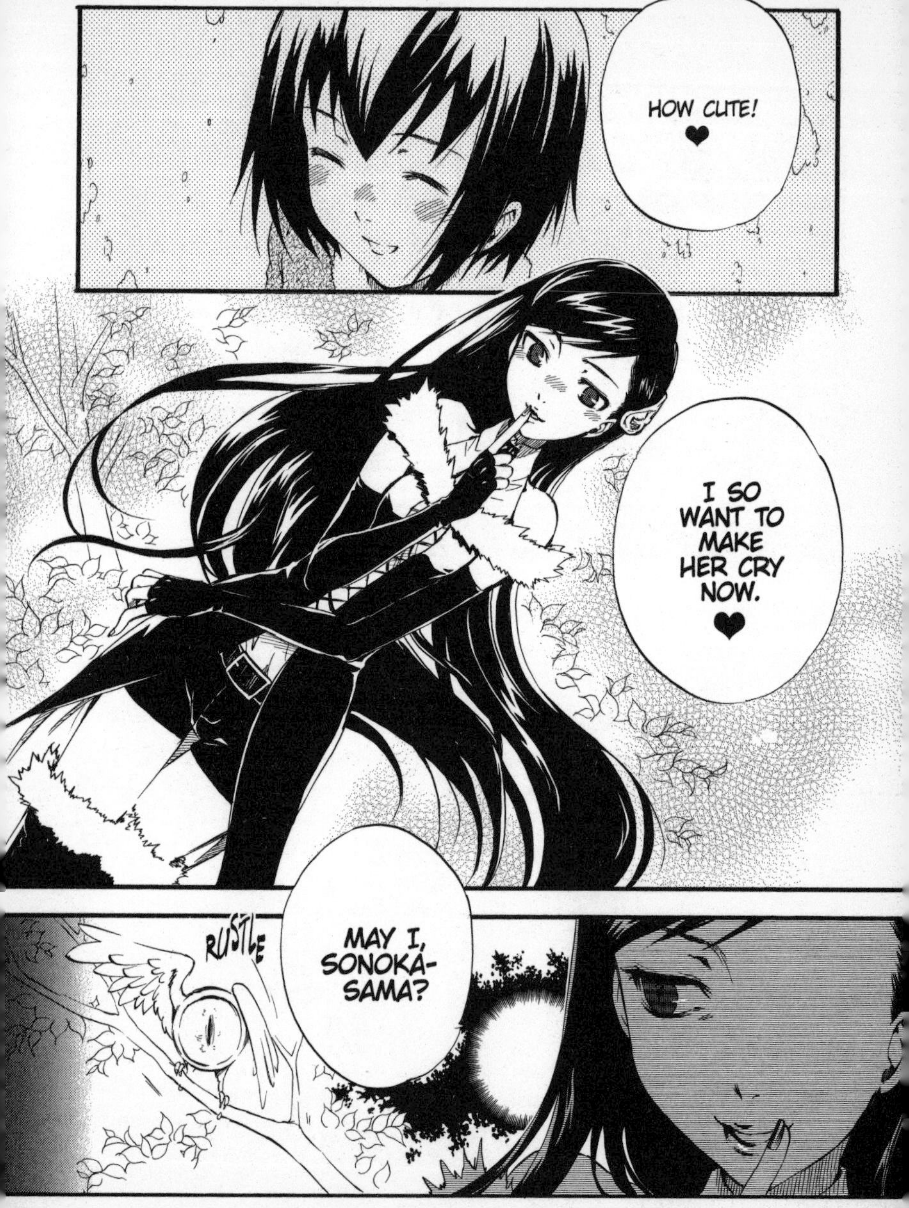
HOW CUTE! ♥
I SO WANT TO MAKE HER CRY NOW. ♥
MAY I, SONOKA-SAMA?
RUSTLE

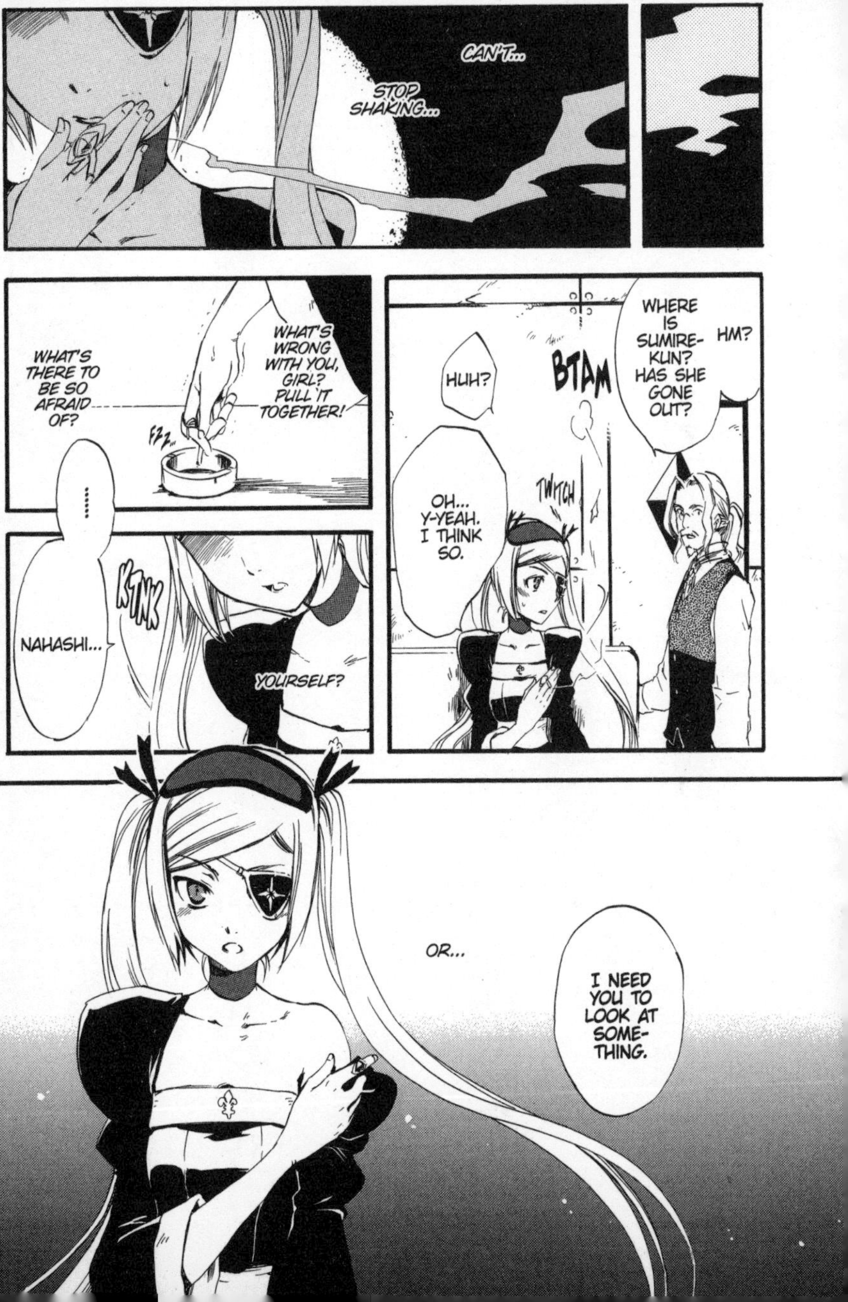
CAN'T...
STOP SHAKING...
HM?
WHERE IS SUMIRE-KUN? HAS SHE GONE OUT?
BTAM
HUH?
TWITCH
OH... Y-YEAH. I THINK SO.
WHAT'S WRONG WITH YOU, GIRL? PULL IT TOGETHER!
WHAT'S THERE TO BE SO AFRAID OF?
FZZ...
......
KTNK
NAHASHI...
YOURSELF?
OR...
I NEED YOU TO LOOK AT SOMETHING.

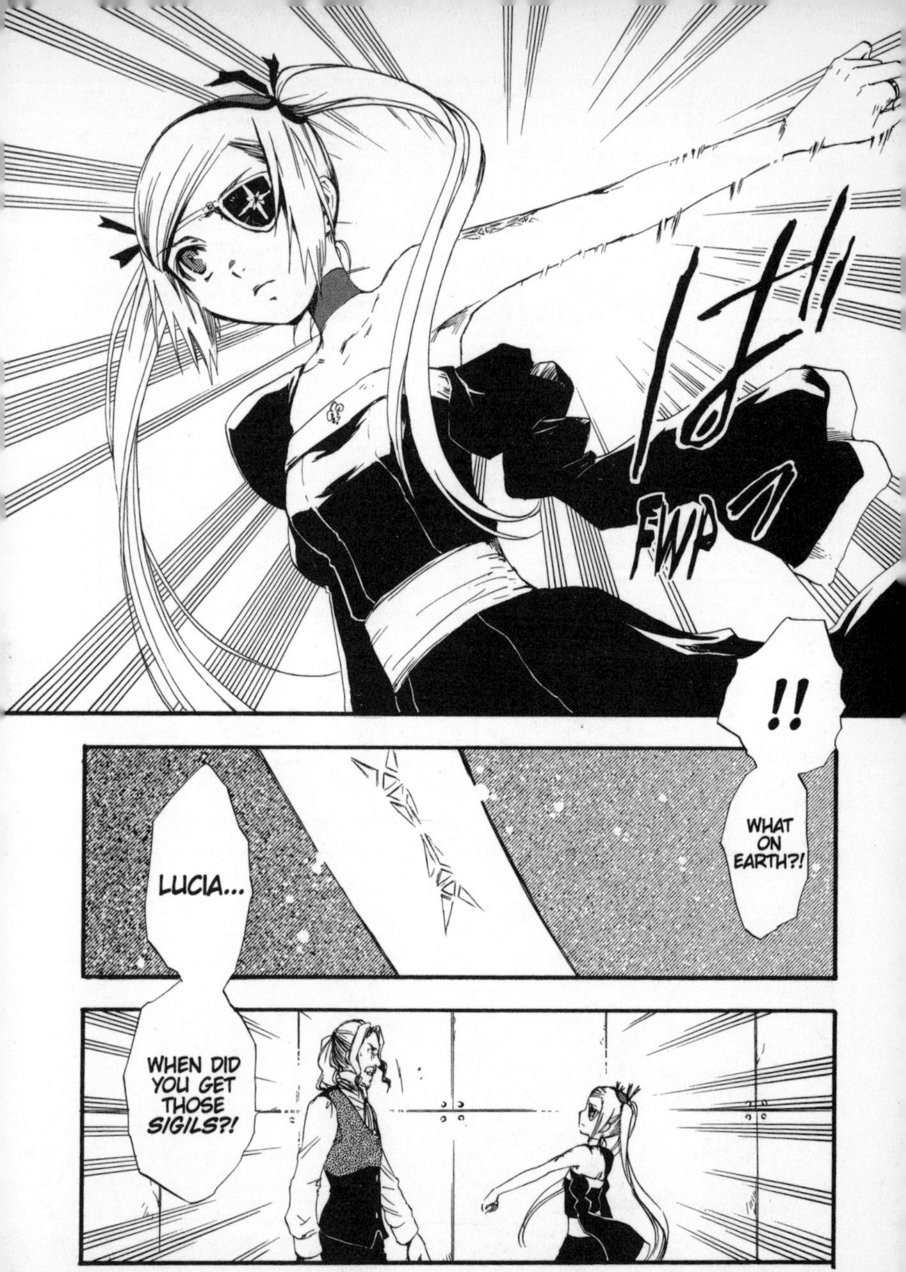
FWP
!!
WHAT ON EARTH?!
LUCIA...
WHEN DID YOU GET THOSE SIGILS?!

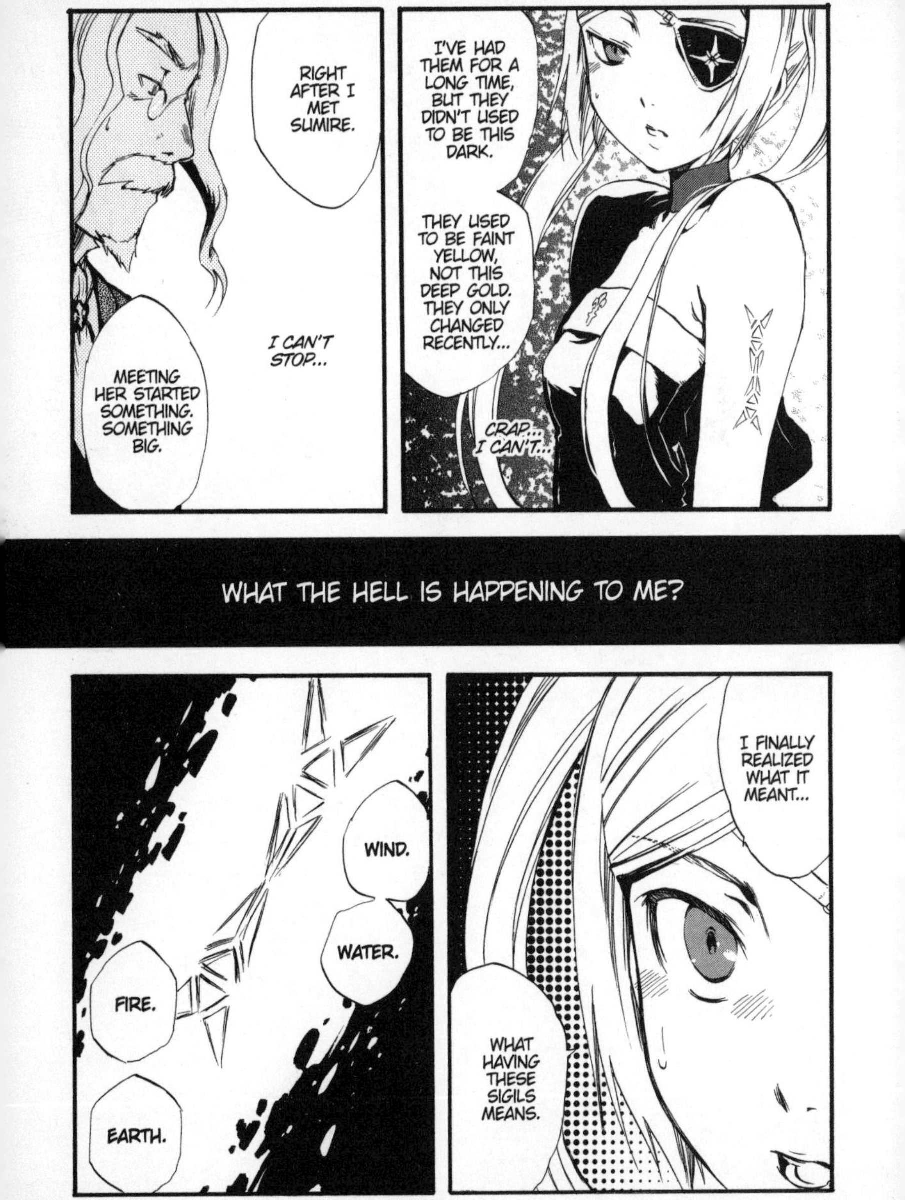
I'VE HAD THEM FOR A LONG TIME, BUT THEY DIDN'T USED TO BE THIS DARK.
THEY USED TO BE FAINT YELLOW, NOT THIS DEEP GOLD. THEY ONLY CHANGED RECENTLY...
CRAP... I CAN'T...
RIGHT AFTER I MET SUMIRE.
I CAN'T STOP...
MEETING HER STARTED SOMETHING. SOMETHING BIG.
WHAT THE HELL IS HAPPENING TO ME?
I FINALLY REALIZED WHAT IT MEANT...
WHAT HAVING THESE SIGILS MEANS.
WIND.
WATER.
FIRE.
EARTH.

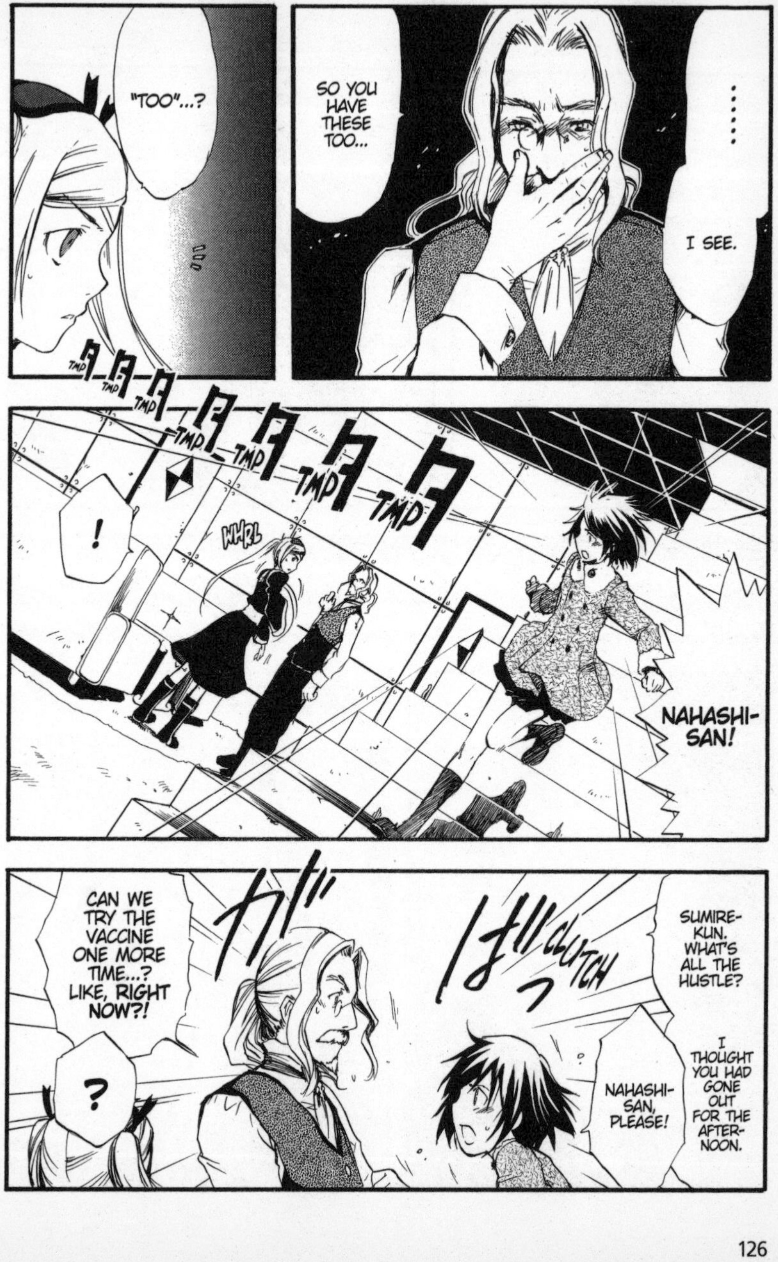
......
I SEE.
SO YOU HAVE THESE TOO...
"TOO"...?
TMP TMP TMP TMP TMP TMP TMP
NAHASHI-SAN!
WHRL
!
SUMIRE-KUN. WHAT'S ALL THE HUSTLE?
I THOUGHT YOU HAD GONE OUT FOR THE AFTERNOON.
CLUTCH
NAHASHI-SAN, PLEASE!
CAN WE TRY THE VACCINE ONE MORE TIME...? LIKE, RIGHT NOW?!
?

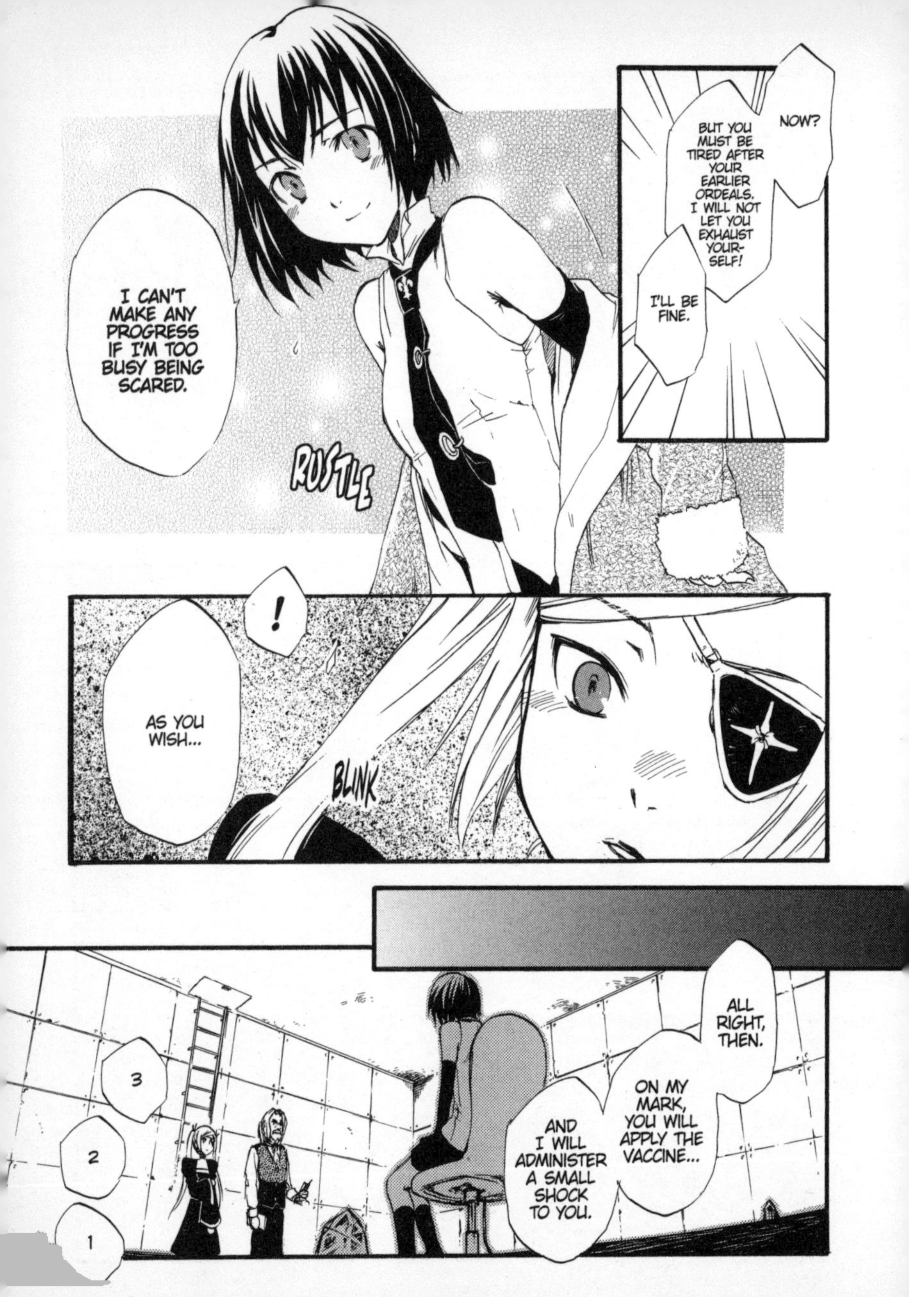
NOW?
BUT YOU MUST BE TIRED AFTER YOUR EARLIER ORDEALS. I WILL NOT LET YOU EXHAUST YOUR-SELF!
I'LL BE FINE.
I CAN'T MAKE ANY PROGRESS IF I'M TOO BUSY BEING SCARED.
RUSTLE
!
AS YOU WISH...
BLINK
ALL RIGHT, THEN.
ON MY MARK, YOU WILL APPLY THE VACCINE...
AND I WILL ADMINISTER A SMALL SHOCK TO YOU.
3
2
1

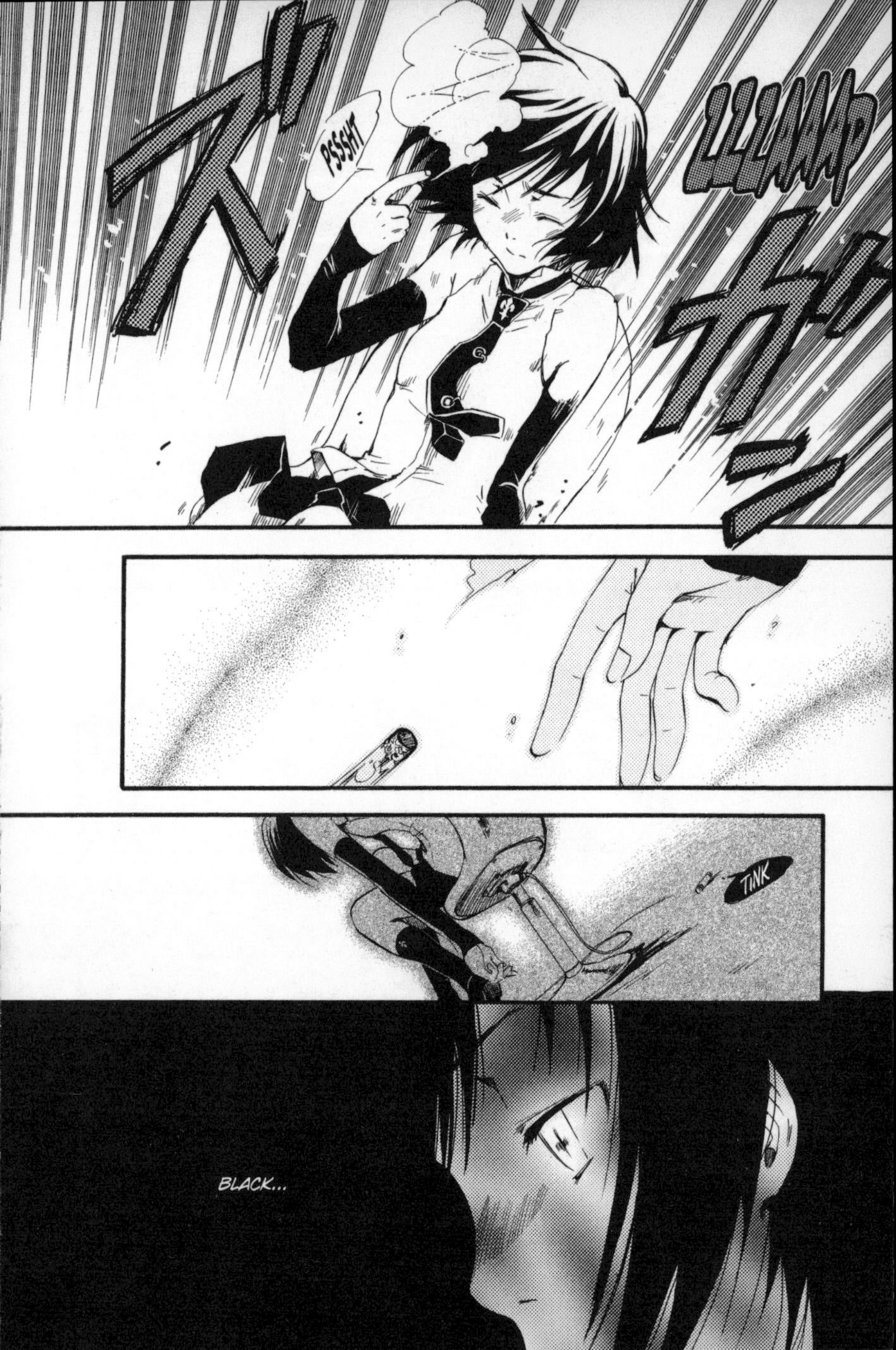
ZZZAAAP
PSSSHT
TINK
BLACK...

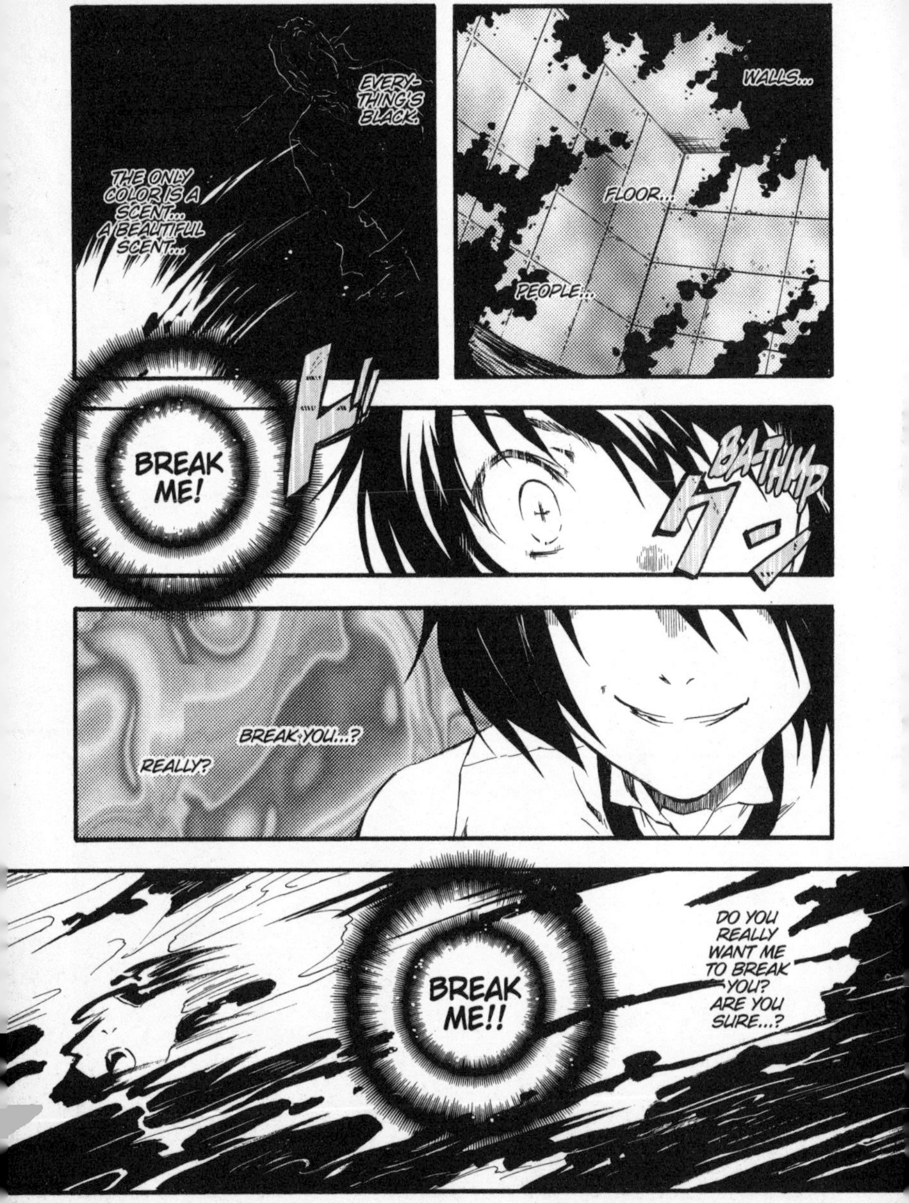
WALLS...
FLOOR...
PEOPLE...
EVERY-THING'S BLACK.
THE ONLY COLOR IS A SCENT... A BEAUTIFUL SCENT...
BA-THMP
BREAK ME!
BREAK YOU...?
REALLY?
DO YOU REALLY WANT ME TO BREAK YOU? ARE YOU SURE...?
BREAK ME!!

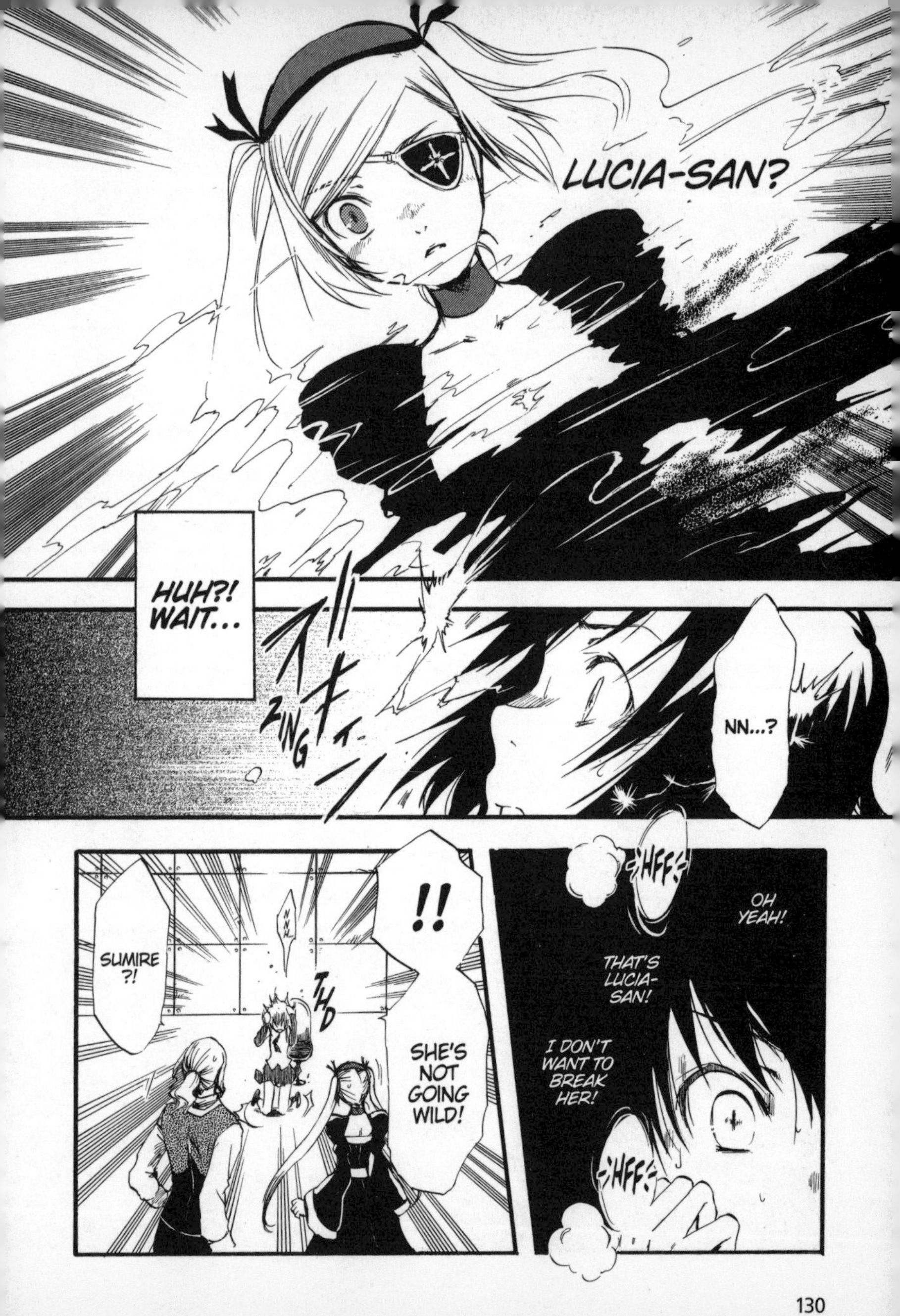
LUCIA-SAN?
NN...?
ZING
HUH?! WAIT...
HFF
OH YEAH!
THAT'S LUCIA-SAN!
I DON'T WANT TO BREAK HER!
HFF
!!
SHE'S NOT GOING WILD!
THD
NNH
SUMIRE ?!

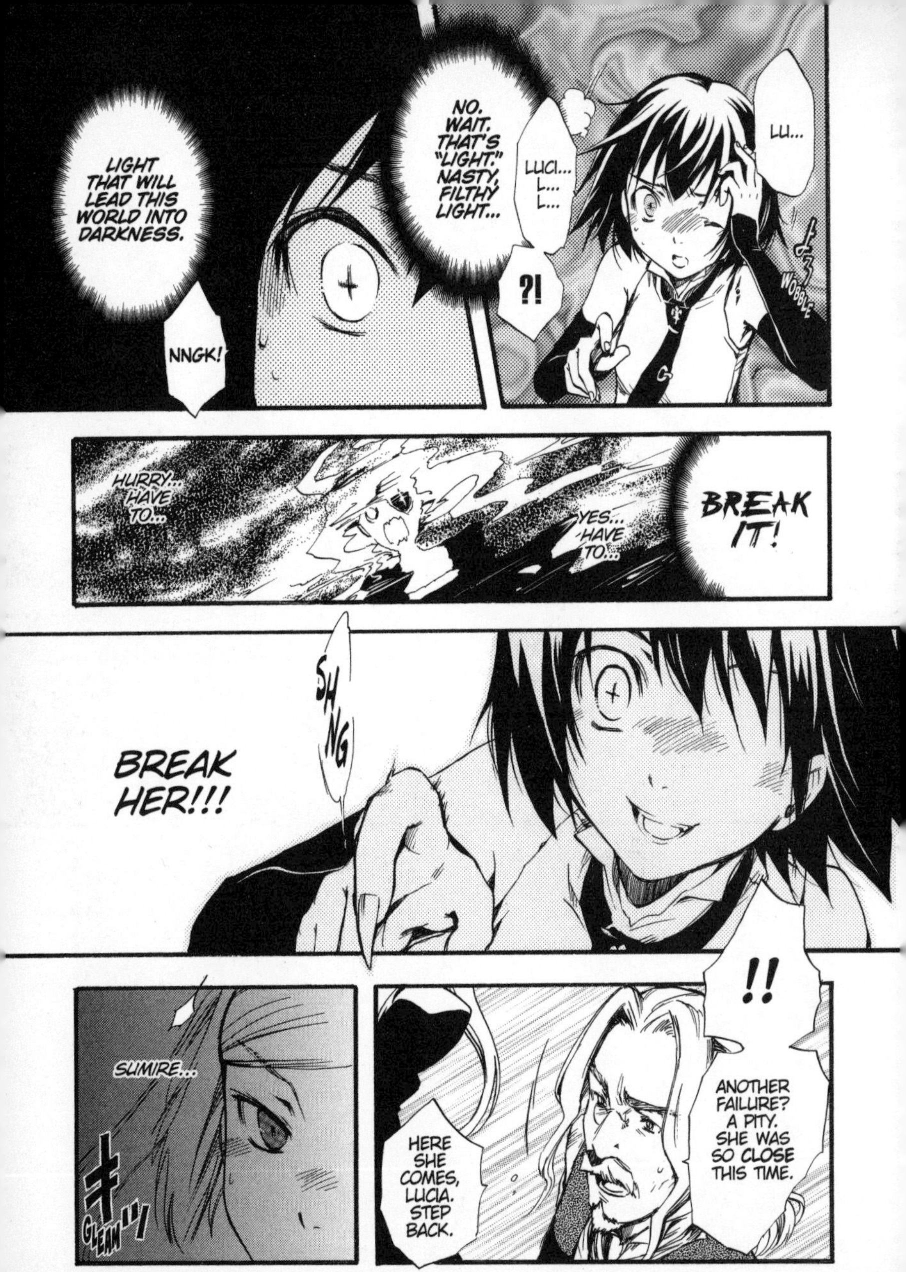
LU...
LUCI... L... L...
?!
WOBBLE
NO. WAIT. THAT'S "LIGHT." NASTY, FILTHY LIGHT...
LIGHT THAT WILL LEAD THIS WORLD INTO DARKNESS.
NNGK!
BREAK IT!
YES... HAVE TO...
HURRY... HAVE TO...
SHNG
BREAK HER!!!
!!
ANOTHER FAILURE? A PITY. SHE WAS SO CLOSE THIS TIME.
HERE SHE COMES, LUCIA. STEP BACK.
SUMIRE...
GLEAM

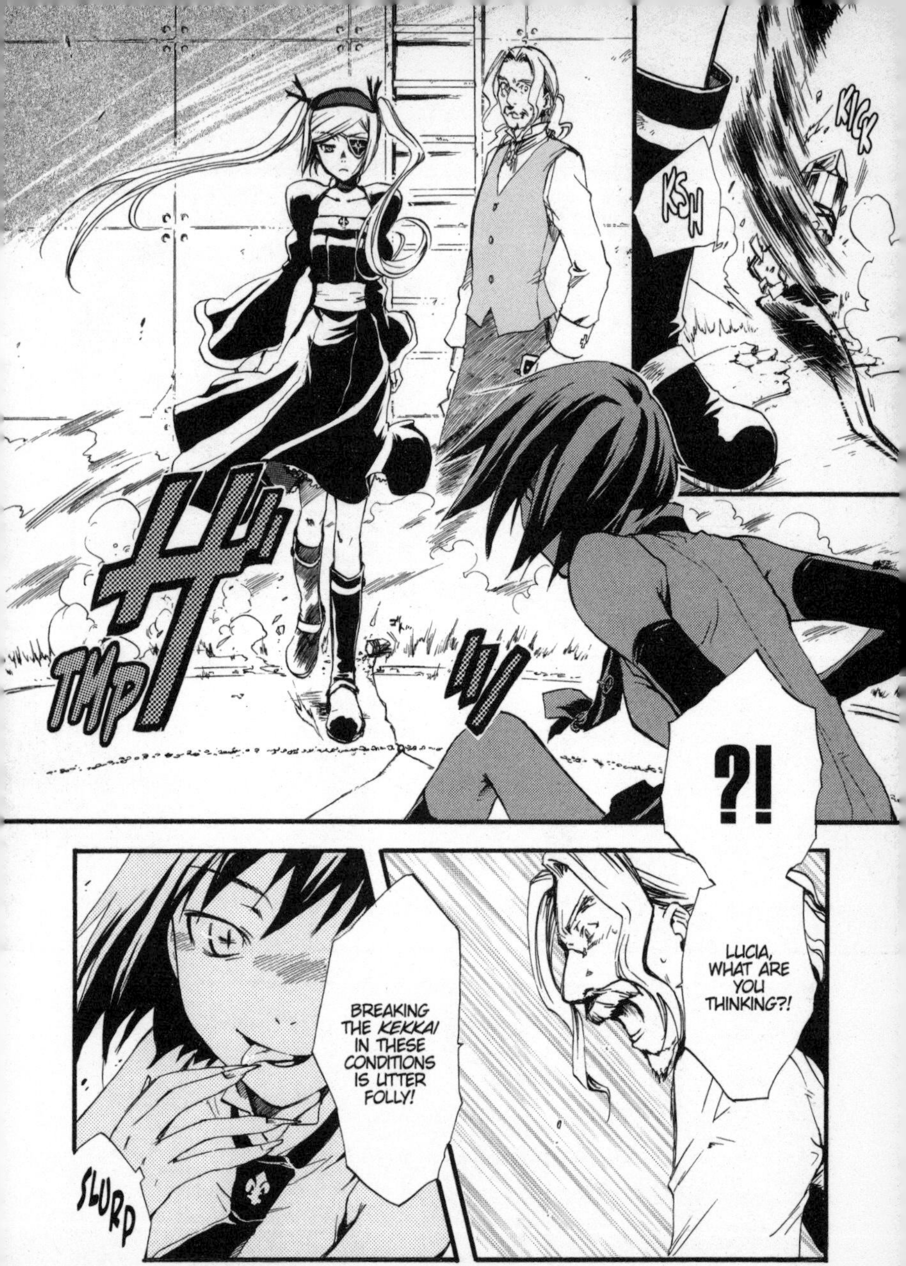
KICK
KSH
TMP
?!
LUCIA, WHAT ARE YOU THINKING?!
BREAKING THE *KEKKAI* IN THESE CONDITIONS IS UTTER FOLLY!
SLURP

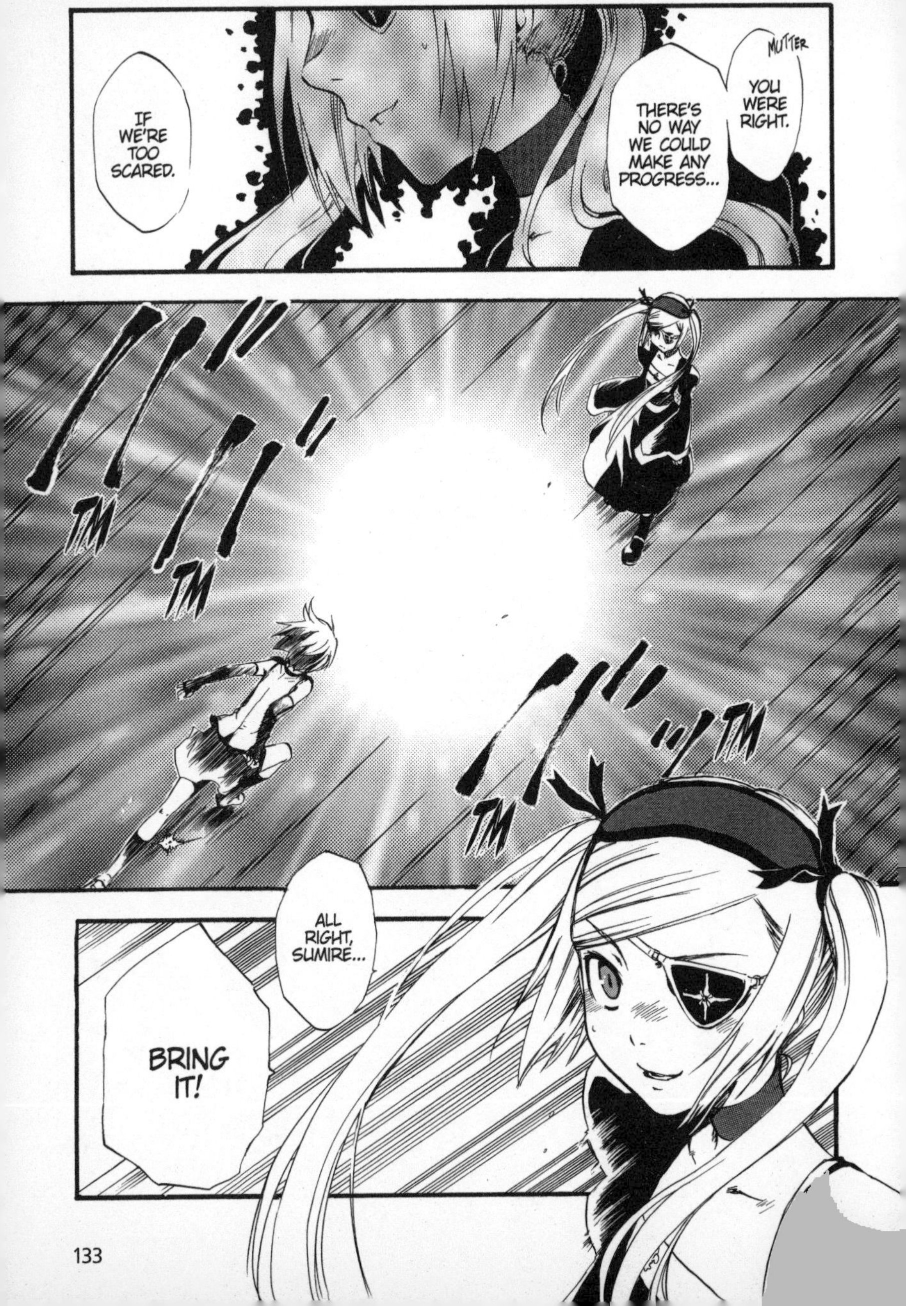
MUTTER
YOU WERE RIGHT.
THERE'S NO WAY WE COULD MAKE ANY PROGRESS...
IF WE'RE TOO SCARED.
TM
TM
TM
TM
ALL RIGHT, SUMIRE...
BRING IT!

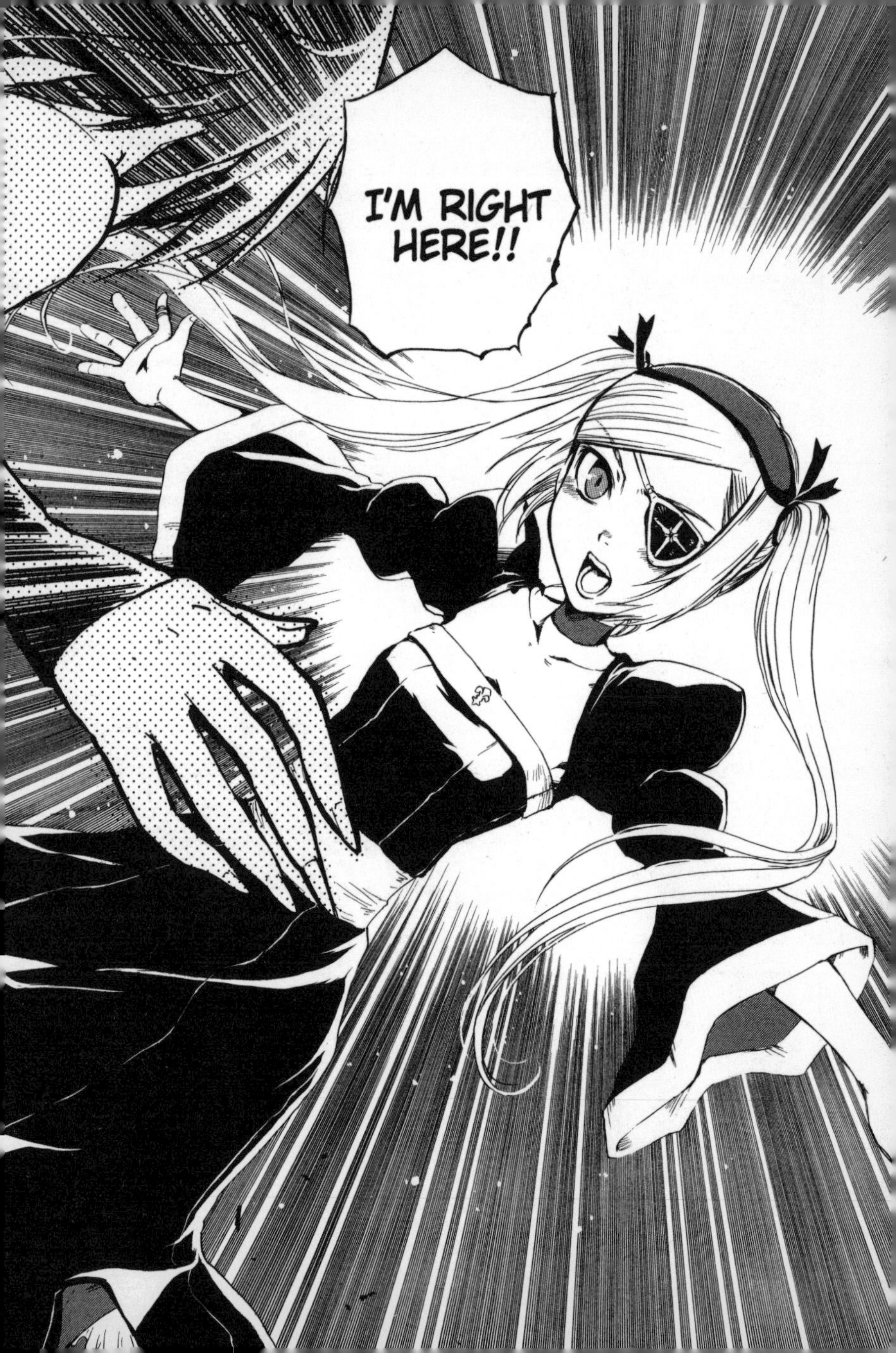
I'M RIGHT HERE!!

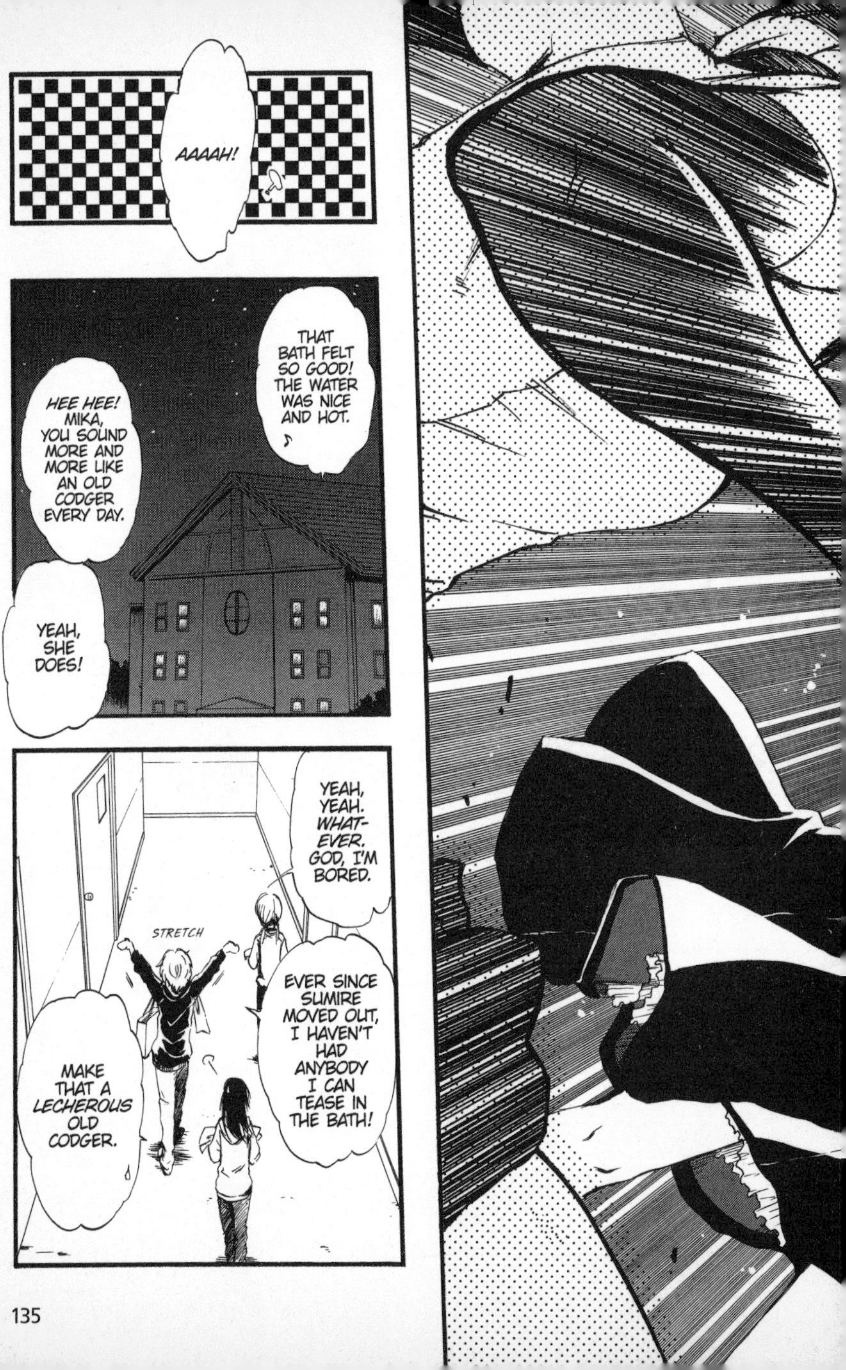
AAAAH!
THAT BATH FELT SO GOOD! THE WATER WAS NICE AND HOT. ♪
HEE HEE! MIKA, YOU SOUND MORE AND MORE LIKE AN OLD CODGER EVERY DAY.
YEAH, SHE DOES!
YEAH, YEAH. WHATEVER. GOD, I'M BORED.
EVER SINCE SUMIRE MOVED OUT, I HAVEN'T HAD ANYBODY I CAN TEASE IN THE BATH!
STRETCH
MAKE THAT A LECHEROUS OLD CODGER.

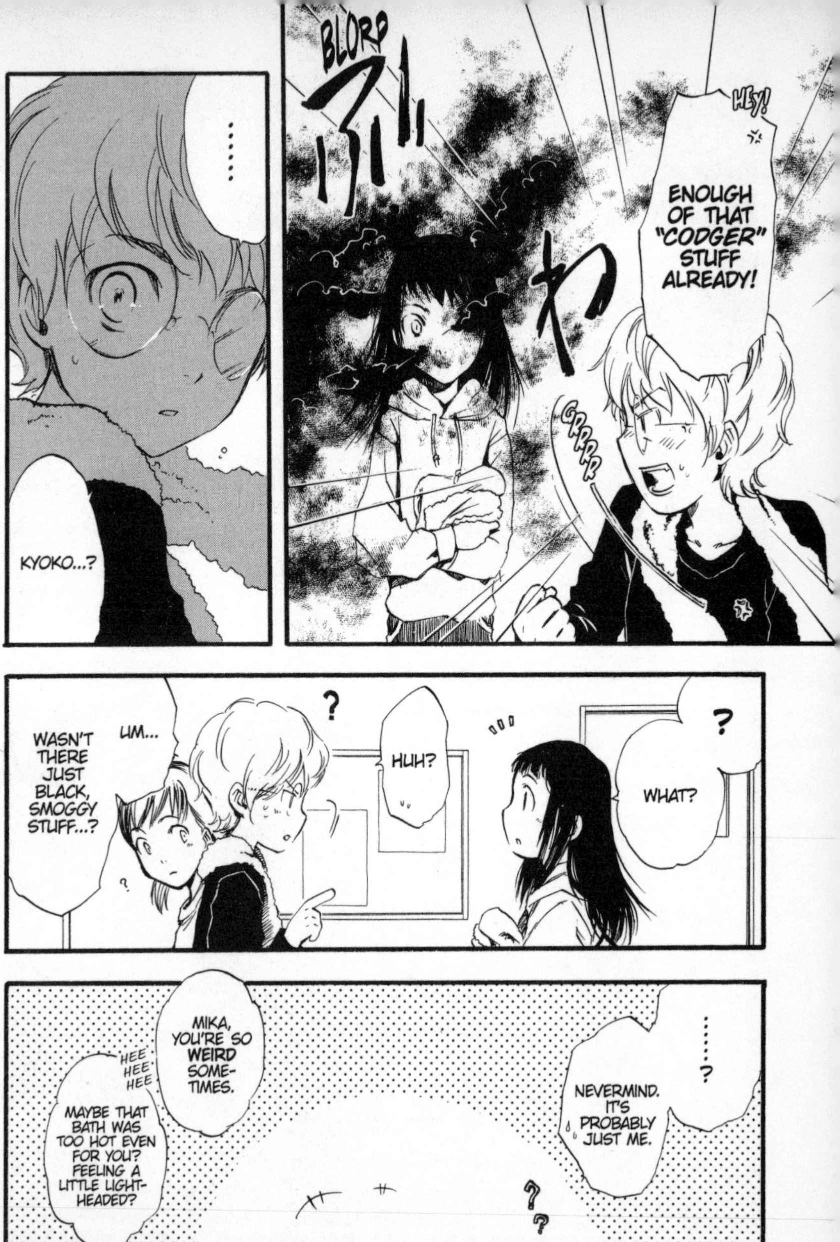
BLORP
HEY!
ENOUGH OF THAT "CODGER" STUFF ALREADY!
GRRRR
......
KYOKO...?
?
WHAT?
HUH?
?
UM...
WASN'T THERE JUST BLACK, SMOGGY STUFF...?
?
......?
NEVERMIND. IT'S PROBABLY JUST ME.
MIKA, YOU'RE SO WEIRD SOME-TIMES.
HEE HEE HEE
MAYBE THAT BATH WAS TOO HOT EVEN FOR YOU? FEELING A LITTLE LIGHT-HEADED?
?
?

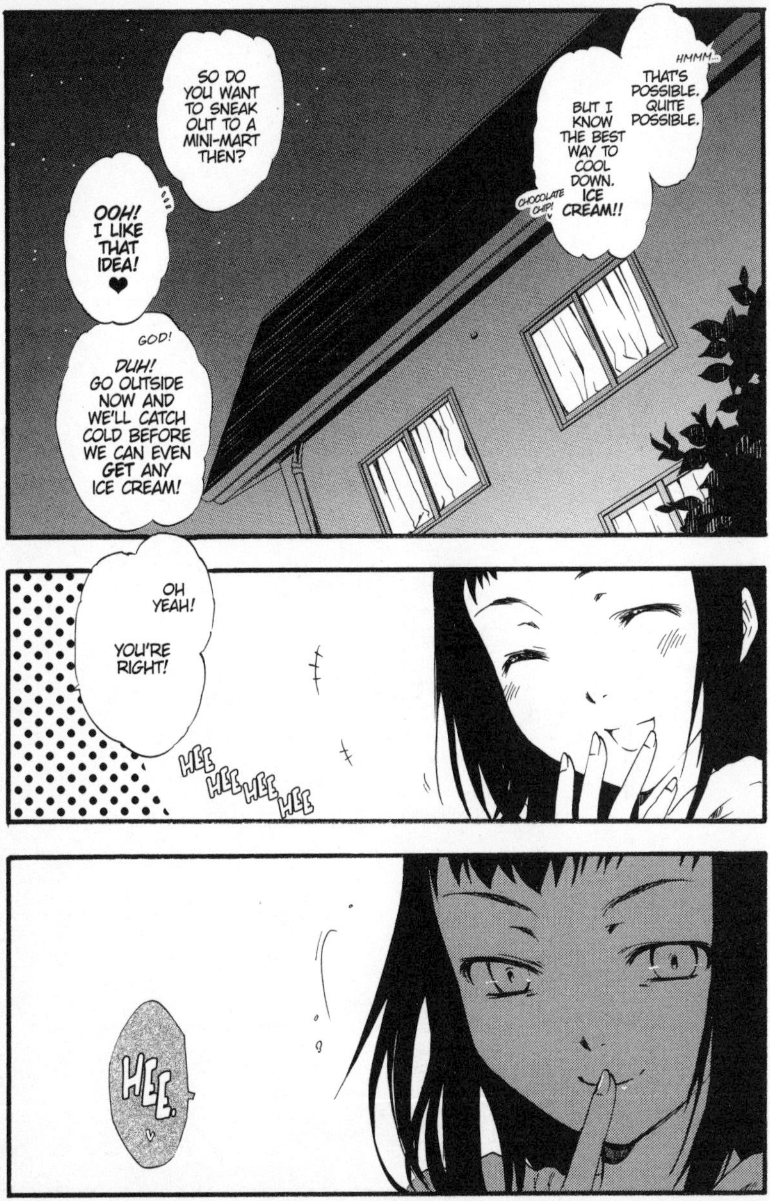
HMMM... THAT'S POSSIBLE. QUITE POSSIBLE.
BUT I KNOW THE BEST WAY TO COOL DOWN. ICE CREAM!!
CHOCOLATE CHIP!
SO DO YOU WANT TO SNEAK OUT TO A MINI-MART THEN?
OOH! I LIKE THAT IDEA! ❤
GOD!
DUH! GO OUTSIDE NOW AND WE'LL CATCH COLD BEFORE WE CAN EVEN GET ANY ICE CREAM!
OH YEAH!
YOU'RE RIGHT!
HEE HEE HEE HEE
HEE.

Jewelry
and
Clothes

Venus Vangard

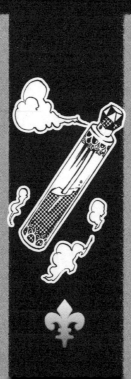

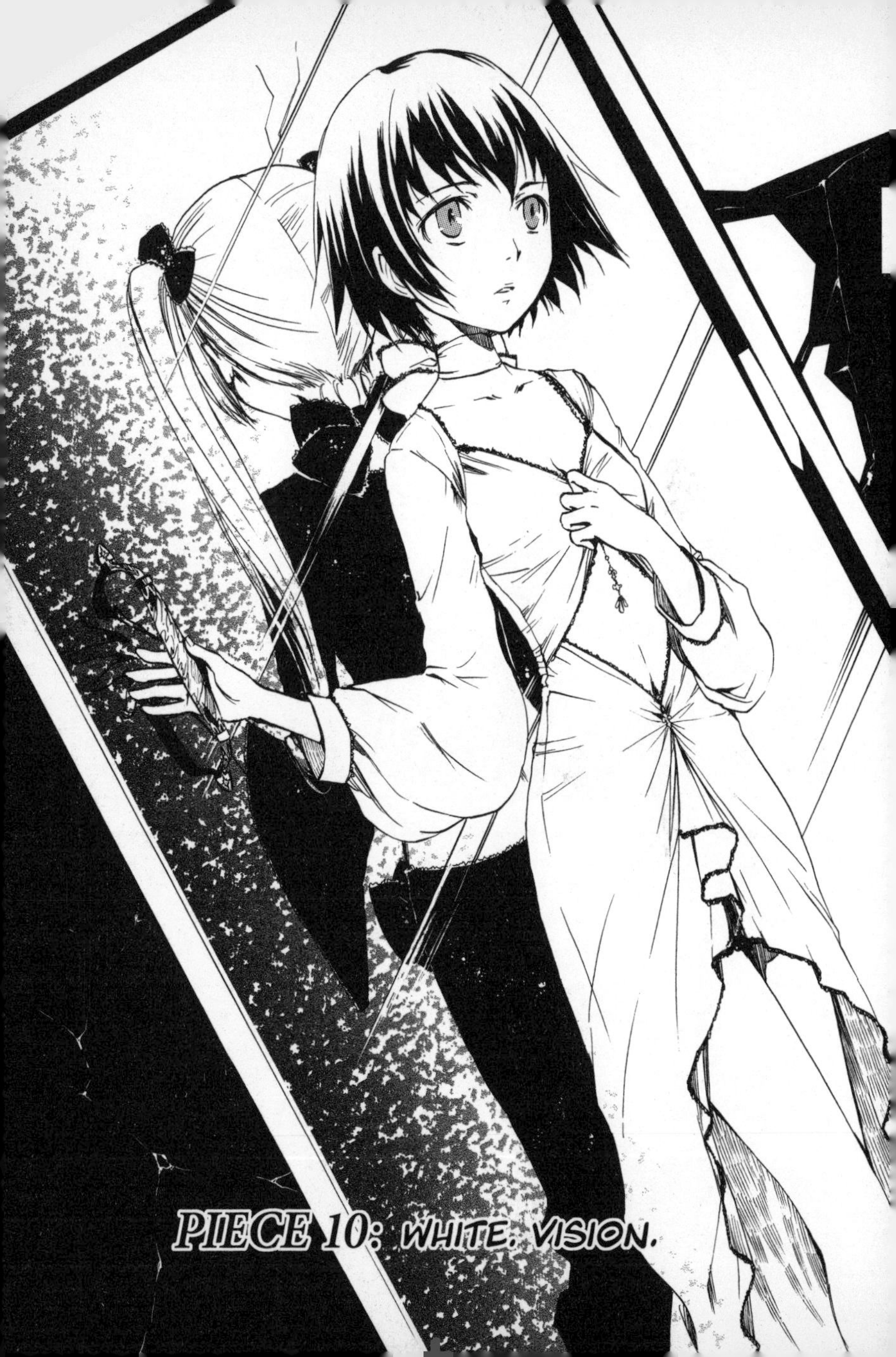
PIECE 10: WHITE. VISION.

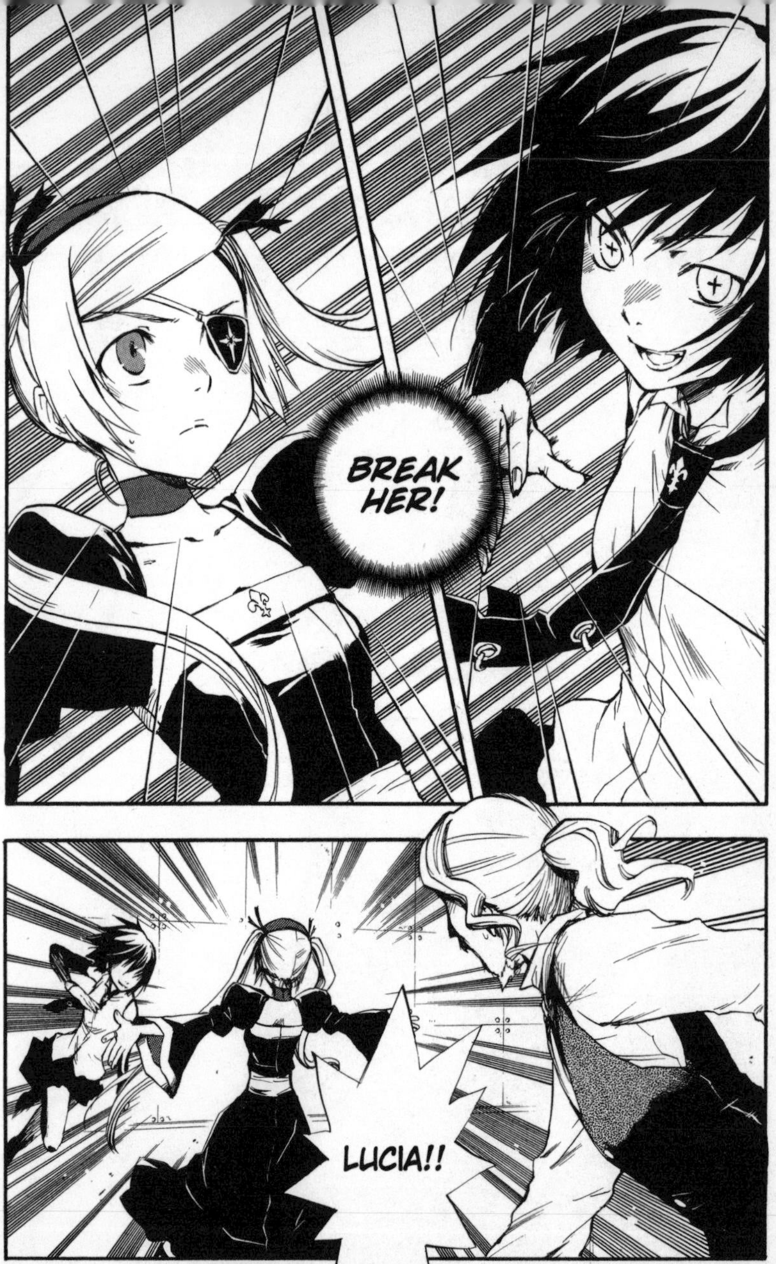
BREAK HER!
LUCIA!!

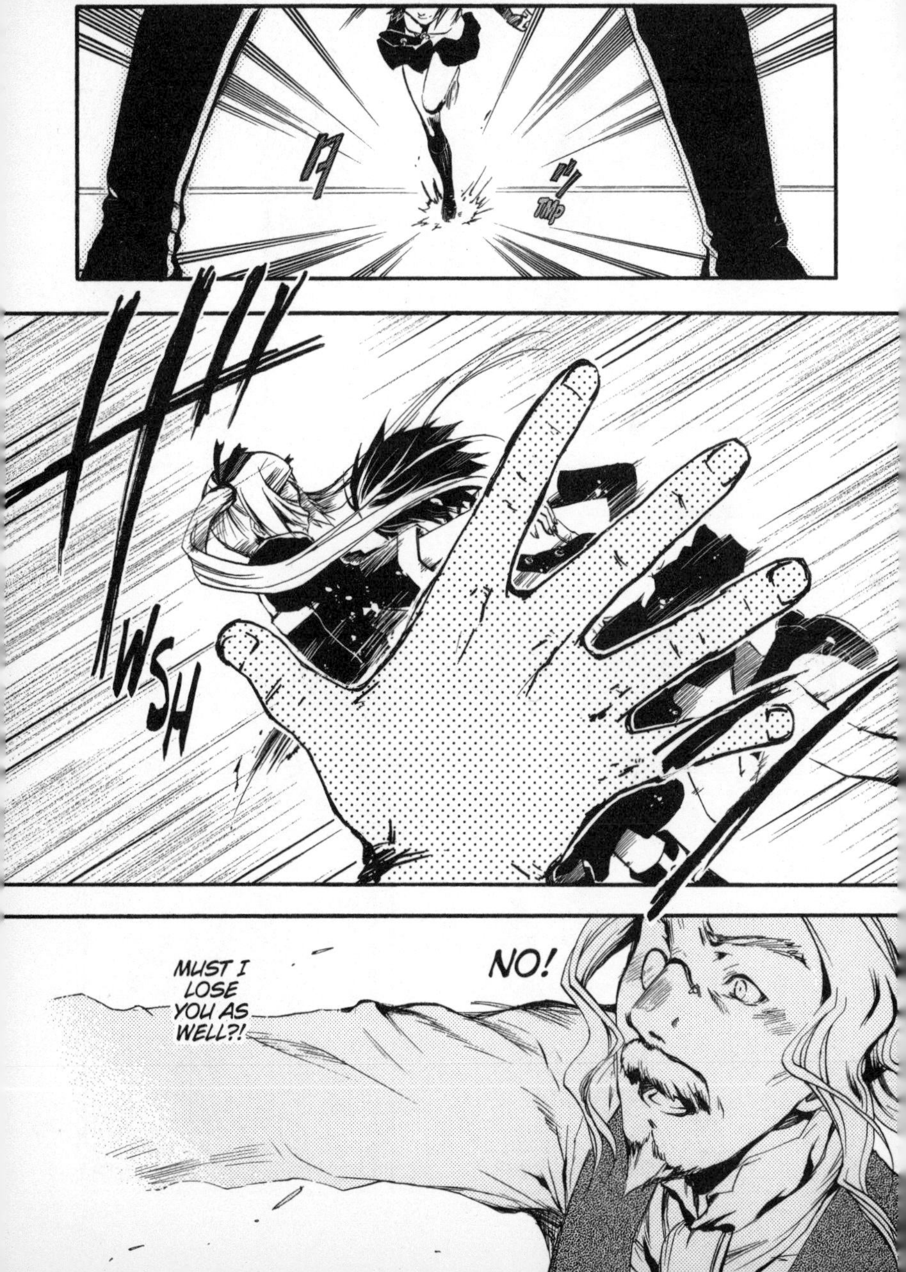
TMP
WSH
NO!
MUST I LOSE YOU AS WELL?!

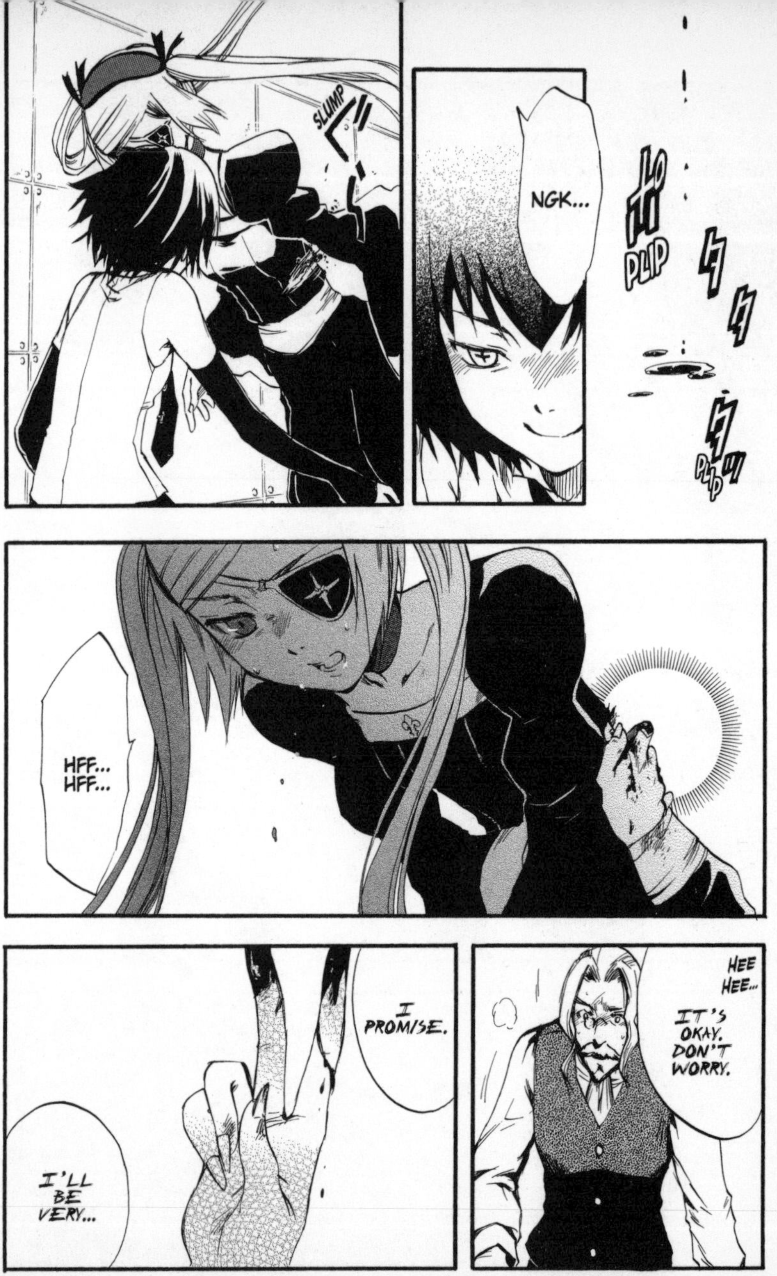
NGK...
PLIP
PLIP
SLUMP
HFF...
HFF...
HEE HEE...
IT'S OKAY. DON'T WORRY.
I PROMISE.
I'LL BE VERY...

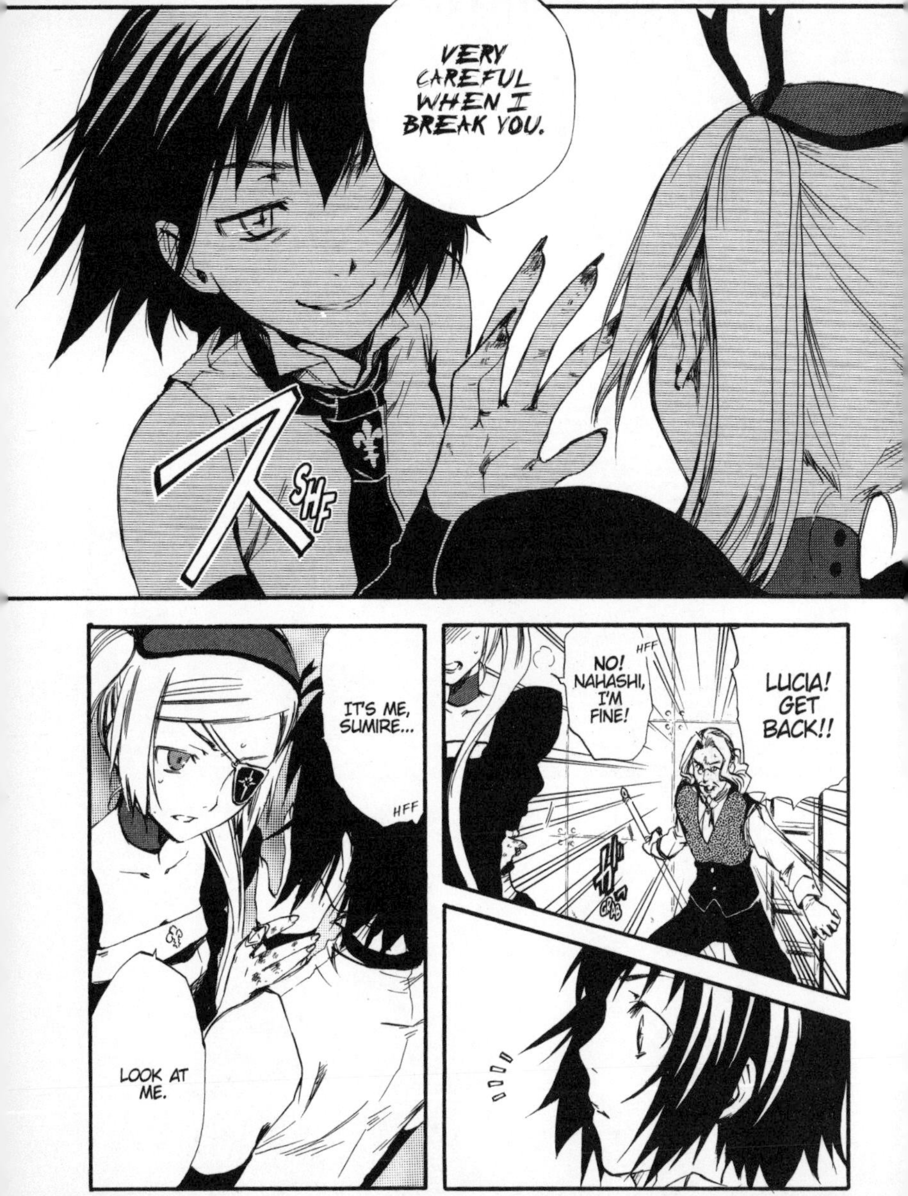
VERY CAREFUL WHEN I BREAK YOU.
SHF
LUCIA! GET BACK!!
NO! NAHASHI, I'M FINE!
HFF
GRAB
IT'S ME, SUMIRE...
HFF
LOOK AT ME.

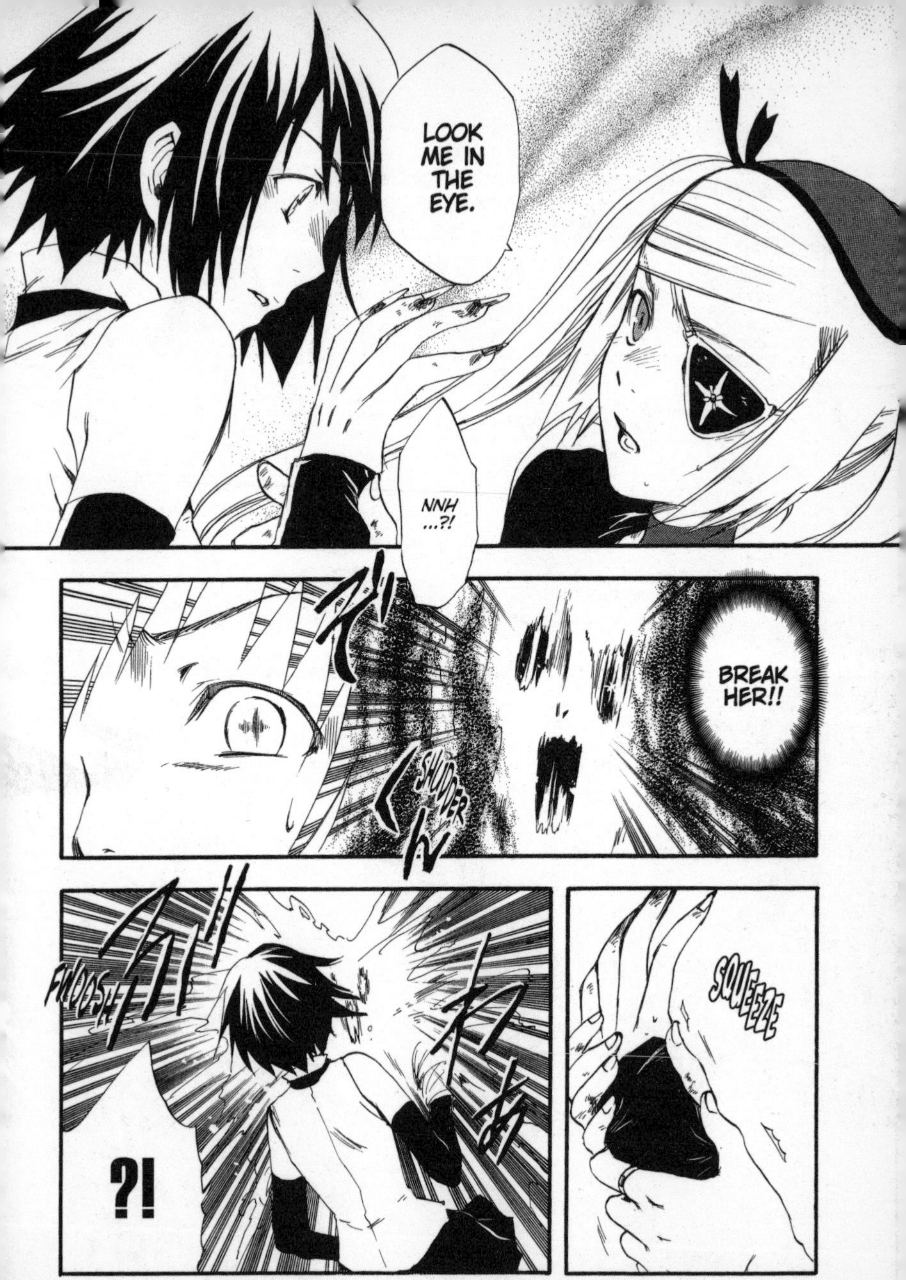
LOOK ME IN THE EYE.
NNH ...?!
BREAK HER!!
SHUDDER
SQUEEZE
FWOOSH
?!

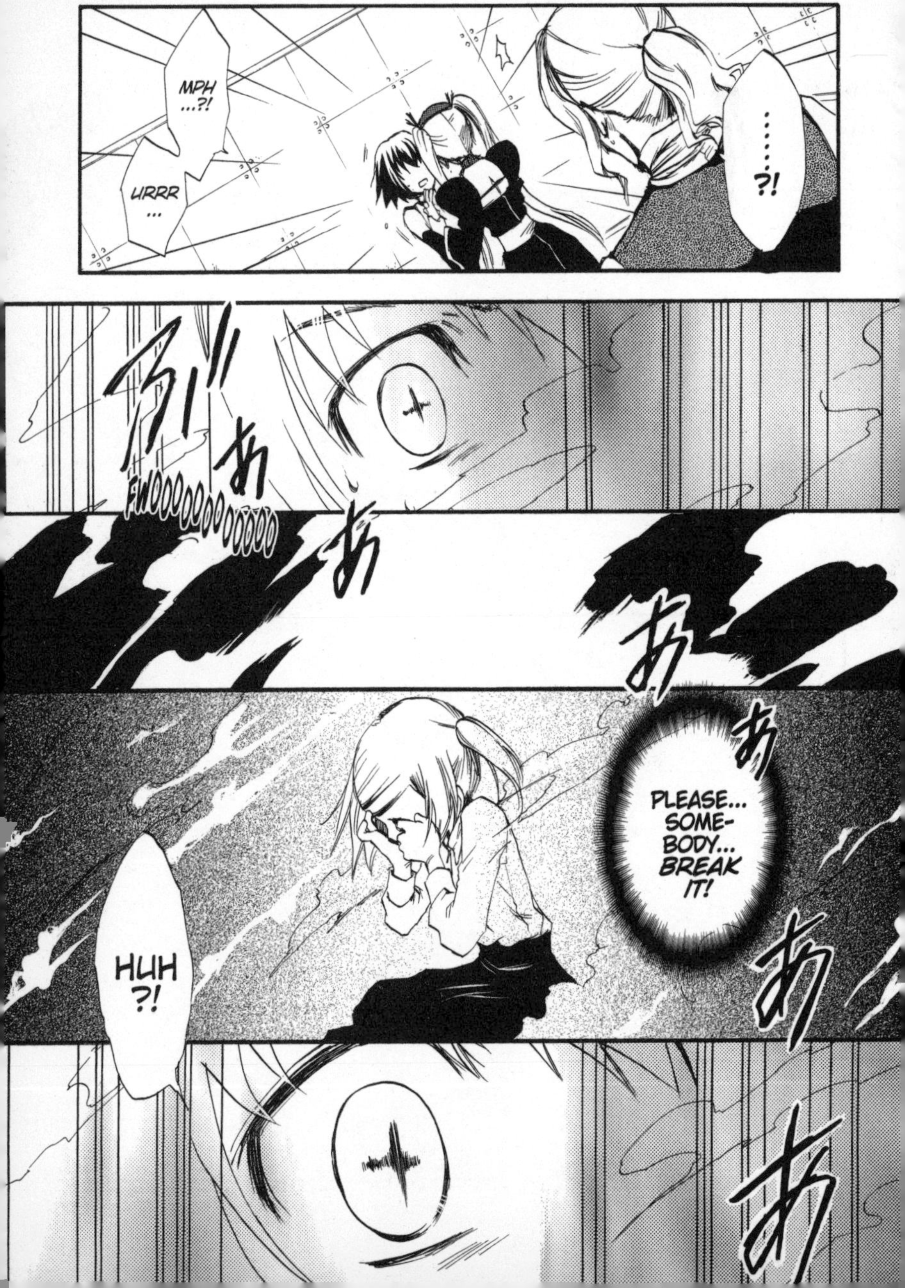
……?!
MPH ...?!
URRR ...
FWOOOOOOOOOOOOO
PLEASE... SOME-BODY... BREAK IT!
HUH ?!

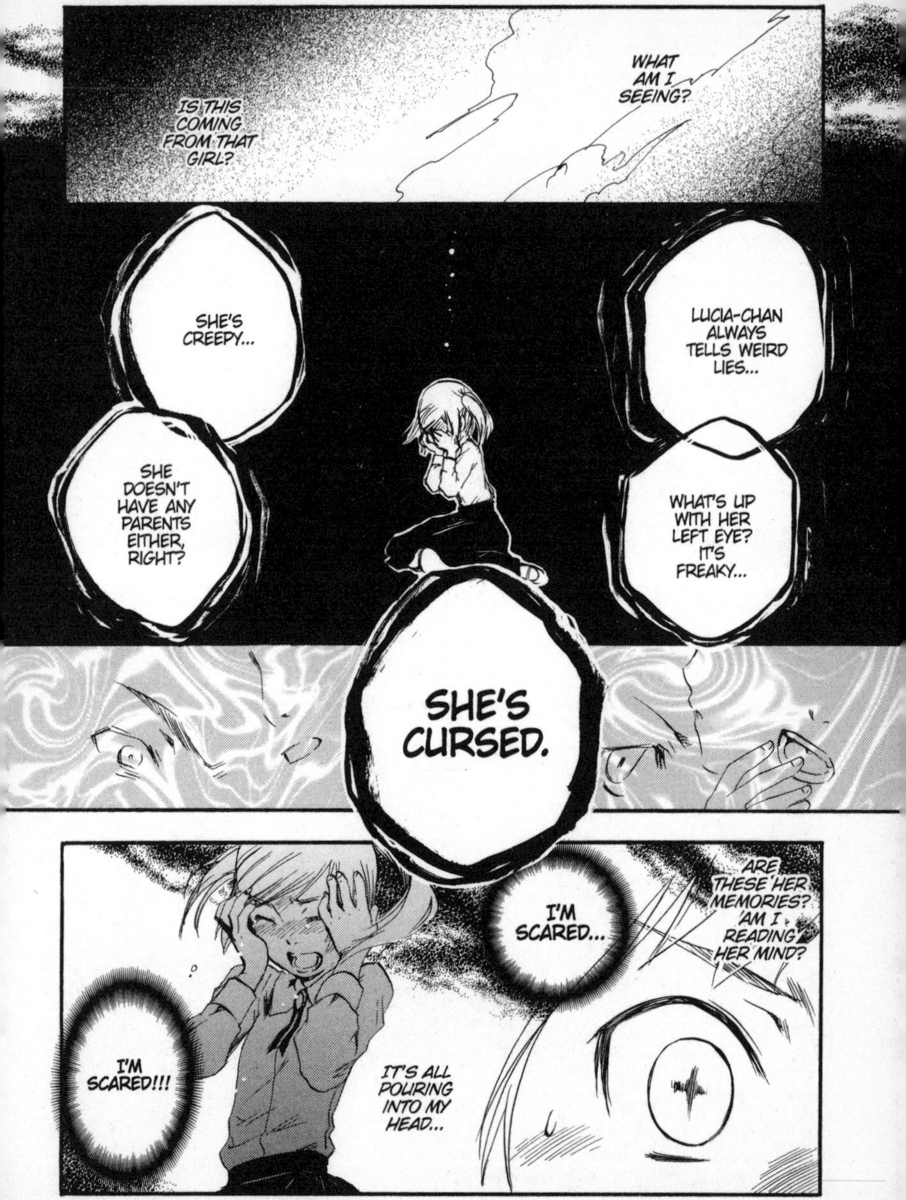
WHAT AM I SEEING?
IS THIS COMING FROM THAT GIRL?
LUCIA-CHAN ALWAYS TELLS WEIRD LIES...
SHE'S CREEPY...
WHAT'S UP WITH HER LEFT EYE? IT'S FREAKY...
SHE DOESN'T HAVE ANY PARENTS EITHER, RIGHT?
SHE'S CURSED.
ARE THESE HER MEMORIES? AM I READING HER MIND?
I'M SCARED...
IT'S ALL POURING INTO MY HEAD...
I'M SCARED!!!

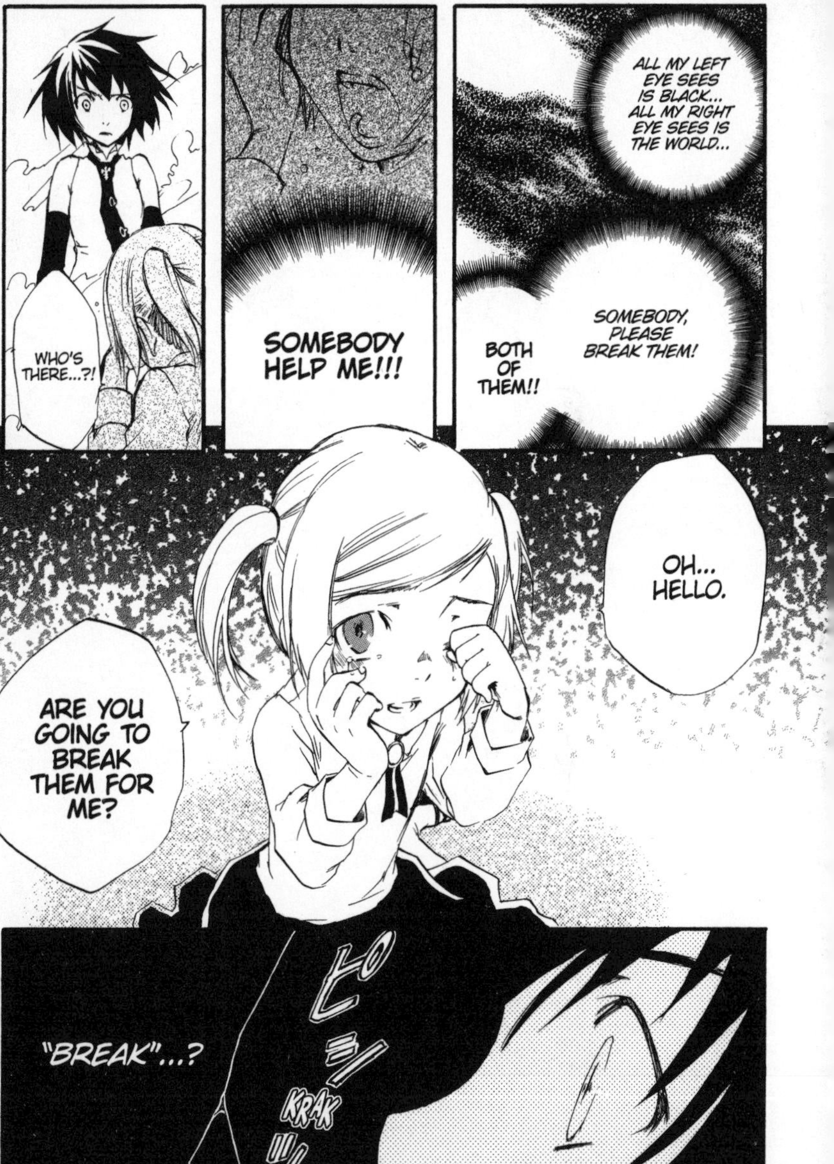
ALL MY LEFT EYE SEES IS BLACK... ALL MY RIGHT EYE SEES IS THE WORLD...
SOMEBODY, PLEASE BREAK THEM!
BOTH OF THEM!!
SOMEBODY HELP ME!!!
WHO'S THERE...?!
OH... HELLO.
ARE YOU GOING TO BREAK THEM FOR ME?
KRAK
"BREAK"...?

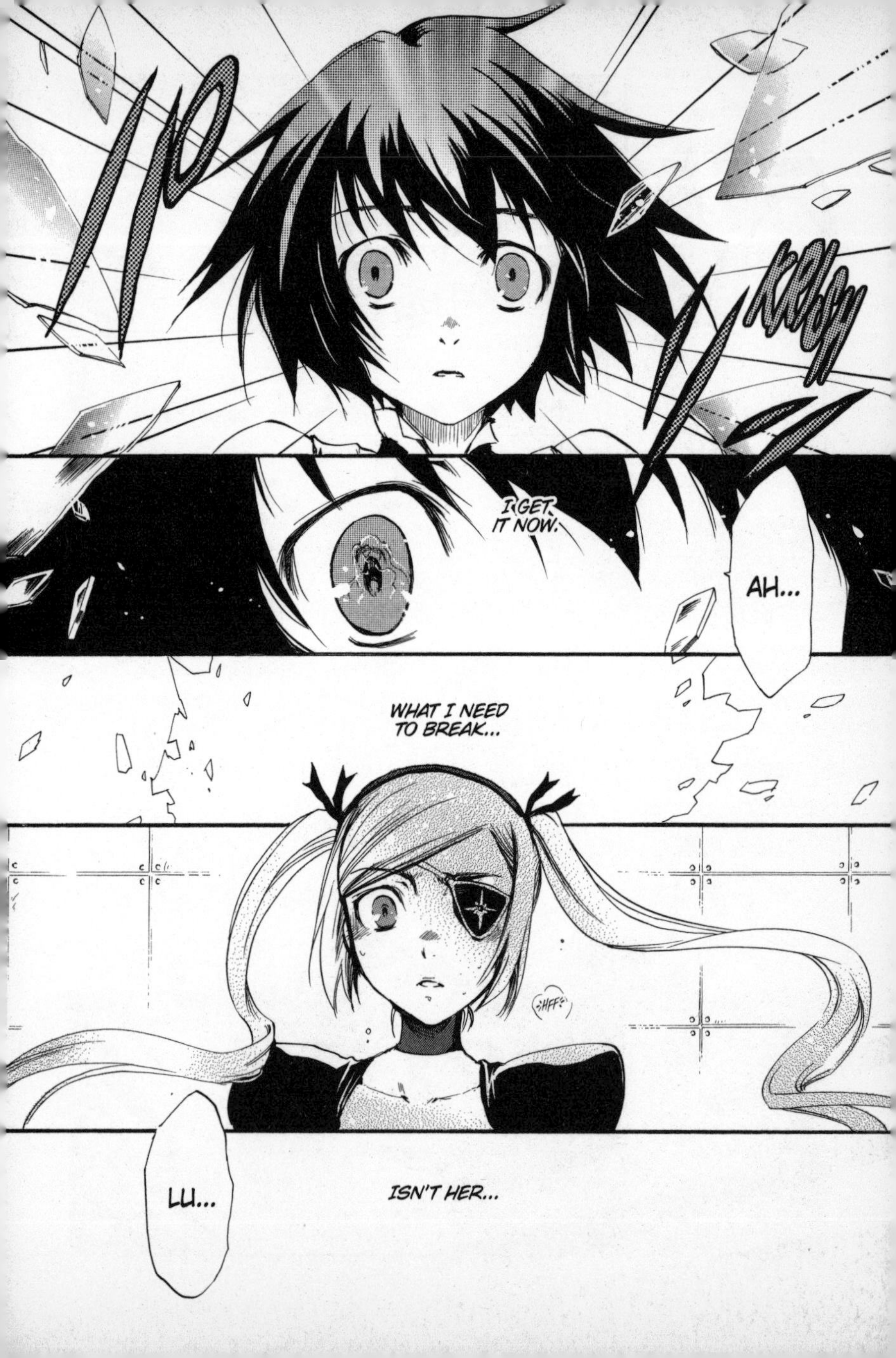
AH...
I GET IT NOW.
WHAT I NEED TO BREAK...
HFF
ISN'T HER...
LU...

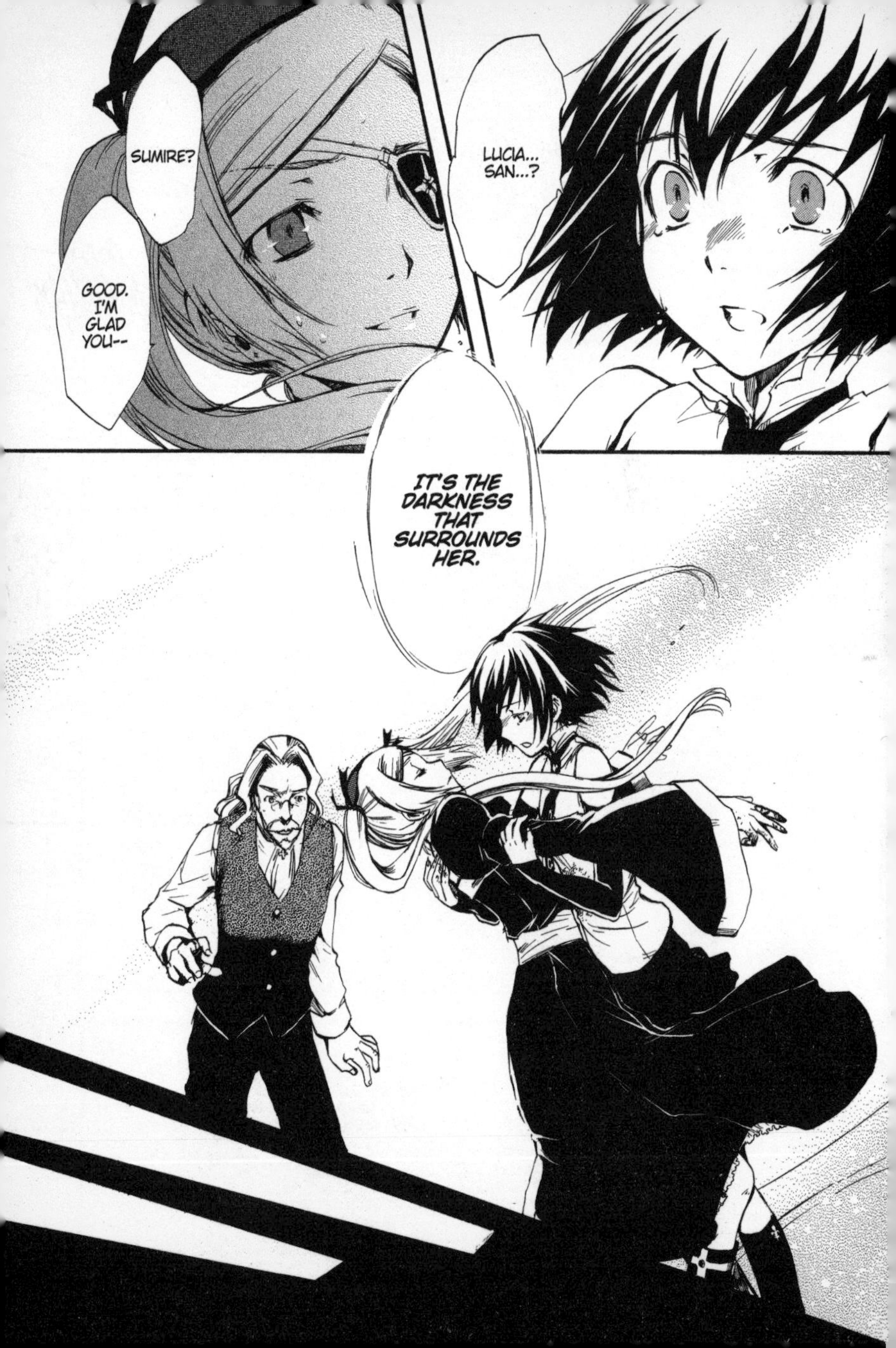
LUCIA... SAN...?
SUMIRE?
GOOD. I'M GLAD YOU--
IT'S THE DARKNESS THAT SURROUNDS HER.

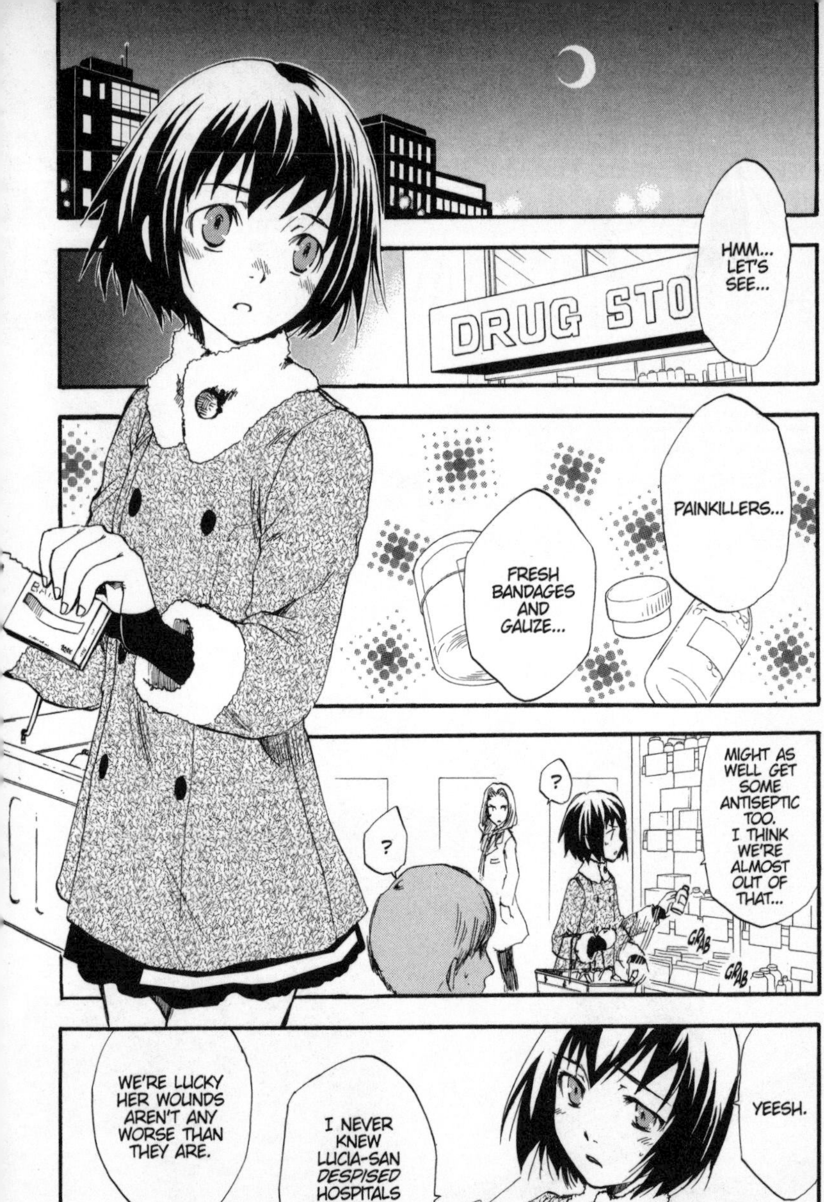
HMM... LET'S SEE...
DRUG STO
PAINKILLERS...
FRESH BANDAGES AND GAUZE...
MIGHT AS WELL GET SOME ANTISEPTIC TOO. I THINK WE'RE ALMOST OUT OF THAT...
?
GRAB
GRAB
?
YEESH.
I NEVER KNEW LUCIA-SAN *DESPISED* HOSPITALS SO MUCH.
WE'RE LUCKY HER WOUNDS AREN'T ANY WORSE THAN THEY ARE.

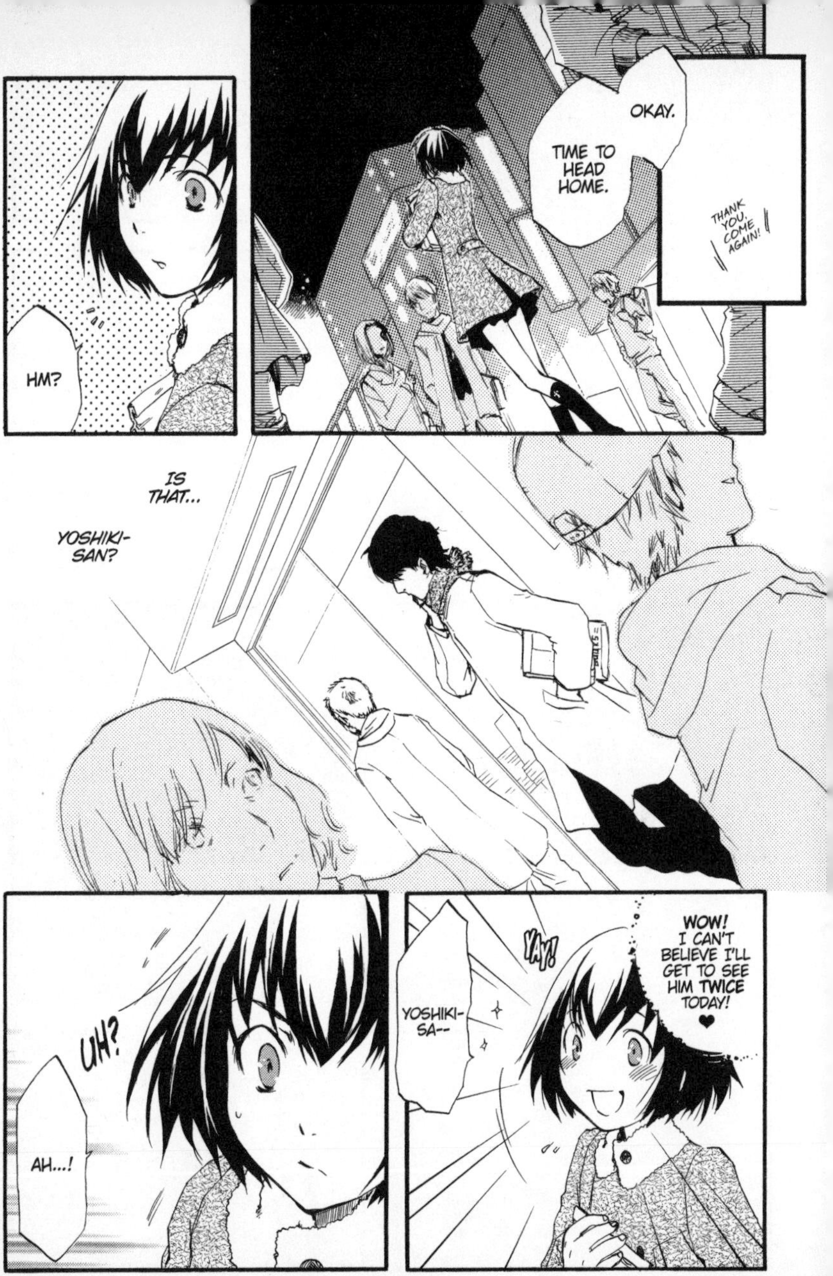
THANK YOU, COME AGAIN!
OKAY.
TIME TO HEAD HOME.
HM?
IS THAT...
YOSHIKI-SAN?
WOW! I CAN'T BELIEVE I'LL GET TO SEE HIM TWICE TODAY! ♥
YAY!
YOSHIKI-SA--
UH?
AH...!

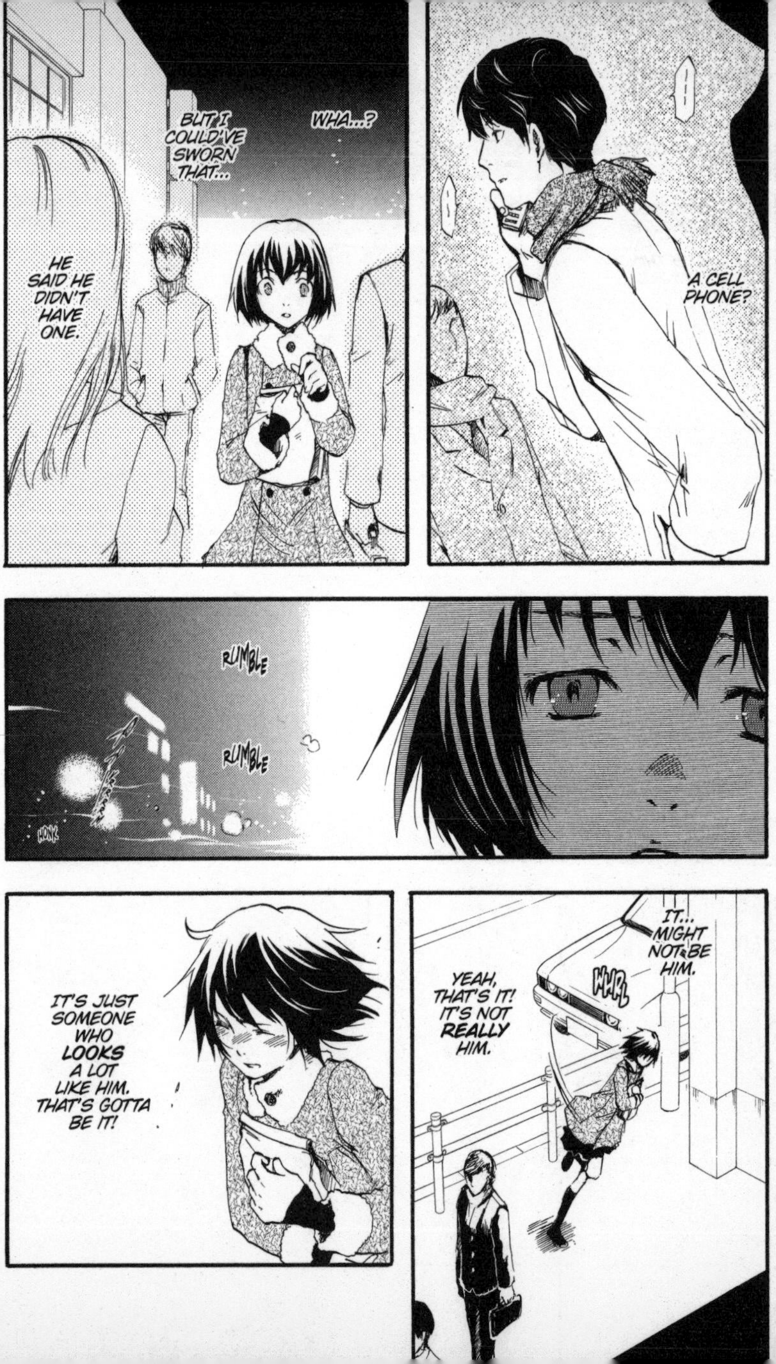
!
!
A CELL PHONE?
WHA...?
BUT I COULD'VE SWORN THAT...
HE SAID HE DIDN'T HAVE ONE.
RUMBLE
RUMBLE
HONK
IT... MIGHT NOT BE HIM.
WHIRL
YEAH, THAT'S IT! IT'S NOT **REALLY** HIM.
IT'S JUST SOMEONE WHO **LOOKS** A LOT LIKE HIM. THAT'S GOTTA BE IT!

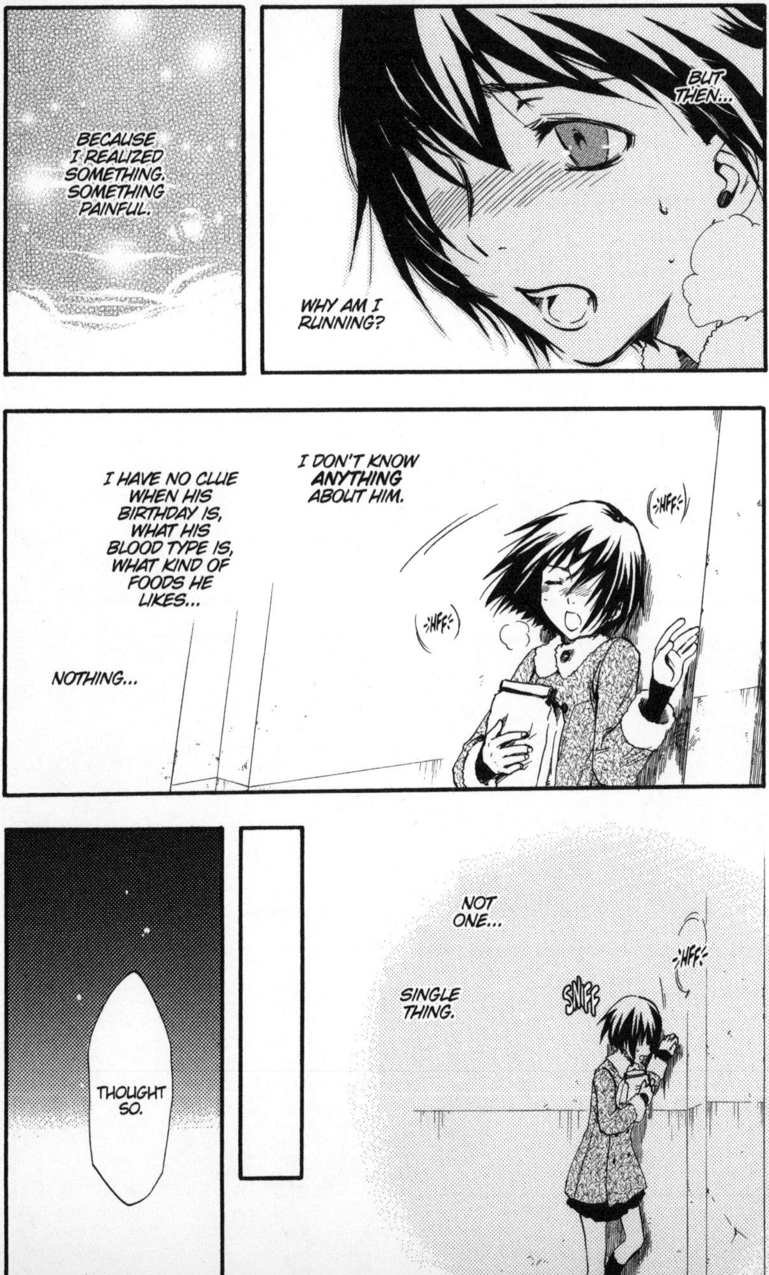
BUT THEN...
WHY AM I RUNNING?
BECAUSE I REALIZED SOMETHING. SOMETHING PAINFUL.
I DON'T KNOW **ANYTHING** ABOUT HIM.
HFF
I HAVE NO CLUE WHEN HIS BIRTHDAY IS, WHAT HIS BLOOD TYPE IS, WHAT KIND OF FOODS HE LIKES...
HFF
NOTHING...
HFF
NOT ONE...
SINGLE THING.
SNIFF
THOUGHT SO.

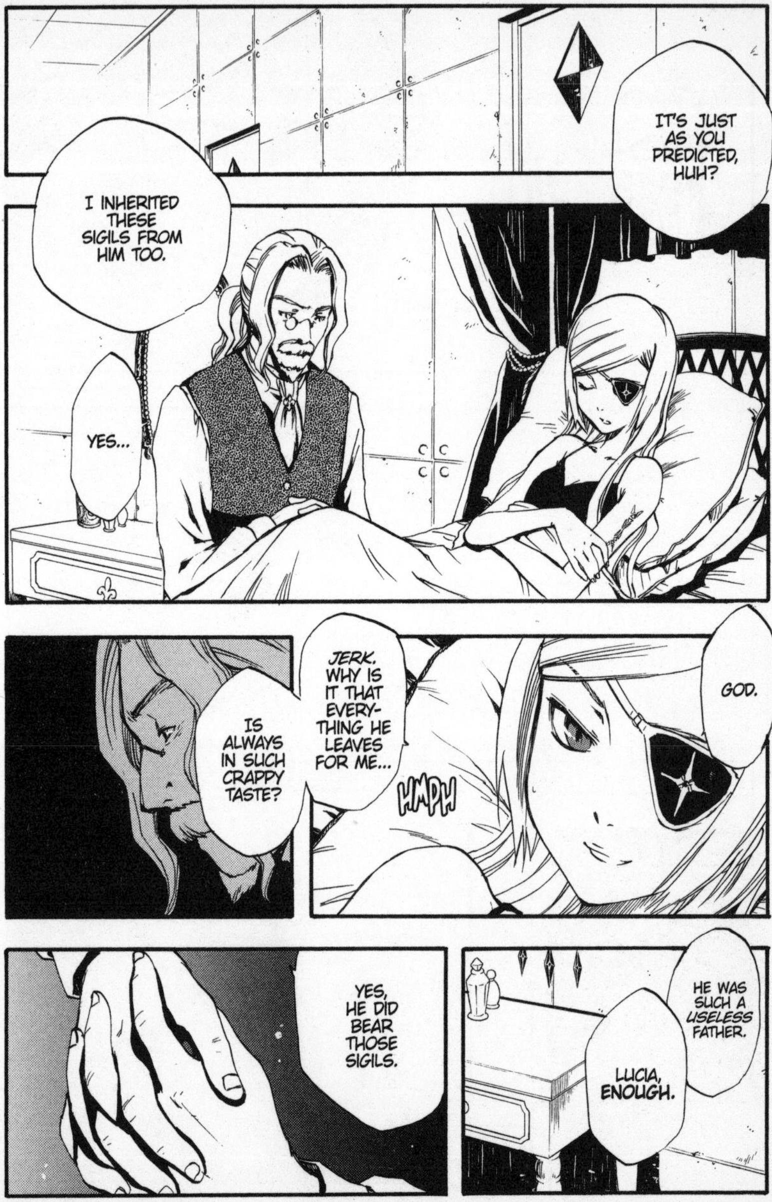
IT'S JUST AS YOU PREDICTED, HUH?
I INHERITED THESE SIGILS FROM HIM TOO.
YES...
GOD.
HMPH
JERK. WHY IS IT THAT EVERY-THING HE LEAVES FOR ME...
IS ALWAYS IN SUCH CRAPPY TASTE?
HE WAS SUCH A *USELESS* FATHER.
LUCIA, ENOUGH.
YES, HE DID BEAR THOSE SIGILS.

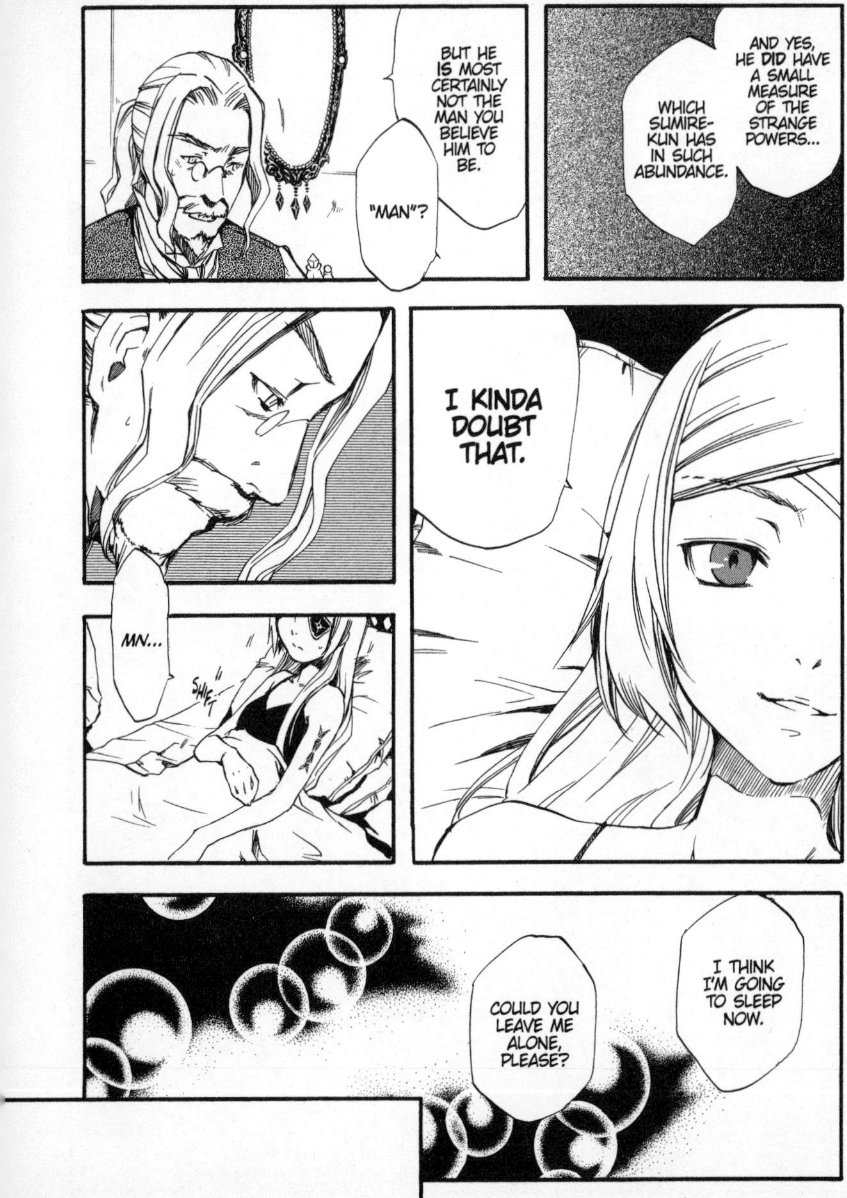
AND YES, HE DID HAVE A SMALL MEASURE OF THE STRANGE POWERS...
WHICH SUMIRE-KUN HAS IN SUCH ABUNDANCE.
BUT HE IS MOST CERTAINLY NOT THE MAN YOU BELIEVE HIM TO BE.
"MAN"?
I KINDA DOUBT THAT.
MN...
SHIFT
I THINK I'M GOING TO SLEEP NOW.
COULD YOU LEAVE ME ALONE, PLEASE?

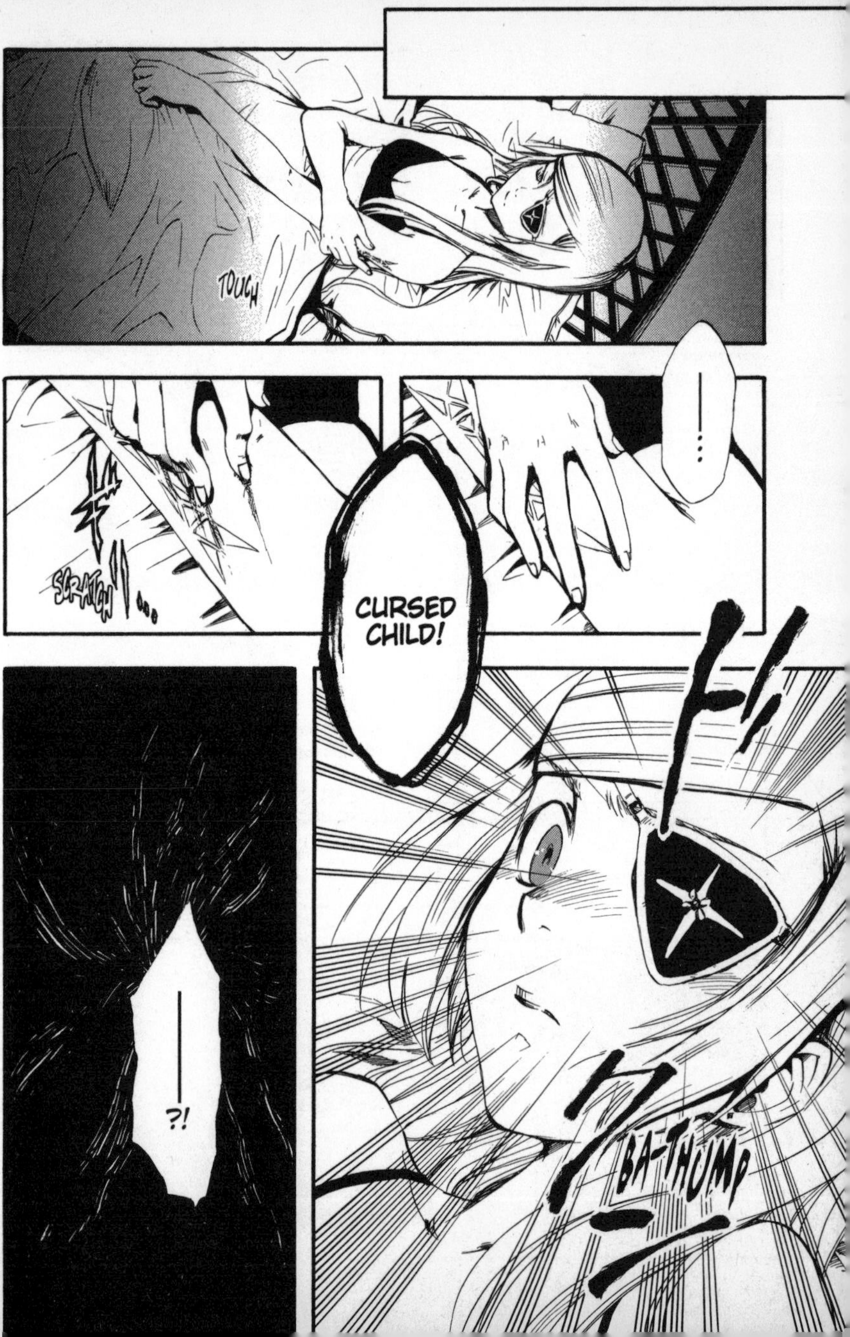
TOUCH
—...
CURSED CHILD!
SCRATCH
BA-THUMP
—?!

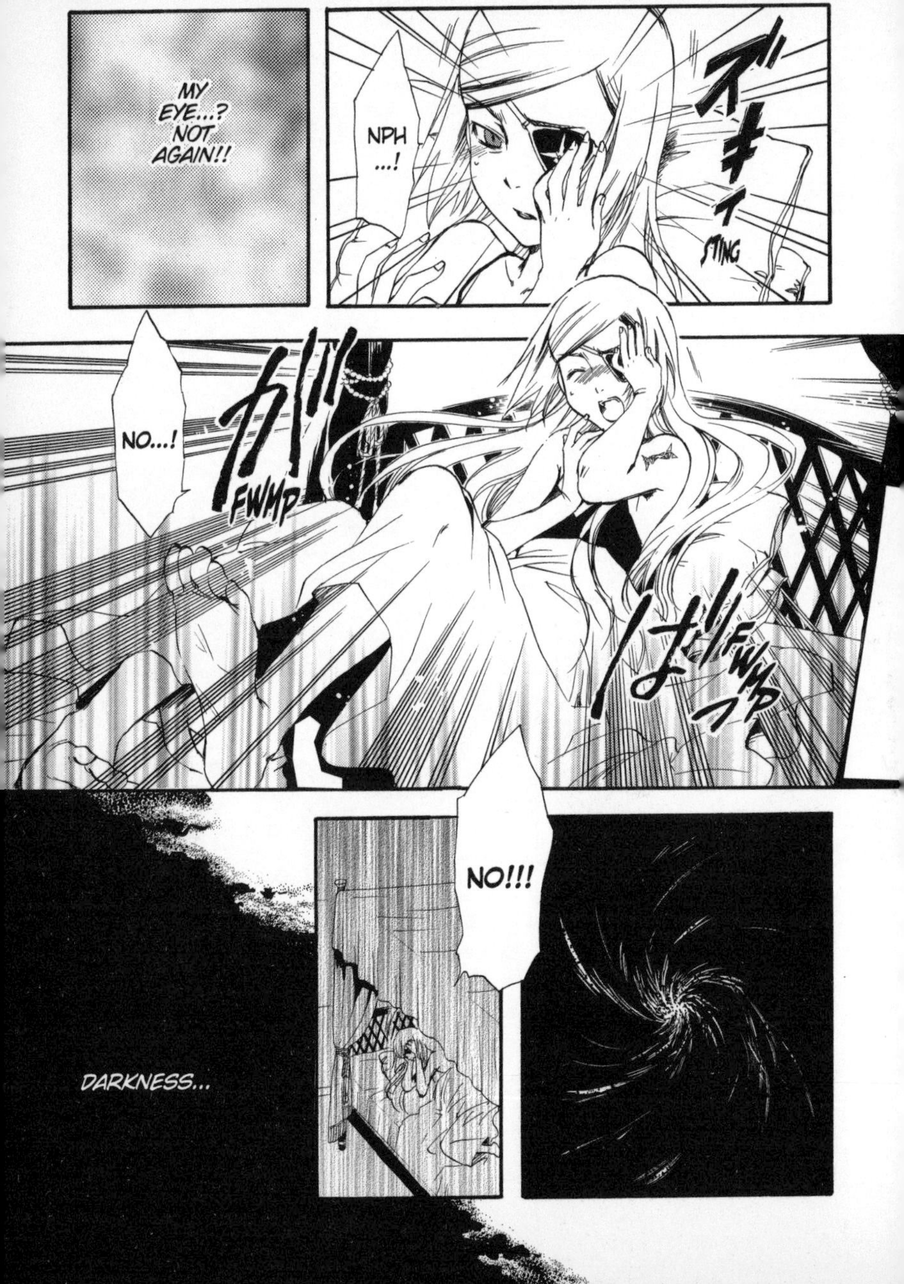
NPH ...!
STING
MY EYE...? NOT AGAIN!!
NO...!
FWMP
FWMP
NO!!!
DARKNESS...

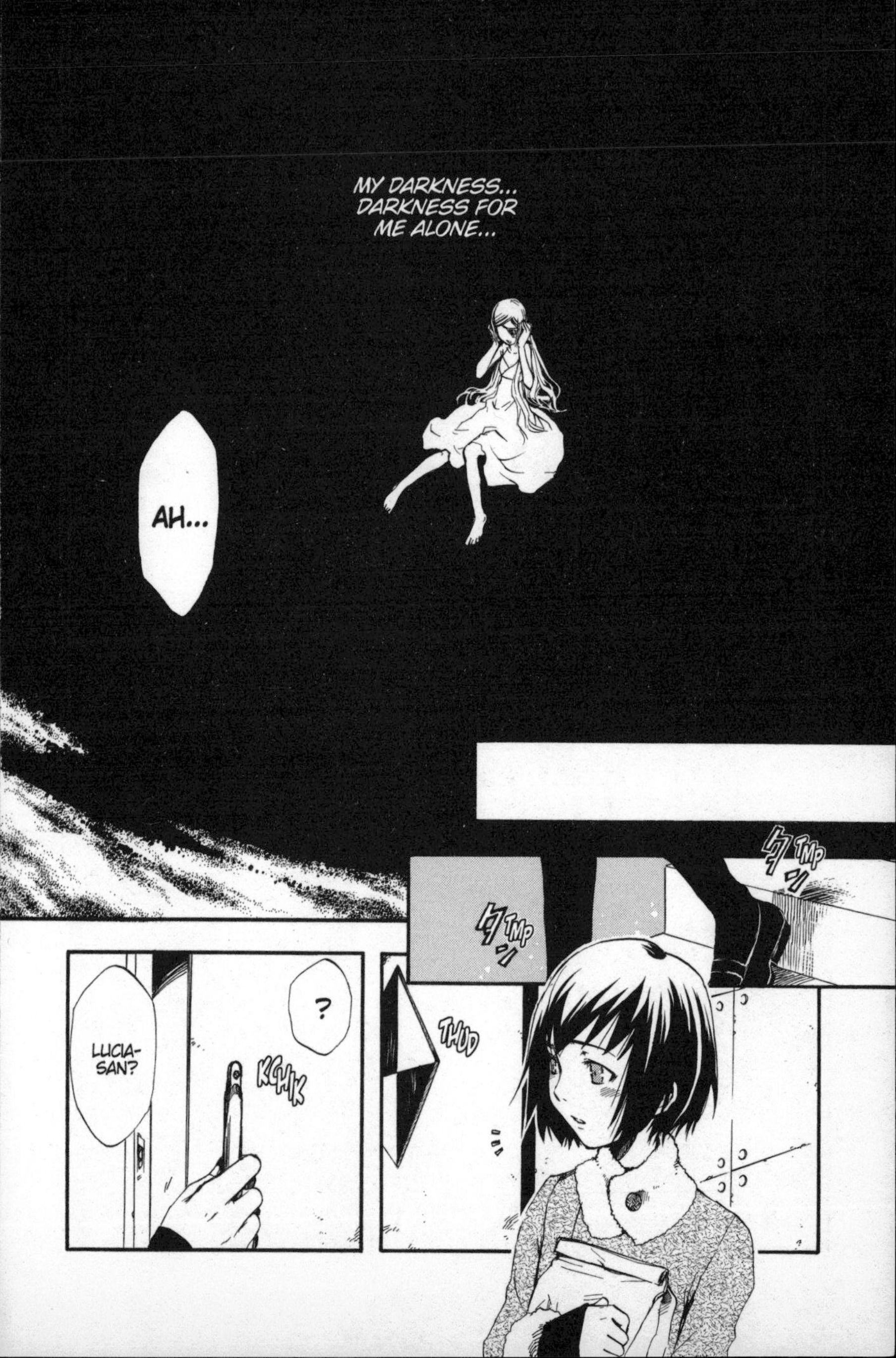
MY DARKNESS... DARKNESS FOR ME ALONE...
AH...
TMP
TMP
THUD
?
KCHIK
LUCIA-SAN?

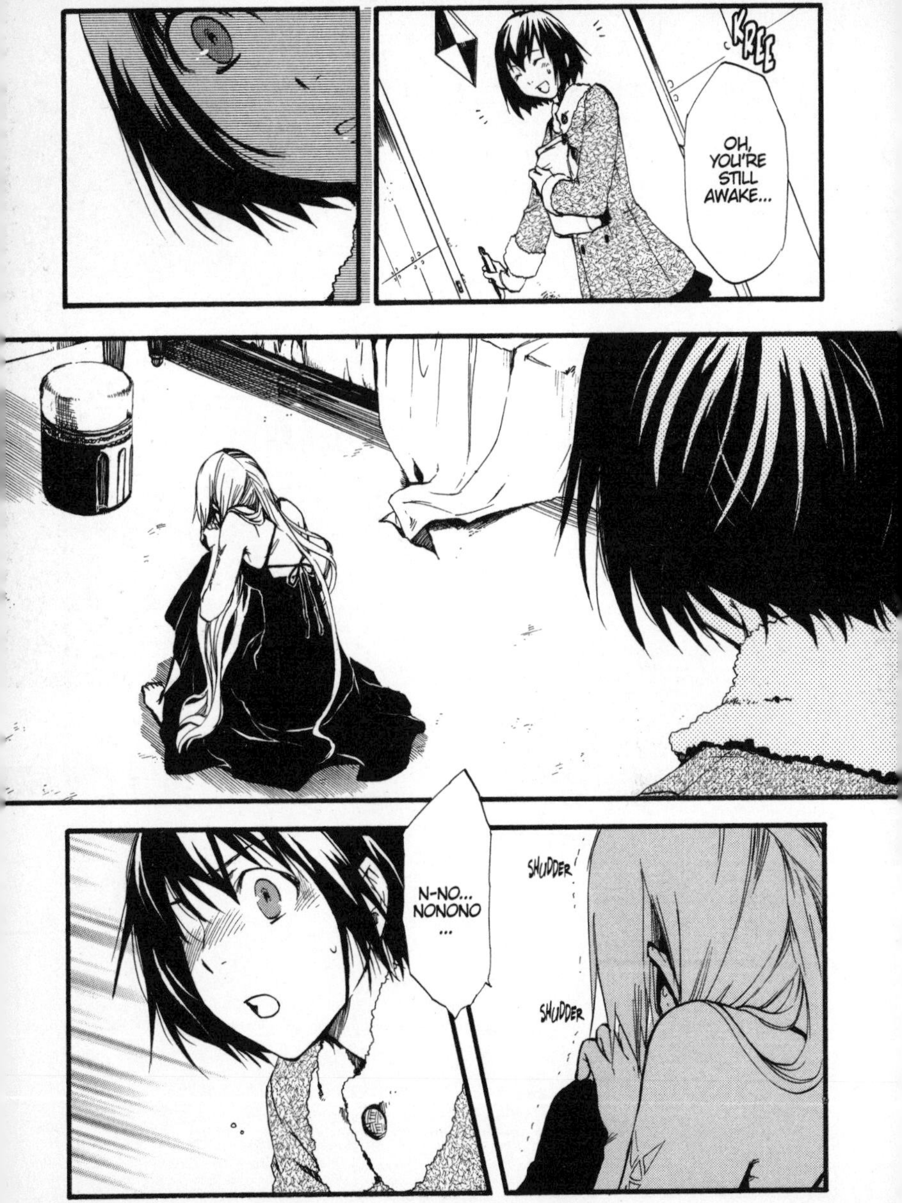

KREE
OH, YOU'RE STILL AWAKE...
SHUDDER
SHUDDER
N-NO... NONONO ...

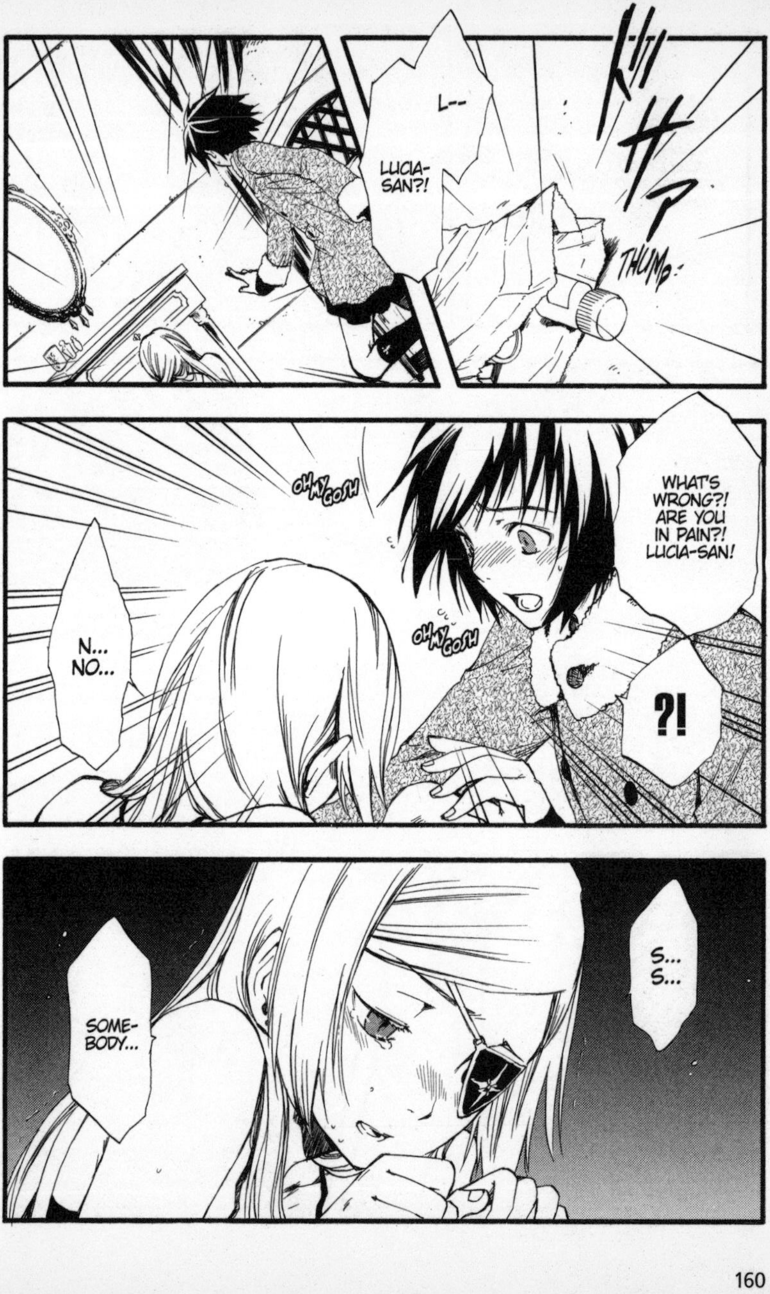
ドサァ
THUMP
L--
LUCIA-SAN?!
WHAT'S WRONG?! ARE YOU IN PAIN?! LUCIA-SAN!
OH MY GOSH
OH MY GOSH
?!
N... NO...
S... S...
SOMEBODY...

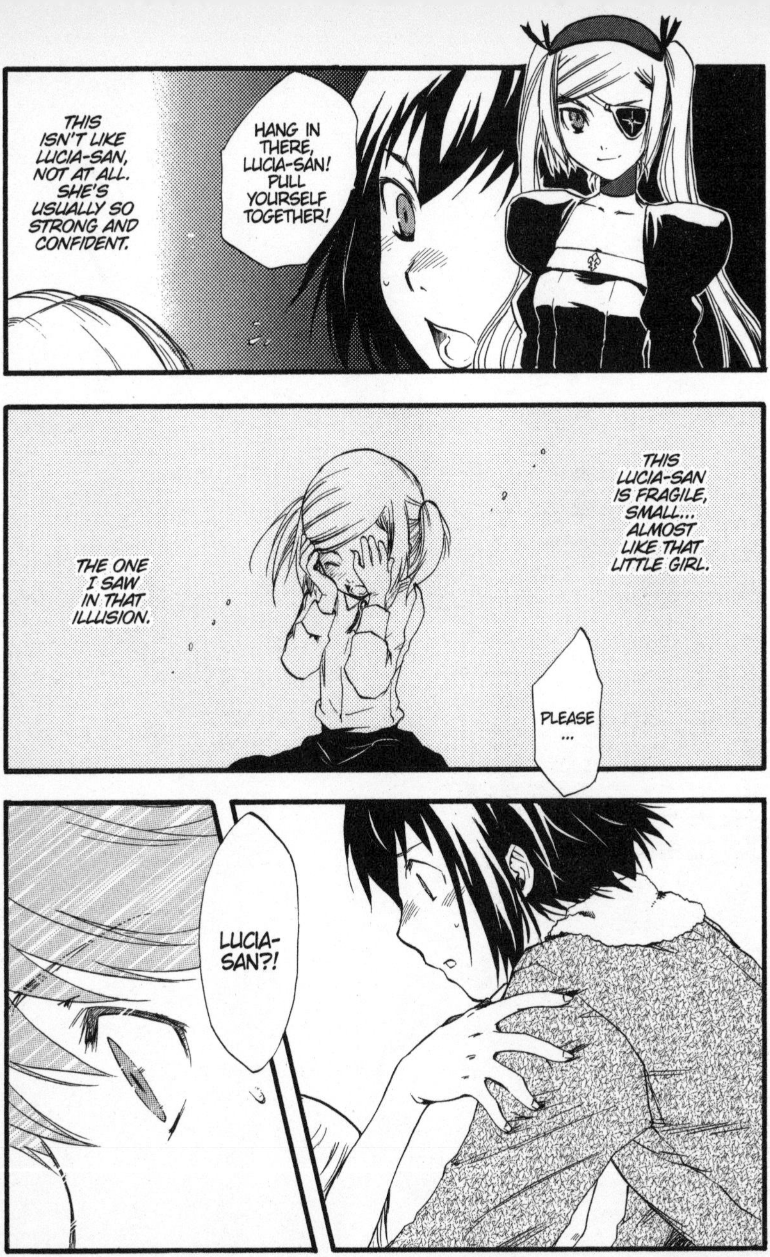
HANG IN THERE, LUCIA-SAN! PULL YOURSELF TOGETHER!
THIS ISN'T LIKE LUCIA-SAN, NOT AT ALL. SHE'S USUALLY SO STRONG AND CONFIDENT.
THIS LUCIA-SAN IS FRAGILE, SMALL... ALMOST LIKE THAT LITTLE GIRL.
THE ONE I SAW IN THAT ILLUSION.
PLEASE ...
LUCIA-SAN?!

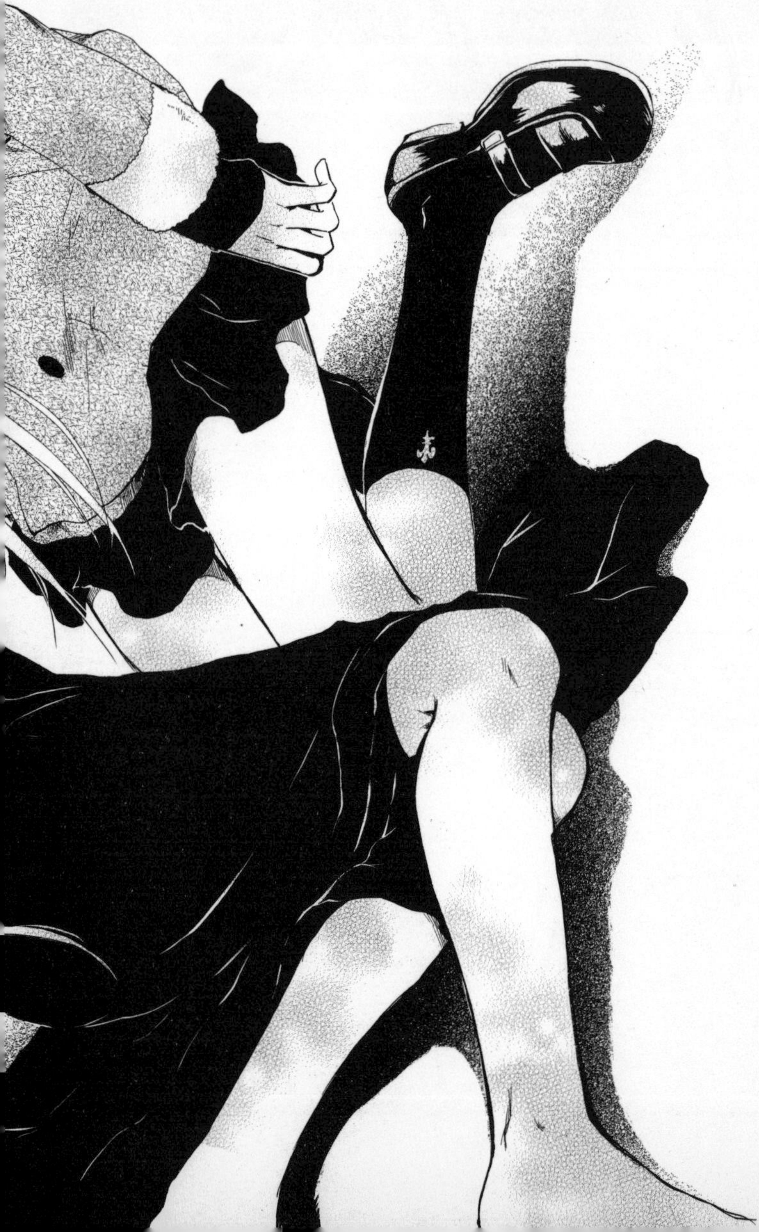

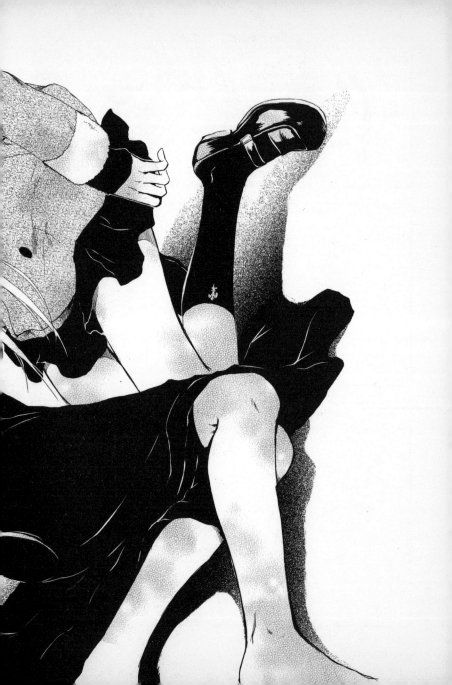

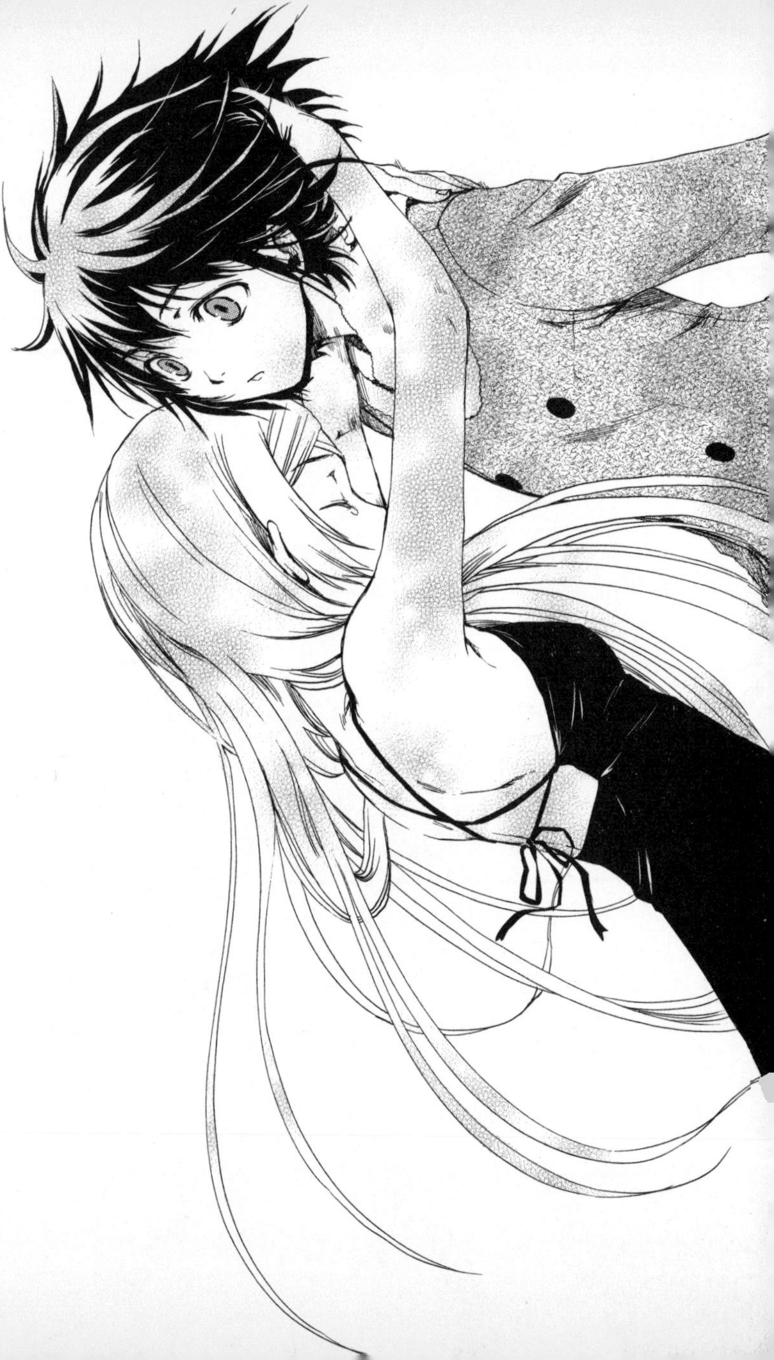

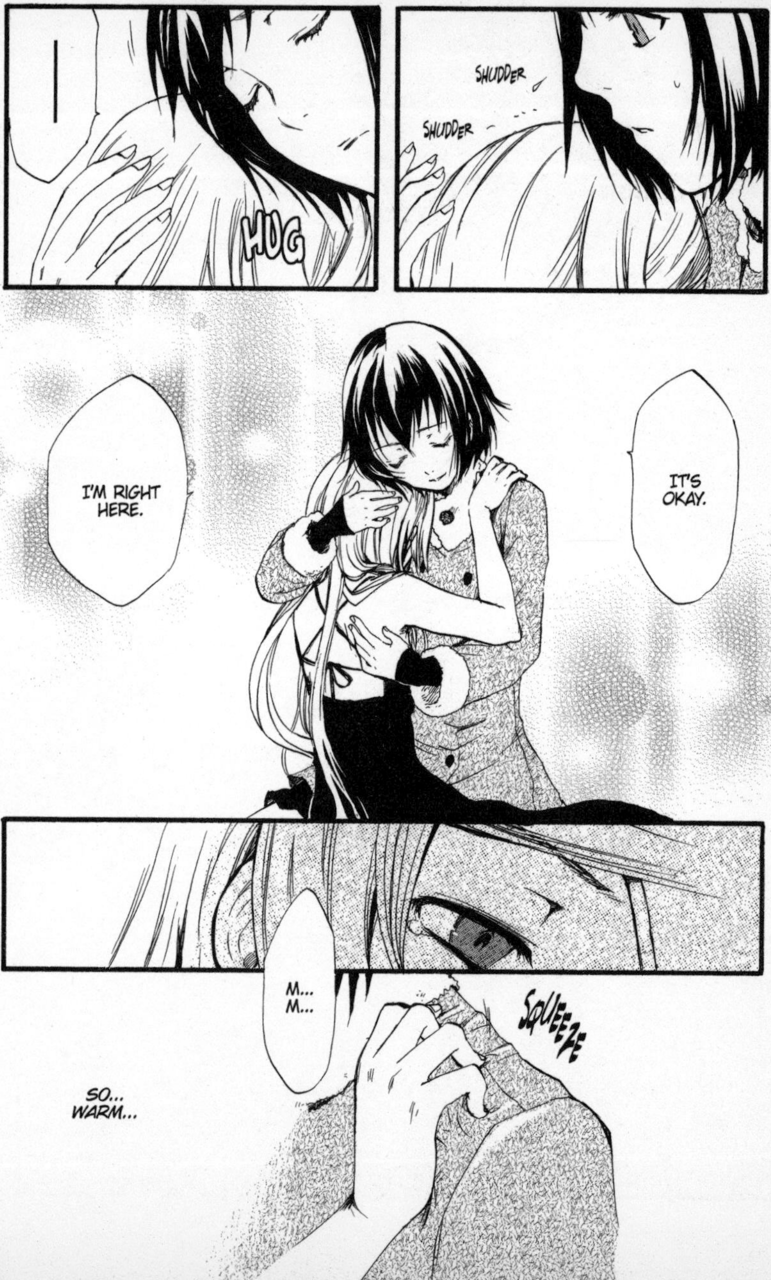
SHUDDER
SHUDDER
HUG
IT'S OKAY.
I'M RIGHT HERE.
M... M...
SQUEEZE
SO... WARM...

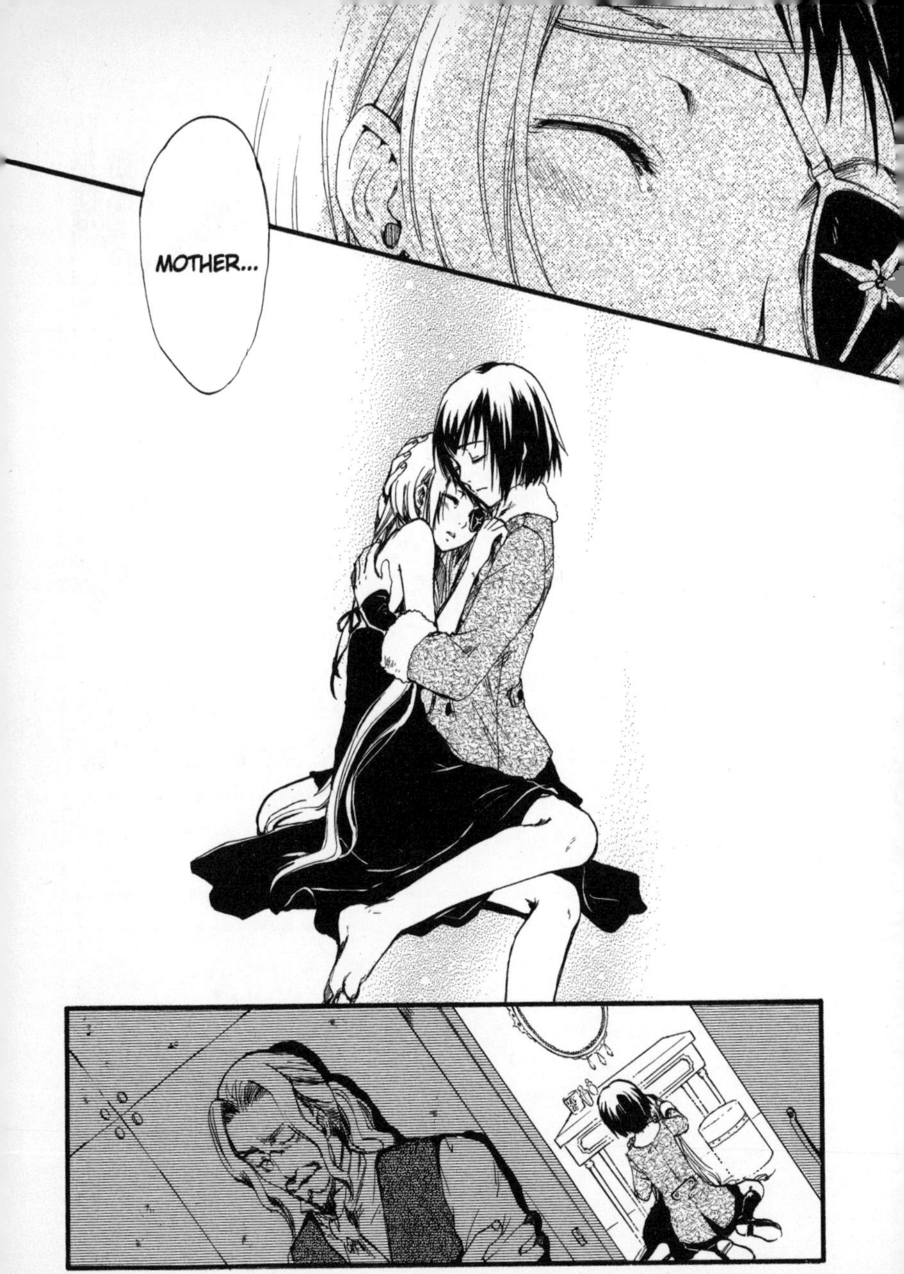
MOTHER...

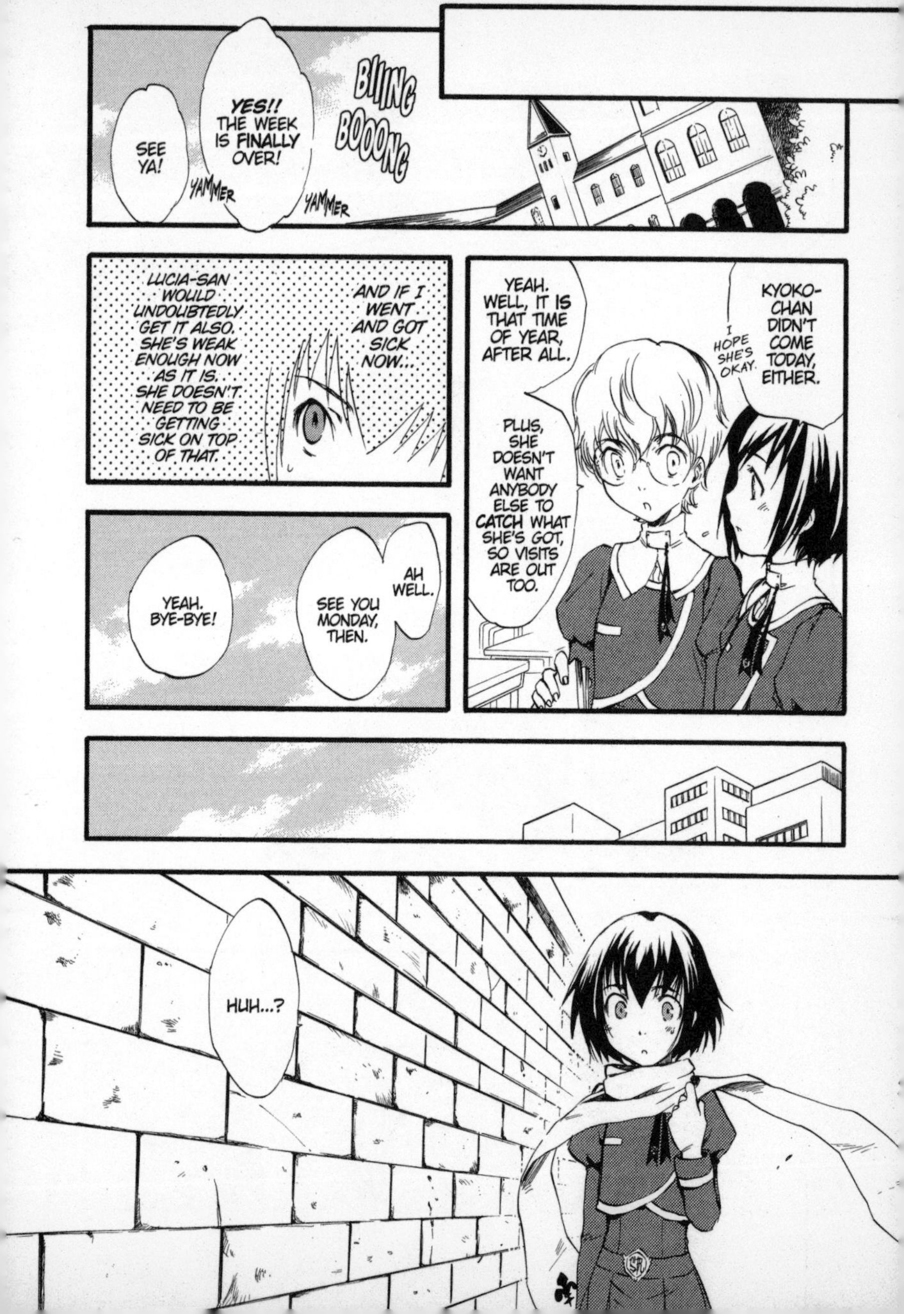
BIIING BOOONG
YES!! THE WEEK IS FINALLY OVER!
YAMMER
YAMMER
SEE YA!
KYOKO-CHAN DIDN'T COME TODAY, EITHER.
I HOPE SHE'S OKAY.
YEAH. WELL, IT IS THAT TIME OF YEAR, AFTER ALL.
PLUS, SHE DOESN'T WANT ANYBODY ELSE TO CATCH WHAT SHE'S GOT, SO VISITS ARE OUT TOO.
AND IF I WENT AND GOT SICK NOW...
LUCIA-SAN WOULD UNDOUBTEDLY GET IT ALSO. SHE'S WEAK ENOUGH NOW AS IT IS. SHE DOESN'T NEED TO BE GETTING SICK ON TOP OF THAT.
AH WELL.
SEE YOU MONDAY, THEN.
YEAH. BYE-BYE!
HUH...?

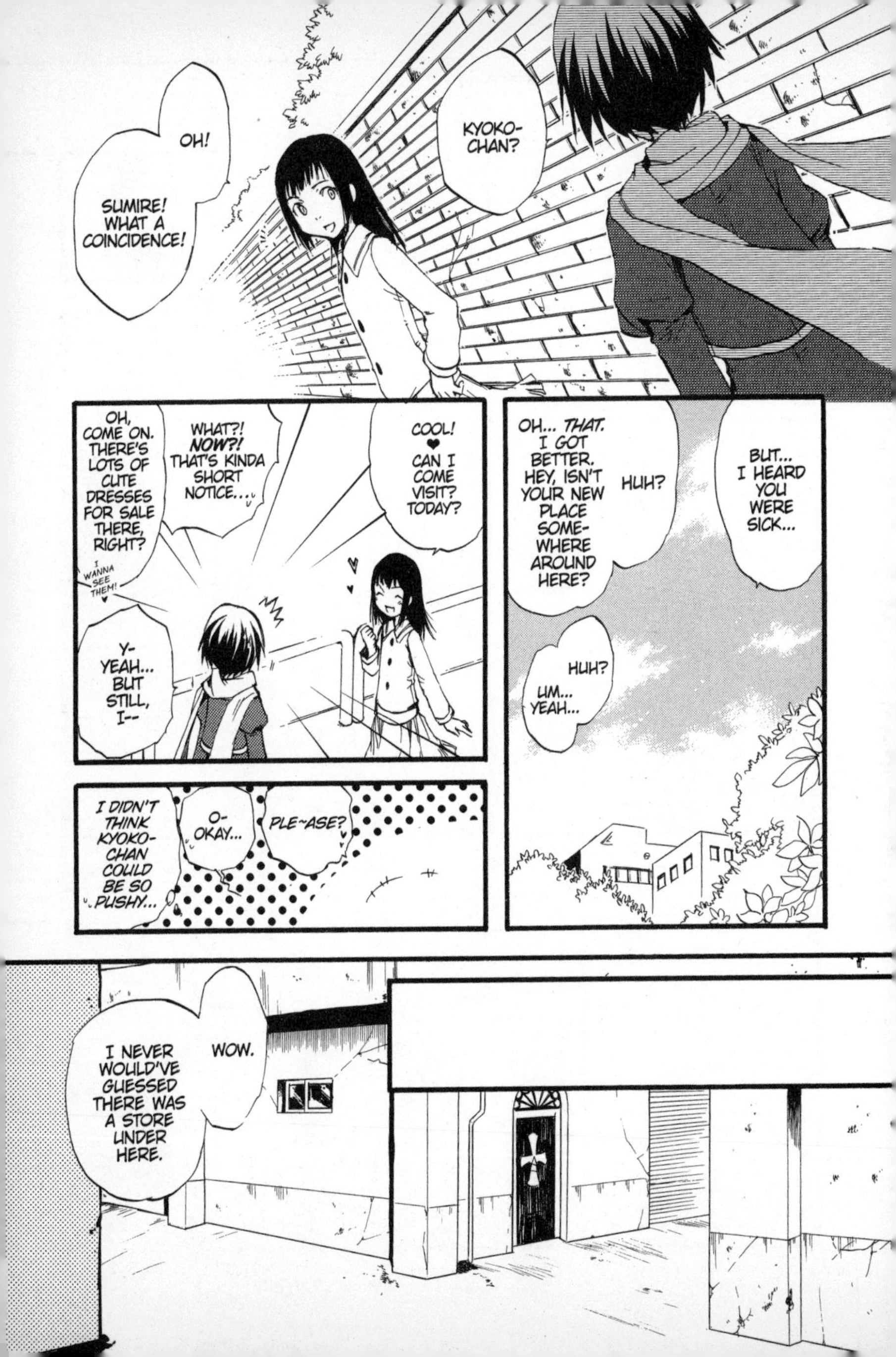
KYOKO-CHAN?
OH!
SUMIRE! WHAT A COINCIDENCE!
BUT... I HEARD YOU WERE SICK...
HUH?
OH... *THAT.* I GOT BETTER. HEY, ISN'T YOUR NEW PLACE SOME-WHERE AROUND HERE?
HUH? UM... YEAH...
COOL! ❤ CAN I COME VISIT? TODAY?
WHAT?! ***NOW?!*** THAT'S KINDA SHORT NOTICE...
OH, COME ON. THERE'S LOTS OF CUTE DRESSES FOR SALE THERE, RIGHT?
I WANNA SEE THEM! ❤
Y-YEAH... BUT STILL, I--
PLE~ASE?
O-OKAY...
I DIDN'T THINK KYOKO-CHAN COULD BE SO PUSHY...
WOW.
I NEVER WOULD'VE GUESSED THERE WAS A STORE UNDER HERE.

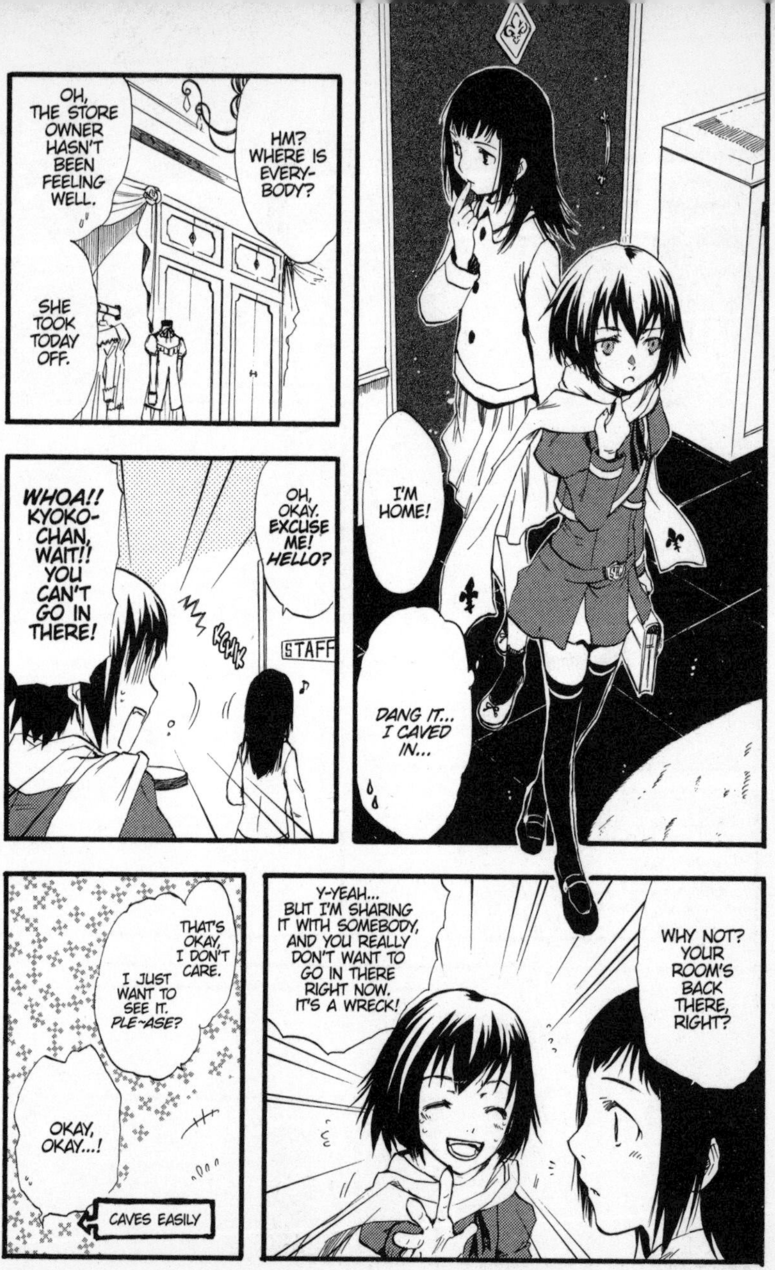
I'M HOME!
DANG IT... I CAVED IN...
HM? WHERE IS EVERYBODY?
OH, THE STORE OWNER HASN'T BEEN FEELING WELL.
SHE TOOK TODAY OFF.
OH, OKAY. EXCUSE ME! HELLO?
KCHK
STAFF
WHOA!! KYOKO-CHAN, WAIT!! YOU CAN'T GO IN THERE!
WHY NOT? YOUR ROOM'S BACK THERE, RIGHT?
Y-YEAH... BUT I'M SHARING IT WITH SOMEBODY, AND YOU REALLY DON'T WANT TO GO IN THERE RIGHT NOW. IT'S A WRECK!
THAT'S OKAY, I DON'T CARE.
I JUST WANT TO SEE IT. PLE~ASE?
OKAY, OKAY...!
CAVES EASILY

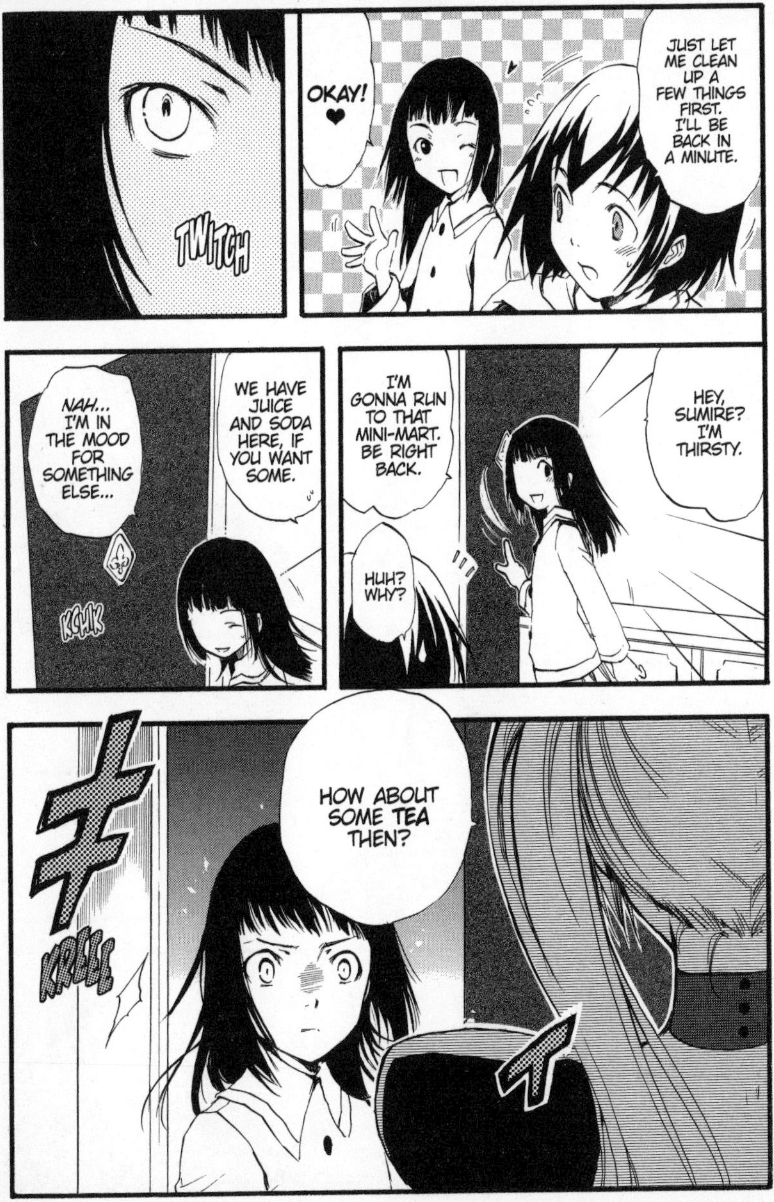
JUST LET ME CLEAN UP A FEW THINGS FIRST. I'LL BE BACK IN A MINUTE.
OKAY! ❤
TWITCH
HEY, SUMIRE? I'M THIRSTY.
I'M GONNA RUN TO THAT MINI-MART. BE RIGHT BACK.
HUH? WHY?
WE HAVE JUICE AND SODA HERE, IF YOU WANT SOME.
NAH... I'M IN THE MOOD FOR SOMETHING ELSE...
KCHIK
HOW ABOUT SOME TEA THEN?

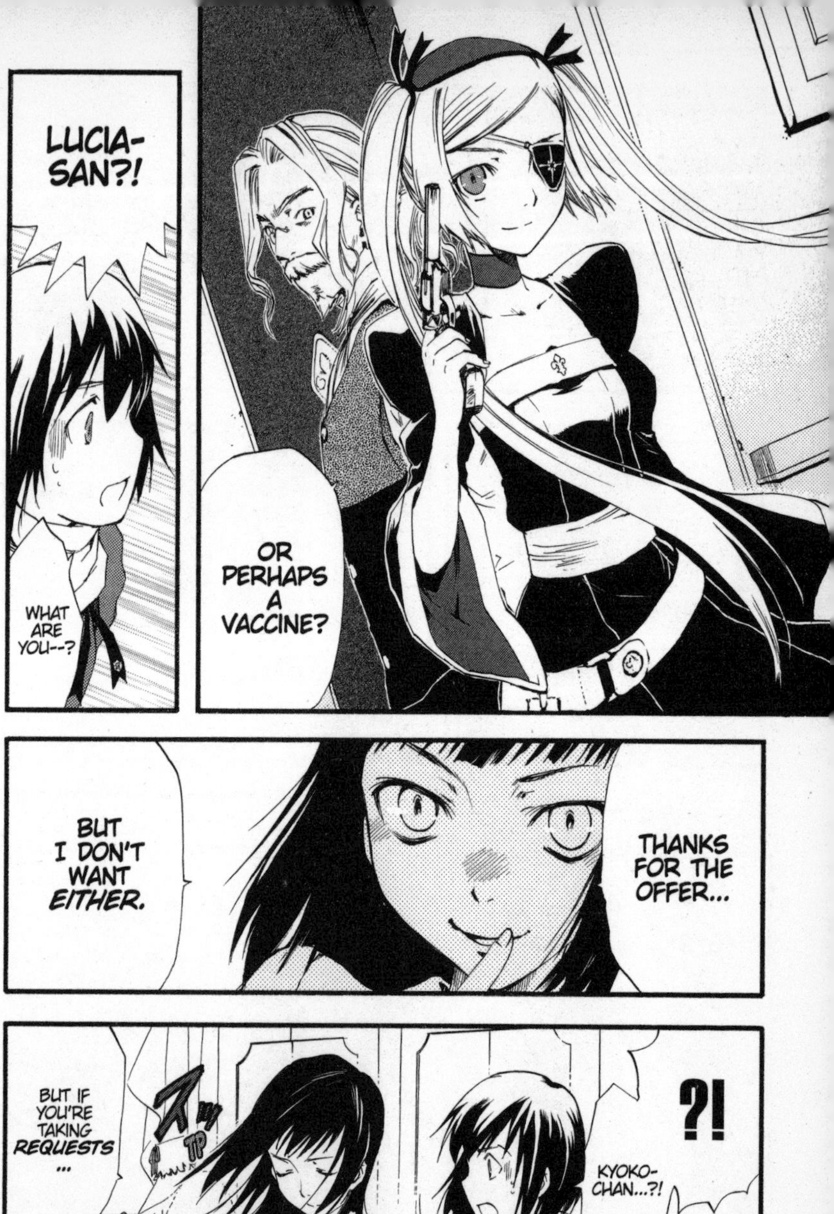
OR PERHAPS A VACCINE?
LUCIA-SAN?!
WHAT ARE YOU--?
THANKS FOR THE OFFER...
BUT I DON'T WANT *EITHER.*
?!
KYOKO-CHAN...?!
TP
BUT IF YOU'RE TAKING *REQUESTS*...

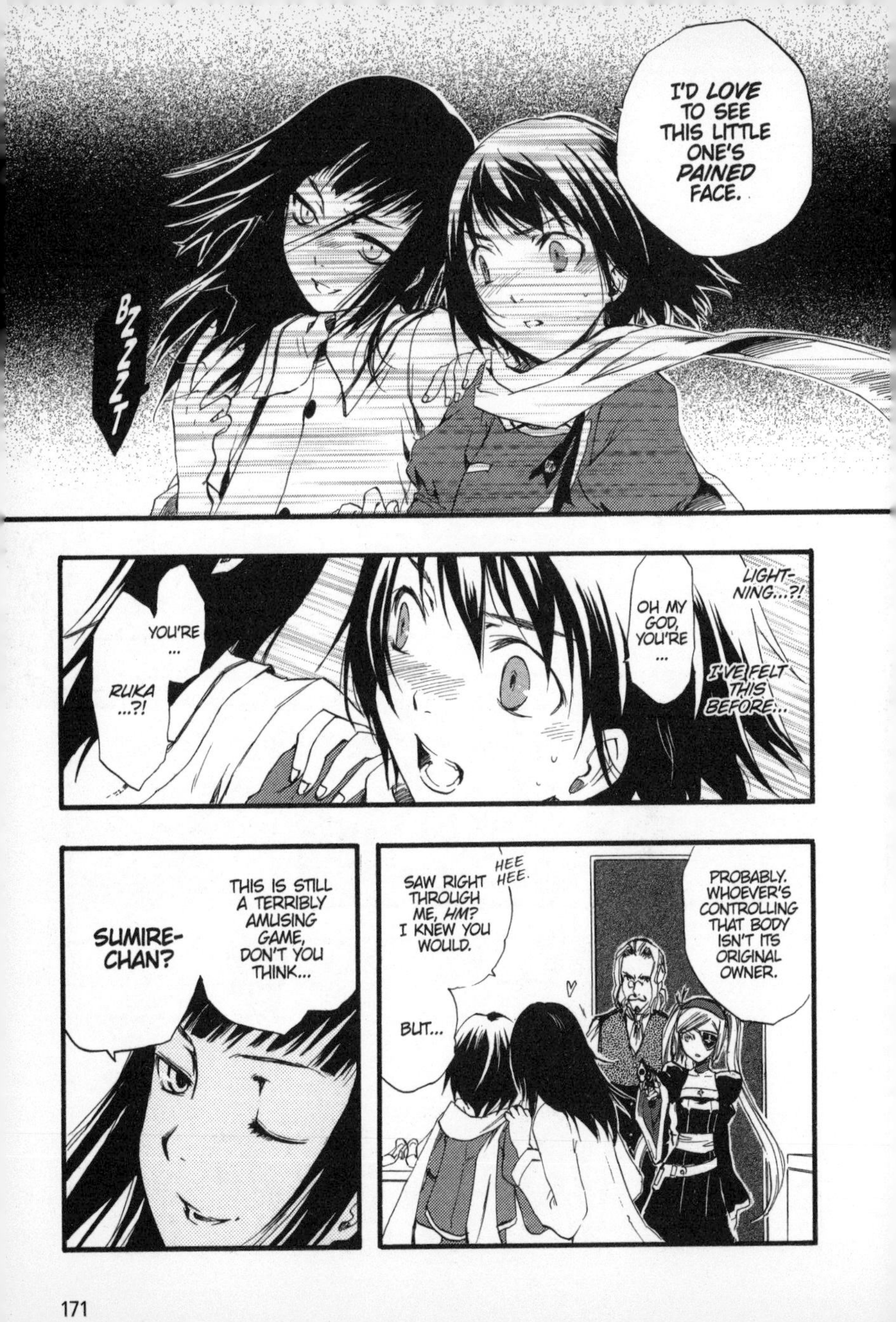
I'D LOVE TO SEE THIS LITTLE ONE'S PAINED FACE.
BZZZT
LIGHTNING...?!
I'VE FELT THIS BEFORE...
OH MY GOD, YOU'RE ...
YOU'RE ...
RUKA ...?!
PROBABLY. WHOEVER'S CONTROLLING THAT BODY ISN'T ITS ORIGINAL OWNER.
HEE HEE.
SAW RIGHT THROUGH ME, HM? I KNEW YOU WOULD.
BUT...
THIS IS STILL A TERRIBLY AMUSING GAME, DON'T YOU THINK...
SUMIRE-CHAN?

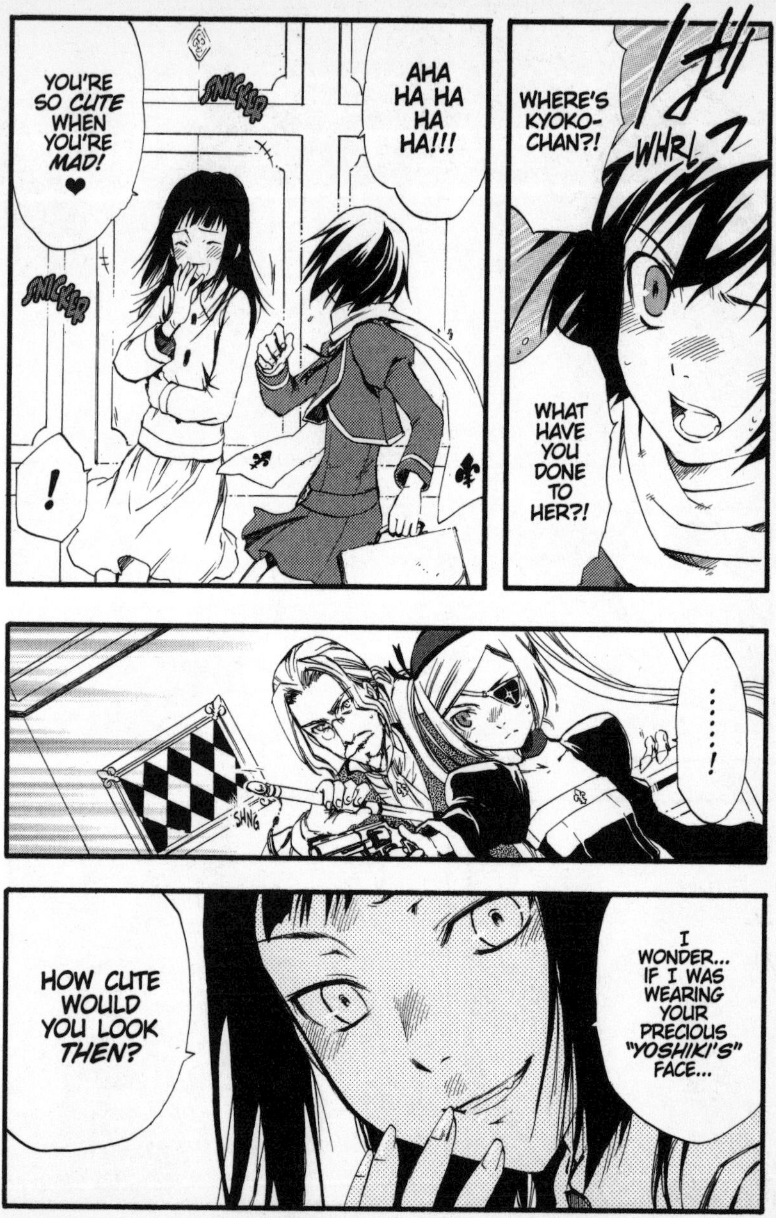
WHRL
WHERE'S KYOKO-CHAN?!
WHAT HAVE YOU DONE TO HER?!
AHA HA HA HA HA!!!
SNICKER
YOU'RE SO CUTE WHEN YOU'RE MAD! ❤
SNICKER
!
......!
SHNG
I WONDER... IF I WAS WEARING YOUR PRECIOUS "YOSHIKI'S" FACE...
HOW CUTE WOULD YOU LOOK THEN?

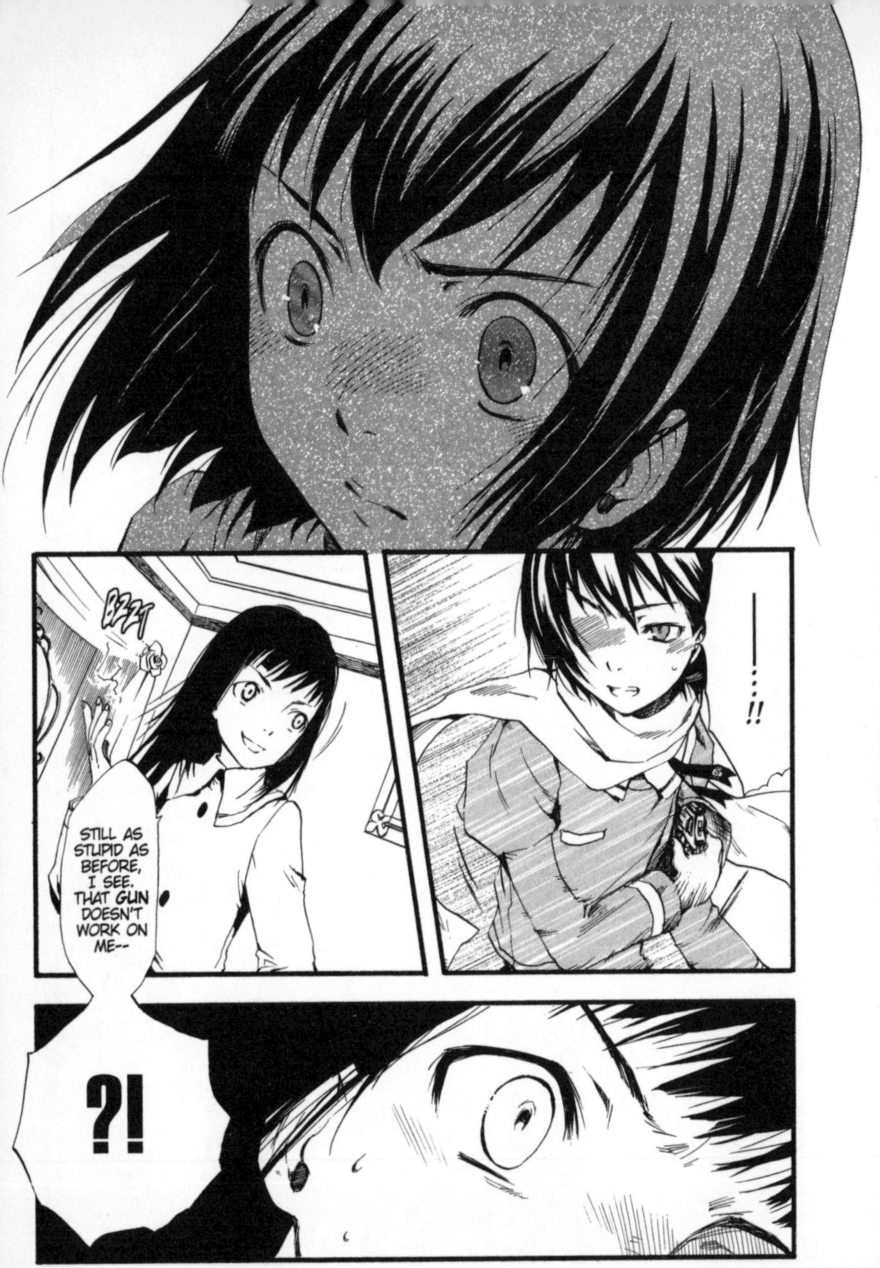
—......!!
BZZT
STILL AS STUPID AS BEFORE, I SEE. THAT GUN DOESN'T WORK ON ME--
?!

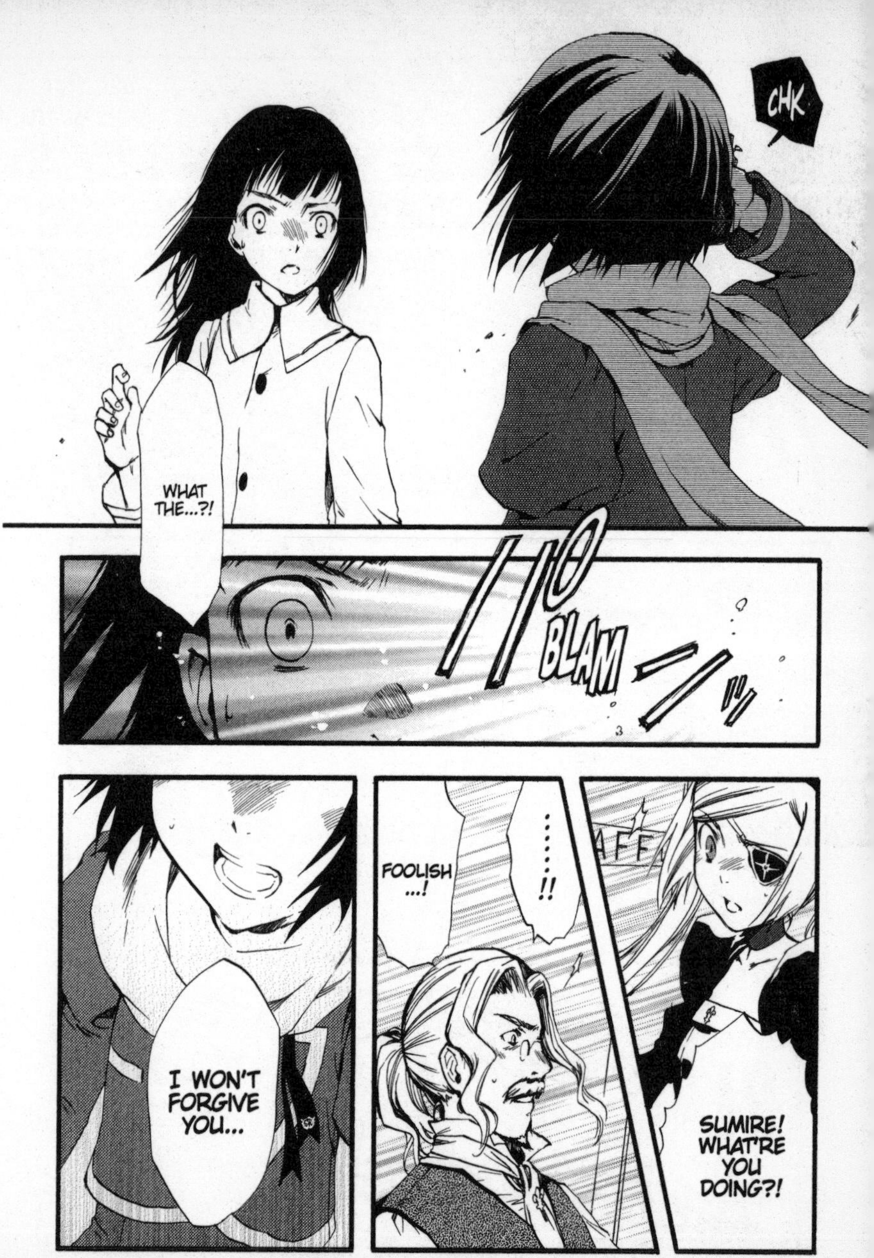
CHK
WHAT THE...?!
BLAM
SUMIRE! WHAT'RE YOU DOING?!
......!!
FOOLISH ...!
I WON'T FORGIVE YOU...

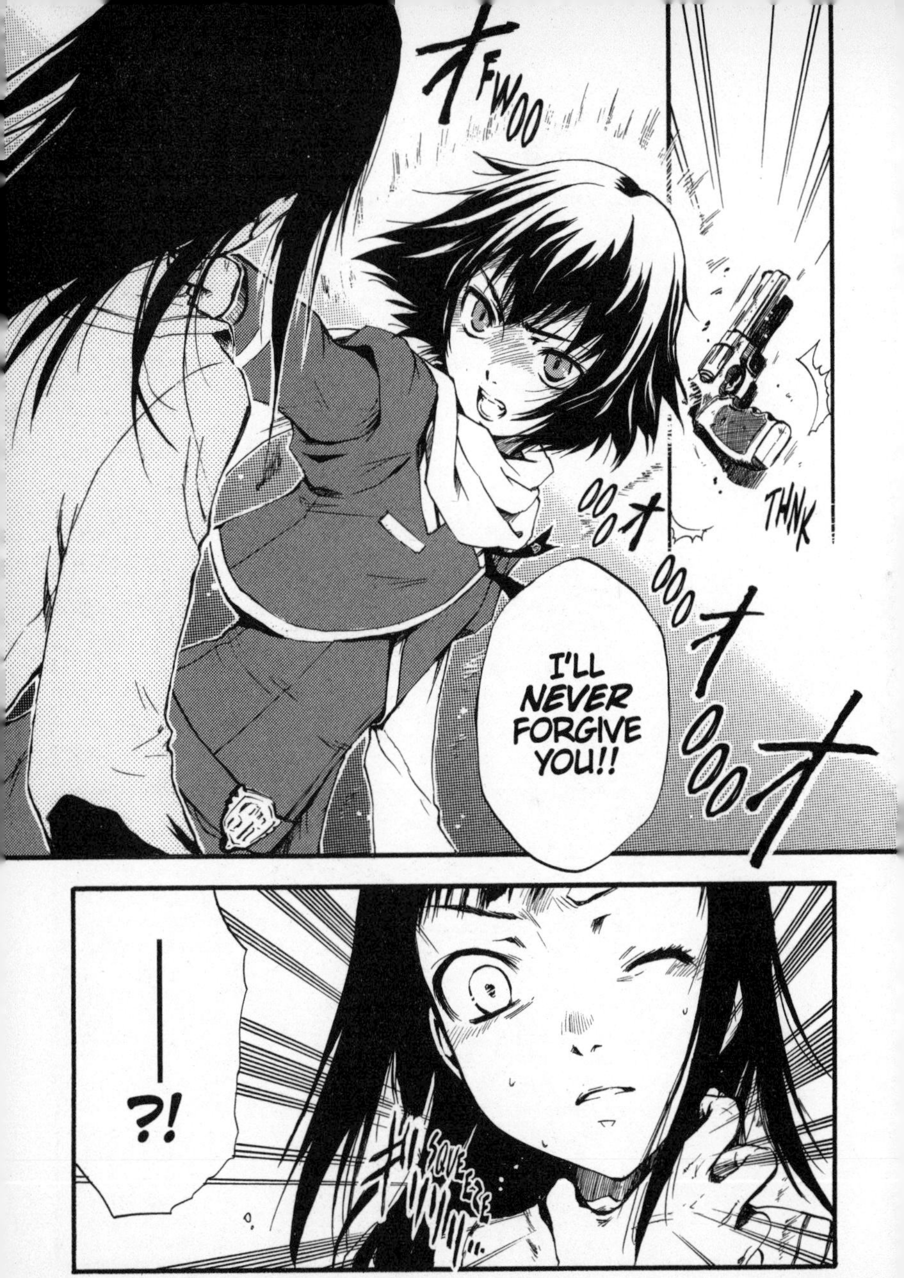
FWOO
THNK
OOO OOO OOOO
I'LL NEVER FORGIVE YOU!!
SQUE-E-ZE
—?!

TO BE CONTINUED...

POSTSCRIPT

HELLO, EVERYONE. THIS IS SUZUMI.
THANK YOU VERY MUCH FOR DECIDING TO PICK UP "V.V.V."
VOLUME 2! AS BEFORE, I COULDN'T HAVE PUT THIS
VOLUME TOGETHER WITHOUT HELP FROM LOTS OF OTHER
VERY GENEROUS PEOPLE. THANK YOU!

I DON'T KNOW ABOUT YOU, BUT TO ME IT FEELS LIKE
VOLUME 1 CAME OUT JUST A FEW DAYS AGO. NOW THAT I'VE
FINISHED UP THE SHORT SERIES I HAD GOING IN ANOTHER
ANTHOLOGY, I HAD THOUGHT I WOULD BE ABLE TO TONE
DOWN MY PACE AND RELAX A LITTLE MORE, BUT THAT DIDN'T
HAPPEN, OF COURSE. I HAD TO MOVE WHILE I WAS
WORKING ON THIS VOLUME, SO I ENDED UP BEING IN A
TOTAL RUSH THE ENTIRE TIME ANYWAY. TIME SURE FLIES
WHEN YOU AREN'T PAYING ATTENTION, DOESN'T IT? I MEAN,
IT'S BEEN AN ENTIRE YEAR SINCE I FIRST CAME UP WITH THE
IDEA FOR THIS SERIES! I DON'T HAVE THE TIME TO MESS
AROUND ANYMORE, DO I...? I SERIOUSLY NEED TO BECOME
THE KIND OF PERSON WHO CAN KEEP A SCHEDULE AND
EFFECTIVELY USE EVERY HOUR OF THE DAY.
(←USUALLY JUST WINGS IT DAY AFTER DAY)

THANK YOU TO MY SUPERVISOR, TAKAJIMA-SAMA,
WHO ALWAYS SUPPORTS ME, DESPITE MY UTTER
INABILITY TO PLAN.

THANK YOU TO ISSEKI-SAMA, WHOSE WONDERFUL DESIGNS
ALWAYS LEAVE ME FEELING GREAT.

THANK YOU TO ALL YOU READERS OUT THERE WHO HAVE
SENT ME LETTERS FULL OF SUPPORT THAT HELP ME KEEP
GOING.

THANK YOU, EVERYONE, FROM THE BOTTOM OF MY HEART.
I HOPE FOR YOUR CONTINUED HELP AND GOOD WILL
THROUGHOUT THE REST OF THE SERIES!

2006.4 鈴見敦
ATSUSHI SUZUMI

Staff & Help

Chisa Mori
Ichihara
Tokishi Nagokawa
Sachi Soutou
Suiren Matsukaze
Maroichi
Hoshikaze

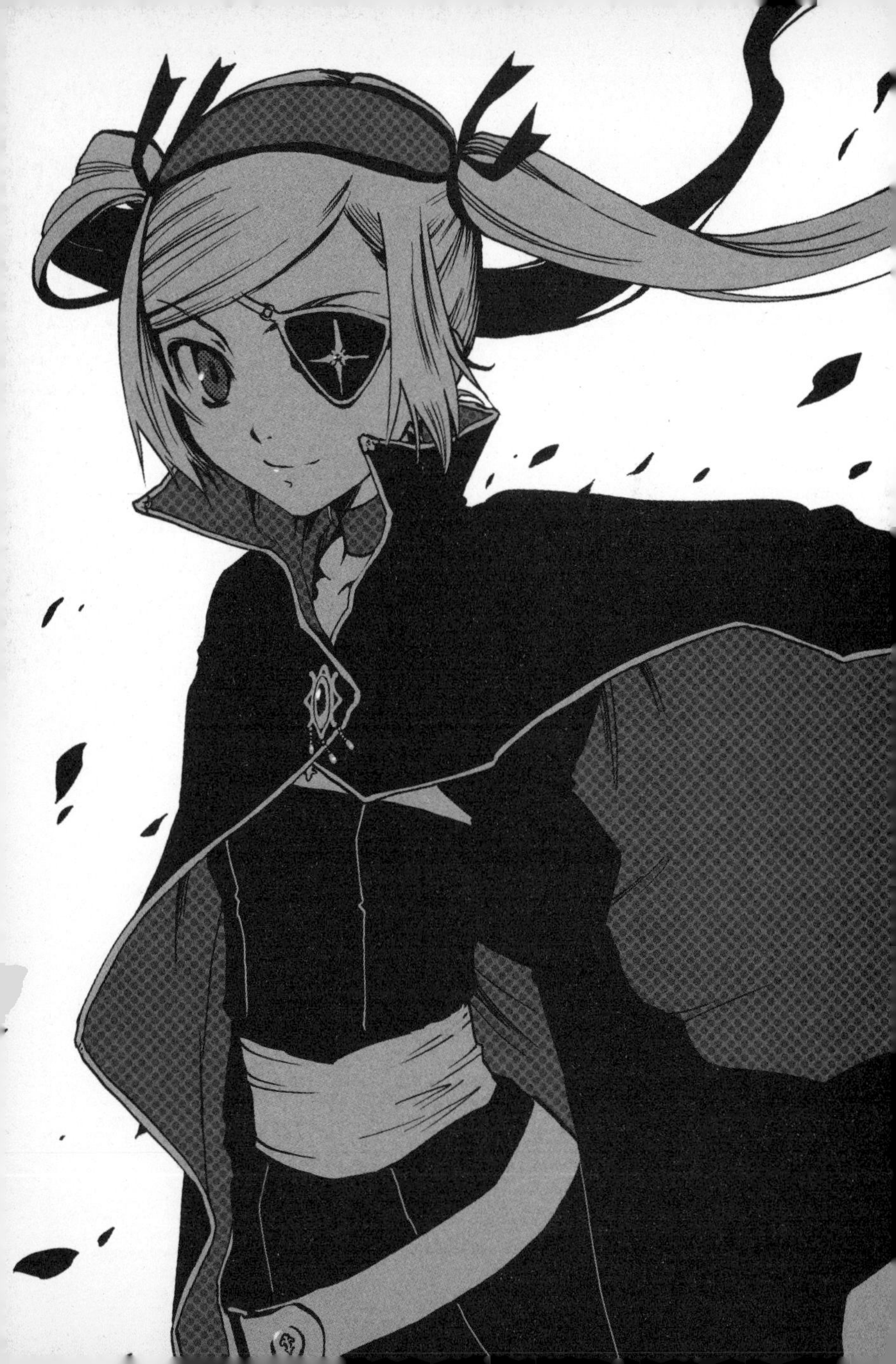

JAPANESE HONORIFICS GUIDE

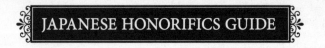

To ensure that all character relationships appear as they were originally intended, all character names have been kept in their original Japanese name order with family name first and given name second. For copyright reasons, creator names appear in standard English name order.

In addition to preserving the original Japanese name order, Seven Seas is committed to ensuring that honorifics—polite speech that indicates a person's status or relationship towards another individual—are retained within this book. Politeness is an integral facet of Japanese culture and we believe that maintaining honorifics in our translations helps bring out the same character nuances as seen in the original work.

The following are some of the more common honorifics you may come across while reading this and other books:

-san – The most common of all honorifics, it is an all-purpose suffix that can be used in any situation where politeness is expected. Generally seen as the equivalent to Mr., Miss, Ms., Mrs., etc.

-sama – This suffix is one level higher than "-san" and is used to confer great respect upon an individual.

-dono – Stemming from the word "tono," meaning "lord," "-dono" signifies an even higher level than "-sama," and confers the utmost respect.

-kun – This suffix is commonly used at the end of boys' names to express either familiarity or endearment. It can also be used when addressing someone younger than oneself or of a lower status.

-chan – Another common honorific. This suffix is mainly used to express endearment towards girls, but can also be used when referring to little boys or even pets. Couples are also known to use the term amongst each other to convey a sense of cuteness and intimacy.

Sempai – This title is used towards one's senior or "superior" in a particular group or organization. "Sempai" is most often used in a school setting, where underclassmen refer to upperclassmen as "sempai," though it is also commonly said by employees when addressing fellow employees who hold seniority in the workplace.

Kouhai – This is the exact opposite of "sempai," and is used to refer to underclassmen in school, junior employees at the workplace, etc.

Sensei – Literally meaning "one who has come before," this title is used for teachers, doctors, or masters of any profession or art.

Oniisan – This title literally means "big brother." First and foremost, it is used by younger siblings towards older male siblings. It can be used by itself or attached to a person's name as a suffix (niisan). It is often used by a younger person toward an older person unrelated by blood, but as a sign of respect. Other forms include the informal "oniichan" and the more respectful "oniisama."

Oneesan – This title is the opposite of "oniisan" and means "big sister." Other forms include the informal "oneechan" and the more respectful "oneesama."

⚜ TRANSLATION NOTES ⚜

98.3
A *"kekkai"* is a magical barrier or protective ward.

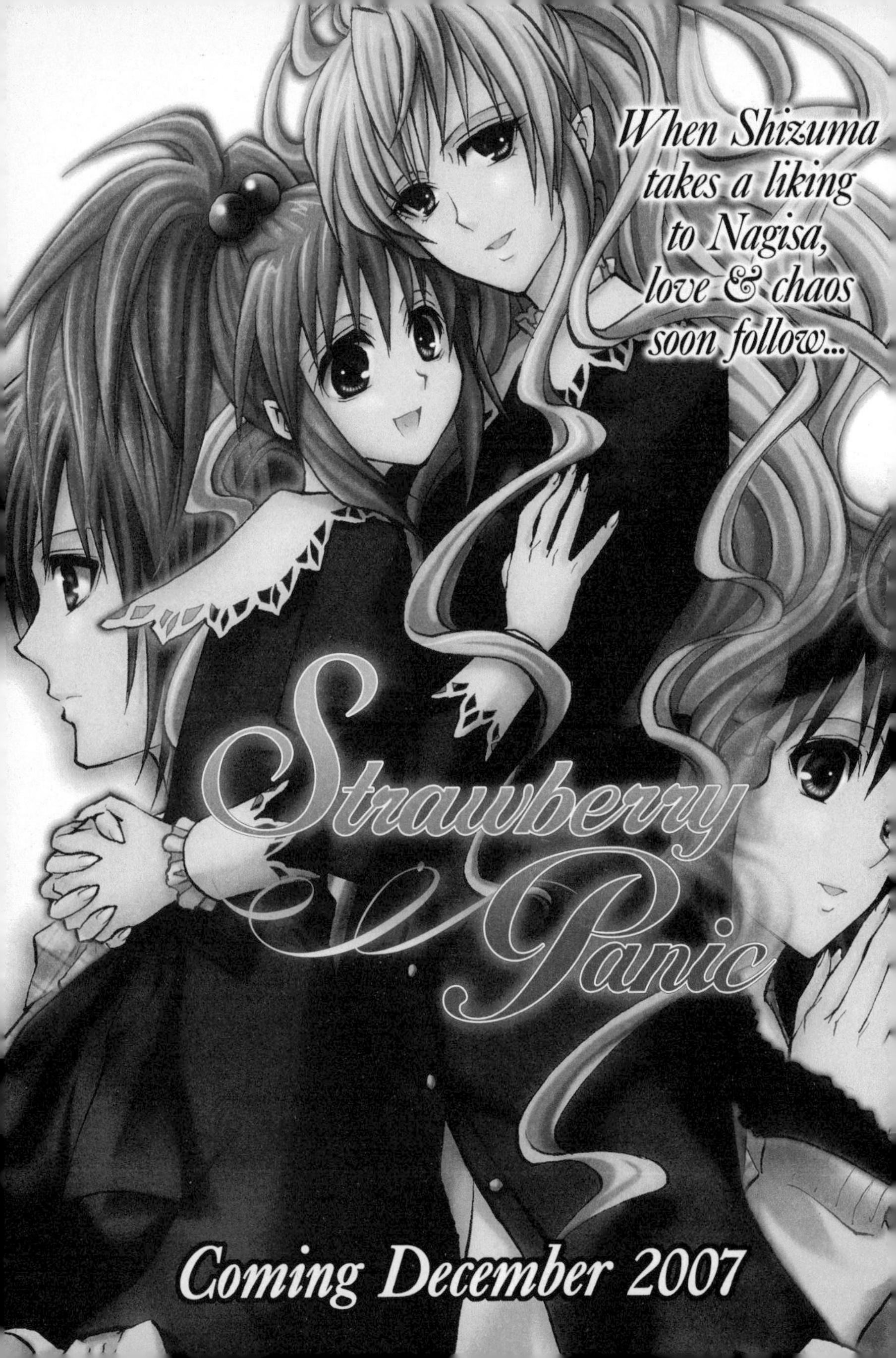

When Shizuma takes a liking to Nagisa, love & chaos soon follow...
Strawberry Panic
Coming December 2007

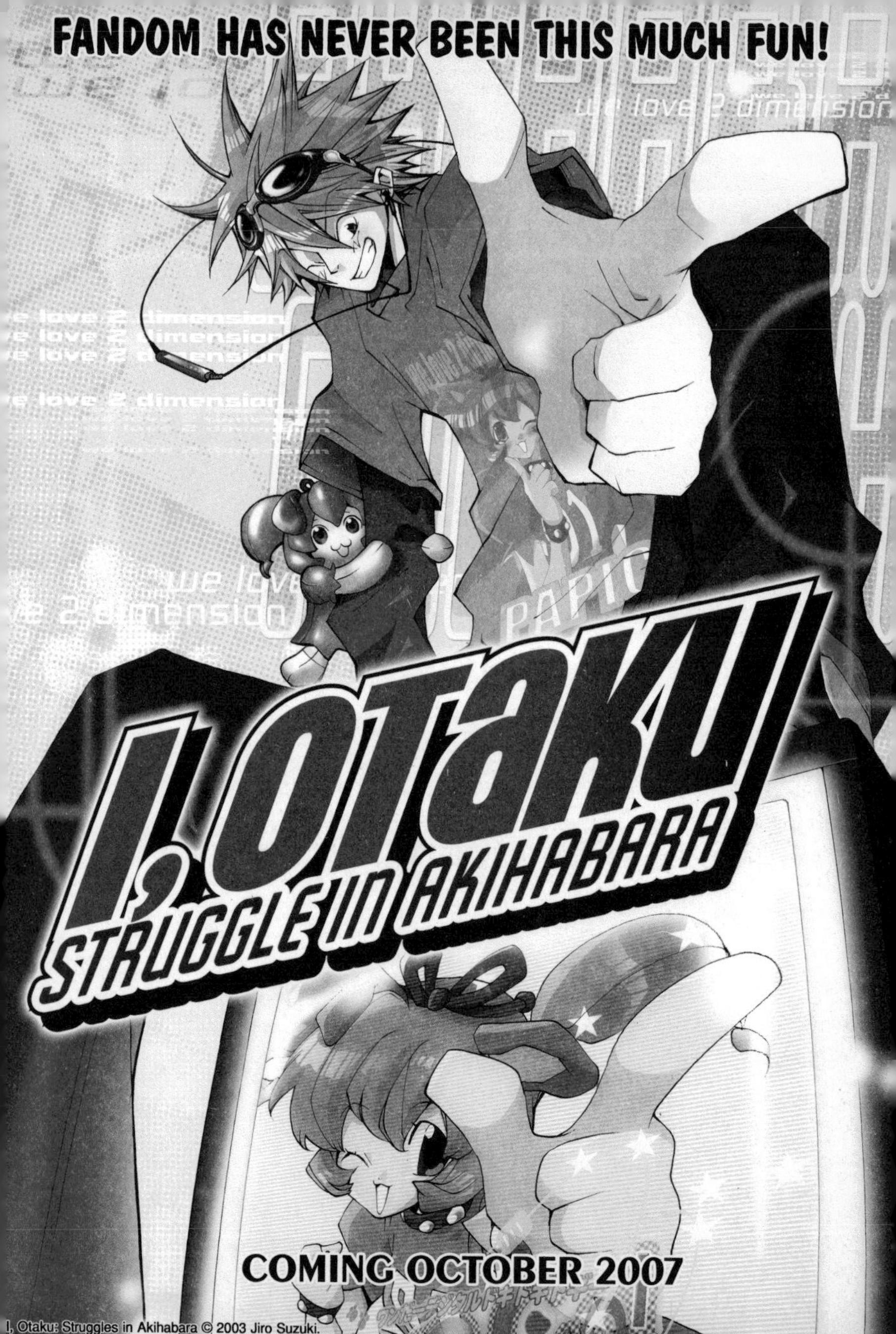
FANDOM HAS NEVER BEEN THIS MUCH FUN!
we love 2 dimension
I, OTAKU
STRUGGLE IN AKIHABARA
COMING OCTOBER 2007

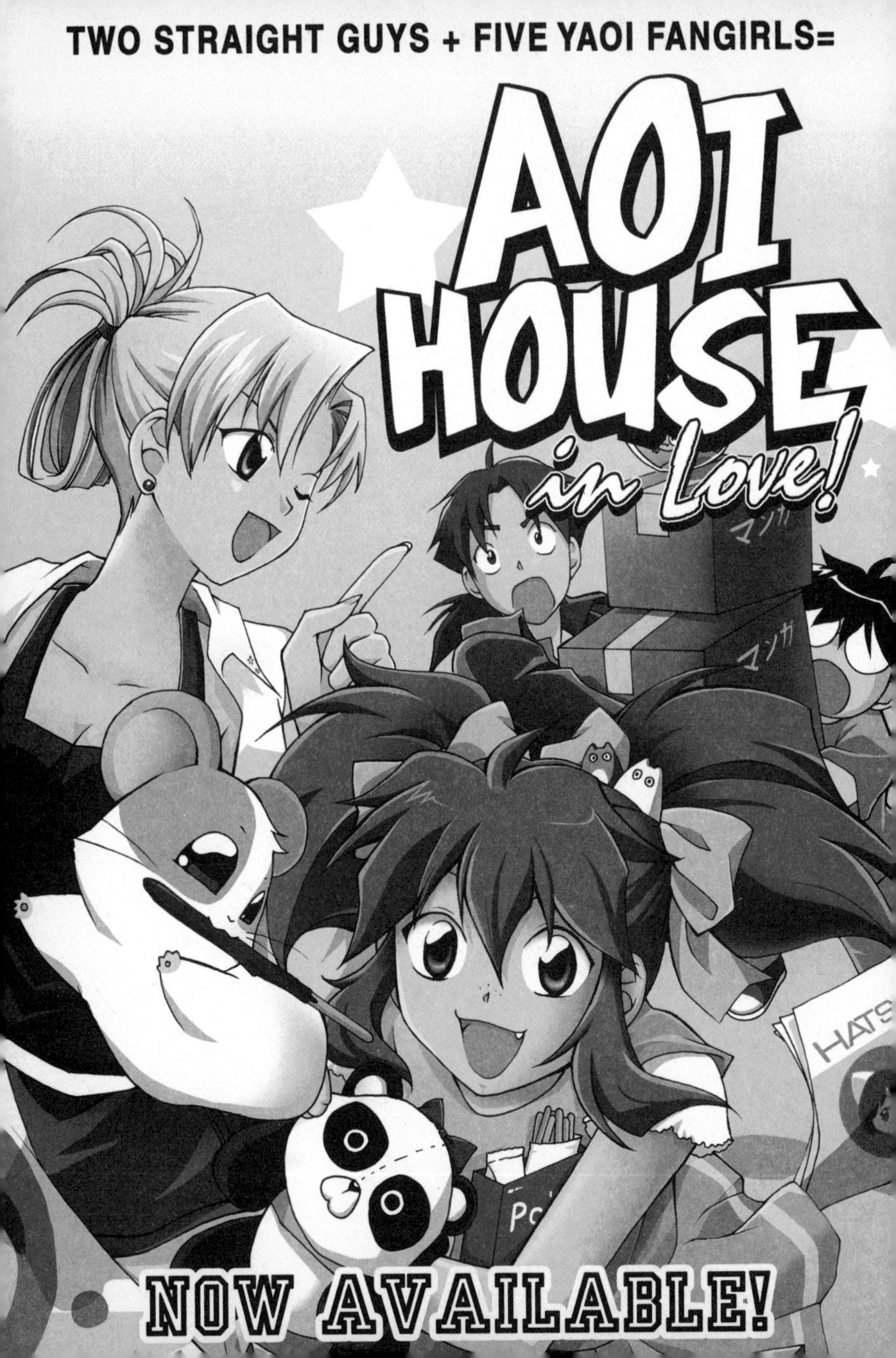
TWO STRAIGHT GUYS + FIVE YAOI FANGIRLS=
AOI HOUSE
in Love!
マンガ
マンガ
NOW AVAILABLE!

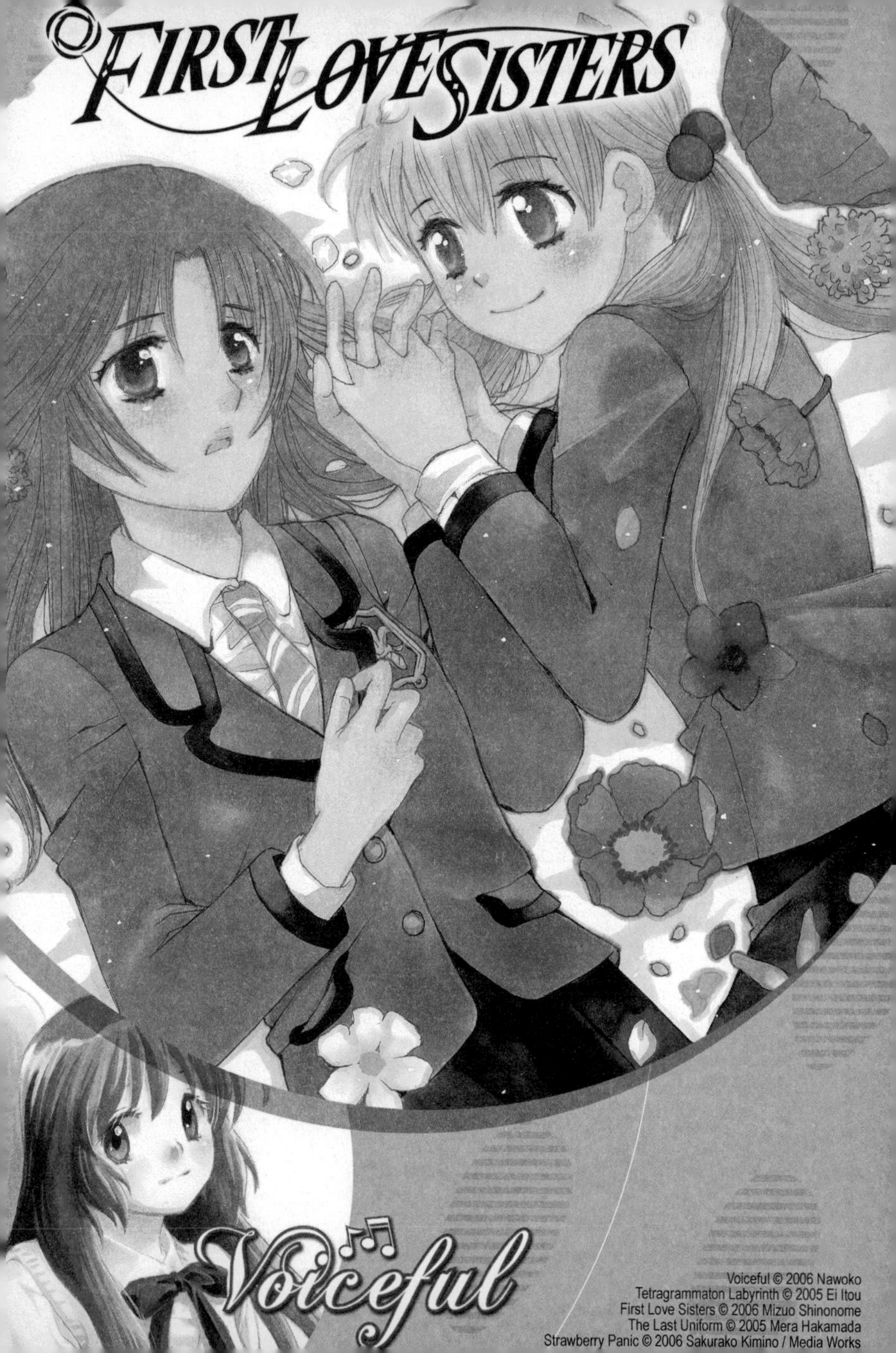
FIRST LOVE SISTERS
Voiceful

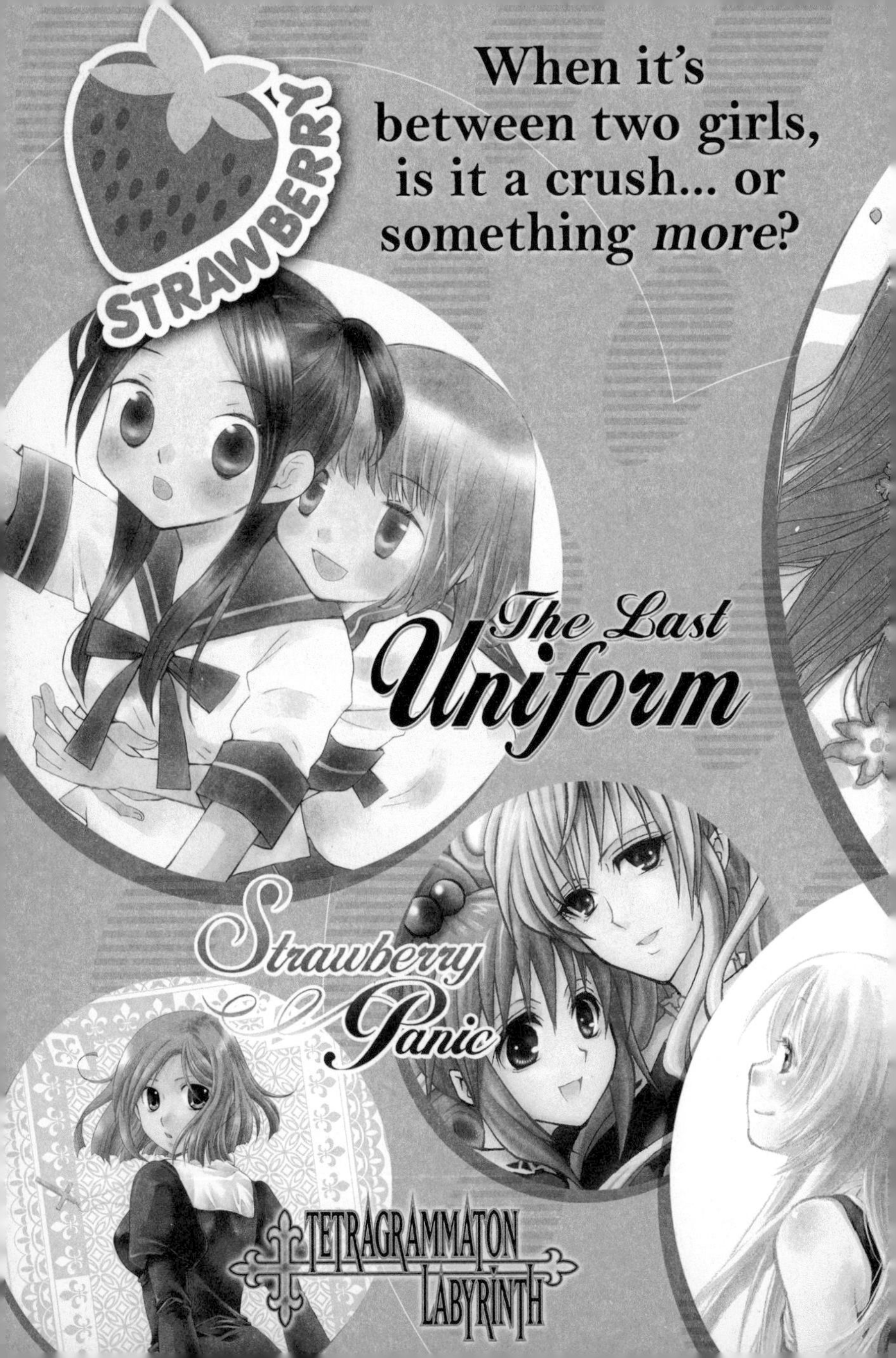
STRAWBERRY
When it's between two girls, is it a crush... or something *more*?
The Last Uniform
Strawberry Panic
TETRAGRAMMATON LABYRINTH

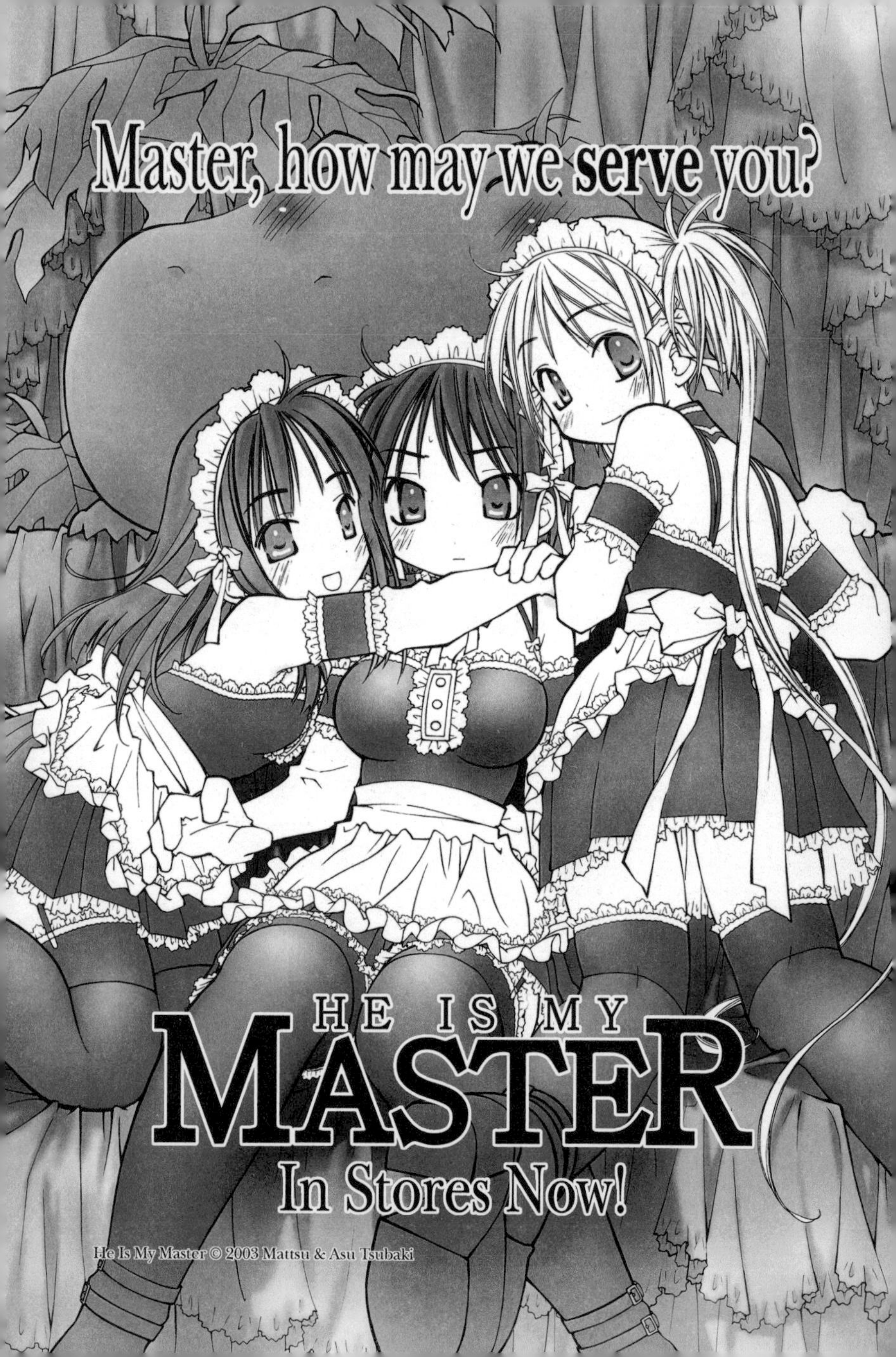
Master, how may we serve you?
HE IS MY
MASTER
In Stores Now!
He Is My Master © 2003 Mattsu & Asu Tsubaki

Amazing_Agent
LUNA
volume 4

From the
artist of
AOI HOUSE

**Volume 1 - 3
In Stores Now!**

Luna: the perfect secret agent. A girl grown in a
lab from the finest genetic material, she has been
trained since birth to be the U.S. government's
ultimate espionage weapon. But now she is given
an assignment that will test her abilities to the
max - *high school!*

story
Nunzio DeFilippis & Christina Weir • *art* Shiei

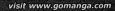

visit www.gomanga.com

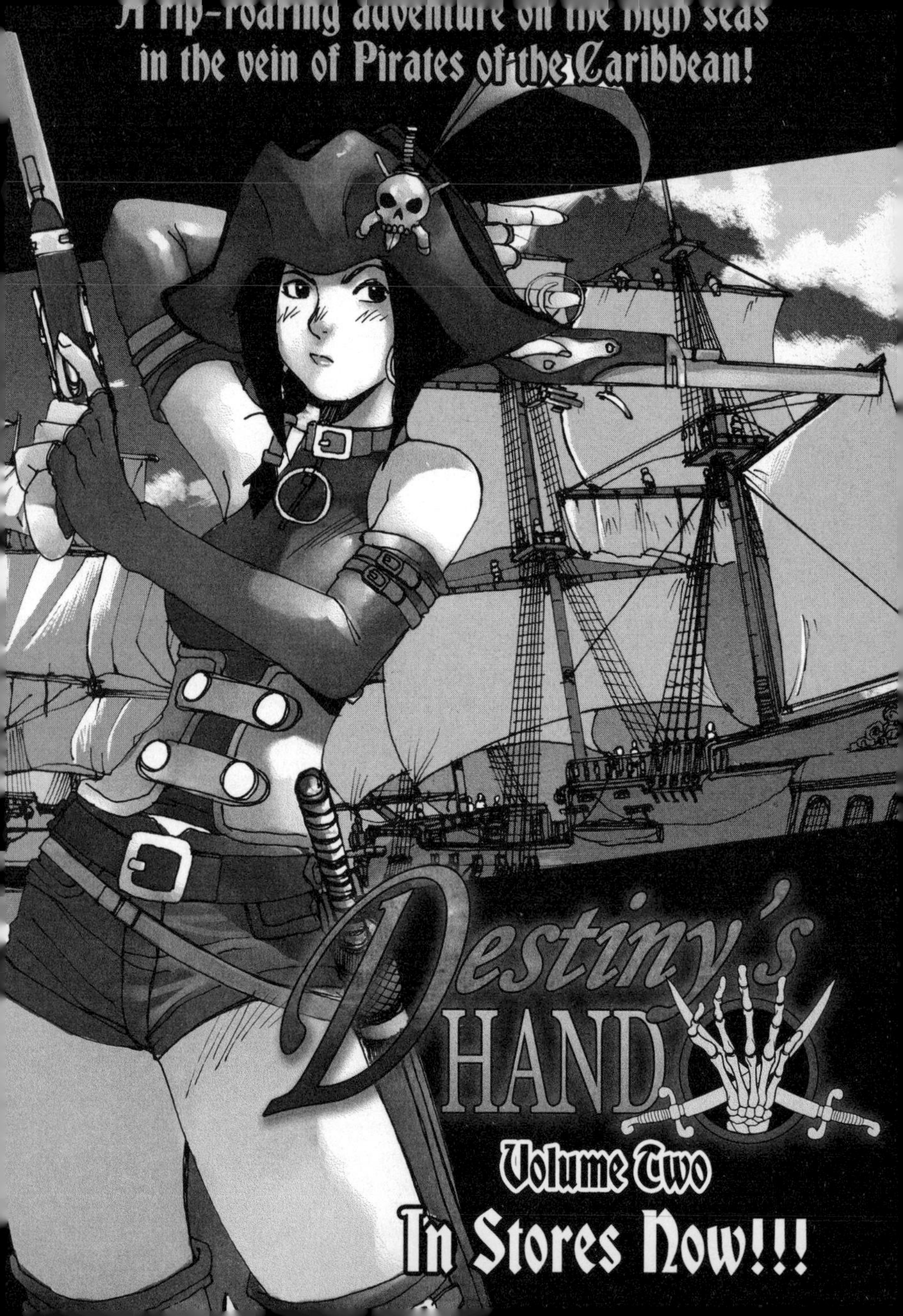

A rip-roaring adventure on the high seas
in the vein of Pirates of the Caribbean!
Destiny's
HAND
Volume Two
In Stores Now!!!

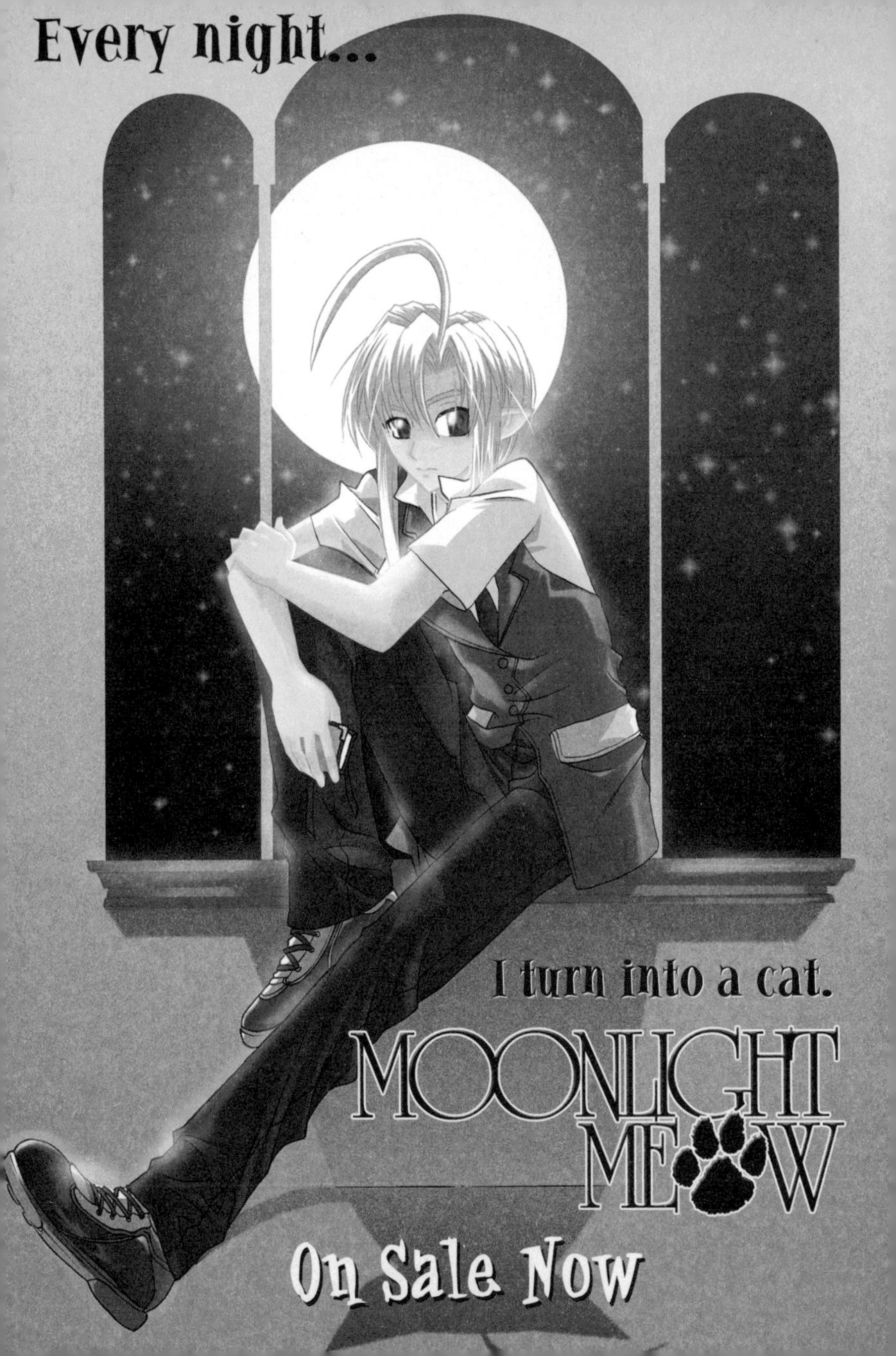

Every night...
I turn into a cat.
MOONLIGHT MEOW
On Sale Now

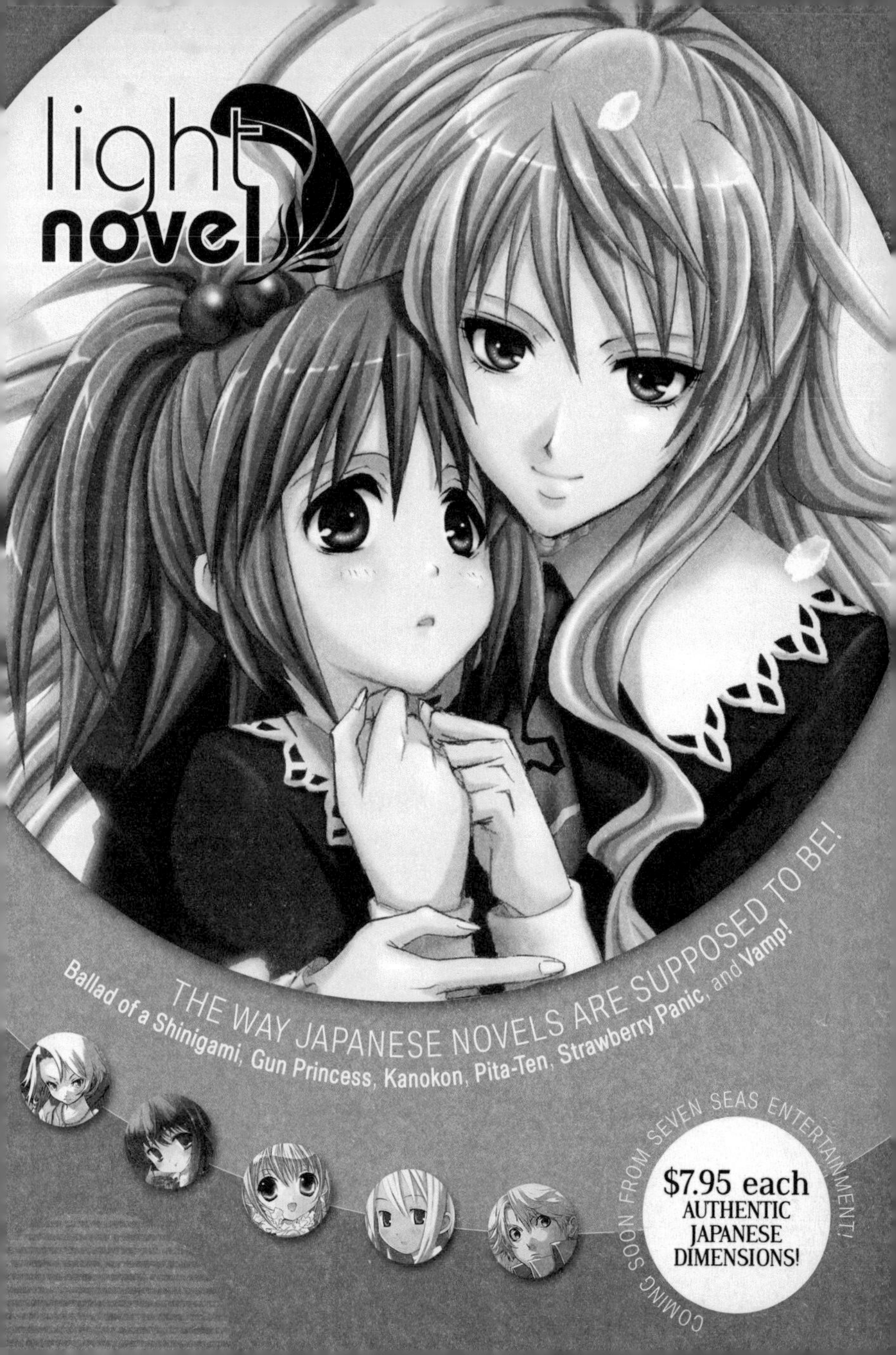
light novel
THE WAY JAPANESE NOVELS ARE SUPPOSED TO BE!
Ballad of a Shinigami, Gun Princess, Kanokon, Pita-Ten, Strawberry Panic, and Vamp!
COMING SOON FROM SEVEN SEAS ENTERTAINMENT!
$7.95 each
AUTHENTIC JAPANESE DIMENSIONS!

VOLUME 2

story & art by Atsushi Suzumi

STAFF CREDITS

translation	**Adrienne Beck**
adaptation	**Janet Houck**
retouch & lettering	**Roland Amago**
design	**Roland Amago**
layout	**Bambi Eloriaga**
editor	**Adam Arnold**
publisher	**Seven Seas Entertainment**

VENUS VERSUS VIRUS VOL. 2
© ATSUSHI SUZUMI 2006
First published in 2006 by Media Works Inc., Tokyo, Japan
English translation rights arranged with Media Works, Inc.

Visit us online at www.gomanga.com

ISBN: 978-1-933164-49-6

Printed in Canada

First printing: October 2007

10 9 8 7 6 5 4 3 2 1

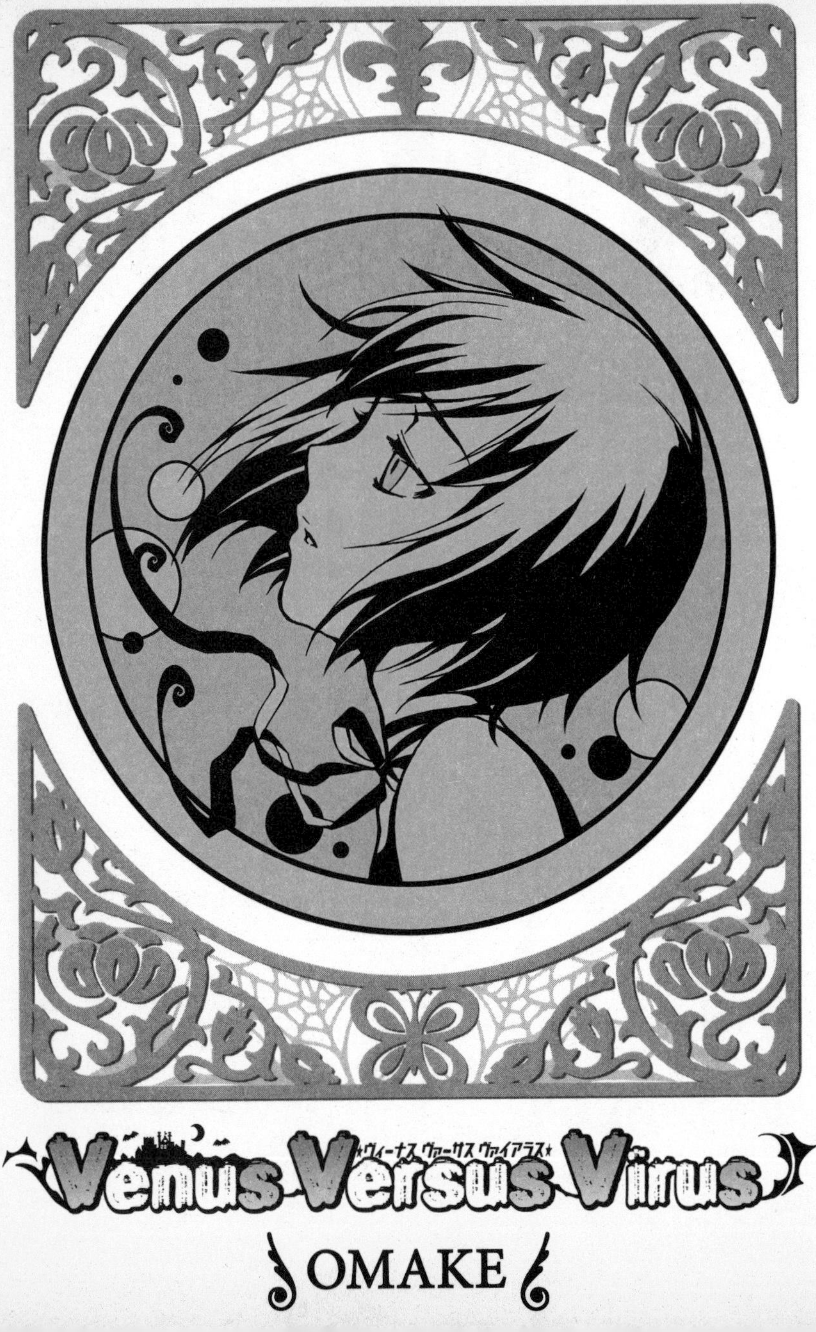

Venus Versus Virus

ヴィーナス ヴァーサス ヴァイアラス

OMAKE

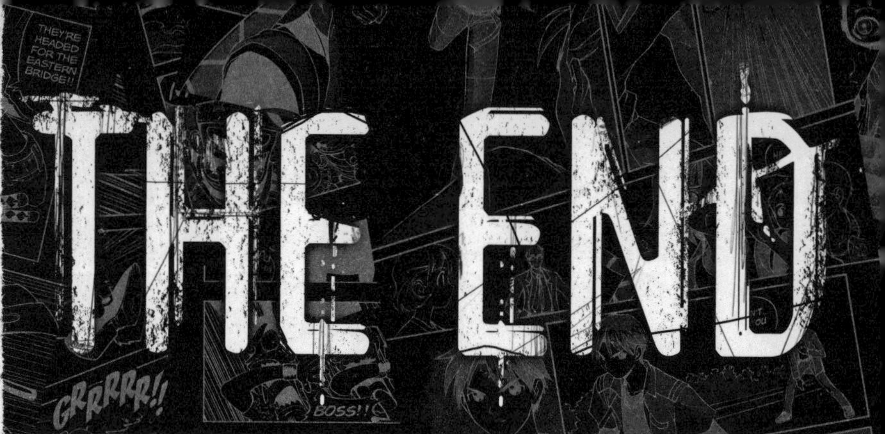
THEY'RE HEADED FOR THE EASTERN BRIDGE!!
THE END
BOSS!!
GRRRRR!!

YOU'RE READING THE WRONG WAY

This is the last page of
Venus Versus Virus Volume 2

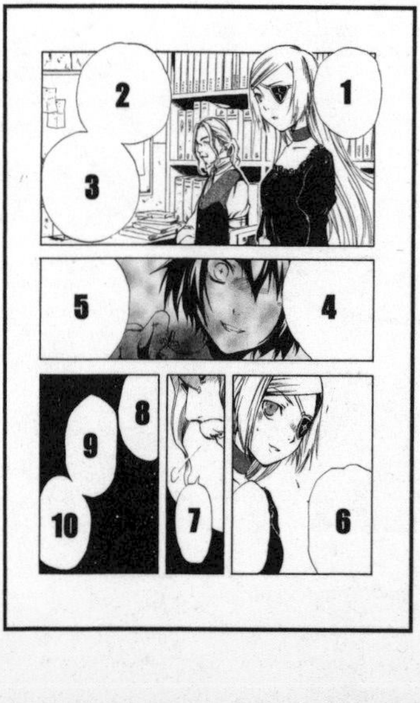
1
2
3
4
5
6
7
8
9
10

This book reads from right to left, Japanese style. To read from the beginning, flip the book over to the other side, start with the top right panel, and take it from there.

If this is your first time reading manga, just follow the diagram. It may seem backwards at first, but you'll get used to it! Have fun!